Character's Theater

Character's Theater

Genre and Identity on the Eighteenth-Century English Stage

LISA A. FREEMAN

PENN

UNIVERSITY OF PENNSYLVANIA PRESS

Philadelphia

10 9 8 7 6 5 4 3 2 1

Published by
University of Pennsylvania Press
Philadelphia, Pennsylvania 19104-4011

Library of Congress Cataloging-in-Publication Data
Freeman, Lisa A.
    Character's theater : genre and identity on the eighteenth-century English stage / Lisa A. Freeman.
        p.   cm.
    ISBN 0-8122-3639-4 (cloth : alk. paper)
    Includes bibliographical references (p.   ) and index.
    1. English drama—18th century—History and criticism. 2. Characters and characteristics in
literature. 3. Identity (Psychology) in literature. 4. Group identity in literature. 5. Literary form.
PS708.C47 F74 2002
822.50927—dc21   2001041543

For my parents
Jack and Ellen Freeman

Contents

Introduction: A Prologue

This book challenges at least two major premises of eighteenth-century literary and cultural studies: first, that the study of eighteenth-century drama can contribute little to how we understand the literary forms and cultural contents of this period; and second, that the subject as figured in the novel emerged inevitably in the eighteenth century as the dominant discursive structure for modeling modern identities. In a genre by genre analysis, I argue not only that the stage functioned as a critical focal point in eighteenth-century cultural discourse, but that in deploying an alternative model of identity based on the concept of character, it marked a site of resistance to the rise of the subject and to the ideological conformity enforced through that identity formation. In elucidating the social, political, economic, and cultural resonances of the various dramatic genres of the period, I illustrate how those dramatic genres manipulated markers of identity such as gender, class, and nation for representation on the eighteenth-century stage. In this introduction, I describe the materials and ideas that inform this project and delineate both its range and its bounds.

To date, the study of eighteenth-century drama has been dominated by what I call the taxonomic impulse, a sustained effort to divide, subdivide, and divide yet again the genres of dramatic production. This taxonomic impulse has been matched by a complementary encyclopedic charge to produce nothing less than a complete historical account of the plays: their plots, their sources, their production and acting histories, their reception, and their box-office receipts. Driven by these dual imperatives, dedicated scholars have amassed a vast historical record of eighteenth-century drama which eclipses that for any other popular form in the period, including the novel. Let me begin, then, by acknowledging that this book would not have been possible if it were not for the work of those dedicated scholars. The vast store of information that has been compiled in multivolume reference works such as *The London Stage, 1660–1800: A Calendar of Plays, Entertainments and Afterpieces* and *A Biographical Dictionary of Actors, Actresses, Musicians, Dancers, Managers, and Other Stage Personnel in London, 1660–1800*, as well as in a number of histories of eighteenth-century drama, provides the necessary foundation for a factually grounded, historically oriented critical study.[1]

At the same time, however, many of the scholars involved in these projects have turned a dubious eye toward the content of their subject matter and have expressed strong resistance to any efforts aimed at literary interpretation. The indefatigable historian of eighteenth-century drama Robert D. Hume has concluded, for instance, that "We must face the unpalatable fact bluntly. . . . Most of the comedies simply need no explication."[2] Earlier, Allardyce Nicoll conceded that with respect to the stage the eighteenth century was in many ways a "period of decay and disintegration . . . perhaps the greater oblivion that could fall on the dramatic productivity of these years the better."[3] Despite these reservations, Nicoll and others still justify the study of eighteenth-century drama insofar as it provides a kind of genealogy for the modern stage. Amid the aesthetic chaos that is so readily apparent to anyone who has read even a handful of these plays, they are intent on locating and identifying the forward-looking traces that anticipate the elements of the well-made play of the late nineteenth and early twentieth centuries.

By contrast, this study approaches the materials of eighteenth-century drama as significant in their own right, that is, as worthy of literary and cultural study neither as a fall-away from the dazzling achievements of the Renaissance stage nor simply as a prelude to the well-made play of the nineteenth century. It aims, in short, at picking up where these scholars have left off by drawing on that immense trove of accumulated knowledge to produce an interpretive account of eighteenth-century drama and its cultural work. To do so requires that we interrogate some earlier assumptions and raise questions about what others may have taken for granted. For instance, Nicoll once asserted in a series of passing observations that the eighteenth-century theater was a "sure index" of "public taste and of almost intangible literary and intellectual movements," and that "it was intimately in touch with nearly all the great men of letters of the time" (2:3). This study takes up questions that Nicoll here leaves unpursued: What was the role of eighteenth-century drama in those "literary and intellectual movements"? Why was the theater the object of so much cultural interest and scrutiny? Why were so many of the major literary figures of the day so "intimately in touch" with dramatic production? What potentialities did they see in that medium which they could not find in other cultural forms? In what sense did eighteenth-century drama act as a "sure index" for larger cultural issues?

To address such questions, we need first to develop an understanding of the kind of lively cultural encounter that a night at the theater proffered to eighteenth-century audiences.[4] Before audience members even entered the theater, they would probably have encountered numerous advertisements and playbills describing the bill of fare for the evening. They would have known whether to expect a comedy, a tragedy, or a farce, which actors and actresses they would see on the stage, and whether any members of the royal family were expected to attend the performance. Their expectations for the evening would have been stoked, moreover, by newspaper and periodical puffs, reviews, and criticisms, and even, perhaps, by the eruption of pamphlet wars and exchanges over the formal merits and moral significance of the play in question. Typically, moreover, the bill of fare for an evening's entertainment would include more than merely a play's performance. At a minimum, the night would be punctuated by a series of dance performances and musical interludes, often occurring between the acts of the play, and the play would be followed by at least one short afterpiece. The presentation of the main play was, at best, discontinuous.

The scene inside the theater was often raucous and filled with spectacular possibility; it was a place to see and be seen. The evening's entertainment would begin around six o'clock, but many of the wealthier audience members would have sent attendants and footmen as early as two or three o'clock in the afternoon to joust for and save prime places in the boxes and the pit. The seating arrangements in the playhouse could be read as a study in social stratification, with the pit and the side-boxes reserved for wealthy gentlemen, both aristocratic and middling, the front boxes for the ladies of quality and fashion and the wives and daughters of wealthier merchants, and the galleries for the lesser middling and serving classes. Indeed, authors regularly took note of these seating arrangements by tailoring sequential appeals to each class of persons in the prologues and epilogues to their plays.

This gesture represents just one of the ways in which the audience was acknowledged as being as much a part of the entertainment as the actors on the stage. Indeed, the playhouse remained fully lit throughout the evening, providing for a performance situation in which audience members attracted at least as much attention as the action on the stage, if not more. The audience, moreover, was hardly docile or quiet. Audience members routinely carried on conversations during the performances, and the sound levels in the playhouse often drowned out the dialogue on the boards. Further, some boxes were actually situated on the sides of the stage, and, until Garrick instituted a series of reforms in the 1760s that ultimately paved the way for the withdrawal of action behind the "fourth wall" of the proscenium, many of the bolder members of the pit took the liberty of sitting on the forestage, attracting attention and interfering with the performance at will. It was not uncommon for wits in the pit to form themselves into claques, cabals, and parties in order to influence the fate of plays, hissing and directing catcalls toward plays they wished to damn and clapping up plays they wished to succeed. On rare occasions these parties in the pit were even able to incite a riot.

One can only imagine, then, how unnerving the prospect of a first performance might have been to a wary playwright. After having run the gauntlet of getting a playhouse manager to look at a manuscript and then accept it for performance, an author could only hope that a fickle and capricious audience would allow the play to become a hit and reach the author's benefit peformance on the third night. Oliver Goldsmith described this experience as a "process truly chymical" in which a play must not only "be tried in the manager's fire, strained through a licenser," but also "purified in the Review, or the news-paper of the day."[5] Those poets who endured such a process were only a fortunate few, for the prospects of getting a new play mounted at all, especially after the Stage Licensing Act of 1737, were very slim. In the course of the main season, which generally ran from mid-September to the last week of May, only a few new plays were produced. The rest of the performance schedule was reserved for a repertory of fifty to seventy revivals and adaptations of stock Restoration and Renaissance plays.

In an age when a run of three performances signaled a success, the audience thus wielded a great deal of deliberative power. By midcentury, this audience was composed of a core of between 12,000 and 15,000 regular theatergoers. While this figure represented only a small percentage of the London population, it increasingly came to encompass a wider socioeconomic cross-section of the city.[6] Moreover, the influence of the theater spread far beyond the theater walls through coffeehouse discussions and debates, periodical and newspaper reviews and critiques, pamphlet exchanges, and acting memoirs and biographies, both scandalous and serious. The eighteenth-century playhouse thus constituted what Lawrence E. Klein, in a different context, has termed a "nodal point in the network of the new urban culture," a place not only where new forms of sociability emerged but also where that emerging culture could develop and test new ways of representing and explaining itself.[7]

This function was facilitated precisely by the conditions I have just described. The repertory system ensured an audience whose theatrical expectations and discursive instincts were sharply honed and whose ability to distinguish among plays, performances, and various genres of entertainment was finely tuned. At the same time, the audience was itself implicated both in the immediate performance and in the performative experience beyond the walls of the theater. As William B. Worthen has observed, "On the architectural scale, the division of the theater into box, pit, and gallery audiences objectified the class distinctions that structured society at large . . . each social group was conscious of the conventional role it performed before the rest of the public."[8] In short, the semiotics of placement within the theater provided for an intense experience of the socioeconomic conditions that regulated society at large and made patently clear the kinds of competing interests that had to be negotiated within that culture. Social rank was as significant an element in the experience of the theatrical space as it was in the meaning of the plays performed.

Finally, and perhaps most crucially, this was not a theater of the fourth wall. The style of play was discontinuous rather than continuous and in ways both conservative and subversive pointed up the uneven effects of performance in everyday life. This was not a theater of absorption in character, then, but a theater of interaction in which the audience was as much a part of the performance as the players. No single controlling gaze regulated the space of performance in the eighteenth century; the power of performance was routinely shared and exchanged between audience and performers. Together they monitored not the depth of a character, but rather the arc of a genre over the course of five discontinuous acts.

This book examines the cultural work performed by the drama across that arc of representation. By cultural work I mean the ways plays functioned in the eighteenth century not only as a form of entertainment but as a medium through which authors could attempt, under the epistemological and formal constraints of genre, to engage with, represent, and make sense of the changing literary and socioeconomic landscape of English life. While in an abstract sense this project has been influenced in its conception by the theoretical work of Victor Turner on the anthropology of drama and performance, for more immediate and historically concrete models it looks to the work of John Loftis, who explored the social and political status of eighteenth-century drama, and to Laura Brown, who first attempted to elucidate generic developments in cultural terms.[9] Critical projects like those of Loftis and Brown, which specifically target eighteenth-century drama and its sociocultural dimensions, have been few and far between, however, in at least two respects. First, it is not uncommon for even the most informed scholars to group eighteenth-century dramas with those of the Restoration, as if together they constitute a consistent and undifferentiated body of works. Yet the periods and the concerns of the drama in each period are quite distinct. In the most general sense, Restoration drama, influenced by the discursive necessities of a new monarchist imperative, concerns itself with the reconstitution of both political legitimacy and the authority of language. Eighteenth-century drama, on the other hand, turns in the wake of the political settlements of 1688 and the financial revolution of the 1690s to considerations of the new social, economic, and political relations among and between the different classes and of the impact of consumer culture and commercial interests on social, moral and, literary values.

Second, those who have taken eighteenth-century drama proper as their subject have often displayed a studied resistance to employing current critical and theoretical methods. In particular, they have shunned any attempts to cultivate an understanding of the ways in which drama regulates the representation of social bodies, that is, how cultural forms such as dramatic genres work to produce historically situated identities of class, gender, and nation. While such modes of understanding have been widely adopted and directed toward the study of the Renaissance and Restoration stages, the materials of the eighteenth-century stage have been largely untouched by these methods and thus remain poorly understood.

I endeavor here to fill these gaps in our understanding, first, by focusing specifically on the dramatic materials of the eighteenth century proper and, second, by bringing current theoretical and critical methodologies to bear on the study of these materials. In staking this claim to a field, however, it is also worth stating clearly both which materials in this period are covered and which are not. I focus on those plays that were originally written in the eighteenth century and prepared for eighteenth-century audiences. This means two things: one, I do not include discussions of the Restoration dramas that made up so much of the eighteenth-century repertory; and two, I do not take up the subject either of Shakespearean adaptations in the eighteenth century or of the rise of Shakespeare's popularity in the eighteenth century. These kinds of exclusions arise both out of a necessity to limit the scope of this study and out of the recognition that these subjects have been covered already by scholars far better versed in those materials than myself.[10] Inevitably, I will make allusions to these fields of study and, from time to time, draw on the insights of these critics. But my primary concern is with the particularities of the dramatic genres of the eighteenth century and the ways that identity was represented on its stages.

In taking up questions about the representation of identity in the eighteenth century, it would be difficult to overlook the precedents set in the large body of work on the rise of the novel in the last fifteen years. In an essay that distills the main arguments of his dialectical account of the rise of the novel, *The Origins of the English Novel, 1600–1740*, Michael McKeon notes that in light of the instability of generic and social categories in the later seventeenth century, two main challenges for representation in narrative forms arose: "What kind of authority or evidence is required of narrative to permit it to signify truth to its readers? What kind of social existence or behavior signifies an individual's virtue to others?"[11] Following the insight offered by Ian Watt in *The Rise of the Novel*, McKeon looked to the rise of the middle class subject as the key to understanding both the emergence of this new form and the effect of its operations upon readers.[12] He argued that, "In its preoccupation with questions of virtue . . . the emerging novel internalizes the emergence of the middle class and the concerns that it exists to mediate."[13] Ever since that moment of critical ferment, "the rise of the modern subject" has become, as William B. Warner notes, the "central payoff" in accounts of the "rise of the novel."[14] This is not to say that there have been no questions or qualms about the strength or accuracy of this thesis. Warner, for example, massages the issue in his own account of the "elevation" of the novel: "Rather than inventing *the* modern subject, novel reading contributes to the expansion of the range and types of subjectivity."[15] Taking a more skeptical approach, Deidre Lynch questions whether we ought to assume that the "history of character and the history of the individual are the same thing" and suggests that "it is a bit too neat how the narrative about characterization's development dovetails with the narrative about culture's long-postponed recognition of the intrinsic significance of the private individual."[16] Yet whether they view the rise of the middle class subject either as a necessary and concomitant condition for the rise of the novel or as coincidental or proleptic to it, all of these theorists agree on at least two crucial points: the novel aspires to produce a representation of interiority and it does so both amid and in reaction to the proliferation of other forms of commercial print media. The promise, indeed the seductive pitch, of the novel, as Deidre Lynch points out, is that it appears to offer its readers the "deepest, truest knowledge of character" (28). Novels, in short, appear to render the inner depths, the conscious and even unconscious motives and thoughts of characters, transparent to the reader, even as, under the cloak of "realism" they conceal the very mechanics of character conveyance.[17]

When I first started working on this project, I assumed that I would be following in the footsteps of these theorists and that I would be examining the status of the subject and subjectivities on the eighteenth-century English stage. Yet the more I studied the plays of the eighteenth century, the more convinced I became that the discourse of "the subject" fails and, in fact, is conceptually inappropriate as a paradigm to figure or assess the representation of identity in the drama of this period. What we can find in the drama and on the stage, however, is a dynamic paradigm for representing identity that derives its force from the concept of "character" as it was elaborated and understood in an eighteenth-century context. To draw these conclusions, one need look no farther than to the basic conditions governing stage representations at the time: the discontinuous presentation of the plays, the disruptions and attractions of the audience, and the absence of a "fourth-wall" that could create the double illusion of separation and transparency between spectacle and spectator. These factors alone, not to mention the culture of celebrity associated with the actors and actresses on the boards, precluded the kinds of discursive operations upon which the novel relies to produce its effects, especially that of subjectivity. At the same time, and perhaps as a reflection of the conditions of the medium, the plays themselves exhibit a curious lack of depth in characterization. Indeed, if there is any sense of coherence in the plays, it derives more from the conventional imperatives of genre than from the persistence or growth of individual consciousness across time.

I want to make clear from the outset, however, that my argument about the shaping and representation of identity on the stage is not meant as a critique of the work that has been done with respect to identity formation in the novel.

Rather, what I will be arguing is that while eighteenth-century drama was concerned with many of the same categories of identity that preoccupied the novel, it offered a structure for those identities and our experience of them that was fundamentally distinct and was particular to the qualities of the theatrical medium. At least implicitly, then, this study will raise the question of why, in our understanding of eighteenth-century literature and culture, we have come to privilege the novel's version of the modern subject when it was neither the inevitable nor the only configuration of identity in circulation at the time. Indeed, in a culture in which it was possible to appear genteel without being gentle and it was increasingly difficult to know whom to "credit" in the marketplace of identities, it could be argued that in turning to "character" the stage registered a kind of resistance to and critique of the illusion of transparency and plenitude that the novel offered in "the subject."

Chapter 1 examines these issues about character in much greater detail. My interest in particular lies in elaborating the historical forces and differences in media that would motivate writers of novels and authors of plays to adopt such distinct models for the representation of identity. The chapter thus describes the semantic resonance of the concept of "character" in the eighteenth century and demonstrates how this semantically complex rubric provided for an understanding of identity that was particularly apposite not only to the conditions that governed eighteenth-century performance but also to the increasingly performative conditions of eighteenth-century life. Through a discussion of John Gay's *The What D'Ye Call It?* (1714/1715) at the end of the chapter, I demonstrate how the eighteenth-century stage looked to the conventions of genre to provide a framework within which to measure, assess, and assign meaning to the characters represented. Refusing the illusory consolations offered in the novel through the figure of the transparent subject, the stage highlighted the multiple, contradictory, and opaque surfaces of character and located meaning instead in the contingencies and contexts that shape perception and recognition. In this respect, the productions of the eighteenth-century stage were not so much character-driven as genre-driven entertainments.

Consequently, if we want to understand the cultural work of drama in the eighteenth century, we need to look both at the ways that dramatic genres were construed in theory and at the ways that genres construed characters in practice. Following the discussion of character in Chapter 1, each subsequent chapter in this study thus focuses on a different dramatic genre: plays about plays; tragedies; comedies of manners, humours, and intrigue; and sentimental comedies. In each chapter, I strive first to theorize the kinds of cultural work traditionally expected of and impressed upon the genre and to explore the intersection of those expectations with historical circumstances in contemporary eighteenth-century culture.

Having established those parameters, I then examine how that form functioned in practice either to facilitate or to constrain both the representation of character and the production of categories of identity such as class, gender, and nation. Although each chapter contains a series of sustained readings, I do not necessarily focus on particular authors or on what might be considered the "best" plays of the period. Rather, based on extensive reading in each of the different genres, I have sought to discern the patterns that characterize each form and to select for interpretation and analysis those plays that best illustrate the significance of those patterns. In short, these chapter-long discussions aim less at being exhaustive than at being representative of the materials in question.

Chapter 2, "Plays About Plays: An 'Abstract Chronicle,'" extends my discussion of the status of character on the eighteenth-century stage by turning to the dramatic genre that was most self-consciously aware of the mechanisms of theatrical representation. I explore how playwrights who took the stage and stage practices as their subject entered into current debates over authorship and situated themselves amid the swirling cultural politics of the day. I discuss how these dramatists took the measure of a culture saturated by suspicions of theatricality and insincerity, and I argue that they deployed an antitheatrical theatricalism in order to establish their own authority. Finally, I examine how they directed that authority and the cultural capital it carried against the rise of female playwrights and the incursions of foreign entertainments.

Chapter 3, "Tragedy's Tragic Flaw: National Character and Feminine Unruliness," examines the particularly heavy burden borne by tragedy in the eighteenth century as the genre responsible for envisioning the nation's posterity. I submit that the growing preoccupation with the demise of tragedy can be read as an index for a national identity crisis. Focusing on conflicts between classical ideals and bourgeois pragmatism in plays from the first half of the century by Addison, Lillo, and Rowe, I show how the crises over tragedy and national identity came to be displaced antagonistically onto the "character" of feminine unruliness rather than being dealt with at their origin in class conflict.

Chapter 4, "Constitutional Parodies of Identity: Manners, Humours, and Intrigue on the Comic Stage," focuses on comedy's role in administering a process of character valuation whereby the economic and social status of each character comes to be identified and the various couples' interests aligned and secured. Through readings of comedies by authors such as George Farquhar, Susanna Centlivre, Hannah Cowley, and Richard Brinsley Sheridan, I demonstrate how eighteenth-century comedies reflect ironically on the ideal of romantic love by dramatizing the social labor required to produce an appearance of motivated disinterest. At the same time, I examine the role of masquerade, deception, and spectacle in producing what I term "constitutional parodies of identity"—performances of historically situated identities that mimic and mark the contours of their gendered and classed counterparts in everyday life.

Finally, Chapter 5, "Sentimental Comedy: Or, The Comedy of Good Breeding," explores the emergence of a new dramatic genre in the eighteenth century, that of sentimental comedy. I examine the conflicts that emerged over the "breeding" of this new genre and demonstrate how those conflicts were implicated in the larger cultural politics of English liberty in the period. In subsequent readings of plays from this new genre, beginning with Richard Steele's *The Conscious Lovers*, I demonstrate how sentimental comedies carried out the same process of character valuation that can be found in the laughing comedies but altered the basis on which that valuation was realized from contests of wit to displays of good breeding in order to accommodate the social and economic merits of the new middling classes. In the course of these readings, I focus particular attention on the proliferation of orphans and long-lost children in this genre in order to illuminate how the prerogatives of patrimony were redefined to satisfy an ideology of patriarchal benevolence in sentimental discourse.

These are the chapters, the concerns, and the ideas that form the central interests of this book. Without further ado, then, let me turn now to the first order of business in this study: the question of character.

Chapter One
Staged Identities
It's Just a Question of Character

It is certain that if we look all round us and behold the different Employments of Mankind, you hardly see one who is not, as the Player is, in an
assumed Character.
Richard Steele, *Spectator*, No. 370,
May 5, 1712

In *Spectator* No. 370, Richard Steele asserts the "certainty" of the
slogan *totus mundus agit histrionem*—the whole world acts the player.[1] Underlin-
ing the apparently theatrical texture of eighteenth-century life, Steele charges:
"Consider all the different Pursuits and Employments of Men, and you will find
half their Actions tend to nothing else but Disguise and Imposture; and all that is
done which proceeds not from a Man's very self is the Action of a Player." While
Steele's confident gesture echoes commonplace observations, it also marks his
own willingness in this instance to gloss over some of the most troubling concerns raised by that commonplace in eighteenth-century social and cultural life.
In particular, Steele fails to address widespread anxieties over how to distinguish
between those actions that proceed from a "Man's very self" and those that
proceed from the "Action of a Player." Indeed, his banal insistence that the stage
and the world "reciprocally imitate each other" frustrates the possibility, held out
at the beginning of the essay, of a more probing inquiry into the relationship
sustained between these distinct realms of experience. More importantly, it begs
the question that forms the central concern of this study: if the "whole world
act[ed] the Player," how did the player act the world? How, in short, did the stage
position itself in relation to the increasingly performative culture of eighteenth-
century England?

As I have already explained briefly in the Introduction, this study argues that
the stage located its response to this situation not in representations of the "subject" as did the novel, but rather in representations of identity that fell under the
rubric of "character," as it was specifically conceived and understood in the
eighteenth century. In this chapter, then, I begin to address the questions I have

raised above by exploring the semantic resonance of "character" in the eighteenth century and by describing the logic governing the dynamic model of identity that it supported. In the course of this discussion, I offer specific observations on the temperamental affinities between this model of identity and the material conditions that held sway over theatrical performances and representations. I thus provide an account of how character functioned as the rubric for shaping identities on the eighteenth-century stage, and I indicate the ways in which the concept of character was implicated in contemporary debates over economic value and epistemological authority. I argue that by representing identity as an effect of character, writers for the stage capitalized upon, rather than compensated for, anxieties over the stability of personal and social identity and thus gained a strategic position from which they could claim to offer a more sincere and trustworthy perspective in those debates. To make these abstract claims more concrete, I turn at the end of this chapter to John Gay's *The What D'Ye Call It?* (1714/1715) to illustrate how the multifaceted concept of character was deployed in dramatic representations and to demonstrate how genre was situated as the epistemological frame for construing this contingent mode of personation. I conclude this chapter by offering a discussion of genre as the ordering principle of the eighteenth-century stage and the social identities it produced. Before we turn to the stage, however, it may be useful, first, to examine how other narrative forms responded to the uncertainties occasioned by what one critic discussed below has termed the "theatricalization of social relations" and, second, to analyze the form of represented identity to which these compensatory strategies gave rise.[2]

Theatricality and Identity in Nondramatic Representation

A number of influential critics of eighteenth-century literature and culture have touted theatricality as both the governing metaphor of social life and the primary filter of psychic perception in the period. Not insignificantly, they have generally done so, without referring either to actual theatrical practice or to the play texts through which that practice was drawn. Three prominent examples will suffice to illustrate this pattern. In *Worlds Apart: The Market and the Theatre in Anglo-American Thought, 1550–1750*, Jean Christophe-Agnew bypasses eighteenth-century drama by asserting, "Once the English stage divested itself of its sociologically heterodox audience, as it did after the Restoration, the source of the theatrical perspective shifted from the public experience of the stage to the private experience of the novel."[3] Agnew's contention that the theatrical metaphor was taken up and deployed in earnest by "authors" rather than by "playwrights" is echoed in David Marshall's study *The Figure of Theater: Shaftesbury, Defoe, Adam Smith, and George Eliot*.[4] Even as he boldly acknowledges that he "does not include specific plays (or considerations of their production or influence)," Marshall writes: "the figure of theater provides a significant cultural paradigm for eighteenth-century English culture. . . . [I]t represents a locus where crucial issues in fiction writing, moral philosophy, aesthetics, and epistemology are addressed and acted out by a surprising variety of influential authors" (4–5). Finally, in *Absorption and Theatricality: Painting and the Beholder in the Age of Diderot*, Michael Fried offers a brilliant counterintuitive account of eighteenth-century French art, arguing that one of the essential projects of pictorial art and art criticism in this period was precisely to efface the theatrical relationship between the spectator and the observed.[5]

Significantly, what these studies have in common is an interest in the "Age of the Spectator" and in the central role played by spectatorship in the historic emergence of what we now recognize as the modern "subject." Whether he invokes David Hume's "theatre of the mind," Adam Smith's "impartial spectator," or Diderot's "tableaux," each theorist describes a process whereby a theatrical logic comes to be internalized and naturalized as the private individual observes and apprehends the self as other, that is, as an object to itself. David Marshall explicitly introduces this topic when he asserts that all of the authors in his study "are concerned with the theater that exists outside the playhouse: the theatrical relations formed between people who face each other from the positions of actor and spectator, and the play of characters created by a view of the self as a persona, a role. . . . Theater, for these authors, represents, creates, and responds to the uncertainties about how to constitute, maintain, and represent a stable and authentic self" (1). Jean-Christophe Agnew also locates a dynamic of internal self-dramatization and stabilization in eighteenth-century discourse and argues that in part this process involved the construction of a kind of "fourth wall" by which an individual could "remove the all too palpable presence of those spectators presumptuously seated on the stage of his text" (169).[6] Similarly, in both the figures of absorption in eighteenth-century French art and Diderot's commentaries, Michael Fried discovers a desire to "neutralize" the gaze of others, "to wall it off from the action taking place" (96). The artist who depicts figures that appear to be conscious to themselves and "declare their aloneness relative to the beholder or at any rate their obliviousness of his presence," achieves, according to Fried, the illusion of realism (103). In the context of representation, this form of "aloneness," a suspension in and separation from an otherwise inexorable world of action, functions as the signature, or proof, of an invisible yet animate and conscious interiority. Behind that illusory, yet profoundly effective, "fourth wall," the represented figure sustains and extends the fantasy of an active inner life in which the self, in isolation and at a distance from the vulgarities and changing tastes of a market culture, can view itself as an object of estimation that can be assigned an authentic and stable value.

Severed from any referential relation to material practice in the eighteenth-century playhouse, theatricality emerges in each of these studies as a constitutive frame of mind, and hence as a productive analog to explain an increasingly performative culture. More importantly, theatricality is consistently identified both as a critical mechanism in the construction of modern subjectivity and as a contrivance that must be internalized and concealed in order to maintain the fiction of the subject's stability. Taken together, these studies suggest that for the eighteenth century, the authority of a given representation, defined as the extent to which it was taken for the "real," depended upon, and could be maintained only to, the extent that the fictionality or artifice of its own enterprise could be concealed, with the subject situated behind a stabilizing fourth wall.

This demand for a kind of "formal realism" in eighteenth-century representation was also recognized and described in Ian Watt's groundbreaking *The Rise of the Novel.*[7] Employing what was then an unprecedented critical strategy, Watt initiated his discussion of the novel by conducting an inquiry into the foundational term that so many critics had previously taken for granted. Realism, he explains, in its classical sense of the truth claims of universal principles removed from the burden of particularities, was abandoned and replaced over the course of the eighteenth century by a philosophical realism formulated by Descartes and Locke that emphasized access to knowledge through individual experiences of empirical data from the senses. Watt describes this reconfiguration of "realism" as one of the more significant "semantic reversals" witnessed by the eighteenth century, one that reflected an increasing willingness in eighteenth-century culture to set aside medieval ontologies in favor of emergent epistemologies as the frames of reference for organizing and interpreting everyday life. Fundamentally, this transition to what we now term modernity involved both the loss of faith in the models of authority and knowledge that were anchored in ahistorical cosmologies and the affirmation of a more secular approach to and experience of knowledge as rationally, temporally, and spatially situated. It marked a diminishment in efforts to provide accounts for appointed ways of being and a growing commitment to understanding how we come to locate, recognize, and attribute meaning to ways of being *as such* in the aggregate of their particularities.

Although Watt foregrounds this development to illustrate the unique conditions enabling the rise of the novel—the circumstances that enabled new "forms" to emerge—his commentary also elucidates a broader concern in eighteenth-century cultural life with the processes by which the elements of those forms were understood to produce or "originate" new meanings. These new forms concerned themselves at least as much with the general structures that enabled "realities" to become known as with the "realities" that ultimately emerged from a particular collection of data. They understood the "real" not as transcendent, but rather as deriving from a dialectic between presentation and perception. Consequently, "reality" came to be approached and understood as an effect of mediation, as something made—a product of the interchange between the connotative structures of representation and the interpretive structures of individual consciousness. Watt thus writes, "the novel's realism does not reside in the kind of life it presents, but in the way it presents it" (11).

Not insignificantly, critics of the novel, like critics of eighteenth-century culture more generally, have identified the modeling of coherent subjectivities as the main "way" or strategy developed by writers of novels to compensate for such perceived instabilities. They have thus extended Watt's thesis to demonstrate that formal realism not only contributed to, but indeed was constitutive of and coextensive with the emergence of modern and, in particular, middle-class subjectivities. For instance, in a point of clarification of the assumptions underlying *Imagining the Penitentiary*, John Bender writes, "I take the novel in general, and the realist novel in particular, to be defined by its unique technical capacity to represent consciousness in the form of unspoken thoughts, subjective responses, and sensations."[8] For Bender, in other words, the representation of subjectivity is not merely an incidental effect of the realist novel. Rather it is both an essential product and a definitive sign of that form. Narrative realism functions *unrealistically* to produce the illusion of continuity of self.

In *Desire and Domestic Fiction*, Nancy Armstrong goes one step further to claim that the modern individual referred to by Bender and others "was first and foremost a woman" and that "one cannot distinguish the production of the new female ideal either from the rise of the novel or from the rise of the new middle classes in England."[9] Drawing upon discourses of desire that are deeply implicated in psychoanalytic and Marxist theories of the subject, Armstrong positions the novel as the master narrative of the period and claims both a correlative and a causal role for the novel in producing "a subject who understood herself in the psychological terms that had shaped fiction" (23). Bender and Armstrong both advance the view, then, that the novel's realism contributed to and depended upon the creation and representation of individual consciousness, that is, on what Leo Braudy has elsewhere described as "character apprehended from within."[10]

In the context of a culture, then, in which even the notion of personal identity was under attack as potentially a mere fiction of human consciousness, what the novel seemed to offer readers was the opportunity to have access to "persons" whose consciousness could be fully known, whose emotions and motives were freely and completely available to scrutiny, and, hence, whose value and meaning could be assessed and fixed. While interpretable surfaces abounded and the value of knowledge about persons was increasingly difficult to assess, the novel generated a "rhetoric of essences rather than surfaces."[11] Thus deploying a compensatory strategy, the novel displaced the reigning sense of identity as theatrically constituted and replaced it with the illusion of a "materially constituted self," a self of substance, depth, consciousness, and self-consciousness—in other words, a subject.[12] The novel, in short, was in the business of manufacturing the illusion of access to other subjects. This illusion provided a reassuring point of access to the interior thoughts and sentiments of another, even if that other was only a fictional character.[13]

Indeed, in her award-winning study of the rise of the novel and its cognitive effects, *Nobody's Story: The Vanishing Acts of Women Writers in the Marketplace, 1670–1820*, Catherine Gallagher argues that this "fictionality" was precisely the point of these representations and the access to sentiment that they provided. "By representing feelings that belong to no other body," She explains, fiction "gives us the illusion of immediately appropriable sentiments, free sentiments belonging to nobody and therefore identifiable with ourselves." By deploying what Gallagher calls "universally engaging subjectivities . . . unmarked by a proprietary relationship to anyone in the real world," the novel created a "species of utopian common property" that every reader could feel free to appropriate.[14] In short, in the context of a culture in which actual bodies were suspected for their theatrical ability to conceal intentions and sentiments, the novel manufactured the double illusion of transparent, material subjects—fictional no-bodies—whose value could be assessed, authenticated, fixed, and appropriated, without resistance, as the property of readers. The rise of the subject as both the means and end of the rise of the novel thus provided a stable form of compensation for the reader's specific labors and for the culture's general anxieties over the instability of identity.

The accounts of narrative forms that I have outlined here are both rich and illuminating and have been instrumental in shaping many of my own ideas about the "theatricalization of social relations" in the eighteenth century and about the complex play—between surface and depth, public and private, and self and other—through which the "subject" is constituted. Yet insofar as these accounts rely heavily on reading back into eighteenth-century representations either a definition of theatricality indebted to late twentieth-century performance theory or a notion of the "subject" that was first articulated in nineteenth-century economic and psychological discourse, the exercise of a healthy degree of skepticism toward the universal applicability of their arguments seems warranted. If the modern "subject" was only just emerging as the dominant mode for imagining and representing a self, as many of these theorists have themselves conceded, then we ought not to assume that we can locate that model of identity in all forms of eighteenth-century representation.[15] Indeed, even if the "subject" had fully emerged in representation, there is no reason to suppose either that it was the only model of identity available or that it would be the one used in all representations. Given these historical circumstances, we ought to begin a study of eighteenth-century plays by asking a series of basic questions that take into consideration the particular contours, conditions, and interests of eighteenth-century dramatic practice. First and foremost, we must ask: how did the stage position itself in relation to a theatrical conception of everyday life? Did the stage seek, as did other forms, to make transparent the very medium of its own representation? Did the stage aspire to formal realism? Was the stage devoted either to the shaping of modern subjectivities or to the exchange of property implicit in the representation of subjectivities? Was there a subject on the eighteenth-century stage?

In the Playhouse of Eighteenth-Century Drama

It might be best to begin such an inquiry with a few basic observations on the state of affairs in the eighteenth-century playhouse. The first thing we notice when we read eighteenth-century dramatic works is that they do not share in that "impetus toward realism" that so many scholars have identified as critical both to the rise of the novel and to the emergence of the subject in representation.[16] From the shifting frames of plays about plays to the formal, declamatory speeches of tragedy to the often improbable and chaotic plots of comedies of manners, humours, and intrigue to the carefully stylized gestures of sentimental comedy, it is clear that realism, in either a mimetic or a formal sense, was simply not an objective or even a consideration in eighteenth-century dramatic representations. Indeed, far from constructing a "fourth wall" behind which the illusion of a "subject" could be produced and commodified, the eighteenth-century stage highlighted its contrivances and celebrated the process of being watched. Rather than efface the relationship between the spectator and the observed, the stage noted those spectators who were, quite literally, "presumptuously seated on the stage" and exploited that dynamic.[17]

The second significant curiosity we notice is that the representations of the eighteenth-century stage appear formulaic and repetitive in a manner that seems less concerned with technical virtuosity than with the blunt fulfillment of generic demands through the movements of fictional individuals who are marked precisely by an absence of consciousness. In short, rather than working toward the "ideological regrounding of intrinsic value," the stage, as I will demonstrate throughout this study, worked to place the ideology of "intrinsic value" under suspicion and focused its attention on extrinsic qualities and their ambiguous value.[18]

That these contrasts between the novel and the drama were recognized by readers in the eighteenth century is evidenced by the following comment from an essay titled *Remarks on Clarissa*: "*Clarissa* is not intended as a Dramatic, but as a real Picture of human Life, where Story can move but slowly, where the Characters must open by degrees, and the Reader's own Judgment form them from different Parts, as they display themselves according to the Incidents that arise."[19] The key distinctions drawn here are between "dramatic" and "real" representation and between the kind, pace, and amount of psychological detail offered to readers of novels as compared to readers of plays. Indeed, the basic constraints of theatrical production in the eighteenth century meant that plays simply did not have the luxury of time or space to develop or "open" a character by "degrees." The brief observation supplied in this essay thus attests not only to distinctions in the texture of fictional personae, but also to the unique cognitive experience proffered by the theatrical event.

Perhaps the single most obvious and consequential feature that distinguishes the theatrical from the novelistic event, at any time, is that which Steele was so eager to point out to readers of *The Conscious Lovers* (1722/1723): "It must be remembered a play is to be seen, and is made to be represented with the advantage of action."[20] Drama involves live performance, and live performance requires the physical presence of actors and actresses on the stage. In the eighteenth century, specifically, this situation was complicated by the possibility that, unlike fictional characters who have no independent existence, an actor or actress could, and often did, step out of character during a performance. Indeed, as I will discuss in much greater detail later in this chapter, the extent to which an actor or actress in the eighteenth century could be said to be "in character" at all represents a point of critical debate. Suffice it to say here that in the eighteenth century—the age of the actor—the fictional persona created by a playwright often had to compete with the persona or public reputation of the actor or actress taking that part. In this very basic sense, the "character" presented to an audience was neither singular nor unitary, but rather manifold and incongruous.[21]

This set of circumstances did not merely complicate, rather it *precluded* the kind of proprietary relationship that Gallagher has identified as so crucial to the experience of the "realist" novel. The theater resisted the forms of appropriation available to readers of novels precisely because the bodies of the actors and actresses presented what Gallagher would term a "proprietary barrier" to the audience (171). As if mimicking the kinds of epistemological confusion experienced over identity in everyday life, the theatrical situation ensured that any attempt to establish a proprietary claim on dramatic character would be frustrated not only by confusion over which aspect of "character" ought to be given priority in establishing value, but also over which aspects of "character" were "authentic" and which were "assumed." In sum, if subjectivity constitutes a form of property both in others and in oneself, then it could and will be argued that for both situational and ideological reasons the eighteenth-century stage actively resisted that form of commodification and the method of valuation of persons it entailed. There was no "subject," nor could there be a "subject" on the eighteenth-century stage.

In light of the fact that the theater resisted both the underlying principles and the "psychological terms" that made the very representation of subjectivities possible, we need to ask and answer a new series of questions. First and foremost, what model of identity was provided for by the particular "technical capacities" of the stage and its generic forms? What logic or idea of representation would motivate playwrights to adopt this model rather than the model that increasingly dominated prose forms? What did the stage have to gain from the repetitive and formulaic, and what about these representations is so oddly fascinating? Finally, if we assume that, like other literary forms, drama serves as a "vehicle for our experience of the real," what experience was offered by eighteenth-century drama that was distinct from the novel and hence what insights into eighteenth-century culture can the stage provide us with that the novel cannot?[22]

The Concept of Character in Theory

To answer these questions, I suggest we return to the place where we began this inquiry—to Steele's essay and in particular to the multiple and divergent ways in which he calls upon "character" in this critical piece.[23] The ease with which Steele associates "character" both with the theatricality of identity in everyday life and with identities on the stage suggests a conceptualization of identity that was in wide circulation in eighteenth-century culture and that ought to be better understood. By examining how the term "character" was defined and used in this period, we can begin to form a better idea of any notion of identity that would take this semantic unit as its conceptual base and to discern why, as I will argue, the stage employed and promoted this alternative concept as its rubric for the representation of identity. More broadly, we will be able to assess how the stage positioned itself both to claim authority in a theatrical culture and to critique the emergence of the subject in representation.

Like many elements of language during the late seventeenth and eighteenth centuries, the term "character" underwent a radical semantic transformation.[24] Prior to the eighteenth century, "character" carried primarily literal denotations alluding most often to a "distinctive mark impressed, engraved or otherwise formed," that is, to a graphic sign or symbol, like a letter in an alphabet. Such designations outline an understanding, within a preexisting system, of a one-to-one correspondence between what we now commonly refer to as the signifier and the signified. As long as "character" referred to a letter or some other graphic sign or symbol—as long, that is, as it referred to a sign in a sign system—its meaning was arbitrary and ascribed and, paradoxically, fixed and naturalized. Conspicuously absent from all early definitions is any suggestion of meaning as mediated by either human sympathy or judgment.[25] Defined strictly and understood with some severity as literal signs, "characters" bore no relation either to subjective interpretation or to human agency. They neither courted ambiguity nor appeared to hold any interest in questions of moral content or meaning. The meaning of a "character" appeared to be contained in its own identity, in the integrity of its visual self-referentiality.

This understanding of "character" applied in particular to the numismatic case of characters impressed upon precious metals such as gold and silver to produce coins. The "face" value of a coin, its extrinsic mark, was understood to be equivalent to its intrinsic value; the sign of value was understood as real value. From the outset, then, character supported an association with value and the representation of value, an association that increased in importance and ambiguity in the late seventeenth and eighteenth centuries. Indeed, as James Thompson has demonstrated at length, the severe debasement and scarcity of English coinage in the late seventeenth century raised into consciousness considerations not only of currency's significance but also of the significance of the characters or symbols found on that currency. Confronted by the practical reality of clipped, shaved, and worn-out coins, not to mention the proliferation of paper money and negotiable financial instruments, political economists and the public at large were forced to consider "just what money was and what it represented" (16). Debates over the Recoinage Act (1695–96) only made explicit what was already implicit in the marketplace: "The very character of the king's image stamped on the face of a silver coin [was] contradictory, for if the regal sign on the coin [was] a mark of its authenticity, the use or history of that coin [did] not reinforce but rather efface[d] the coin's authenticity" (16). In short, "character" as a "distinctive mark engraved, impressed or otherwise formed" upon metal came under scrutiny for its "truth" value and was shown to be less than reliable as an indicator of that metal's value. Considerations of the value of a "character" thus referred not only to questions of representation but also to questions of authority and authenticity in representation.

In a broader context, this crisis over what Thompson terms the "concept of value" can be understood as an epiphenomenon of a more general concern in eighteenth-century culture over how extrinsic signs relate to intrinsic value. This historical situation has been understood by many theorists as a consequence of the changing philosophical, economic, and political climate in eighteenth-century England. J. G. A. Pocock, for instance, writes of an ideological confrontation between classical idealism and the new commercial politics. He writes, "it was the individual as classical political being whose capacities for self-knowledge and self-command—expressed in the ideal of virtue—were rendered uncertain and dissolved into fantasy, other-directedness, and anomie by the corruptions of the new commercial politics."[26] Under siege, that "classical political being" was salvaged and reinvented in the eighteenth century, emerging, as Pocock argues in another essay, as a "commercial humanist" whose status was secured and sustained by the rearticulation of virtue as "manners."[27] John Brewer concurs, writing, "Overall, the entire credit system engendered a highly speculative and volatile economy, full of enterprise and initiative, open to an extraordinary degree to the vagaries of fashion and fad, encouraging quick returns and setting a premium on highly flexible and imaginative business strategies."[28] He goes on to argue that "manners" were adopted as a form of social regulation for these volatile relations, a way of controlling and minimizing risk by codifying behavior. Insofar as "Presentation of self as sober, reliable, candid and constant was not merely a question of genteel manners, but a matter of economic survival," he writes, "One needed to be, or at least, needed *to appear as* a man with such characteristics in order to carry on trade" (214, emphasis added). In sum, the exigencies of nascent capitalism combined with a novel emphasis on individualism provided the occasion for the institution of stratagem, or the "theatricalization of social relations," in the presentation of self in everyday life.[29]

In the eighteenth century, then, the problem of defining an individual, or the formation and attribution of what we term "identity," involved conflicts over the value of outward appearances, or surfaces, as "real" indices of persons. Claims to identity lost their self-evident power and were instead subjected to profound scrutiny and distrust. These changes were reflected as well in the literal reversals and figurative splinterings of the language applied to the problem of identity and the delineation of persons.[30] There is perhaps no case more illustrative of this phenomenon than the case of "character."

Indeed, even as "character" was transformed in its monetary register to indicate nominal rather than real value, the term also experienced an explosion in the number of figurative meanings with which it was associated in eighteenth-century discourse. In this case, moreover, the proliferation of meanings was marked by an almost chaotic dissociation from physical or objective points of reference. Of particular interest, we find that where "character" had been tied earlier to claims of rank in a fixed social order, by the early eighteenth century character was increasingly applied to designate, "A personality invested with distinctive attributes and qualities by a novelist or dramatist; also, the personality or 'part' assumed by an actor on the stage."[31] With this modification in meaning, character lost its self-evident or transparent signature and entered into the gray area of fiction, fabrication, forgery, and fraud. Understanding "character" now required skills in observation, penetration, and interpretation because it could be imaginatively modeled as well as "assumed," or mimetically reproduced, without respect to any particular hierarchy or system of representation. The one-to-one correspondence between signifier and signified that had once been embodied by this term was cleaved apart because the outside of a "character" no longer bore any necessary or meaningful resemblance to its inside. Like the splitting in the value of a coin, the relationship between individual and title moved away from the certainties of permanence, probity, and orderliness toward the more transient postures of imaginative composition, calculated deceit, and social irregularity. Immediate visual recognition gave way to mediated misprision, and the gap between perception and meaning widened into the space of fiction and theatricality.[32]

This matter of "character" was made all the more complicated by the increasingly common enlistment of the term to delineate and distinguish moral quality. That is, at the same time that "character" was being applied to fiction, it was also called upon, paradoxically, to designate a kind of "truth." This latter usage had its origins in the seventeenth century, when it was known to denote: "The sum of moral and mental qualities which distinguish an individual or a race, viewed as a homogeneous whole; the individuality impressed by nature and habit on man or nation; mental or moral constitution." Providing for standards of judgment that result in general and reductive summations of persons, this definition maintained a claim to at least some modicum of self-evident "proof" in its insistence on recognizing "character" as an "impressed" or visually identifiable mark.

This, of course, was the account of character that supported Theophrastan character sketches, a popular seventeenth-century genre derived from the classical sketches of typical individuals by Theophrastus.[33] Yet where Theophrastus relied on concrete, physical detail to produce general types, his seventeenth-century imitators gradually adapted the character sketch for the purpose of drawing exemplary and specific moral or polemical types.[34] By the eighteenth century, "virtues and vices [were] exemplified in clearly defined social types and [were] so depicted as to demonstrate their importance, for good or ill, within their particular social sphere."[35]

These new literary modelings thus reflected and took part in the general evolution of "character" to denote: "Moral qualities strongly developed or strikingly displayed; distinct or distinguished character; character worth speaking of," as well as, "The estimate formed of a person's qualities; reputation: when used without qualifying epithet implying 'favourable estimate, good repute.' " "Character" unmodified by descriptive adjective now stood alone signifying worth and value in society; to have character was to possess moral integrity without qualification. "Character," in this sense, appeared to lay claim to the same kind of self-evident signature as the term's original graphic denotation.

Yet if we direct a critical eye over this claim, we find that it was troubled on at least two levels—one a matter of representational theory, the other a matter of representational practice—suggesting that "character" in a moral sense was every bit as illusory and plural as the poses or "characters" assumed by actors and actresses on the playhouse stage. From a theoretical perspective, the presentation of "character" as a singular and uncompromised articulation of identity rested on shaky ground. Its tenuous standing was illustrated by the experience of character-writers whose efforts gave rise to more uncertainty than certainty about social and moral types. For the more character-writers strove to concretize each discrete social type, the more they perceived both the abstractness or nominal quality of the language of concretization and the infinite divisions to which those social types could be subjected. As Deidre Lynch has demonstrated: "In striving to encompass the increasingly quirky assortment of social particulars, the character collections . . . stymied the cataloging capacity that had been established for their genre. . . . The book of characters makes it apparent that the social and ethical divisions set out in preceding representational schemes—divisions regulating the relation of the individual to the totality, and asserting the permanence and unity of character beneath contradiction and transitory appearances—have the potential to be subdivided *ad infinitum*."[36] In other words, the harder character-writers worked to establish the moral efficacy of "character," the more it became clear that the moral types they created lacked authority and provided insufficient explanations for the problems of identity and identification in eighteenth-century culture. Like the "characters" on coins, the epistemic structures responsible for distinguishing moral character proved to offer an inadequate and unstable measure of value.

The imposition of a practical perspective on the problem yields similar results. It is abundantly apparent that a "display" of moral character depends upon the same delicate negotiation between representation and perception as the "display" of character by an actor or actress on the stage. Indeed, if an actor in "character" could assume a pose of moral integrity on the stage, why couldn't an individual assume such a fictional pose in everyday life? In each case, the audience or spectator had to form an estimate of the persona on display. That is, while morality per se could not be "acted," social conventions or, as noted earlier, "manners" could be identified and adhered to in such a way as to enable a person to gain the appearance or the "character" of moral good. In short, theatricality mediates the very assignment of character in this moral sense because the articulation of such a claim requires both the ability to conceal the vagaries of estimation and the capacity to assume the confident posture of one who claims to penetrate to, and to speak the objective truth about, the essence of an individual. It requires no less than the imposition of an evaluative judgment under the guise of self-evident "truth." Like "character" on a coin, then, the idea of moral character also came to occupy that site between the desire to claim the existence of an intrinsic truth and the skeptical eighteenth-century understanding that all truth in itself is only a product of the epistemological orderings of language. At best, the status of "character" as a measure of an individual's internal moral value was confounded by its dependence upon external appearances and the susceptibility of external appearance to counterfeit. On both representational and etymological levels, character was too protean to hold a stable value.

Remarkably, this condition did not prevent "character" from assuming a place as a desirable good in the marketplace of identities. Indeed, character as public reputation came to function in the eighteenth century as a prominent form of credit and credibility in social and economic transactions. Subject to exchange, acquisition, and possession, it constituted what Jean-Christophe Agnew might term, "a social and economic form of capital sufficiently liquid to meet and defeat the vicissitudes of a placeless market" (175). In this sense, what many critics have referred to as the "crisis of character" can be understood as a synedochic effect of the more general crisis in credit or value.[37] What remained ambiguous and thus most at stake in this crisis were precisely those networks that could structure or contain the liquidity of "character" so that it could be coined and placed in circulation with tenable claims to self-evident worth.

It is no surprise to find, then, that philosophers and theologians labored in unprecedented numbers during this period to produce inquiries into the origins and nature of character. At the same time, an emerging class of literary critics and critical thinkers generated systems and stratagems for reading or detecting the character of men and women. One such effort to produce a reliable way of assessing character can be found in Henry Fielding's "An Essay on the Knowledge of the Characters of Men," and it is worthwhile examining this essay for the illustrative ways in which Fielding attempts to negotiate the many meanings of "character."[38]

Fielding opens the essay by offering himself as a champion of the naive and impressionable who unselfishly offers a procedure for discerning the "characters" of men. Setting himself up as a benevolent defender of the less perceptive, and therefore more vulnerable, members of society, Fielding points out the perils that face one who cannot properly discern "character":

Thus while the crafty and designing part of mankind, consulting only their own separate advantage, endeavour to maintain one constant imposition on others, the whole world becomes a vast masquerade, where the greatest part appear disguised under false vizors and habits; a very few only showing their own faces, who become, by so doing, the astonishment and ridicule of the rest. (283)

Character disguises are motivated, according to Fielding, by self-interest, by a desire to gain material advantages over others in a competitive market culture.[39] To combat this "craft," this "Art of thriving," he proposes, in turn, three different methods for ascertaining character.

The first method Fielding proposes for discovering the characters of men is set against the adage "Fronti nulla fides," or "no trust is to be given the countenance." While Fielding acknowledges that an "austere countenance" may not be a "token of purity," he still argues that the "passions of men do commonly imprint sufficient marks on the countenance; and it is owing chiefly to want of skill in the observer that physiognomy is of so little use and credit in the world." Calling upon a definition of character as something that is irreducibly stamped or "imprinted" upon the face, Fielding disregards his own prior assertion that very few "[show] their own faces" and insists, moreover, that the problem is not whether character shows itself in faces, but whether we have the right "rules" or skills to regulate how faces are read (284). Subsequently, he endeavors to provide a sample series of rules for distinguishing between real and false casts of face. But he is finally compelled to concede, first, that an "accurate and discerning eye" is "the property of few" and, second, and perhaps even more troubling, that none of the rules he has outlined is "without some exceptions" (288–89).

Troubled by the inadequacy of his initial efforts, Fielding drops this first diagnostic procedure and counsels, "let us see if we have not a more infallible guide to direct us to the knowledge of men; one more easily to be attained, and on the efficacy of which, we may with the greatest certainty rely" (284, 289). He then goes on to propose not one, but two, other methods for attaining a "knowledge of men." First he advocates observing the actions of men because "the actions of men seem to be the justest interpreters of their thoughts, and the truest standards by which we may judge them" (289). Yet no sooner does Fielding offer this method than he finds himself compelled to present a series of warnings about how vulnerable this method of assessment is to bias and corruption. To combat this hazard, Fielding admonishes his reader neither to take someone's "own words against their actions" nor to "take the colour of a man's actions . . . from his public character," and he offers an extended catalogue of hypocritical types who work their deceits "on easy, credulous, and open dispositions" (290, 301). Yet even then, Fielding remains uncertain about the efficacy of the methods he has offered. Thus he offers his third and last diagnostic, "one more certain rule" to "extirpate all fallacy out of the world," which is, "to observe the actions of men with others, and especially with those to whom they are allied" (301). Surely, Fielding seems to hope, this last procedure will eliminate all possibility of deceit and therefore remove all doubts from the business of assessing the characters of men.

By the end of his essay, however, Fielding seems to realize just how misplaced is this hope, for no matter how many rules or warnings he might supply to his reader, the efficacy of the last two methods of assessment remain as dependent on the perceptive abilities of the observer as the first one. He wants to construe character as an internal truth, marked self-evidently on the countenance and imprinted indelibly on behavior. Instead he finds all efforts to gain access to "character" blocked by potentially misleading displays of "character" and frustrated by the infirmities of human discernment. In the end he is forced to concede: "however useless this treatise may be to instruct, I hope it will be at least effectual to alarm my reader . . . sure no honest undesigning man can ever be too much on his guard against the hypocrite, or too industrious to expose and expel him out of society" (305).

Like Richard Steele, Fielding wants to stake a claim for "real" character yet finds himself compelled to admit that "nothing remains but the outside" (298). Despite Fielding's initially confident tone, the essay reveals not only the semantic confusion associated with "character" in the eighteenth century but also his own uncertainty about whether the methods he proposes can cut through that confusion. This uncertainty is most apparent in Fielding's vacillations over the course of the essay between an account of character as innate, an "original distinction, in the nature or soul of one man, from that of another," and an account of character as something that can be formed "by art" when "man is yet soft and ductile, and the unformed character susceptible of any arbitrary impression you please to make on it" (282, 304). In short, even as Fielding attempts to devise a system for assessing "character," his own understanding of the concept remains divided between at least two of character's many meanings—as a sign of a fixed moral truth and as a mutable product. While he reveals how the concept of character retained a nostalgic connection to a notion of singular identity in the eighteenth century, he also demonstrates the extent to which that connection was not only tenuous but also subject to the kinds of skeptical inquiry that located a radical disjunction between inside and outside. In this manner, and despite his attempt to provide a practical system for distinguishing "true" from "false" character, Fielding provides us instead with an excellent illustration of the almost unavoidable semantic slippage that doomed any such effort to enlist character as the conceptual basis for modeling *coherent* identities in the eighteenth century. Indeed, the concept of character raised the frightening possibility either that there was no true "inside" or that if there were, we have no "real" access to it. The only basis for assessing others consisted of multiple, contradictory, and competing "outsides," that which can be observed but never confidently "known."

What the concept of character offered in the eighteenth century, then, and what the theater could exploit by taking it up, was an understanding of identity not as an emanation of a stable interiority, but as the unstable product of staged contests between interpretable surfaces. Hence, as I will demonstrate throughout this study, when we turn to eighteenth-century drama we find a medium obsessed not with the tensions between interiority and exteriority but with the conflicting meaning of surfaces in themselves. On the stage there was no public/private split; there was only public space and public displays. In contrast to the novel, we will find that the stage offers us a medium in which public exteriors were taken not merely as symptomatic of an interior, but rather as the *only* basis upon which judgments about character could be formed. Indeed, while the novel and other prose forms worked to resolve or at least to compensate for the semantic conflicts of character, the stage sought to exploit the dissonant effects that emanated from that concept of identity. Where the novel worked toward producing the stabilizing illusion of coherent identities, the stage worked to expose literary character as a fiction, questioning the authority with which it was increasingly invested by playing it against other aspects of "character." Delighting in the at least duplicitous play of the many meanings of "character," the eighteenth-century stage could enact the "crisis of character" by staging it precisely as a competition in which actions, words, figure, and reputation could all be weighed against one another. Put another way, while the production of identity in the novel relied upon the process of developing a psychological conjunction between being and behaving, figured through the presentation of an individual mind capable of taking itself as an object, the stage eschewed such self-consciousness and, through the representation of identity as a contingent effect of character, concerned itself with cultural anxieties about the psychology of knowing.

The Concept of Character in Practice

Up to this point, my discussion of character and its place in eighteenth-century culture has touched only tangentially on its role in the theater. In this section, I provide a more extensive description of the particular stage practices that influenced the shape of dramatic representations and regulated the production of identity on the eighteenth-century stage. My purpose in doing so is to demonstrate how these practices were implicated in and drew upon the fluid "concept of character" that I have just described.

In the field of eighteenth-century studies, theater historians have been instrumental in reminding us of the particular circumstances that define the theatrical medium as a space of live performance and as a dynamic testing ground for an ongoing process of interpretation. Cutting across the dimensions of space and time, theater confronts us with an inherently confusing interpretive situation in which, as Peter Holland cautions us, "Every fragment of the event potentially carries meaning."[40] In the Restoration and eighteenth century, this situation was complicated by the fact that when the audience entered the theater, they did so with a "set of preconceptions, of patterns, of predictions that the playwrights could fulfill or frustrate" (18). While these expectations were in large part the result of the conventions of genre, a critical determinant of eighteenth-century dramatic experience that I will discuss in the concluding portions of this chapter, they were also directly related to, and inseparable from, the status of the actors and actresses involved in the production. As many critics have pointed out, the eighteenth-century theater was "an actor's theater, attended by an experienced and discriminating public."[41] Audiences attended the theater frequently and were deeply aware not only of long traditions in acting technique but also of current management policies. In their evaluation of the drama, eighteenth-century audiences "paid close attention to the formal structure of the actor's performance."[42]

This kind of attention followed from the employment practices of acting companies. In the eighteenth century, actors and actresses were generally hired by contract to perform certain kinds of parts. These were known as the "lines of business," and actresses or actors who played against this "type" would be recognized for stepping "out of line." As a result of these practices, audiences could shape their expectations about a night's bill of fare around their knowledge of the particular company behind the production. Managers would advertise new plays in playbills that listed only the names of the actors and actresses who would appear in the production (see Figures 1 and 2). Depending on whether the play advertised was a comedy or tragedy, the audience, with their knowledge of the company, could anticipate precisely what kind of play and what kind of action they would witness that evening. Those who violated such expectations were

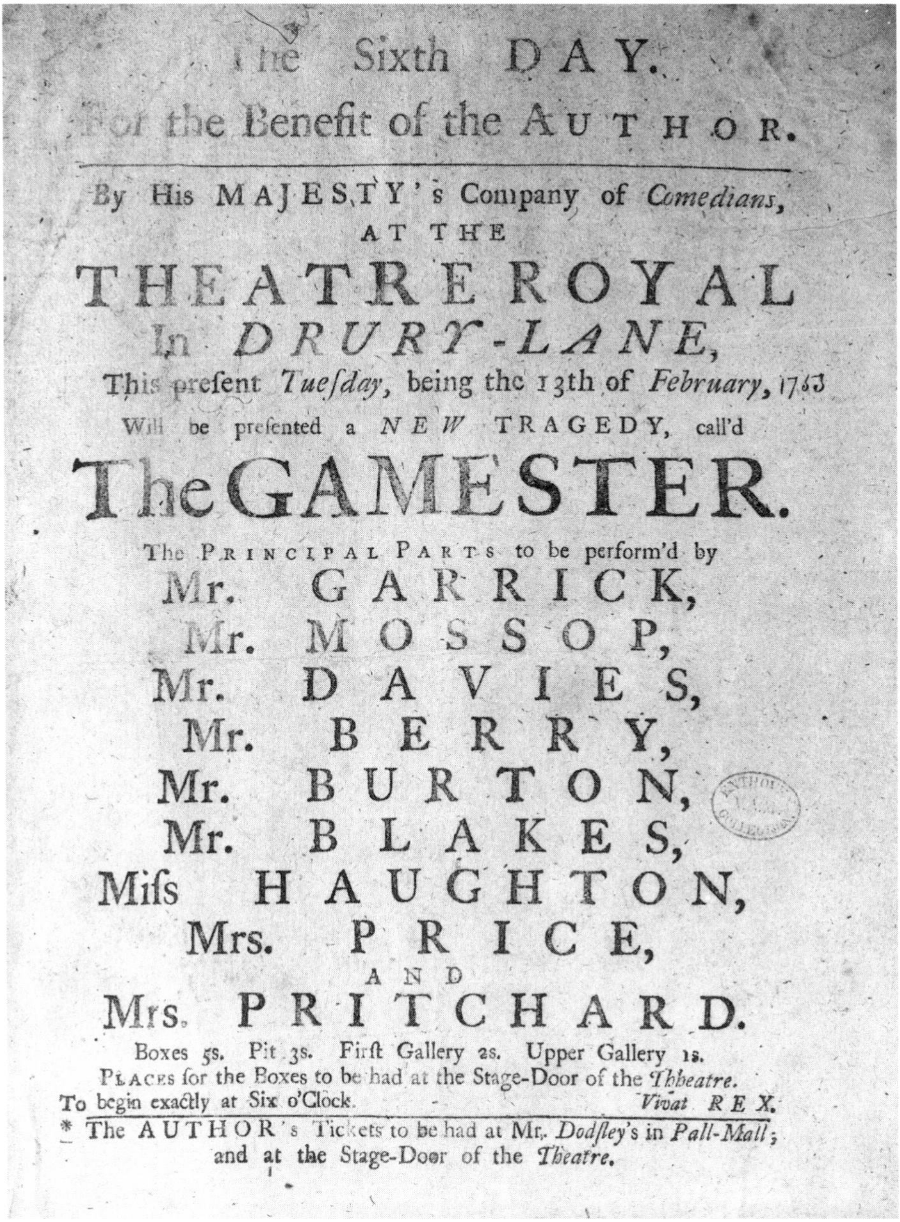

The Sixth DAY.

For the Benefit of the AUTHOR.

By His MAJESTY's Company of *Comedians*,
AT THE

THEATRE ROYAL

In *DRURY-LANE*,

This present *Tuesday*, being the 13th of *February*, 1753

Will be presented a NEW TRAGEDY, call'd

The GAMESTER.

The PRINCIPAL PARTS to be perform'd by

Mr. GARRICK,

Mr. MOSSOP,

Mr. DAVIES,

Mr. BERRY,

Mr. BURTON,

Mr. BLAKES,

Miss HAUGHTON,

Mrs. PRICE,

AND

Mrs. PRITCHARD.

Boxes 5s. Pit 3s. First Gallery 2s. Upper Gallery 1s.
PLACES for the Boxes to be had at the Stage-Door of the *Thheatre*.
To begin exactly at Six o'Clock. - *Vivat REX.*
* The AUTHOR's Tickets to be had at Mr. *Dodsley's* in *Pall-Mall*;
and at the Stage-Door of the *Theatre*.

Figure 1. Playbill for *The Gamester*, 13 February 1753. By permission of the V & A Picture
Library.

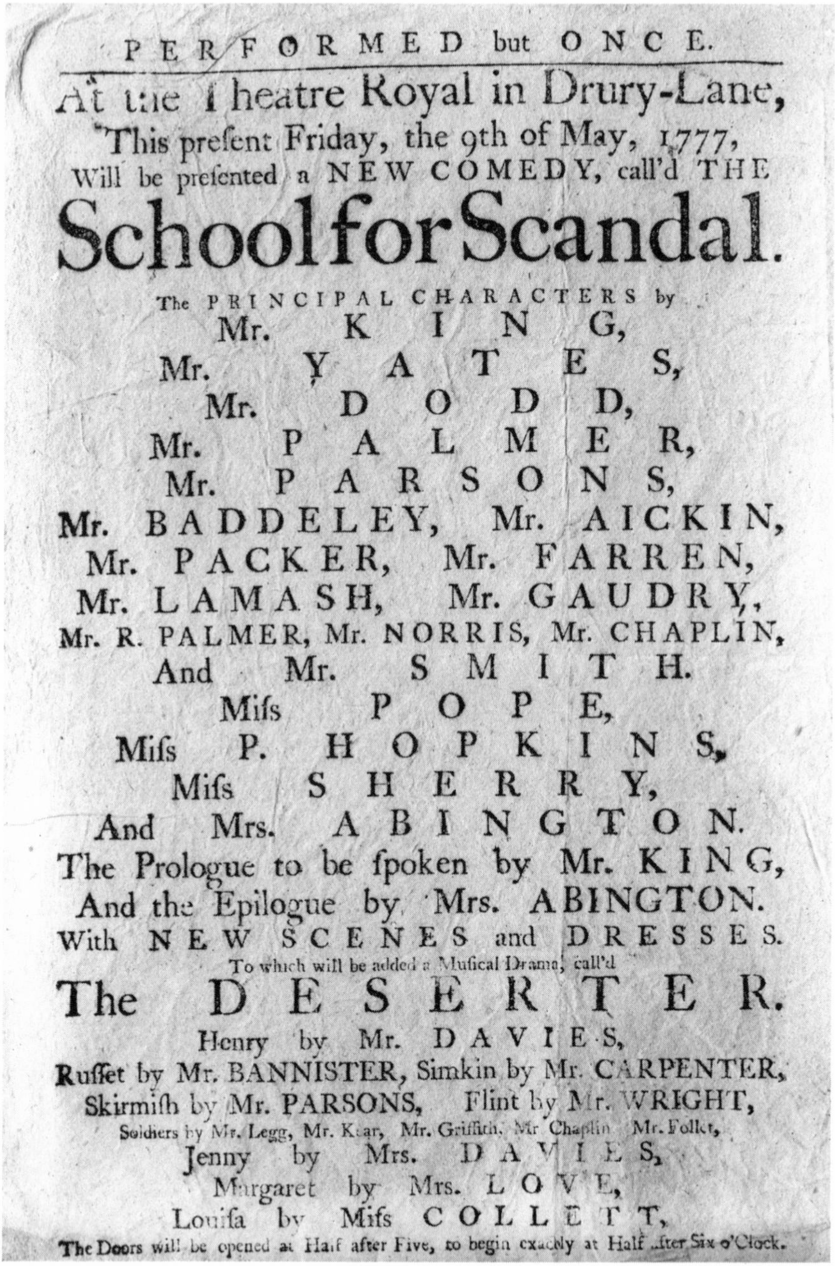
PERFORMED but ONCE.

At the Theatre Royal in Drury-Lane,

This preſent Friday, the 9th of May, 1777,

Will be preſented a NEW COMEDY, call'd THE

School for Scandal.

The PRINCIPAL CHARACTERS by

Mr. KING,

Mr. YATES,

Mr. DODD,

Mr. PALMER,

Mr. PARSONS,

Mr. BADDELEY, Mr. AICKIN,

Mr. PACKER, Mr. FARREN,

Mr. LAMASH, Mr. GAUDRY,

Mr. R. PALMER, Mr. NORRIS, Mr. CHAPLIN,

And Mr. SMITH.

Miſs POPE,

Miſs P. HOPKINS,

Miſs SHERRY,

And Mrs. ABINGTON.

The Prologue to be ſpoken by Mr. KING,

And the Epilogue by Mrs. ABINGTON.

With NEW SCENES and DRESSES.

To which will be added a Muſical Drama, call'd

The DESERTER.

Henry by Mr. DAVIES,

Ruſſet by Mr. BANNISTER, Simkin by Mr. CARPENTER,

Skirmiſh by Mr. PARSONS, Flint by Mr. WRIGHT,

Soldiers by Mr. Legg, Mr. Kear, Mr. Griffith, Mr Chaplin, Mr. Follet,

Jenny by Mrs. DAVIES,

Margaret by Mrs. LOVE,

Louiſa by Miſs COLLETT,

The Doors will be opened at Half after Five, to begin exactly at Half after Six o'Clock.

Figure 2. Playbill for *The School for Scandal*, 9 May 1777. By permission of the V & A Picture Library.

liable to confront not only confusion on the part of audience but also a potentially violent reaction.[43] Such incidents suggest that audiences did not attend performances to see how well a "character" was developed so much as to see how well a particular performer played against his or her "line."

This should not lead us into thinking, however, that eighteenth-century drama was regulated by the kind of "type-casting" that audiences in the twenty-first century associate with realism. For while physical characteristics might be taken into consideration in casting, they were not always determining factors. Changes in an actor's or actress's physical appearance rarely resulted in casting alterations, even if those changes signaled circumstances that directly undermined the pretensions of the fictional character he or she portrayed. Perhaps one of the most egregious instances of this practice occurred when, in the original production of Addison's *Cato*, Anne Oldfield played Marcia, the virgin daughter of Cato, while she was nine months pregnant.[44]

While pregnancy did not prevent an actress from playing a virgin, neither was age necessarily a significant factor in determining the distribution of parts. As Peter Holland points out, "age was unimportant because the style of acting was not one in which the identification with the part was total; the actor never stopped being the actor . . . as an expression of the audience's recognition of the actor as individual, the actor kept his own parts" (60). Holland refers here to the fact that when an actor or actress was contracted to perform a "line" in a company, such as first lady or second lady, he or she would receive the "sides" or "parts" that corresponded to their "line" in the company. For each play, these "parts" consisted only of their lines and adequate cues; performers were not given complete copies of the play. These "parts" were then considered the property of the actor or actress, and they retained that property interest during their tenure in the company. "Parts" could be lent out upon request and, generally, were given up only upon retirement or departure from the company or in the event of death. Under these conditions, audiences formed close associations over the course of a lifetime between particular actors and actresses and particular roles.

Significantly, this distribution of "lines" and "parts" formed the basis for an eighteenth-century obsession with drawing comparisons in the art of "pointing." The dramatic technique of "pointing" refers to the practice of bracketing off a set speech from the course of action and directing that speech, along with a set of gestures, at the audience. Once plays were established in the repertory, particular roles and speeches or "points" achieved privileged status in the course of performance and were associated with the technique of a particular actor or actress who either originated the role or attempted innovations in that role.[45] As William Worthen explains, "As a device emphasizing technique rather than meaning, pointing naturally provided the opportunity to compare the talents of various actors in the performance tradition" (72). Indeed, Colley Cibber follows this protocol throughout his *Apology* to illustrate the achievements of each actor or actress in "Their several Theatrical Characters."[46] Comparing the late Robert Wilks's Hamlet to that of Thomas Betterton, for example, he laments the former's habit of "straining Vociferation" while he "[tore] a Passion into Rags" at the "first appearance of his Father's spirit" and praises the latter for the "Light into which [he] threw this Scene":

he open'd with a Pause of mute Amazement! then rising slowly, to a solemn, trembling Voice, he made the Ghost equally terrible to the Spectator, as to himself! and in the descriptive Part of the natural Emotions which the ghastly Vision gave him, the boldness of his Expostulation was still govern'd by Decency, manly, but not braving; his Voice never rising into that seeming Outrage, or wild Defiance of what he naturally rever'd. (60–61)

Later in the century the German visitor Georg Lichtenberg would provide a now famous description of David Garrick as Hamlet in the same moment (see Figure 3):

Suddenly, as Hamlet moves towards the back of the stage slightly to the left and turns his back on the audience, Horatio starts, and saying: "Look, my lord, it comes," points to the right, where the ghost has already appeared and stands motionless, before any one is aware of him. At these words, Garrick turns sharply and at the same moment staggers back two or three paces with his knees giving way under him; his hat falls to the ground and both his arms, especially the left, are stretched out nearly to their full length, with the hands as high as his head, the right arm more bent and the hand lower, and the fingers apart; his mouth is open; thus he stands rooted to the spot, with legs apart, but no loss of dignity, supported by his friends, who are better acquainted with the apparition and fear lest he should collapse. . . . At last he speaks, not at the beginning, but at the end of a breath, with a trembling voice: "Angels and ministers of grace defend us!"[47]

What becomes clear as we review contemporary accounts of these "points" —and "Hamlet's first meeting with the ghost of his father" was considered "one of the actor's most telling points"[48]—is that they were treated as discrete moments in the course of a production and were not considered part of a larger, more "organic" whole. "Points" constituted abrupt and prolonged breaks from the course of action. Indeed, as Joseph Roach notes of the "point" described above, "Garrick held this tableau for so long that some spectators wondered if he needed prompting."[49] Further, when Garrick left the scene to follow the ghost, the applause, as Lichtenberg reports, "[began] as soon as the ghost [went] off the stage and last[ed] until Hamlet also disappear[ed]" (11). Thus it appears that these episodic set pieces, which broke the momentum of plot and story, were directed, much like opera arias, not toward the other characters in the play but rather toward the ever-watchful audience.

Figure 3. David Garrick as Hamlet. By permission of the Harvard Theatre Collection.

Such a finding is significant with respect to our investigation of the stage practice of character for it undermines claims about character "development" on the eighteenth-century stage and suggests instead that eighteenth-century stage practice was devoted to virtuoso performances of set pieces. Under this regime, as George Winchester Stone, Jr., and George M. Kahrl write in their admiring biography of Garrick, "The spectator's enjoyment came from viewing the 'passions' going through their paces, or being exquisitely delineated in a series of isolated actions and declamations, rather than from enjoying the development of a 'whole' character, or the complication of a full plot. Set speeches were helpful, and soliloquies seemed made for exhibiting virtuosity. The star performer could declaim both, and rivet attention on his individual performance. Supreme art showed in his doing it well."[50] But even as they try to champion Garrick as an innovator in the area of character development, Stone and Kahrl are forced to concede that "One senses from abundant generalizing of foreign visitors, as well as by inveterate theatre goers of London that audiences lagged in commentary upon total performance, seeing brilliancies still in spots and commenting upon specifics with more vivid recollection than they did on total effects—Lear's curse and Macbeth's air-drawn daggers stuck in their memories" (49). In sum, the power of the "point" and the power of the theatrical experience in the eighteenth century depended not on a consistently or coherently developed sense of a character's interior life—something, that is, that we would associate with subjectivity—but rather on the agility with which an actor or actress could convey the passions visually and episodically through a conventional series of facial, gestural, and vocal postures. Although twenty-first-century critics may argue about the degree to which the display of passions or the "art of the gesture" were meant to provide a kind of shorthand for internal emotional states, the reception of these displays in the eighteenth century suggests that actors and audiences in this period were interested in drawing attention not so much to the "character" portrayed as to the *portrayal* of the character by the actor.[51]

Indeed, I would argue that this was even, and perhaps especially, the case for Garrick, the actor whom many critics view as a great innovator who brought a more natural style to the stage.[52] I do not seek to diminish Garrick's accomplishments or his genius in any way. Yet I would submit first, as George Taylor has already suggested, that Garrick's "naturalism" needs to be viewed within an eighteenth-century context and, second, that we ought to look more carefully at Garrick's methods for conveying character and at how the effects of those methods were received.[53] Simply put, in a context where few actors or actresses bothered to remain in character when they were not speaking (indeed they might even look around the theater and drop bows and curtsies of acknowledgment to wealthier patrons), Garrick's insistence on "maintaining" character might appear more "natural" by comparison.[54] Yet, as I will suggest below, this hardly means that his mode of expression would be viewed as "natural" on the twenty-first-century stage.

Garrick's great skill resided in his ability to display the passions in a series of expressive tableaux, shifting with great efficiency from one to another. In *The Player's Passion*, Joseph Roach has discussed at length the psychophysiological theories of nature that provided the foundation for Garrick's style of acting, and he has illustrated the extent to which Garrick relied as a consequence on a "mechanical" understanding of the body and the passions. Not insignificantly, Roach points out that one of the primary effects of such a "mechanistic view of nature" was that it "objectified and exteriorized the passions, draining them of their subjective content" (71). This systemic effect—one that diminished the significance of interiority and privileged the role of exteriority in the presentation and reception of an actor's performance—provides a critical point of perspective from which Garrick's performative practices can be better understood. Whether one agrees or disagrees with the position that the key to Garrick's characterizations lay in his conceptualization of individual psychological complexities, his methods for conveying those complexities suggest the extent to which Garrick himself understood the dramatic necessity of making those aspects of character visible through action.

In fact, Garrick's indebtedness to "mechanical" theories is evidenced in his own definition of acting as "an Entertainment of the Stage, which by calling in the Aid and Assistance of Articulation, Corporeal Motion, and Occular Expression, imitates, assumes, or puts on the various mental and bodily Emotions arising from various Humours, Virtues and Vices, incident to human Nature."[55] Relying, as Roach points out, on a Cartesian "interactive dualism" between mind and body, Garrick goes on to elaborate a series of postures that offer *ekphrastic* equivalents to illustrations of the passions in influential painting manuals. He seems to imply that like the "characters" stamped on metal to signify value, the passions impress themselves upon the human form to signify an emotional state.[56] This emphasis on exterior appearances does not necessarily preclude the contribution of "feeling" to an actor's performance, but it does reveal that in the eighteenth century what actors like Garrick and others stressed in practice was "the formal surface of the actor's performance."[57]

In this respect, we may be able to make more sense out of the debates over whether an actor or actress truly feels the emotions he or she exhibits by understanding them as debates about how a performance ought to be valued, that is, about whether artificial, external signifiers, like the nominal value stamped on coins or the gestures of an actor, offer a reliable index to an essential, internal state. While a number of eighteenth-century theorists may have insisted that the actor's expression could "move the audience only if his own feeling sustained the character's passion," it appears in practice that, when actual audiences went to see Garrick perform and when Garrick prepared his performances, they and he were more concerned with how well he "put on" the passion than with whether he actually felt it.[58] Indeed, as Henry Fielding so cannily illustrates when he sends Tom Jones and Partridge on a visit to Drury Lane, audience members did not attend Garrick's performances to see Hamlet, but rather to see Garrick as Hamlet. The point of eighteenth-century dramatic representations was not for the actor to transcend character, nor the character the actor, but rather for each to be constituted in performance as visible planes of "character" that competed with and against one another for control over meaning. Only the naive theatergoer like Fielding's Partridge would have thought or "seen" otherwise.[59]

In order for Garrick's performances to be taken as "natural," members of an audience thus not only had to be aware of the elaborate conventions or gestures regulating the expression of the passions, but also had to accept those conventions as signs of feeling.[60] Whether the latter condition meant "feeling" as experienced by a fictional character or "feeling" experienced by an actor or actress portraying that fictional character constituted a point of heated debate among acting theorists and critics. Either way, the problem of "feeling" only underlines the extent to which the theater complicated and frustrated the desire for authenticity. Those who championed Garrick usually insisted on the sincerity and authenticity of his stage representations, arguing that his genius lay in his ability to truly feel the emotions of his characters.[61] Those who opposed Garrick usually highlighted the exaggerated conventionality of his performances and cast the figure of the actor as a duplicitous hypocrite who pandered to vulgar interests.[62] In short, whether they looked for the rigged fright wig he wore or the more subtle series of facial expressions he produced in his portrait of Hamlet, audiences came to expect certain contrivances in a Garrick performance. They were at least as much aware of Garrick as an elaborate producer of expressive passions as of the emotional states those gestures were meant to indicate for a particular fictional character, and they measured Garrick as much against their expectations as against any developed sense of the characters he was meant to portray.[63] What is clear, moreover, is that theatergoers did not engage in extended commentaries on overall character development; rather they commented upon and compared isolated "points" among actors and actresses.

My intention in this extended discussion of Garrick has been to illustrate just a few of the relevant senses in which "character" was on display at any given moment on the eighteenth-century stage. Critics today may argue over whether Garrick's display constituted "an observable quantity which existed on the surface of dramatic character and whose essential meanings could be seen and understood by anyone" or whether "those added touches" constituted "a surplus threatening sense."[64] But in any event the evidence for both arguments suggests that Garrick's "person" competed with the "persona" he represented, as audiences distinguished between and then conflated personal character and fictional character—Garrick himself and the role he played. It is worth recalling, too, that

Garrick—the most "natural" actor of his time—was also an anomaly. While critics tend to highlight his "naturalizing" achievements, it remains the case that the declamatory style, or old school of acting, persisted throughout the eighteenth century and dominated the practice of many actors and actresses. Overall, as Alan S. Downer writes, "it is safe to conclude that the typical actor was not too conscientious about being the thing he represented" (1037). The idea of being "in character" was one that had only limited merit and little appeal.

Still, Garrick's attempts to produce "legible" performances were not without motive. Indeed, the one thing that most critics can agree upon is that Garrick sought to elevate the status of his profession and endeavored to do so, in part, by attempting to produce morally instructive spectacles on the stage. Responding especially to anxieties over potential disjunctions between actions and feelings, Garrick offered spectacles in which the body, disciplined by the art of the gesture, could appear to function consistently as an instrument of sincere expression.[65] By adopting an iconic acting style, Garrick in theory could "accommodate the kinetic imperative of theatre to an ideal moral and ontological stasis."[66] In practice, however, these goals were confounded precisely by the complicated epistemological problem presented by the actor's or actress's body, and in particular, by the moral "character" of that body.

Let me try to illustrate this point at greater length by turning to considerations of "character" and the eighteenth-century actor or actress not yet discussed. In theory the association of particular actors with particular kinds of roles was often extended to the point where actors' names could serve, much like allegorical types, as emblems in manuals of conduct. We find precisely this odd conflation of actor with fictional type in Steele's *Spectator* No. 370. Calling on the authority of literary typology, Steele argues: "As the Writers of Epick Poems introduce shadowy Persons and represent Vices and Virtues under the Characters of Men and Women; so I, who am a SPECTATOR in the World, may perhaps sometimes make use of the Names of Actors on the Stage, to represent or admonish those who transact Affairs in the World" (3:393). Steele goes on to argue that an actor in a role could serve as a kind of exemplum either encouraging or discouraging certain behaviors and attitudes. Yet if an actor's name became the sign of a social character type, what became of the actor's person and how, in practice, might personal character have contributed to or detracted from the status of the actor or actress as emblem on the stage?

Colley Cibber offers us one skeptical index of judgment for this dilemma when he discusses the moral character of an actress who made a point of demanding that she be allowed to play only virtuous roles on the stage. He offers from experience:

I am apt to think, that if the Personal Morals of an Actor, were to be weighed by his Appearance on the Stage, the Advantage and Favour . . . might rather incline to the Traitor, than the Heroe. . . . Because no Man can naturally desire to cover his Honesty with a wicked Appearance; but an ill Man might possibly incline to cover his Guilt with the Appearance of Virtue.[67]

Cibber thus presents us with the possibility that an actress might try to cover up private indiscretions by taking on the character of virtue on the stage.[68] In this case, the representation of fictional character would come into conflict with the moral character of an actress.

Indeed, as Kristina Straub has demonstrated at great length, an actor or actress's sexual reputation could have a tremendous impact on the reception and interpretation of stage performances.[69] The private morals of actors and actresses and the respectability of the profession as a whole were frequent subjects of discussion, debate, and scrutiny as she notes: "despite repeated interdictions throughout the century, against too great a curiosity about what players did off the stage, what they did in bed is a constant theme in biographies, theatrical histories, and pamphlets on the players" (13). Straub cites the case of Jane Rogers and Robert Wilks, who, while having a love affair, were frequently cast opposite one another as lead hero and heroine. Of their performances she writes: "Wilks's and Rogers's theatrical love scenes were often most interesting for what they told about the course of their offstage love affair; audiences thrilled to the spectacle of their 'real' passion at the height of their amour, just as they thrilled to the spectacle of Rogers biting Wilks on the cheek after discovering his unfaithfulness to her" (13).[70] Certainly this form of interest was so pervasive in the eighteenth century that John Hill was compelled to aver in his treatise, "we shall find that the highest scenes of love in our best plays have never been so expressively represented as when the actor and actress were not only of amorous tempers, but were actually at the time of their playing these parts heartily in love with each other."[71]

This conflation of publicly acted with privately lived character in the reception of stage performances was especially marked for actresses, who were first allowed to appear onstage only after the Restoration. Their sexuality was considered open to both public inspection and public consumption.[72] In his *General History of the Stage* (1749), William Chetwood provides us with a vivid illustration of how these conditions impacted on Restoration stage performances. He recounts that when Anne Bracegirdle, "a virtuous Actress, or one reputed so," played Cordelia and referred to her "Virgin Innocence," she "[received] a Plaudit from the Audience, more as a Reward for her reputable Character, than, perhaps, her acting claimed." In contrast, he claims, when Elizabeth Barry, an actress notorious for her sexual libertinage, played Cordelia, she elicited a "Horse-laugh" at the same line "and the Scene of generous Pity and Compassion at the Close, turn'd to ridicule."[73] This kind of scrutiny and its effects on performance reception in the Restoration continued through the eighteenth century and clearly motivated actresses such as Catherine Clive and later Sarah Siddons to cultivate scrupulous reputations, while others like George Anne Bellamy and Charlotte Charke attempted to capitalize in their performances and autobiographies on their less-than-pristine offstage reputations.[74]

In sum, eighteenth-century audiences were not only obsessively aware of aspects of an actor's or actress's personal life. Rather, as Hogarth's wry placement of Lavinia Fenton and the duke of Bolton in his illustration for *The Beggar's Opera* reveals, they were also persistently encouraged to draw associations between those private lives and the roles players played (see Figure 4).[75] Audiences, in short, were keenly aware of how public and private "character" either converged or diverged in performance. Hence, while the selection of an acting style like Garrick's could carry a series of coded extratextual moral meanings, those meanings had to compete for control over the intelligibility of the action with other potentially disruptive signifiers brought to a performance through the player's bodily presence. Indeed, even something as innocuous as the placement of a beauty spot on an actress's face could give rise to a series of contrary meanings with respect to the sexual and social status of an actor or actress and the figures he or she might represent in a play.[76] In other words, even as the actor or actress took on the role provided by the playwright, they also retained their own bodies and their own personalities. The persona or "character" created by a playwright for public consumption had either to compete with or to play upon the various public images or "characters" of the actor or actress playing that role. In the course of assigning value to a character, audiences had to weigh fictional characters represented in words against character represented both in physical gestures and in actual bodies.

What the discussion above has revealed is that at any given moment in the course of a performance the actor's protean body presented, rather than concealed, a variety of surfaces to the viewer, each of which vied for control over the intelligibility of the action. This condition, with its tenacious emphasis on readable surfaces and its resistance to notions of "sincere" depths, drew on the concept of character in all its semantic complexity to form an alternative rubric for shaping and apprehending identity. Unlike its prose counterparts, the stage revealed, rather than concealed, the gap between what is seen and what is perceived when character as fiction and character as a sign of "real" moral integrity

Figure 4. *The Beggar's Opera*, William Hogarth, 1729. Lavinia Fenton achieved a kind of celebrity in her role as Polly Peachum, when the married Duke of Bolton fell in love with her during the first performances of *The Beggar's Opera*. She soon became his mistress, and at the end of the season she retired from the stage. Hogarth exploits that scandal by portraying Lavinia Fenton as Polly, looking away from Macheath and toward the Duke of Bolton, sitting in a box to the side of the stage. This image vividly illustrates the extent to which the boundaries between audience and performance were blurred as well as the extent to which an actress's public reputation was understood either to play upon or to play against the roles she played on the stage. By permission of the Yale Center for British Art, Paul Mellon Collection.

cannot be differentiated or entirely separated. Indeed, the stage suggested that any effort at concealing this instability constituted a kind of dangerous, because illusory, practice. Displaying a temperamental affinity for the transient and episodic, the stage thus mirrored, rather than compensated for, the very qualities of contingency that marked the understanding of character in society at large. Through its unique capacity to bring to life the disjunctions and competing priorities of character's multiple meanings, the stage provided a place where the problematic nature of seeing and knowing character could be tested and explored. In this manner, as Kristina Straub has noted, "the theater's discursive space" not only made "a particular demand for 'rules' of spectating," it also "[foregrounded] the difficulty of fixing those rules" (7).

In the next section, I will turn to John Gay's *The What D'Ye Call It?* first, to illustrate how the concept of character was taken into consideration in the representation of staged identities and, second, to identify the kinds of "structures" or "rules of fixity" that playwrights deployed to resolve the problem of the intelligibility of character on the stage and in the theatrical culture at large. In particular, I will suggest that the eighteenth-century audience was not absorbed in plumbing a character's depths, but rather it was interactively engaged in tracing character in relation to generic conventions over the course of three to five acts.

The Question of "Character" in John Gay's The What D'Ye Call It?

One could argue that the "difficulty of fixing" the rules of spectating formed the central idea motivating John Gay when he presented *The What D'Ye Call It?* to Drury Lane audiences in 1715. Subtitled *A Tragi-Comi-Pastoral Farce*, *The What D'Ye Call It?* was a huge success on the London stage, with as many as seventeen performances in its very first season. In the most reductive sense, this mock-heroic rehearsal play represents the tale of Kitty, a Steward's daughter, who has been made pregnant by Squire Thomas, the son of Sir Roger, who is the patron of the play. Sir Roger has arranged for the presentation of a play-to-order so that his country neighbors who have never seen a play before might see "all sorts of Plays under one."[77] Determined to see his daughter receive her due, however, the steward arranges, by substituting a real curate for a play one, for Kitty to be legally married to Thomas within the frame of the fictional play, in which they represent Kitty Carrot and Thomas Filbert. Although this play provides for a number of interesting and even bizarre twists, my main objectives in the reading below will be to capture a sense of the play's tone and to offer a brief account of what might have made this play so oddly fascinating for eighteenth-century audiences. By doing so, I hope to highlight the implications of Gay's metatheatrical burlesque on genres with respect to the idea of character and its perception in eighteenth-century culture.

The What D'Ye Call It? opens as the so-called actors and actresses prepare to take up their roles in the amateur theatricals that they have prepared for Sir Roger and his cronies. The Steward, played by Mr. Quin, enters roaring at the players: "So, you are ready in your parts, and in your dress too, I see: your own best cloaths do the business. Sure never was Play and actors so suited. Come, range your selves before me, women on the right and men on the left" (opening scene, p. 1). The scene continues as the Steward calls upon the actors and actresses by their character names and demands that they identify the roles they will play in Sir Roger's command performance. Strangely, and despite the obvious theatrical markers, the situation in this opening scene remains ambiguous and confusing. That Gay must have had at least some interest in creating this effect is evidenced by two particular details in the reading text. The first can be found in the design of the dramatis personae, where some, but not all, of the actors are listed by both their play name and their play-within-the-play alias. It seems that some of the actors and actresses will play only a character in the play-within-the-play; others will play the same character in both the play and the play-within-the-play, that is, the play character will play himself, and still others will play different, though related characters, in the play and the play-within-the play respectively. If this unevenness in the distribution of parts sounds confusing, it is made even more so by Gay's stage directions following the Steward's lines: "The Actors range them-selves" (opening scene, p. 1). At first we remain unsure whether these directions refer to the professional actors and actresses who appeared on the Drury Lane stage or to those same actors and actresses who were already "in character" as the amateur "actors" who will participate in the Steward's drama. Indeed, for all practical purposes, the stage directions could reasonably refer to either alternative. Here, then, as in most rehearsal plays of the period, we see the illusions of stage productions laid bare as Gay satirically displays both the entry of actors into characters and the kinds of epistemological dissonance that can result from an inability to distinguish the "real" from the "play" world of the stage, or, analogously, the "real" from the "assumed" characters. Gay subsequently maintains this chaotic sense of dislocation by ensuring that in any one scene in the theatrical presentation that follows, any two characters may converse across the different frames of reference that indicate what counts as "reality" in any given moment, for any given character. Ultimately, the conflation of play with reality in *The What D'Ye Call It?* finds its fullest realization in that most natural, because most conventional, of all comic endings: the marriage of Thomas and Kitty. It is a marriage, indeed, of fictional as well as real convenience.

This is as much to say that while Gay swings wildly, not to mention scandalously, through a series of dramatic conventions, each authorized by one of the genres alluded to in the subtitle, the play ends in an almost wholly conventional manner with a wedding. Indeed, we are meant to pay attention to just how deeply conventional this marriage is when we are told that we will "see what was never shewn upon the *London* stage," that is, a marriage ceremony (II.ix, p. 38). As Sir Roger pragmatically insists, "what's a Play without a marriage? and what's a marriage if one sees nothing of it?" (II.ix, p. 39). Subsequently, we do "see" the marriage ceremony, yet we do not hear it, for it is performed in the recesses of the backstage as if it were a pantomime narrated by Sir Roger and we were the uninvited voyeurs. At one and the same time, then, Gay violates the decorum of comedy by offering us a view of a marriage ceremony and makes us uncomfortably aware of just how unfamiliar such a seemingly innocuous sight was on the eighteenth-century stage.

Indeed, in the course of Gay's tragi-comi-pastoral farce we are treated to a variety of such violations of generic expectations—some satirical like the peripeteia that results in Thomas Filbert's last minute release from a death sentence, others farcical like the lyrical ballad Kitty Carrot pronounces on a gardening rake. The result is a disconcerting, even chaotic mélange of arbitrary causes and effects that outraged a number of Gay's critical contemporaries and motivated them to publish a "Key" to the burlesque in which they demanded that Gay provide clarification of his own motives, the motives of each of the genres in his play, and even of his casting decisions.[78] Was it a tragedy, a comedy, a pastoral, or simply a farce? If the genre could not be determined, how could any sense be made of the narrative and the characters that acted in that narrative?

Yet as Gay intimates in the tongue-in-cheek preface that supporters like Pope and Congreve urged him to offer with the printed play, these critics missed the central figure of irony in the burlesque.[79] Indeed, what is significant about their demands is that they only underline the point Gay seems most interested in making with both his chaotic parody and his preface: the "rules of fixity" that we depend upon for interpreting and understanding character on the eighteenth-century stage derive first and foremost from that epistemological frame of reference we call genre. In other words, Gay's project in both pieces is less about claiming genres for his repertoire, as his critics enviously intimated, than about defamiliarizing dramatic genres and dramatic conventions in order, precisely, to demonstrate how important such forms are for making meaning. As Brean Hammond and Peter Lewis have also argued, Gay's object in confounding genres was precisely and paradoxically to critique such mixing.[80] Hence, as Gay inflates and then deflates generic conventions in *The What D'Ye Call It?* he reveals just how deeply characters are motivated and shaped by the generic narratives in which they are found. Where dramatic characters lacked interiority or consciousness, genre could supply internal motive and agency. Where the various signifiers and signifieds of character came into conflict, genre could supply an interpretive framework within which those competing claims could be prioritized and assessed. Gay thus discloses how genres not only supplied an interpretive framework for eighteenth-century audiences, but also supplied agency to characters and to actors and actresses who assumed characters. He dramatizes how "character" can occupy a series of diverse and uneven positions and illustrates the fact that the production of knowledge about character is necessarily an interpretive act and one that depends much less on a belief in essence than upon the empirical data of appearances and situation. For the stage, that data was supplied by genres and the meanings they either gave voice to or silenced. Genre functioned as the double lens through which the narratives and social identities of character could be projected and construed.

Genres: Or What Can be Known

Gay's heightened awareness of genre in *The What D'Ye Call It?* was hardly unusual for an eighteenth-century play. Indeed, if one had to identify a distinguishing trait of eighteenth-century drama and dramatic criticism, it would be difficult to find one more dominant and telling than the intense self-consciousness about, and sensitivity to, genre and generic concerns. One might even go so far as to say that eighteenth-century drama offers a case in excess of what Jacques Derrida has posited as the "genre clause" of the "law of genre."[81] For eighteenth-century dramas more than fulfill this condition of genre by incessantly, conspicuously, and literally "re-marking" on their generic protocols and their generic interests. As Derrida points out, this "re-marking" signals a kind of belongingness without belonging, in this case, I would argue, a means by which eighteenth-century dramatists could signal an awareness of the normative claims made by genres even as they naturalized those claims by reposing in them the unique condition for making meaning out of character.[82]

Genres could be expected to perform these functions because by definition they reflect particular cultural logics; they offer ways of constituting narratives and directing readers how to read. These cultural logics have been described by the influential theorist Hans Robert Jauss as the "horizons of expectation" that mediate literary experience and must be taken into consideration in any full account of literary history.[83] In such accounts, it must be recognized, moreover, that though genres might achieve institutional status, this does not mean that they are static or unchangeable over time or that the reception of a genre by readers does not vary in relation to historical conditions.[84] Rather, as Tzvetan Todorov points out: "each epoch has its own system of genres, which stands in some relation to the dominant ideology. . . . Like any other institution, genres bring to light the constitutive features of the society to which they belong."[85] In this respect, genres do not only set the "rules of fixity" that make character intelligible; they also have the potential to adapt to and address new social needs and anxieties. The formal outlines of a genre thus provide a discursive pattern or epistemological frame of reference within which the particular cultural and ideological contents of a specific time and place can be articulated and evaluated.

In my account of the concept of character, I have tried to provide a broad, yet pointed, perspective on the complicated matrix of motives, tensions, and contingencies that impacted on the production and perception of identity in eighteenth-century English culture. I have suggested that those who thought of themselves as fit arbiters for these questions of "how to know" faced the at least twofold challenge of producing an epistemological system that would provide a reliable predictive index of persons without disclosing that very system as merely another code for prescribing a practice of manners. That is, they had to compete with one another to generate and articulate new ways of seeing and reading that would provide consistent and incisive ways of knowing while minimizing the visibility of both their own interests and the contradictions attending the splintering of "character." Indeed, the less visible the interests of the arbiter, the more authority and legitimacy would accrue to the system generated.

As I have pointed out, novelists responded to this "crisis of character" by producing the illusion of sincere protagonists to whose inner life readers could have unmediated access. In contrast, I have argued, dramatists emphasized a rhetoric of surfaces, refusing to represent "subjects" vested with individuality or an active inner life. To this end, the inherent and long-disputed hypocrisy of the dramatic medium became an asset rather than a liability, as dramatists could claim to be mirroring a culture in which hypocritical appearances were thought to predominate. Deploying a counterintuitive strategy, dramatists could "prove" their sincerity and thus their trustworthiness by never alleging to present anything but appearances. Likewise, the stage could be positioned as a cultural site in which the crisis of character would not be hidden under a veil of formal realism; indeed, it could appear to resist and to critique those motivated investments in character and the "subjects" to which they gave rise. In short, if "the whole world acted the player," then the stage deployed its players to act "the world" as a place in which any representational claims to either the transparency or the accessibility of the individual would be understood as necessarily specious.

By calling attention to genre, moreover, dramatists shifted responsibility for meaning away from the vagaries of human motivation and self-interest, which could be viewed with suspicion even in fictional characters, and assigned it to the apparently less capricious, and therefore less suspect, motives of form. Even as particular plays in a given genre promote the social values of a culture, genres per se appear to represent disinterested and general narrative patterns. Like the fictional "nobodies" that Catherine Gallagher points to in the novel, genres too belonged to no one in particular. Yet unlike the nobodies of the novel, genres carried no association with personal psychologies, even fictional ones, and hence no tie to individual interests. Consequently, as befitted a public rather than a private medium, dramatic genres could institute a kind of community property in which audiences and readers could form an interest. Indeed, as the numerous pamphlet exchanges and newspaper accounts that I will review in subsequent chapters indicate, audiences entered the theater with a set of generic expectations against which they judged each play; and they protested vehemently when those expectations were violated. Audiences were able to claim a kind of proprietary interest in the drama; their approval or disapproval of a play created and sustained that play's value.

In the chapters that follow, I will outline the general contours of each dramatic genre and discuss how, within that general epistemological framework, plays negotiated the crisis of character and promoted or discredited particular cultural values. By considering a variety of critical responses to the plays, moreover, I will demonstrate how audiences took a proprietary interest in eighteenth-century dramas and how they, like the plays themselves, either participated in or refused the emerging ideologies—of gender, of class, and of nation—that we associate with eighteenth-century culture. I will begin with plays about plays, the most self-conscious, chaotic, and provisional of all eighteenth-century dramatic genres.

Chapter Two
Plays About Plays
An "Abstract Chronicle"

In the opening scene of Richard Brinsley Sheridan's *The Critic* (1779/ 1780), the lead character Dangle defends his addiction to theater and provides a justification for "affect[ing] the character of a critic" by arguing, "the stage is 'the mirror of nature,' and the actors are 'the abstract, and brief chronicles of the time' . . . pray what can a man of sense study better?"[1] Later, in the opening scene of the second act, Puff—a self-avowed "practitioner in panegyric"—declares, almost as if addressing Dangle's prior claim, "No, no, sir; what Shakespeare says of actors may be better applied to the purpose of plays; *they* ought to be 'the abstract and brief chronicles of the times'" (I.ii, p. 147; II.i, p. 155). Although Dangle and Puff are to be viewed with some suspicion, Sheridan's management of these characters ensures the introduction of basic questions that had been rehearsed again and again in eighteenth-century plays about plays: what is the relationship between the stage and society and what "ought" it to be? Is the governing principle of theatrical representation mimetic or metadramatic? Should the stage act merely as a reflective mirror, or should it act more like a microscope, turning a discriminating and indeed critical eye on society? Should the player or the play's purpose operate as the predominant figure shaping our understanding of the play's meaning? And finally, if we determine what is meant by "player" and "purpose," in what sense can we say that either acts as the "'abstract and brief chronicles of the time'"?

In the previous chapter, I made the case that the stage not only presented identity as an effect of character, but that in so doing it reflected and capitalized upon, rather than concealed and compensated for, the general "crisis of character" that was of such widespread concern in eighteenth-century culture. In this sense, "character," as it was produced on the stage and represented by "players," can be viewed as an "abstract" of the particular anxieties over the stability of identity and identification that were in circulation at the time. In this chapter, I focus on plays about plays in order to begin the process of elucidating the kinds of "purposes" that were engaged by eighteenth-century dramatists and to demonstrate how those "purposes" constitute an "abstract chronicle of the time." In beginning my exploration of the dramatic genres of the eighteenth century with plays about plays, rather than, say, with tragedies or comedies, I have at least two related goals in mind. First, I want to continue to illustrate how the concept of character circulated on stage and in play texts by taking it up in the genre that was most explicit about acknowledging and exploring the significance of form. Second, I want to explore how the stage capitalized on the crisis of character to position its own authority and to begin to detail the kinds of cultural and ideological values that were promoted from that position. Before we can arrive at such an elaboration, however, we need to establish the basic contours and interests of plays about plays in the eighteenth century and to situate the genre more fully and more particularly amid the hurly-burly of eighteenth-century cultural life.

The Interests of Eighteenth-Century Plays About Plays

It might be best to begin this process by examining the general presumptions made about this genre across time and investigating whether those suppositions held in the eighteenth century or whether we need to reorient our perception of the genre in this period.[2] As a genre, plays about plays, and more specifically plays with a play within, have often been relished by theorists and critics as occasions for explicating the ontological concerns of a particular era. Indeed, the expression of ontological anxiety has often been taken not only as the very mark of the genre, but as the generic crux to which all discussions and judgments of such plays must ultimately refer. On this score, as one might already anticipate from my discussion of character in the previous chapter, eighteenth-century plays about plays have often been judged not merely as deficient, but as wholly devoid of any intellectual or aesthetic merit. This occurs because an investigation into the experience of ontological anxiety generally presumes, and indeed is dependent upon, representations of forms of subjectivity and consciousness that cannot be found on the eighteenth-century stage. Yet if, as I am contending in this chapter, eighteenth-century plays about plays provide a kind of "abstract chronicle of the time," we might gain a better sense of the project they undertake by situating them in relation to the particular concerns about theatricality in everyday life that marked this period.

In his discussion of eighteenth-century plays about plays, Jean-Christophe Agnew describes a world and a stage whose relation to one another had been fundamentally transformed from that which sustained and regulated Elizabethan performance. Extending the work of Richard Sennett on public culture in the eighteenth century, Agnew delineates a secular urban world in which "the capacity to distance oneself from one's social role no longer inspired any deeper doubts about its authority or authenticity."[3] He argues further that such a transformation of public culture was the result not merely of the adaptation of mannerisms in public life, but rather of the "fundamental political, social, and economic settlements of eighteenth-century Britain," where formerly "unquestioned and immemorial rights and obligations" were more and more "seen to rehearse claims on negotiable prerogatives and perquisites" and where the "reality conferred on the new government notes more closely resembled the reality conferred on the drama . . . an artifact of the audience's collective suspension of disbelief" (154–55, 158).

What Agnew describes, in short, is a world in which the idiom of *theatrum mundi*, which had had the potential to be " 'ontologically subversive' " in Elizabethan times *precisely because* of its limited exposure, had now spread beyond the walls of the theater to take up a position as the ubiquitous, indeed governing, assumption of public life.[4] The new reality of eighteenth-century culture, with its expanding economic base, was one in which new money could buy status and such fluidity meant that anyone could assume a role in exchange at any time. In the absence of a controlling orthodoxy or hierarchical perspective, epistemological authority was diffuse and speculation about identities and status ran rampant.

Yet despite his description of a world in which epistemological concerns had taken center stage, Agnew maintains the category of the ontological as his investigative measure for eighteenth-century plays about plays. For instance, he cites John Gay's *The What D'Ye Call It?*—a play that, as we have just seen, concerns itself with the epistemological problem of character—as a case in point for the failings of this genre in the eighteenth century and concludes that while it could, "within limits, be 'politically skeptical,' it could not . . . be 'ontologically subversive' " (154). Indeed, what stands out in Agnew's dismissal "of the seventy or so plays that took the theater as their subject in the years before the Licensing Act of 1737" is that he fails to engage the question of how the eighteenth-century stage itself adapted to the new cultural conditions he describes (153). In short, he overlooks the obvious alternative that, like other forms in the period, plays about plays took the measure of a culture saturated by suspicions of theatricality and insincerity and, in response, adopted both a new strategy of presentation—what I will characterize as an antitheatrical theatricalism—and a new set of interests and themes.

Once we allow for an engagement with this body of work on its own terms it will become increasingly apparent, first, that the driving force behind eighteenth-century plays about plays consisted not so much in a fear of ontological collapse as in a desire for epistemological authority. Second, and perhaps more significantly, once we acknowledge that plays about plays treated the sheer ubiquity of theatricality in everyday social and economic life as an assumed value, rather than as a point of crisis or dramatic expression in and of itself, we will be able to begin to discern the ways that the stage played with theatricality both to gain audience trust and to distinguish its authority from that of other popular forms. The discussion below will thus be devoted to developing a more extensive account of eighteenth-century public life and to elucidating how a strategy of antitheatrical theatricalism provided plays about plays with a way to distinguish the voice of the stage amid the general cacophony of voices clamoring for attention and authority.

Dominated by a satirical impulse and often ranging into the burlesque, eighteenth-century plays about plays ran the gamut from plays featuring intermittent commentaries on stage practices and local conflicts to the more sustained focus and critique of the rehearsal play, a form that first came into prominence during the Restoration with *The Rehearsal* (1671/1672) by the second duke of Buckingham, George Villiers. While the former type of plays functioned as vehicles for theatrical gossip and theatrical quarrels, the rehearsal form provided for a play-within-a-play format in which, typically, the pretense of an author going to watch the rehearsal of his or her new play in the company of a number of acquaintances created an occasion for both an extended examination of the nature of theatrical practice and a satirical excoriation of the taste of the town and the excesses of the age. In this respect, plays about plays provide us not only with a sustained and revealing glimpse into the working world of eighteenth-century dramatists but also with further evidence for the arguments already advanced in Chapter 1. As these dramas anatomize and expose theatrical techniques, highlighting the entry of an actor or actress into a role or, in a few more unsettling cases, featuring an actor or actress "playing" himself or herself, they also bring the problem of character into the forefront of representation.[5] Indeed, as plays about plays shift from one frame to another, what they "discover" to their audience is that there is no fourth wall behind which the "subject" can be constructed. Instead, there is only another frame, genre being perhaps the most potent kind, within which character can be provisionally situated and read for meaning. As we shall see, plays about plays emphasize and exploit a world of surfaces even as they mock the pretenses of forms that claim to portray characters "in depth."

At the same time, through their constant reference to the larger cultural contests in which the theater participated, plays about plays offer us a dynamic, though clearly biased, view of the battlegrounds in the cultural wars that dominated so much of eighteenth-century representation (see Figure 5). Indeed, for much of the early part of the century, and particularly in the period leading up to the Stage Licensing Act of 1737, this genre was dominated, as were other satirical forms, by political satire directed against the perceived corruptions of Walpole's

Figure 5. The Theatrical Steel-Yards of 1750. This image from mid-century illustrates the kinds of cultural contests that were waged between rival entertainments and theaters. Here we find a triumphant Garrick on the right of the steel-yard, weighed against the performers of Covent Garden: Woffington, Barry, Quin, and Cibber. On the ground, the manager of Covent Garden, Rich, in harlequin garb, laments his defeat and looks toward Woodward, also in harlequin garb, as a formidable rival in that entertainment form. Copyright © The British Museum.

regime. In these timely attacks, the theater was transformed analogically into a microempire where the forces of Dulness predominated as much as they did in the wider realm of English politics. Resonating with the same "moral" outrage and aesthetic horror that saturates Pope's *Dunciad*, these plays burlesque and assail the mixing of dramatic genres in popular entertainments, catalogue the effects of degenerate taste, chastise the egos of unruly actors and money-hungry theatrical managers, and identify all of these ills with the corrupt and corrupting government of the "Great Man" himself, Robert Walpole, whose only principle of government was thought to be the principle of individual and petty self-interest. Hence we find that a play such as *Stage Mutineers, or, A Play-House to be Lett* (1732/1733), features not only a specific attack on Theophilus Cibber's pompous

Pistol and his self-promoting revolt against the management of Drury Lane, but also an ongoing commentary that likens the "Little Great Men, on this Mimic Stage of Life" to the "Great Men on the Grand Theatre of the World."[6] In each realm the "God of Riches" has conquered the "God of Wit," and the politics of raw commercialism has become the most potent ally of both the Grub Street hack who styles himself an author and the theatrical manager who seeks greater and greater profits (21).

We can attribute these last charges, at least in part, to the anxieties and concerns generated by a burgeoning print culture in which, as Marlon Ross has so eloquently explained, print, which had formerly emanated from authority, had now become a source of authority in itself. Ross paints a vivid portrait of the effects of this new accessibility and argues that the eighteenth-century author was "caught in the swivel moments of this process of reversal, not only when print begins to give the stamp of authority, but also when authority begins to become fragmented by the possessibility of private knowledge."[7] In a culture in which it seemed as if almost anyone could suddenly claim to "own" the authority of print, the issue of legitimate authority, what Ross refers to as "authenticity," came to the forefront and raised a number of disturbing questions. If anything appearing in print immediately bore the "imprint" of authority, how could a public audience distinguish and discriminate among the various claims? Did the very proliferation of potential authorities result in a devaluation of the currency of print as cultural capital? What strategies did an author have to deploy in order to ensure that his or her voice would be heard above the general cacophony of voices, all clamoring for authority and the ultimate reward of cultural capital? How could an author's competence be situated and evaluated in a marketplace where the commodity was everything and any aesthetic interest appeared to be a merely secondary consideration?

Authors of plays about plays situated their works at the very center of these controversies. Implicit, and often explicit, in plays about plays is a concern for the status of authority and a desire for control over the means of cultural production. Plays about plays were thus used to draw distinctions between legitimate and illegitimate forms of print and entertainment. And, in this sense, we can read plays about plays throughout the century as dramatic vehicles for an aesthetic and cultural politics. We can read beyond the immediate personal and political agenda of the moment for the arguments these plays make not just about the nature of representation, but also about the kinds of representation, dramatic and nondramatic, that ought to be in circulation and the kinds of the authors from whose pens those entertainments ought arise. Indeed, as I shall make clear in the sustained readings below, the fundamental interest of eighteenth-century plays about plays was with the representation of authority and with the circulation and ownership of the cultural capital that such authority entails.

To illustrate the ways that plays about plays undermined supposedly commonsensical understandings of character and authority by revealing them as subject to purchase and market manipulations, I turn first to a play titled *The Mad-House* (1736/1737). Subsequently, I examine Henry Fielding's *The Author's Farce* (1729/1730; 1733/1734), in order to demonstrate how, in assailing conventional forms of authority, plays about plays also created a space in which to make a case for their own offerings of "truth." I argue here that to the extent that plays about plays functioned as extended addresses to the audience, they also provided an opportunity for playwrights to align their interests with those spectators and thus gain a share of cultural capital. In the sections that follow these illustrative readings, I turn my attention to the cultural and ideological values in which playwrights like Henry Fielding invested their accumulated capital. First, I demonstrate how in plays such as *The Female Wits* (1696/1697) and *Three Hours After Marriage* (1716/1717) male playwrights campaigned against female playwrights by casting them as a kind of culturally queer grotesque. Second, I examine satirical attacks on foreign entertainments in plays such as *The English Stage Italianiz'd* (1727) and demonstrate how charges against these forms were dressed in the kind of patriotic garb that would appeal to the audience's nationalistic sensibilities.[8]

Locating the Frame in Plays About Plays; Or, The Problem of Competence, Authority, and Knowledge

Like its well-known and oft-written-about precedent, John Gay's *The Beggar's Opera* (1727/1728), Robert Baker's *Rehearsal of a New Ballad-Opera burlesqu'd, called The Mad-House* dramatizes the problem of authority and conventional ways of knowing in a world where "truth" was the purchase and plaything of private interests. Performed at Lincoln's-Inn-Fields during the 1736/1737 season, *The Mad-House* poses the basic question: what constitutes "competence" in a world preoccupied with profit?[9] In this play, Tom Friendly, an escaped inmate of Bedlam, presents a rehearsal of his new two-act entertainment. His dramatic piece presents the tale of Lucy, the daughter of Solomon Testy, who is locked up in Dr. Hyppo's madhouse in order to prevent her from running off and making a financially disadvantageous marriage. Happily for Lucy, the play concludes with her engagement to a soldier named Peacock, who has managed to save her from imprisonment by having the authorities put Hyppo out of business.

In this, his only recorded play, Baker, a "gentleman of the Inner Temple," avowedly takes up the poet's profession and the play-within-a-play format to render a critique of the ways in which distinctions as to who is and who is not mentally sound have been perverted by schemers who by declaring rich relatives insane stand to inherit wealthy estates (Dedication). Reflecting on a number of current inmates at Bedlam, he inquires, "Wretches who have ruined themselves by squandering away their Patrimony, green Girls in Love, and Men of Consequence merely so in their own Imaginations, may properly be said to be prejudiced; but shall we therefore call them Lunatick?" (Dedication). Baker's rehearsal play goes on satirically to depict and critique a world that suffers from money madness and conspicuous consumption—a world in which, as the practices of Dr. Hyppo, the quack physician/entrepreneur who runs the rehearsal play's madhouse, indicate, the right to declare another person mentally incompetent belongs to the highest bidder. "Competence," in fact, acts as the signature term throughout the representation as Baker deliberately highlights and manipulates its discordant usages in eighteenth-century culture as a referent for both mental and financial status.[10] Rather than separate these meanings, Baker holds them in constant tension with one another precisely to make the larger point that the interest and wealth commanded by those in socially sanctioned positions of authority, rather than objective standards, determine the paradigms through which individuals are perceived and judged. Character, in other words, is situational rather than immutable.

In the very first scene of the rehearsed play, for instance, Sir Solomon Testy enters discoursing on the matter of how best to dispose of his daughter Lucy in marriage and prevent her in the meantime from squandering his hard-earned "competency" by giving herself away to some unworthy beau. Ultimately he resolves to pay Dr. Hyppo (as in hypocrisy) to diagnose and to confine Lucy as a mad "hysteric" for reading romances and going to plays, a common charge against female consumers in the eighteenth century. Wielding paternal power tyrannically, Testy uses his economic "competence" as a means to incriminate his daughter's mental capacities. Lucy is not mad; she merely lacks both the public and the private authority to challenge her father's actions. As Testy himself puts it, he is "Emperor in [his] own House, and accountable to nobody" (II.vii). Madness is thus a mere pawn in a power play, the trump card as it were that cannot be topped so long as the right persons are properly remunerated for delivering so-called professional diagnoses. As Testy acts within his legal rights in relation to his daughter, Baker plays upon the newest usage of "competence" as a term designating, "the quality or position of being legally competent; legal capacity or admissibility."[11] By doing so, he indicates how social separations or cultural ways of seeing, knowing, and judging are determined not only by personal interests, but also by conventional norms and institutionally sanctioned forms of authority and power.

Baker further illustrates his point that declarations of insanity can be bought by introducing a number of other prisoners at Hyppo's for-profit venture. As Hyppo goes over the pay schedule for his "clients" with his assistant Whipcord, we find among others Mrs. Henpeck, who has been committed by her husband on the grounds that she is a termagant, and Aaron Circumcision, a "rich Jew of the Poultry," presumably held because relatives had an eye to his fortune. It appears, moreover, that an inmate named Rag "is come to his senses" and is to be discharged, for, as Hyppo explains, "his Wife has lost all sense of Payment" and thus "'tis impossible he can be mad any longer" (II.ii). In each case, diagnosis and prognosis are decided by two factors considered in conjunction with one another: relative cultural influence—a wife and a Jew in eighteenth-century England were hardly figures of power—and ability to pay the boarding expenses by those in whose interest incarceration occurred.

Yet Baker's indictment of such capricious distinctions does not end with those individuals who manipulate the system. In an almost macabre scene featuring patients chained to the wall at Hyppo's Mad-House, he extends the charge of culpability to public interest at large. As Baker makes a spectacle of the popular eighteenth-century entertainment of visiting Bedlam, he turns an ironic gaze back upon his theater audience engaged at that very moment in the presumptive activity of judging his representation as they might regard the inmates of the hospital. The first purported madman points at the audience and declares: "'tis our Misfortune to be the Monsters in the Fable, while the Man is the Painter;—for, according to the Fable, had the Monster been the Painter, then would you have seen the Lion strangling *Hercules*, and not *Hercules* the Lion" (II.x). Invoking the classical comic device of inversion, Baker disrupts a normative paradigm of perception in order to undermine the audience's sense of social and moral superiority. He continues to assail viewer confidence in this scene by questioning the grounds for assuming that the spectators have any greater degree of mental competence than the inmates they see confined in the asylum. A second so-called madman offers the following address:

Here we languish in Disquiet,
While the World abroad does not
Deck'd out in their splendid Luxury!
We are Mad, for they will have us so;
Yet spite of them we very well know
That the World is much madder than we! (II.x)

The second inmate of the asylum performs the operation of leveling as he contrasts the indefinite injunction that "they will have us so" against the firm and exclusive knowledge that "we very well know." In casting doubt upon the conventional authority of the spectator, Baker unmasks what Ian Donaldson has termed "the artificiality of all social distinctions in the face of human passion and incompetence."[12] Indeed, by highlighting the passionate interest of members of the audience in maintaining the distinction between themselves and the inmates of Bedlam as a means of securing their own sense of competence, Baker ironically manages to undercut their conceit that they are in any position of "competence" to judge either the inmates of Bedlam or the dramatic spectacle within which Bedlam is represented.

In this manner, *The Mad-House* presents just one example of the ways in which plays about plays deployed a redoubled structure in order to suspend audience belief in conventional ways of knowing. As the players play actors playing madmen in a play about a rehearsal play written by Tom Friendly, an escaped inmate of Bedlam, the location of sure knowledge recedes into the overlapping folds of representation. Character per se is neither secure nor self-evident, but rather uncertain and situational. The system for forming both rational meanings and meanings about rationality collapses as it becomes more and more apparent that the only evidence maintaining the separation between the spectators and the asylum inmates is the shackles that bind the inmates to the wall and the economic power that follows the market. In this sense *The Mad-House* does not merely draw the allegory of a paradigm shift or reversal of meaning in which the sane are mad and the mad sane. Rather, it moves beyond what Donaldson astutely classified as the thematic of "the world upside-down" to dispute the very premise of standard techniques such as inversion or leveling— the premise that there is a determinate or set order that inevitably governs all relations. Baker's play works to obscure the very distinctions that can be made between order and disorder in the new commercial world. There is no return to some conventional model at play's end; there is only a provisional accommodation or a change in interest as Solomon Testy becomes the new proprietor of Hyppo's moneymaking establishment.

Borrowing freely, as most eighteenth-century playwrights did, from the innovations of better-known colleagues such as Gay and Fielding, Baker places his work firmly in line with the critique of the conventional idea of order generally rendered in many eighteenth-century plays about play. Moreover, with its specific play on "competence" as a signifier for both mental capacity and financial wherewithal, the *Mad-House* explicitly traces the otherwise concealed relationship between private interest and the constitution and representation of public standards and distinctions that Jürgen Habermas has argued was so fundamental to the establishment of the "bourgeois public sphere" in eighteenth-century England. As Habermas explains, the rationale that enabled "public opinion [to claim] . . . legislative competence" was sustained by the "fictitious identity of the two roles assumed by privatized individuals who came together to form a public: the role of property owners and the role of human beings pure and simple."[13] In effect, private vested interests structured and limited the kinds of meanings that could be publicly produced and recognized. As the example of *The Mad-House* suggests, who is considered mad and what constitutes mad behavior is a function not of a transcendent and inevitable social order, but of the collection of interests that shape the frame of reference within which an individual is perceived and judged.

Like many other eighteenth-century plays about plays, then, *The Mad-House* uses and identifies the stage as a medium for exposing an age in which calculated shows could figure as the inflated form of currency for social and economic commerce. Construing character was revealed to be a speculative activity dependent upon a context or frame of reference that could collapse at any moment; absolute knowledge of character was radically in doubt. Plays about plays were thus positioned to be understood, on the one hand, as mimetic displays of a culture in which reality is "staged"—mirrored images of what has already been described as a ubiquitous performative impulse. On the other hand, and far more significantly, these plays offered satirical allegories of that same culture—representations that shattered the illusion of everyday sincerity by exposing it as a theatrical performance motivated by private interest and supported only by prevailing, but not permanent, social values and conventions.

Plays about plays thus functioned not merely as "passive chronicles" of the times, as Dangle and Puff might have it, but also as histories—narratives that bring an interpretive point of view to bear dialectically on events as a means of producing a sustained critique of the times. In this respect, we need to keep in mind that while plays about plays may have been dedicated to a critique of conventional authority and competence for being tainted by graft and shows of insincerity, they were not without their own interests both in authority and in gaining a cultural competence. Indeed, authors of plays about plays contracted for audience trust precisely on the basis of this antitheatrical theatricalism, a technique whereby they critiqued the insincerity, that is, the disguised performances of other forms, while locating their own sincerity in the admission that they offered and celebrated nothing more than a performance. The act of exposing the theatrical contrivance of actors and actresses entering into "character," that is, into the roles they played, thus conferred strategic advantage on their plots. What we still need to discern in relation to this genre, then, are the ways that playwrights capitalized on their exposure of character and on their critique of other interests as a means to enter with an aspect of disinterest into the ongoing struggle for control over cultural capital and interpretive authority. For that instructive turn, we can look to Henry Fielding's *The Author's Farce* (1729/1730; 1733/1734).

Fielding and the Epistemology of Sincerity and Nonsense

For Henry Fielding, reality in plays about plays was not so much a theatrical ideal as it was a theatrical idea to be played upon in order to substantiate his own authority as an arbiter in the realms of judgment and taste. Perhaps the most successful playwright during the period prior to the Licensing Act of 1737, Fielding's genius consisted in his witty and innovative usage of a plays-about-plays format. In this capacity he has been referred to variously as "the master of the puppet-show," a "puppet-master of dazzling skill," and "the Master . . . manipulating his characters and retaining control over them."[14] These character-izations celebrate Fielding's ability, as Anthony Hassall puts it, to "stoop only to conquer," that is, his capacity to incorporate and to wrestle valiantly with the inanities and incoherencies of the forms of his time in order to reveal truth, sense, and order (76). Susan K. Ahern extends this praise, concluding her article on *The Author's Farce* by writing that Fielding "has discovered a vehicle that not only conveys but creates meaning."[15]

Such claims for Fielding's mastery usually occur, however, either in the course of a developmental account of Fielding's novelistic techniques or in the context of a defense of his theatrical career against those who contend that he found his true artistic niche only after turning to the novel.[16] As a result, they often fail to examine what motivates Fielding to generate a system for the making of meaning. What were the anticipated effects of those meanings in eighteenth-century English culture? What, in other words, is at stake for Fielding when he engages in this kind of cultural production? What did he stand to gain from "mastery"?

In the previous chapter, we saw how Fielding endeavored in his "An Essay on the Knowledge of the Characters of Men" to gain a position of spectatorial author-ity, placing himself beyond those who seek to disguise their motives and offering himself as the champion of the naive and impressionable. In this essay, he gains an interest as a cultural authority in relation to his audience by appearing to situate himself discretely outside the field of advantage. In the reading below, which takes *The Author's Farce* as its example, I will argue that Fielding was up to something similar in many of his plays about plays. I will show how he exploits confusion over how to construe characters and their actions in order to attain a position of authority from which he can act as a cultural Spectator, legislating taste and judgment and distinguishing between legitimate and illegitimate forms.[17]

During the period 1729–37, when *The Author's Farce* first appeared on the London stage, Fielding was not only one of the most prolific playwrights of what is commonly termed "irregular drama," he was also the most effective in the use of experimental forms within the more basic frame of rehearsal plays. Many critics have been quick to fault Fielding for his indulgence in experimental forms, complaining as Dane Farnsworth Smith does in the case of Fielding's later play *Pasquin* (1735/1736): "In his overloading of the rehearsal . . . and in his complication of the burlesque on pantomime by making it likewise an abstruse allegorical attack on his enemies, Fielding has but added to the conglomeration of genres . . . and has left the confusion in the realm of the dramatic still more confounded."[18] First presented at the Little Theatre in the Haymarket during the 1729/1730 theatrical season and revised in 1733/1734 for a new production on the Drury Lane stage, *The Author's Farce* might appear equally confused with its strange presentation of a life-size allegorical puppet show titled *The Pleasures of the Town* as its featured play-within-a-play.[19] Yet if we explore, rather than dismiss, the significance of Fielding's use of "abstruse allegorical attack," we can begin to make sense out of this so-called confusion. We can begin to see how Fielding's allegorical satire provides a vehicle not just for an attack on particular individuals but for a commentary on larger cultural issues. At the same time, moreover, we will find that Fielding's complicated and at times confusing intermingling of dramatic forms functioned, much as it did in John Gay's *The What D'Ye Call It?* both as a means to assail the decline of genres in the burgeoning theatrical marketplace and as a calculated intervention to point up the importance of generic form for the production of meaning. Together these modes of attack offer him a strategically effective, because oblique, way to promote a cultural politics that would bolster his own authority as well as his own cultural capital and interests.[20]

As early as the Prologue to *The Author's Farce*, Fielding introduces the critical content of the production and encodes the logical key for understanding the significance of that content in the narrative. He writes:

Like the tame animals designed for show,
You have your cues to clap, as they to bow.
Taught to commend, your judgments have no share;
By chance you guess aright, by chance you err.

But handkerchiefs and Britain laid aside,
Tonight we mean to laugh and not to chide.

In days of yore, when fools were held in fashion,
Though now, alas all banished from the nation,
A merry jester had reformed his lord,
Who would have scorned the sterner Stoic's word.
Bred in Democritus his laughing schools,
Our author flies sad Heraclitus' rules.
No tears, no terror plead in his behalf;
The aim of farce is but to make you laugh.
Beneath the tragic or the comic name,
Farces and puppet shows ne'er miss of fame.
Since then in borrowed dress they've pleased the town,
Condemn them not, appearing in their own.[21]

Although some aspects of Fielding's work here are subtle, his message is clear. His is a laughing disrespect as he constantly modulates the temporal thrust of his opening enunciation and critiques the audience's pretenses to judgment by comparing their applause to the cued bows taken by animals in popular entertainments on the London stages. Even though he offers parenthetically that the "times when fools were in fashion" have long since passed "in days of yore," his parable of reform through laughter neatly aligns contemporary audiences' mindless clapping responses with the kind of fashionable foolishness that in the past demanded reform. Yet Fielding also willfully downplays any threatening intimation that he means to impose upon the audience, repeatedly insisting, "we mean to laugh and not to chide" and "the aim of farce is but to make you laugh." In the final four lines, he presses his case for the benevolent hand of farce by offering his play as a site of full disclosure. As opposed to the farces and puppet shows that pass speciously on the stage for tragedies and comedies, he promises a puppet-show farce that claims to be nothing more than farce. Through this artfully deployed claim to candor in his laughter, Fielding represents farce as a genre that can be trusted to be frank and ingenuous. On this basis he contracts not only for the praise but also for the trust of the audience. Thus initiating the rhetorical strategy upon which he stakes his interest throughout the production, Fielding offers a surface of full disclosure in order, paradoxically, to gain a veiled position through which he can authoritatively shape audience taste.

The outer frame for Fielding's allegorical puppet show features a hapless and poverty-stricken playwright named Luckless who must struggle to get his play mounted because he lacks the insider's influence or "interest" to coerce playhouse managers to take his play. As Luckless makes the rounds of publishing concerns and playhouses to meet with booksellers and managers, Fielding executes a systematic exposé of the parties and institutions that exerted a virtual stranglehold on the market in theatrical goods. Indeed, as a struggling writer at an early point in his career, Fielding was no stranger to this set of circumstances. As Peter Thomson has noted, Fielding thought his theatrical career had been thwarted when Colley Cibber rejected two of his plays (45).[22] His hits in this section, which were aimed for the most part at Colley Cibber and his confederates, were thus motivated at least in part by a certain amount of personal animus. Still, Fielding had other reasons to despise Cibber. Like Pope, Fielding would come to view Cibber as an incompetent whose rise to prominence in the theater world was made possible through the corrupt politics and influence of Robert Walpole.[23] He held this cabal responsible for the "sunken status of literature," including the degenerate and chaotic condition of plays and entertainments for the stage.[24]

Luckless's best friend and supporter, Witmore, spells out the situation when he advises and admonishes Luckless:

In an age of learning and true politeness, where a man might succeed by his merit, it would be an encouragement. But now, when party and prejudice carry all before them, when learning is decried, wit not understood, when the theaters are puppet shows and the comedians ballad singers, when fools lead the town, would a man think to thrive by his wit? If you must write, write nonsense. (I.v.26–32)

In this passage, Fielding displays the connections between governmental politics and theater politics and uses the metaphor of a puppet show to suggest that the theaters have become as much a vehicle of political propaganda under Walpole as has government itself. In a market culture shaped by interest as much in the theater as in the court, wit and merit have become undervalued currencies. Driven by economic necessity, the author who wants to survive must trade in nonsense, or, as Luckless eventually concedes, "Who would not then rather eat by his nonsense than starve by his wit?" (III.9–10).[25]

By targeting the economic and political strings that privately control a puppet government in the theater, Fielding positions his farce as publicly in opposition to those forms of cultural corruption. Again, he underscores the point of his antitheatrical theatricalism: while other contemporary representations on the stage work to conceal their performative motives, his farce consistently offers to expose its own theatricality. More significantly, he extends that point beyond the theater to the performances of everyday political life. Indeed, while many other plays about plays merely analogize the governing forms of authority in the theater and in the country, rendering each complacently and banally as just the "way of the world," Fielding insists on decisive critique. He thus prepares his audience for a critical allegory that will literally enact the nonsensical lack of distinction between the fictions of everyday life and the fictions of the stage.

Luckless introduces this allegory as his recently accepted play titled *The Pleasures of the Town*, the absurd plot of which he justifies by explaining in an odd echo of Sir Roger in Gay's *The What D'Ye Call It?* that "since everyone has not time or opportunity to visit all the diversions of the town, I have brought most of them together in one" (III.34–39). In fact, the kind of complicated fusion of genres for which Dane Farnsworth Smith chides Fielding reaches its highest pitch here; Luckless's play consists of an allegorical puppet show that proceeds through a series of musical interludes modeled after the ballad opera form initiated by Gay. Each ballad outburst is assigned to one of a series of allegorical figures who represent the most egregious offenders in a variety of popular print and entertainment forms, including Italian opera, the novel, punch shows, pantomime, and tragedy. Yet the aggregate effect of this generic explosion is neither confused nor, I would argue, purposeless. For to the extent that Fielding urges generic distinctions toward a point of collapse, he also abstractly foregrounds the extent to which those generic structures function as necessary bulwarks in the staging of meaning. In a more immediate respect, this original choice furnishes Fielding with the vehicle he needs to capitalize on the critique leveled in the Prologue. Where other authors fashion tragedies and comedies that amount in his opinion to no more than mere farce or puppetry, Fielding literalizes the folly and blatantly commodifies it by offering a life-size puppet show, *The Pleasures of the Town*, in which a fictional author, Luckless, acts as a master of ceremonies who commands a troupe of actors playing allegorical puppets.

Set on the far side of the River Styx, Luckless's *The Pleasures of the Town* features the puppet Goddess of Nonsense at court receiving slavish tributes from what John Loftis terms "personifications of the ruling London pleasures" as they contend not only for the poet laureateship of her kingdom but also for her hand in marriage (40). In this *Dunciad*-like contest for interest and favor in the land of the dead, the contenders include Don Tragedio, Sir Farcical Comic, Dr. Orator, Signior Opera, Monsieur Pantomime, and Mrs. Novel.[26] Each of these satirical portraits serves Fielding's purpose of anatomizing and illustrating the extent of cultural decay in early eighteenth-century England. Yet as the figures each explain how they died of overkill in a particular genre, they also become recognizable as Fielding's competitors in the cultural marketplace from whose mortification he stands to gain.[27] For instance, as the commonly acknowledged stand-in for Eliza Haywood, Mrs. Novel first testifies regretfully that she died defending her virginity, singing on the journey across the river Styx, " 'Twas hard t'encounter death-a / Before the bridal bed. / Ah! Would I had kept my breath-a / And lost my maidenhead" (III. Air V). This remarkable extension of the swoons of maids in romance novels at the threat of a ravisher miscarries, however, as she is later compelled to confess that she in fact died in childbed while bearing the out-of-wedlock child of Signior Opera, a figure for the famous castrato Senesino. In his catalogue of the represented individuals, Charles Woods suggests, "That a castrato should be the father of Mrs. Novel's child need trouble no one in a play in which one ghost almost kills another and in which the heroine turns out to be a brother to a puppet" (Appendix B, 103). Yet, it is precisely the fact that Mrs. Novel claims a eunuch as the man who "ought" to be her husband and the father of her child, but who neither is the former nor can be the latter, that enables Fielding to treble the emphasis on sexual depravity and moral vacuity and thus by specious association to illustrate the depraved vacuousness not only of Mrs. Novel's (Eliza Haywood's) writing but also of the novel in general. Even more significantly, Fielding's technique of rendering Mrs. Novel and the other sycophantic supplicants to the Goddess of Nonsense either as self-exposing hypocrites or simply as self-evidently absurd provides the foundation upon which he forges an alliance in judgment with his audience and readers. For the more he appears to be laughing with the audience at others, the less he appears to be directing their responses or, more importantly, to be laughing at them. His ability to gain spectatorial trust thus depends on the subtlety with which he casts their laughter as an objective response to nonsense. His taste gains credibility to the extent that it becomes that of the audience; he accrues interest to the extent that he compels members of the audience to invest the authority of their own judgments in his critique.[28]

The most significant transaction of the puppet show ultimately takes place, however, in a parodic scene of discovery in which, as Charles Woods so dryly puts it, "what may be called non-realistic elements are juxtaposed or mingled with realistic elements" (Intro., xvi).[29] In this scene a stranger arrives and announces that Luckless is the long-lost son of the King of Bantam. No sooner does Luckless recall his identity in a sudden memory flash than another messenger arrives: the King of Bantam is dead, long live Luckless the new King of Bantam! These timely revelations are followed by an equally unmotivated series of disclosures by the puppet character Punch. Luckless's fiancée Harriot, he reveals, is also of royal blood; not only is she the missing princess of the house of Brentford and therefore worthy of marriage to a king, she is also his (Punch's) long-lost sister. Woods editorializes that "Fielding's purpose . . . is to make his denouement as incredible as possible. . . . [A] more fantastic series of unmotivated discoveries which reveal unsuspected relationships in ludicrous scenes of recognition would be hard to imagine" (72 n). But his earlier hedging that the denouement "may" involve the mingling of realistic with unrealistic elements suggests that the text merits closer examination.

Indeed, given the multiple frames of dramatic reference that have been introduced into the drama by this point, it is difficult to determine where the ground of realism stands. The frame of the puppet show itself had already been disrupted earlier by the arrival of the parson Mr. Murdertext with a constable to arrest Luckless on charges of "abusing Nonsense" (III.693). Here it is not entirely clear whether this is meant to be part of Luckless's play, with Mr. Murdertext as one of his characters, or whether the actors playing the allegorical puppets step out of their roles to defend Luckless against the threat of arrest. The line between the "real" and the "not real" within the representation begins to blur, as does the distinction between "character" as role and "character" as person. This effect is heightened when, in the moments that follow the recognition scene, it not only appears that the "flesh-and-blood" characters have a familial relationship to the allegorical "puppet" characters, but, as Luckless goes on to appoint each of those puppet figures to a position in his court, it becomes unclear whether the outer frame has collapsed into the internal allegory or the internal allegory has displaced the outer frame. That is, as the staged "reality" comes to be both disrupted by and indistinguishable from its own framed fiction, it becomes increasingly apparent that in a pattern of spiraling regression even the "real" is only the constituted or manifest representation of yet another theatrical frame. Indeed, this appears to be the moral or rather the joke of Fielding's allegory; as he relentlessly empties out the content of theatrical performance and entertainment, we are left only with a series of hollowed-out or collapsed frames—that is, with non-sense as the content of eighteenth-century culture.

In his discussion of Fielding's rehearsal plays, J. Paul Hunter maintains that "Fielding emphasizes the radical factitiousness of the form, its tendency to isolate, and compare, the fictional and the 'real' worlds. . . . Traffic between these worlds . . . underscores the separation and enables a concentration upon responses to art which may parallel responses to action and events, especially political ones, in real life" (50). Hunter's reading concentrates attention on a dialectic in which separations and parallels between fiction and reality remain persistently visible. While such a dynamic clearly marks at least one level of structured meaning in *The Author's Farce*, Fielding's efforts to highlight such separations precisely as the product of factitiousness suggest an alternative interpretation. Indeed, as the multiple frames collapse one into another, he destabilizes what we thought of as our definitive understanding of the characters in performance. Our knowledge of where to place each figure along the divide between fiction and reality slips away as the discrete categories of identity with which we began the drama lose their explanatory power. The very distinctions we think can be made between real and merely fictional experience become manifestly fluid and arbitrary as we find ourselves on a continuum where we can only say that something or someone is more or less "real" depending on which factitious pole is dominant in that particular moment. In short, the farce eschews mimesis, or the imitation of nature, to offer a contrived mimicking of the very contrivances by which "nature" is designated. Fielding betrays the circular logic governing such relations; the boundaries that distinguish natural or real from unnatural or fictional experience in everyday life are exposed as merely the provisional or temporary fictions by which we organize, and by default come to say that we "know" the real or that we "know" character.

In short, the allegory that Fielding fashions in *The Author's Farce* emerges as a tale of an epistemological crisis in which distinctions between realities and fictions become increasingly opaque and the conventional representations of meaning *as* truth are exposed as intentionally misleading conflations. The promise of stable meaning or truth is emptied out in the allegory and replaced with the stark new "realism" that meaning is no more or less than a product of a particular epistemological framework that can be displaced or overruled. In this context, meaning itself paradoxically becomes "meaningless," except insofar as it is understood to emerge from a system of articulation that has either been assimilated to belief or, more critically in eighteenth-century culture, captured the public trust.

As in his "Essay on the Knowledge of the Characters of Men," Fielding emerges as our "champion" here insofar as he positions his dramatic allegory strategically to gain audience trust. Rather than offer an absolute truth, he rests his claim for sincerity on his deconstruction of truth as a category. Where other cultural media may go to great lengths to disguise their artifice, *The Author's Farce* takes as its subject the full disclosure not only of its specific deployment of conventional theatrical contrivances but also of those used more generally in society. Fielding's rhetorical pose thus stands in stark contrast to the configuration of authority assumed in other cultural forms of the day.[30] Rather than veil theatricality, Fielding blatantly advertises its ubiquitous presence in *The Author's Farce* in order to intimate that in a competitive market culture inflated by theatricality the theater is the only place that may, in the final analysis, be honest. In this posture of antitheatrical theatricalism, he appears to serve public interest even as he shapes narratives that serve his own particular social values and interests. His hectic but controlled orchestration of nonsense transforms his private interests into self-evident mandates of public opinion.

While I have noted some of the specific targets of Fielding's sharp wit in the discussion above, I have left largely untouched the question of what kinds of interests consistently prevail both in Fielding's plays and in plays about plays in general. In the sections that follow, I want to turn my attention to tracing two of the main interests pursued by plays about plays: first, the problem of gendered authorship and second, the problem of foreign entertainments and the state of the nation's stage. As J. Douglas Canfield has already pointed out, it is one thing to take pleasure in following the almost infinite regress into art through which Fielding establishes his authority; it is quite another matter altogether to consider the targets toward which this authority is directed and, where warranted, to critique its exercise.[31] As we shall see below, authors of plays about plays took as their subject not only the question of authority in general, but also the questions of who ought to have access to the means of representation and what kinds of representations ought to be offered on the eighteenth-century English stage.

Authority, Interest, and Female Authorship

In one of the most insightful essays on Fielding's particular interests, Jill Campbell has argued that "Fielding repeatedly links the significance of gender . . . to matters of 'government,' both political and literary" and that "much of this satiric use of gender works to protect or enforce certain historical notions of masculine authority."[32] Campbell's analysis of Fielding's interests suggests the extent to which many of his plays about plays, in particular *Pasquin* and *The Historical Register*, can be read as dramatizations of Fielding's vexed attempts to police what he considered culturally out of place with respect to gender status.[33] This anxious preoccupation with the status of masculine authority, coupled with a general hostility to female involvement in literary government, places Fielding in accord both with contemporary attitudes toward female authorship and with one of the predominant interests pursued in plays about plays. For just as "Woman's appropriation of male 'empire,' the threat of 'petticoat government,' is the most general and persistent topic of sexual satire in Fielding's plays," the petticoat playwright— or the threat of a female pretender to the male empire of wit—is also consistently subjected to particular disciplinary action in plays-about-plays.[34]

Male playwrights were of course also subject to farcical, parodic, and satirical representation on the stage, and such attacks often played on the resonances of various cultural interpretations of gender. Yet the fact of their sex was never the definitive criterion in these renderings or in judgments on their work. At the same time, the conflation of women writers' sex with their ideas and craft was, and often still is, taken for granted as a convention of eighteenth-century satire and criticism. Woods, for instance, blandly notes this imbalance in Fielding's *The Author's Farce* when he writes that "Mrs. Novel is less identified with her art than the others in her group, though what we learn of her life suggests the scandal and sentimentality of fiction" (Appendix B). This habit of extending an indifferent nod to an historical, yet clearly suspect, premise finds its most curious manifestation in a gossipy but well-intentioned volume titled *Five Queer Women*.[35] Published in 1929 by Walter and Clare Jerrold, a husband and wife team, this text features literary biographies of five women writers from the late seventeenth and early eighteenth centuries.[36] In what is supposed to be a celebratory defense of what these women achieved as writers, almost no effort is made to explain or problematize the title designation "queer" as a descriptor. Indeed, the assumption that a woman who wrote in the eighteenth century was somehow culturally out of place is as solidly entrenched here as is the presumption that an account of each woman's purported sexual escapades both justifies that designation and illuminates her writing. We are still left, then, with the question as to what it was, precisely, that constituted the "queerness" not only of these five women, but of women playwrights and authors in general. In the pages that follow, I attempt to address this question by offering an analysis of the strategies repeatedly invoked both by their satirists in plays-about-plays and by women playwrights in their prologues and prefaces to their plays. By doing so, I hope to demonstrate that what was culturally "queer" about the eighteenth-century female playwright was not her sexual status per se, but rather her refusal to accept the ideologically "normative" role assigned to her in an economic system that was increasingly dominated by a gendered division of labor.

One clue to this alterity comes to us in the form of the title to Kitty Clive's 1749/1750 farce about women playwrights: *The Rehearsal: Or, Bays in Petticoats*.[37] As the title dresses the male protagonist of Buckingham's *The Rehearsal* in female attire, so too did the woman playwright of the eighteenth century inhabit the space of a cultural cross-dresser. That is, she cloaked herself in or assumed the mantle of authorship, an appearance that was considered either a strictly masculine prerogative or one that women could wear only in the private sphere. Indeed, as Kathryn Shevelow has pointed out in her study of women and print culture, "During the eighteenth century, as upper- and middle-class Englishwomen increasingly began to participate in the public realm of print culture, the representational practices of that culture were steadily enclosing them within the private sphere of the home. That is, at the same historical moment that women were . . . becoming visible as readers and writers, the literary representation of women . . . was producing an increasingly narrow and restrictive model of femininity."[38] The cultural transgression effected by the woman writer thus came in the field of the gendered division of labor. A woman's work was supposed to be confined to the private sphere and her products reserved for private consumption. Instead, the woman writer, like the female actress, entered the public sphere and directed her labor toward the production of goods for public consumption.

Transgressing the gendered division between public and private realms, women's writing was thus "defined as a threat to the existing social order."[39]

In the realm of theater, this trespass into masculine territory was perceived as even more dangerous and troublesome, for it intersected with and was reinforced *as* transgression by antitheatrical discourses that, as Jill Campbell observes, "used cross-dressing as a paradigm for the moral dangers of the theater, making gender the ultimate preserve of natural identity to be broached . . . and setting up the theater as the forum in which the boundaries of gender might be tested" (65–66). Exhibiting some of the same cultural potentialities that Terry Castle has identified with the masquerade, the theater provided an alarming opportunity for fluidity of character and the proliferation of identities and thus threatened to disrupt the severe economy of social roles that was beginning to take shape in the early part of the century.[40] Ironically, however, while the theater may have represented a site for acute gender play to its critics, in its day-to-day operations it actually reflected and participated in the consolidation of an ideology that insisted upon the split between masculine and feminine spheres of labor and influence. The threat of female usurpation of male prerogatives was constantly rehearsed and policed on the eighteenth-century stage, with the most virulent aggression aimed at enforcing what Nancy Cotton terms the "Salic Law of Wit."[41] Like the Salic Law of France that barred women from the throne, the Salic Law of Wit was meant to bar women from the bays of authorship.

The precedent for the intentionally malicious and acerbic quality of eighteenth-century efforts to lay down the Salic Law of Wit was set in the late seventeenth century by the notorious dramatic satire *The Female Wits* (1696/1697). During the 1695/1696 theatrical season, Mary Delarivière Manley, Mary Pix, and Catherine Trotter all enjoyed success that was unprecedented for women playwrights as together they saw no fewer than five of their plays through production.[42] Apparently their achievement was perceived as enough of an incursion into the male empire of wit to merit disciplinary action in the form of an anonymous attack at the very beginning of the 1696/1697 season in a play titled *The Female Wits; or, The Triumvirate of Poets at Rehearsal*.[43] Briefly, this three-act satire consists of the action before, during, and after a rehearsal of an inane parody of Manley's *The Royal Mischief* attended by figures for the three satirized playwrights. Its explicit purpose, as laid out in the Prologue accompanying the 1704 edition, was to reform those "Strumpets that would mask'd appear . . . now in their True Colours see 'em here." In short, the prologue frames the play in conformity with the narrow conditions of judgment deemed suitable for women's writing during this period. As Nancy Cotton succinctly characterizes them, "If the woman playwright was ipso facto a whore, then ipso facto she wrote bawdy plays. . . . If a woman's play was not lewd absolutely, it was lewd relatively, that is, too lewd to be written by one of the modest sex" (186).[44] Capitalizing thus on this commonplace equation of female playwrights (and actresses) with prostitutes and bawdiness, the author of the Prologue to *The Female Wits* praises the play for setting out to unmask the "character" of women who sold their nefarious wares to the public from the boards of the playhouse stage.[45]

A number of feminist scholars have now critiqued this play for its concentrated indictment of female authorship as sexual misconduct.[46] Much earlier, however, in the only study that treats the drama as a play about plays, Dane Farnsworth Smith wrote in a defensive tone bordering on approbation that the play's preface:

fails to mention that Mrs. Manley, the chief victim, had in 1696 given ground for the attack in a tribute in verse to Mrs. Trotter which was virtually 'a challenge to the male sex to a race for poetic honours,' and that this flaunt, together with the appearance, unprecedented on London boards, of five plays by three women in a single year was more than the conservative gentlemen of the time could easily bear.[47]

Playing on Mrs. Manley's so-called "queer" reputation for sexual promiscuity as well as on the insinuations of the prologue, Farnsworth's comment seems to suggest that the charge of sexual misconduct was deserved, that Mrs. Manley was "flaunting" herself publicly and such behavior combined with the affront of commercial success by women in the public sphere simply was not acceptable. Significantly, what is coming under attack here, as it did in the eighteenth century, is not only the femaleness of these authors, but also the woman writer's ambition to establish playwrighting as a legitimate profession for women.

In contrast, an examination of Manley's tribute, and those by Trotter and Pix to Manley on the occasion of her play *The Royal Mischief*, reveals that the women were quite self-consciously engaged in an attempt to establish the ground of their dramatic authority by identifying, representing, and supporting a tradition of women playwrights. Pix urges, for instance:

You snatch laurels with undisputed right,
And conquer when you but begin to fight

. . . .
Your self must strive to keep the rapid course,
Like Sappho, charming, like Aphra, eloquent,
Like chaste Orinda, sweetly innocent.[48]

By tracing a female genealogy of dramatic authorship, Pix establishes a historical rationale for the radical claim by women playwrights to an "undisputed right" to the laurels of success on the stage. She urges Manley to stay the course, even as she acknowledges that those successes must be snatched on a battlefield that is unfriendly to female soldiers.

Trotter also invokes the battlefield metaphor when she writes of woman's entry into the dramatic sphere as a declaration of war. She hails Manley:

For us you've vanquished, though the toil yours,
You were our champion, and the glory ours.
Well you've maintained our equal right to fame,
To which vain man had quite engrossed the claim.[49]

For Trotter, the success of one woman playwright created the possibility of the success of all, and she regarded each triumph in the theater as collective property. Shrewdly, she opposes that claim to collective ownership of fame, gained through labor or "toil," to the exclusive "engrossment" of fame by individual men. Moreover, she plays one signification of engrossment against another when she pits the engrossing proprietary claim to authorship by men against the engrossed, or writ large, inscriptions of her own pen. In so doing, she juxtaposes privilege against right and establishes grounds for the legitimacy of female authorship.[50]

Thus it comes as no surprise to find that the anonymously penned *Female Wits* levels its satirical attack with full force against the legitimizing claim of a professional community among women playwrights. As Constance Clark notes, the satire predictably "exploits the cliché of cattiness and competitiveness among the women" (199). The text is riddled in the opening scenes with nasty comments made by Marsilia, the figure for Manley, about each of her female associates, Calista for Trotter and Wellfed for Pix, even as she hypocritically embraces them with great enthusiasm when they enter her dressing room. While the strategy here appears to be superficially playful in its rehearsal of cultural stereotypes, the underlying seriousness of the attack hits its target by exploiting anxieties about the incursion of women into a male-dominated profession. For example, while Marsilia's proclamation of a "Female Triumvirate" is weakly undercut by the spectacle of female hypocrisy, the success of the women playwrights during the previous season is raised and transformed into a perpetual threat of "petticoat government" in the theater world when she continues: "Methinks 'twould be but civil of men to lay down their pens for one year and let us divert the Town. But if we should, they'd certainly be ashamed ever to take 'em up again" (I.i).

The idea that women would mishandle such government comes to be played out through the stunning application of another cliché that strikes at the most significant aspect of the women's claim to professional status: female wit. That is, while Peter Stallybrass and Allon White have described the deployment of satiric wit in the production and regulation of the bourgeois public sphere, they neglect to point out that this territorialization of poetic authority and professional authorship was carried out not only with respect to class but in relation to gender as well.[51] To the extent that satiric wit was championed as both the weapon of choice and the mark of an increasingly bourgeois poetic authority during the early eighteenth century, it was also marked solely as a proprietary right and province of male authorship. In *A Comparison Between the Two Stages* (1702), for instance, Critick provides concrete evidence for the banal authority of this sentiment when he protests to Ramble, "Sir, I tell you we are abus'd: I hate these Petticoat-Authors; 'tis false Grammar, there's no Feminine for the Latin word, 'tis entirely of the Masculine Gender."[52] Indeed, both in *The Female Wits* and, ironically, in Clive's *Bays in Petticoats*, the woman who aspires to wit is cast as a cultural grotesque insofar as she embodies this "grammatical" oxymoron. The "intellectual woman," as Constance Clark pointedly writes, "became a new Jonsonian humor in the comedies of the time—a female fop, affected, arrogant, her self-esteem far in excess of her capacity" (12). Like the effeminized male fops who are her sycophants and with whom she is constantly associated in each of these satires, the female playwright is construed as a false pretender to wit, a culturally queer grotesque who must be driven out of the public sphere of representation. Thus her claim to wit is constantly ridiculed and, more significantly, her work is never valued as productive labor.

This, of course, is the joke that regulates and disciplines the female playwright in the 1716/1717 comedy *Three Hours After Marriage*, penned by a striking "Male Triumvirate" of wits: John Gay, Alexander Pope, and John Arbuthnot.[53] The satire portrays an old dupe named Dr. Fossile, who within three hours of his marriage to Mrs. Townley discovers that she has numerous lovers, an illegitimate child, and at least one other husband. The play revolves around the plots hatched by Townley's beaux Underplot and Plotwell to cuckold Fossile. Consummation of these "plots" never occurs, nor does consummation of Fossile's marriage. The play ends, however, with Fossile gaining custody of the illegitimate child and packing Mrs. Townley off to her other husband. In a parallel plot that runs throughout the course of action, Fossile's niece, Phoebe Clinket, races about the house (turning it into a playhouse on the wedding day), constantly chattering on about her plays and the composition of couplets. One of the most significant elements to emerge through this secondary story line is the satiric contrast between the positioning of Phoebe Clinket as female playwright within the playtext, and Gay, Pope, and Arbuthnot's own posturings as authors in the Prologue and Epilogue to the play.[54] This distinction is particularly revealing insofar as each of those representations depends upon the production of posterity as its critical mediating value.

In the case of Phoebe Clinket, the issue of productivity comes to a crisis when her Uncle Fossile mistakes her plays for offspring, a mistake that is extended to a promiscuous joke when Phoebe unabashedly announces: "I have had one returned on my hands every winter for these past five years. I may perhaps be excell'd by others in judgment and correctness of manners, but for fertility and readiness of conception, I will yield to nobody" (V.402–5). As the joke conflates production with reproduction, Phoebe's poetic activities are sexualized and degraded; her pretensions to wit, according to Fossile, only reduce her to a "wretched creature" (V.396–97). Indeed, though Phoebe may have a fertile mind, the satire suggests that she is ultimately impotent. Because they lack wit, her plays or "breedings" never come to full maturity on the stage. With respect to the production of her own posterity, Clinket has applied her fertility to the wrong profession. She was supposed to give birth to children, not plays. As the drama's unremitting puns on labor insist, she has violated the normative division of labor and consequently is barren not merely as a playwright but also, and more shamefully, as a woman.

In a play dominated by the joke or rather the fantasy of reproduction without women, as Fossile celebrates his newfound posterity without the burden of sex or a wife (V.460ff), it is not surprising to find that Phoebe's impotence is set in direct contrast to the potency of her metaphorical fathers in the epilogue to their play. Gay, Pope, and Arbuthnot rehearse Phoebe's shortcomings in their appeal to the audience—her offense a "harmless want of wit"—even as, per the conventions of the genre, they stake their claim to posterity and authority on the basis of their own well-bred wit (Epilogue, 21, 44–45). In essence, they associate their wit with poetic potency, even as they identify it as the quality that the female playwright invariably lacks. Barred thus from the challenge initiated in the prologue, in which wit is marked as both the weapon of engagement as well as the privileged term of production when Gay, Pope, and Arbuthnot throw down a "fool's cap," daring other "gallants" to pick up the challenge of playwrighting, the female playwright can only, as Roy Porter points out, "run the gauntlet."[55] That is, if the eighteenth-century woman playwright dared to pick up wit as her weapon, she risked at the very least what Elizabeth Montagu politely termed, "bad consequences" for "like a sword without a scabbard, it wounds the wearer and provokes assailants."[56]

Although *Three Hours After Marriage* does not operate exclusively as an attack on female playwrights, its studied efforts to illustrate and then to galvanize the general interests served by proscribing female wit constituted neither a veiled nor a merely fictional threat to women writers. If wielding the pen was represented as a frivolous and dangerous luxury for the triumvirate's Phoebe Clinket,

Clive's Mrs. Hazard, and the anonymously satirized "Female Wits," for actual women playwrights who earned much of their living by the pen these public attacks amounted to no less than a serious menacing of their livelihoods. This reality could not help but inform the dedications, prefaces, prologues, and epilogues of plays by women writers, for conventionally those framing devices were used by dramatic authors both to proclaim their interests and intentions and to stage preemptive strikes against anticipated criticisms. For women playwrights, particularly those in the first half of the eighteenth century, these extratextual opportunities to establish authority were taken up and dominated by defenses of their sex. Even Susanna Centlivre, who was not only the most successful woman playwright, but also one of the most successful playwrights period in her time, felt constrained in many of the direct addresses associated with her dramatic texts either to mount her own argument for her sex or to sanction such declarations by those who authored some of the prologues and epilogues to her plays. Her prologues reveal the kinds of discourses mobilized by female dramatists in defense of their own character and illustrate the extent to which they staged their own authority by taking advantage of the other controlling interest of eighteenth-century plays about plays: an antipathy to foreign entertainments and persons.

Although written by various champions of her work, the prologues to *The Beau's Duel* (1701/1702) and *The Cruel Gift* (1716/1717) best illustrate the general pattern followed by Centlivre when she undertook that labor in her own defense.[57] The prologue to *The Beau's Duel*, written by a Gentleman, concludes with the following declaration:

Our Female Author, tho' she sees what Fate
Does the Event of such Attempts still wait;
With a true *British* Courage ventures on,
Thinks nothing Honour, without Danger won.
She fain wou'd shew our great Fore-Fathers Days,
When Virtue, Honour, Courage, wore the Bays;
Fain wou'd she kindle up those fading Fires,
That warm'd their Noble Blood to fierce Desires.
When the Bold Hero, after tedious wars,
With Bleeding Wounds adorn'd, and Glorious Scars,
From Conquest back return'd with Laurels Crown'd,
Where from the Fair, their just Rewards they found.

In his prologue to Centlivre's tragedy *The Cruel Gift*, Mr. Sewell (presumably George Sewell, who wrote a number of tracts on English drama in the eighteenth century) strikes similar chords when he protests:

Our Woman says, for its a Woman's wit,

. . . .

If she must sue, she scorns those vulgar Arts,
But fain by nobler Means would in your *Hearts*;
Tell you she wears her Country in her Breast,
And is as firmly *Loyal*, as the best.

Significantly, each of these prologues mobilizes a narrative with at least two interconnected strands. The first refers to the vulnerable status of the female sex with respect to authorship and publicity; the second represents national reputation and posterity not merely as contingent upon, but rather as coextensive with, the female author's plight. In *The Beau's Duel* prologue, for instance, a broadly conceived parallel is drawn between those who win the laurels of war and Centlivre, who, despite all of the risks particular to women writers, ventures with "Virtue, Honour, [and] Courage" to win the bays from the "fair." The rich linguistic play with the intersecting rhetorics of war and poetry situates Centlivre as a paragon of "true British courage," who, as a matter of national interest, reputation, and conscience, must and should be judged *fairly*.

This appeal to national honor and pride was later extended and explicitly exploited in the preface to the first edition of Centlivre's collected works. Published in 1760/1761, the plays were introduced by "no other than a Woman" in an address "To the World."[58] The address opens with an expression of dismay over the fact that Centlivre was not honored upon her death, as were so many male writers of her time, with a monument in Westminster Abbey. The author, who is "not a little piqued" at what she takes to be a purposeful oversight, then goes on to mobilize what Linda Colley has identified as perhaps the most effective discourses and images for forging national identity over the course of the eighteenth century: those portraying Protestant Britain as a nation embodying the very essence of liberty, locked heroically in a vital struggle against the tyrannical governments and peoples of Catholic nations such as France and Spain.[59]

Accordingly, our mediator declares, "See here the Effects of Prejudice, a Woman who did Honour to the Nation, suffer'd because she was a Woman. Are these Things fit and becoming a free-born People, who call themselves polite and civilized!" Having raised the doctrine of British liberty as the banner under which to convince her (male) contemporaries to rectify the "sins of the Father," she adeptly invokes the specter of the Salic Law and implies through this juxtaposition that the imposition of a Salic Law of Wit upon Centlivre and other women writers not only constitutes a gross act of male tyranny, but also, and more portentously, it registers and perpetuates a significant source of national shame in its congruence with French principles.[60] She pleads thus for the sake of the

English soul that since "*English* Men . . . have been more sensible of our natural Abilities, and not so barbarous as to exclude us from the Chance of Reigning," they should allow for the same liberty with respect to women's writing. In short, she reasons, "These Doctrines are unreasonably inconsistent, and arise only from Prejudices which it is high Time should be exploded, and our Sex enjoy the Liberty which they have a natural Right to." She concludes with the astounding claims that "probably the next Age may be taught by our Pens that our Geniuses have been hitherto cramped and smothered, but not extinguished, and that the Sovereignty, which the male Part of the Creation have, until now, usurped over us, is unreasonably arbitrary: And further, that our natural Abilities entitle us to a larger Share, not only in Literary Decisions, but that, with the present Directors, we are equally intitled to Power both in Church and State."

As the address described above indicates, for women writers and their advocates in the eighteenth century the struggle to provide a space from which they could speak with authority was clearly understood to be ongoing. It was a cause that required the weighty forces of rhetoric and moral suasion. Because plays about plays were so consistently directed against the exercise of female wit, women writers had to adopt an alternative idiom that could supersede the overwhelming appeal of a gendered hierarchy in authorship and provide a legitimate basis for their voices.[61] If it is true, then, as Peter Stallybrass and Allon White have argued, that "An utterance is legitimated or disregarded according to its place of production," then women writers, in their efforts to gain recognition, had not only to defy the sexualization of both their persons and their work, but also to initiate a discourse that could detract from the cultural "queerness" of their claims to authorship and authority (80).

As the tracings above intimate, the most compelling and comprehensive discourse available at the time was that of national identity. This evidence supports Linda Colley's claim that in the eighteenth century, "Britishness was superimposed over an array of internal differences in response to contact with the Other, and above all in response to conflict with the Other" (6). It suggests that the best way to undermine the charge that women writers were "culturally queer" was to reframe the question of authorship as one of national reputation and conscience. Thus women playwrights and their defenders portrayed efforts to suppress their work as a general affront to the almost sacred value of English liberty, a particularly grotesque violation when it was carried out by others of English blood. Capitalizing on a nationalist discourse that was already in circulation, women writers thus attempted to attain legitimacy by negotiating the cultural hierarchies that defined each speaker's "place of production." To make their products viable in the marketplace, they mobilized a rhetoric of national solidarity and made it clear that the defense of the English soul and the maintenance of English liberty ought to transcend all other considerations of judgment. The female playwright thus assumed the character of a patriot in order to defend both her interests and her value.

Defending "National Interests"

The displacement effected by women writers of gendered authorship for national identity coincided with, and took advantage of, charges of illegitimacy leveled against the other general object of derisive interest in plays about plays: foreign entertainments. Indeed, the treatment of women writers in this genre may even seem mild when compared with the outright vilification of imported theatricals. As early as the first half of the eighteenth century, the English stage was reeling at the success of foreign entertainments such as harlequinades and Italian opera. Anxious and concerned by what they both perceived and then represented as a foreign invasion of a native province, many satirists responded on the stage with grotesque, gender-inflected satires of those forms. As Dane Farnsworth Smith has noted, "Indigenous amusements [were] held up as virile, while Continental innovations [were] frowned upon as degenerate and effeminate." Such representations "express[ed] in a literary form a nationalistic temper and a determination to save English theatres for English performers."[62] Not insignificantly, one of the main tactics adopted in these satiric representations to lure the English public away from foreign spectacles was an emphasis on the shameful loss of English revenue and currency to foreign companies. Further, the economic chauvinism advocated in these satires appeared to agitate for theatrical reform not merely for the sake of English fortunes, but also for the sake of the English soul. Indeed, these often violently parodic hits were portrayed as having purgative, remedial benefits for the improvement of the English stage as well as therapeutic advantages for improving English character and reversing the deformation of English taste. In short, these satires offer us a potent example of the way that cultural products were aggressively advertised as patriotic goods in the eighteenth century.

Antagonism to what were characterized as foreign dramatic arts was registered early in the century in *A Comparison Between the Two Stages*. In the course of this three-party dramatic dialogue, which touches on every aspect of business and performance at Drury Lane and Lincoln's-Inn-Fields, the most serious and pessimistic figure, Sullen, reacts with disgust at Critick's descriptions of the absurd inventions of a night piece with Harlequin and Scaramouch: "'S'death I am scandaliz'd at these little things; I am asham'd to own my self of a Country where the Spirit of Poetry is dwindled into vile Farce and Foppery" (47–48). Amid the constant chatter and witty repartee of this ongoing dialogue, it is possible to take Sullen's commentary as a hyperbolic effect of posturing. Yet as the discussion continues, it becomes increasingly clear that it is calculated to cultivate and elicit an almost visceral response of paranoid concern for the debasement of the English stage by foreign infiltrators.

Picking up on the earlier allusion to the audience and income that such entertainments generated, Ramble observes of an Italian castrato, "he got more by being an Eunuch than if he had the best Back in Christendom; the Ladies paid more for his *Caponship* than they wou'd ha' done for his virility" (49). Although at this point it still appears that Ramble and Critick would prefer to keep the conversation buoyant, Sullen again interjects with his usual seriousness, warning, "this Evil increases upon us every day; there are more of the *Circumcision* come over lately from *Italy*" (50). Later, in reaction to Ramble's attempt to console him with the thought that at least the English themselves did not invent such frivolities as the intrusion of music into drama, Sullen protests vehemently:

that which pardons the *Italian* does not pardon us: They are all Idolaters of Musick, an effeminate Nation, not relishing the more masculine Pleasures; their *Theatres* are meer Musick meetings, and the little hodge-podge, which is their *Drama*, is little better than a continu'd Song, without action, incident or variety: But in *England*, where Poetry has been in perfection, where our Passions are more manly, I see no more reason for following 'em in this Custom than in their Dress or romantick way of Intriguing. (52)

The rhetoric mobilized here paints the Italians as a threat to the order of the sexes. The contagion or "evil" which the *castrati* bring to England is not merely envisioned as the effeminization of English culture; rather, it is horrifically imagined as its emasculation, the loss of all virile passion and power. At the same time, these passages allude obliquely to the larger force behind this gradual weakening of a distinctly English "Spirit of Poetry." The unusual characterization of the castrated opera singers as "of the *Circumcision*"—an allusion that associates the castrati with one group of non-Protestants, the Jews—as well as the reference to the Italian penchant for musical interludes as "idolatrous," converges with other passing remarks to direct the discourse toward an understanding that these entertainments mark a critical moment in the Protestant struggle against Catholic treachery. The use of a gender-coded discourse mediates and thus paves the way for more blatant and vociferous allegations against the popish threat concealed in these spectacles.

Indeed, this is the very issue raised when Critick remarks, "We are so fond of every thing that comes from *France* or *Italy*, 'tis God's Mercy we han't their Religion" (50). In contrast to Critick's effort to find some small source of comfort under the circumstances, Ramble seems instead to revel in the possibility of such a conversion, immediately offering the riposte:

O'lard! if they wou'd send over their *Pope*, we shou'd have rare Sport: The *Pope* and the *Cardinals* wou'd make the finest Scene in the World; what running there wou'd be from all Parts to see the *Conclave* kept in *Drury-Lane* or *Lincoln's-Inn-Fields!* Or at *Charing Cross* with the Tyger; or in *Fleet-Street* with the Elephant: But if Mr. *Rich* had 'em, what an Emperor wou'd he think himself with all St. *Peter's* Patrimony, his *Holiness* and all his red *Hats* in Pension. (50)

Although this passage should be read as in the laughing spirit, its humor and Ramble's enthusiasm for a popish spectacle are mitigated by an ambivalent tension. On the one hand, Ramble presents the possibility of Catholicism in performance as a grotesque and degraded spectacle comparable to the animal entertainments in prostitute-ridden Charing Cross and on the festering corners of Fleet Street. On the other hand, his vision of the hordes running willy-nilly to pay to witness such an extraordinary exhibition intimates a kind of slavish submission to mindless follies. More significantly, the placement of such a production under the aegis of the entrepreneurial Christopher Rich draws a parallel between the dumb-show harlequinades that were influenced by the Italian *commedia dell'arte* and the dumb shows of Catholic ritual to which England once submitted. Despite Rich's management, fees paid for admission to foreign spectacles are considered here as no more or less than a new, yet more covert, form of tribute. The endless fascination of spectators approaches the former enslavement of the English mind and soul to Catholic theatrical shows. As Sullen so mournfully concludes, " 'Tis owing to the depravity of our Fancies: Our Judgments are not at all exercis'd in't" (52).

The particularly powerful resonance of this nationalistic discourse grounded in religious conflict has been demonstrated in great detail by Linda Colley in *Britons: Forging a Nation 1707–1837*. England, of course, had a long prior history of acrimonious relations with the Church of Rome; and as England found itself locked in what Colley has termed a "protracted duel" with France, this enmity toward Catholicism only intensified (24). Actual wars such as the Nine Years War (1689–97), the War of the Spanish Succession (1702–13), and later the Seven Years War (1756–63) helped to focus the energies of this hostility. Even more significantly, the threat of a return to power of the Stuarts, who were deposed because they were devoutly Catholic, continued to menace and, according to Colley, to shape national consciousness. As she explains:

the prospect in the first half of the eighteenth century of a Catholic monarch being restored in Britain by force, together with recurrent wars with Catholic states, and especially France, ensured that the vision that so many Britons cherished of their own history became fused in an extraordinary way with their current experience. To many of them, it seemed that the old popish enemy was still at the gates, more threatening than ever before. The struggles of the Protestant Reformation had not ended, but were to be fought over and over again. (25)

In this context, the proliferation on the English stage of entertainments with ties to Catholic nations such as Italy and France was all too easily and opportunistically exploited as the alarming motive for a call to arms. The popish conspirators, it could be argued, were not merely at the gates; they had already squeezed past the guard and were in the process of making the English stage their first conquest. Although these kinds of chimeras were often invoked for no more than rhetorical purposes, they still formed the stage into one of the front lines in a perpetual struggle against Catholic forces. The infiltration of the stage by agents of these insidious forces, in the apparently innocuous form of entertainments, was cited as the cause of the very emasculation of English culture, a condition that would only render the population that much more susceptible to an all-out invasion. In short, the relentless subjection of the stage to these spectacles constituted no less than a monstrous contamination of the "Spirit" of English Poetry and thus a threat to the very soul and existence of the nation.

On the stage the assault on entertainments associated with the French *Opera Comique*, the Italian *commedia dell'arte*, or the Italian Opera was sustained in a variety of productions, including Gabriel Odingsells's *Bay's Opera* (1729/30) and Francis Lynch's *The Independent Patriot; or, Musical Folly* (1736/1737). The former portrays a struggle between dramatic poetry, Italian music, and pantomime to become the heir to the throne of wit in the British Nation. With dramatic poetry, personified by Tragedo, already deposed, the conflict is resolved when Parliament proclaims Pantomime the lawful heir and grants him a military force led by General Briton to lay siege to Italian Music represented in the figure of Cantato. The play concludes as Pantomime celebrates his ascendancy by luxuriating in the grotesque splendor of an inaugural parade. Similarly, Lynch's production features a barbed attack on contemporary English taste for Italian music. Characterizing this affection as an elitist taste and an effeminate affectation brought on by infection or contagion from abroad, Lynch offers an outspoken patriot named Sanguine to defend native, masculine interests. While each of these plays obviously mounts a patriotic attack on foreign entertainments, they at least make some attempt to distinguish among the various foreign forms. In the most vicious of this kind of play about plays, however, no attempt was made on any level either to register any difference among the types or to divert attention away from an overwhelming sense of foul contamination.

This exacting and harsh method is best illustrated in a mock-heroic, mock-pantom, mock-opera fully titled *The English Stage Italianiz'd, in a New Entertainment, Called Dido and Aeneas: Or, Harlequin, a Butler, a Pimp, a Minister of State,*

Generalissimo, and Lord High Admiral, Dead and Alive Again, and at Last Crown'd King of Carthage, by Dido.[63] Published fraudulently in 1727 as the latest work of the already dead Thomas D'Urfey, this play, though apparently never performed, appears at first to meet all of the conventional criteria of dramatic satire: grotesque exaggeration, the fantasy of allegory, and the rhetorical devices of irony.[64] Yet it is necessary to remember that satire generally, and plays about plays in particular, purchased authority in the eighteenth century only to the extent that they maintained an appearance of disinterested distance from their objects. In this respect, *The English Stage Italianiz'd* may not only have played the "Briton" hand, but tipped it and betrayed the very interests that, as earlier portions of this chapter illustrate, plays about plays were designed to disguise.

Deploying both a Swiftian irony as well as a Swiftian propensity for the scatological, *The English Stage Italianiz'd* presents a grotesque allegory of the legendary tale of Dido and Aeneas. The title page introduces the "dramatic entertainment" as a "Tragi-Comedy, after the Italian Manner; by way of Essay, or first step towards the farther Improvement of the English Stage." Within we find an introductory address that features, as the first bold step towards such an "Improvement," a modest proposal to banish from the playhouse stage all "old fashion'd Stuff" that offers too "ponderous Sentiments," including Shakespeare, Jonson, Dryden, Otway, Wycherley, Congreve, Rowe, and Addison (iii). First the author implores his fellow countrymen to "cast away our native heaviness, and soar to the very tip-top of human Excellence . . . [to] become light and spiritous, as those generous People, who are now come in pure Charity to refine us, and make us fit for human Conversation." Then he asserts with great confidence: "They come not with the selfish Views of their Ancestors, to carry our Consciences and our Purses to *Rome* to convert us, but with a view of enriching the Papal See. No, they are now upon quite another Footing: For whereas we formerly were forced to carry our Money to *Rome*, these good natured Souls take the trouble off our Hands, and carry it for us" (ii). The odd syntax of the first sentence, which causes the emphasis to fall on the "enriching of the Papal See," coupled with the blatant sarcasm of the second sentence, ironically undercut this statement of assurance. The proposal, in fact, is anything but modest as we are constantly reminded of both the financial stakes involved in the pursuit of this particular "taste" and the papal, rather than English, interests that may be served by it.

In addition to this conventional rehearsal of chauvinistic, anti-Catholic sentiment, the introduction appeals as well to another class of increasingly resonant cultural distinctions. Alluding to a time when Italian might replace English as the language of the stage and advertising a translation of the performance text into Italian, "For the benefit of the English Quality, and others who have forgot their

Mother-Tongue," the entertainment is cynically marketed as being in the taste indulged and promoted by an elite, rather than a representative, cultural group. The "much injured Bard" appeals in high-minded posture:

Let us judge therefore, of these *Italian* Comedies and Comedians, not by the Report of illiterate and peevish Criticks, but by their full Houses, and their noble Audiences, composed of the best of our People. . . . Shall any Man persuade me, that so many powder'd Perukes, would spend so many Hours in vain? no, no, there is more in it than the generality of shallow Pates can yet imagine: They must live and learn, e're they be able to make any Thing of these Dramatic Mysteries. (iv–v)

The ironical exhortation to judgment in the passage registers a general hostility to aristocratic pretensions to taste, and it contests the cultural authority claimed by those "powder'd Perukes" to ascribe cultural value. This is not to say, of course, that these types of entertainments were subscribed to exclusively by members of the upper classes; to the contrary and despite the higher prices charged for admission, they received across-the-board spectatorial support.[65] Rather, the passage further illustrates the complex mingling of discourses dedicated to reducing the interests of foreign entertainments and adding to "the Interest and Glory of *Great Britain*" (iii). While this marked class discourse rose to prominence in associated genres in the second half of the century, here it remains relatively muted.[66] It merely intimates a basis for the grotesque critique rendered of Italian classical origins and moral degeneracy in what is represented as an exemplary pantomimic performance text for the improvement of the English stage.

Briefly, the argument or action of the text consists of a distorted rendition of the tale of Dido and Aeneas in Carthage. In this re-version, Aeneas does not leave Dido in order to found the great Roman state. Instead he runs off in the middle of the night to be with Colombine, whom he has just pimped from Harlequin. Broadly speaking, unadulterated lust rather than honor and destiny drives Aeneas in this pantomimic spectacle. The high culture of the great thus loses its "dramatic mystery" as its motives are recast in a less than brilliant light. The mythic, classical origins of Italian culture are demystified; its birth is elaborated as no more or less than an accidental and secondary effect of libidinal rather than heroic character.

Yet the method for effecting this satire becomes increasingly suspect as the full course of the pantomime unfolds to include a dumb-show contest in which Aeneas heroically drinks the contents of a chamber pot in order to win and gain sexual favors from Harlequin's mistress Colombine (II.xii); the stabbing of the breechless Aeneas in the backside as he flees with Colombine for fear of Dido's wrath (III.vi); the cowardly retreat of Dido's army at the sound of a herd of swine (IV.x); the cure of Dido's madness at Aeneas's departure when Scaramouch drinks the strained contents of a "Close-stool Pan" (V.viii–ix); the revival of the dead Harlequin by the blowing of wind up his "fundament," and his immediate need upon his resurrection, to urinate "with a Vengeance" in the course of which he displays his ample "Wherewithal" and literally "piss[es] out Scaramouch's Eyes" (V.xi). Finally, rather than ending tragically with Dido's suicide, as tradition would dictate, this grotesque display concludes comically with the marriage of Dido and Harlequin and his subsequent crowning as King of Carthage (V.xii).

In his summation of the action of the play, Farnsworth Smith writes: "The piece which follows [the introduction] is nothing more than a description of an unbelievably vulgar pantomime. . . . The author's idea seems to have been to ridicule that (also Italian) form of amusement by pouring into its framework material of revolting grossness and almost incredible repugnance."[67] Indeed, this unmitigated and unrelenting attack on the mythical origins of Roman and Italian culture was meant to effect a confirmation of English culture and identity. The representation of Italian culture as fundamentally monstrous, vulgar, and corrupt was coupled with the introductory assertions described above in order to draw upon deep-seated suspicions of and hostility towards the popish Catholic church as a hotbed of perverse appetite and extravagant display. The grotesque and degraded bodies of foreign entertainments were, by contrast, to imply the stronger claim of native English plays to the simplicity and moral purity of the idealized classical body. Cast as practically unintelligible action, pantomime and Italian operas were to be repudiated as illegitimate and morally degenerate action.

In order to compete for audience share, defenders of native English dramatic productions endeavored to find a way to project pantomime and Italian opera as what Stallybrass and White might term a "raging set of phantoms and concrete conditions to be forcefully rejected" (105). The desire of forming observers' habits and improving English taste was understood not so much as a problem of representing English drama as high as it was of representing any alternative entertainments as profoundly low. These forms were thus attacked for confounding the classical with the modern to produce cultural grotesques. Foreign entertainments were then construed as wielding a monstrous tyranny over the English soul; they had not only to be overthrown but thoroughly reviled, often by means of an ugly countergrotesque. While it could be argued that plays such as The English Stage Italianiz'd stooped too low, producing a surfeit of vulgar spectacle and betraying the hand of their interests, the fact remains that in powerful ways these plays policed the stage and guarded its boards against the "barbarians" at the box-office gate.

An old school of criticism would have us believe of eighteenth-century plays about plays that the "tendency on the dramatist's part was to play with the theatre and not to use it for any serious purpose."[68] As the discussions above have demonstrated, this is far from the case. Eighteenth-century plays about plays were, in point of fact, marked to perform important cultural work, articulating a cultural and aesthetic politics that would reshape the limits and contours of authority, police the privilege of professional authorship, and proscribe certain forms of entertainment. In this manner they provide us with a kind of "abstract chronicle" of the times, as they elaborate wider eighteenth-century preoccupations with the problem of epistemological authority in a commercial culture, the production of gendered divisions of labor, and the articulation of a discourse of national culture and national identity. Most important, they illustrate how the stage deployed a strategy of antitheatrical theatricalism that put into question the integrity of individual character and privileged the prerogatives, interests, and authority of generic forms.

I have concentrated my focus on plays about plays from the early part of the eighteenth century because those plays set precedents for the genre that were sustained throughout the period. While the Stage Licensing Act of 1737 severely curbed opportunities to deliver fierce satires of the political butts of the day, playwrights continued to avail themselves of the structural dynamics of plays about plays to highlight the problem of authority and to level scathing critiques of the commodification, fluidity, and theatricality of truth. Indeed, if anything, the positions and interests pursued in these earlier plays hardened over the course of the century, as if playwrights who took up the genre later in the period still envisioned themselves doing battle with Grub Street hacks, ambitious female playwrights, and the incursions of foreign entertainments.

Hence at the end of the century we find in George Colman the Elder's play *New Brooms* (1776/1777) a hero named Sprightly who moves against the reign of Dulness to assert the continued greatness of the English stage and to promote the powers of English discernment against the incursions of Dunciad-like forces. Similarly, and slightly earlier at midcentury, we find a play such as Aaron Hill's *A Snake in the Grass* (1760), which features the conversion of a poet from Mr. Fightfashion into Mr. Lightfashion, a slave to Harlequin.[69] Not insignificantly, one of the major symbols of cultural decay in this vignette is the mixing of genres as embodied by the figure of "the Genius" himself, who appears

dressed on the right side, like a man, in the habit of a *Scaramouch* (with a wand)—on the left side like a *Columbine* (with a fan)—the face neatly cover'd with a flesh-colour'd masque, representing on one side a grave *man's* countenance, with black hair and whiskers; and on the other, a gay young *woman's*, with fair locks and complexion; half a hat, or cap, on the right of the head, and the proper headdress for a woman on the left half: and so, in like manner, the whole dress divided quite down to the shoes—the petticoat rounded in, and concealing the left leg and thigh, to the girdle. (91)

As in earlier representations, the generic threat associated with foreign entertainments becomes inextricably implicated in a kind of gender dysfunction, a nonsensical this and that. More an effeminated man than a masculine woman, this harlequin figure, who vacillates between a tragic and a comic tone, capers like a monstrous grotesque displaying the horrors resulting from the mixing of generic forms.

The sense of revulsion for foreign entertainments and the mixing of generic forms they precipitated was not the only lasting hobbyhorse of eighteenth-century plays about plays. Indeed, one could argue that the figure of the female dramatist constituted an even more objectionable subject as the gendered divisions of labor hardened over the course of the eighteenth century. Thus, in an eerie echo of her predecessors, Frances Sheridan felt compelled in the prologue to her sentimental comedy *The Discovery* (1762/1763) to beg pardon for the trespasses of this "Female culprit" onto "poetic grounds." Extending the pattern we observed in our discussion of the strategies of female dramatists, she goes on to invoke the totem of English liberty when she protests against the judgment of "men, / Those lordly tyrants who usurp the pen!" and demands the right guaranteed by "old magna charta . . . / That British subjects by their peers be try'd." In short, she demands not only that she have the opportunity to write but that "her own sex" act as the judges of her works.[70]

That Frances Sheridan had good cause to believe she had violated some kind of gendered division of labor in taking up pen and ink is evident from the portrait of the female playwright we find in George Colman the Younger's *The Female Dramatist* (1781/1782).[71] Here, as in representations from the earlier part of the century, we find a mad female playwright, Mrs. Metaphor, who takes all occasions as hints for generating new play plots. Mrs. Metaphor and her fortune are being courted by a hack named Dash who flatters her sense of her writerly abilities and trumpets his own. The situation is so dire that her niece Harriet's suitor, Beverley, feels compelled to plot her cure. When "her conversion is compleat," he brags, "You shall see me transform her into a downright housewife—and by a single stroke of my Art, turn her Pen into a Needle, and her Tragedies into Thread papers" (II.i, p. 20). Here, as in earlier plays-about-plays, the female playwright must be turned away from the pen and ink she desires and turned toward that other genre of inscription that was available exclusively to women in the domestic sphere: the needle and the thread. A woman's writing was to be limited to the cottage forms that she found in the home.

Returning now to where we began this account, with a sketch of the general contours of the genre, we find that, through their self-conscious willingness to rehearse the conventions, contrivances, and artifices of their own trade in theatrical production, in a culture increasingly dominated by acts of speculation and subterfuge and in which representation itself had become a devalued commodity, authors of plays about plays paradoxically positioned drama as a site of full disclosure within the culture. By deploying metadramatic spectacles, moreover, they created a space in which drama and dramatists could act as critical spectators on the contrived dramas, or nonsense, of everyday life. In this respect, eighteenth-century plays about plays appear to support Victor Turner's thesis that the relationship between performance and society is, "not unidirectional and 'positive'—in the sense that the performative genre merely 'reflects' or 'expresses' the social system or the cultural configuration . . . but that it is reciprocal and reflexive—in the sense that the performance is often a critique, direct, or veiled, of the social life it grows out of, an evaluation . . . of the way society handles history."[72] Turner argues, moreover, that in studying drama, we must examine texts not only as mere texts, but as texts in context, and "not in a static structuralist context but in the living context of dialectic between aesthetic dramatic processes and sociocultural processes in a given place and time" (28).

Plays about plays in the early eighteenth century enact a dialectic that lends itself particularly well to such an examination because their internal structures situate them in a dynamic, though precarious, relation to one of the larger cultural movements of the period. Specifically, through the structural emplacement of the role of spectatorship, as many of these plays enact another play in rehearsal with various observers, the genre intervenes in and confounds the drive to construct and to secure the objective authority of the Spectator. At the same time, such plays enact and participate in a rigorous dialectic whereby they mimetically represent and critique cultural processes on the basis of theatricality, even as they deploy the theatrical allegorically, to legitimate their own position as spectators of that culture. Through this strategy of antitheatrical theatricalism, dramatists produced and provided themselves with a form of cultural capital and authority that could be invested in corrective narratives for the culture—narratives, that is, within which they could personally shape a variety of cultural identities that would appear to be purely in the public's best interests.

These interests are what constitute the abstract and brief chronicles of the time that are eighteenth-century theater: abstract because they are part of larger cultural movements, brief because they are part of a moving, changing montage

of ideas. Although I have traced these interests in plays about plays predomi-
nantly from the first half of the century, I have also shown how the policing of
gender roles and foreign competition can be observed in this genre throughout
the century. Female authorship was persistently subjected to scrutiny and condemnation, and the bodies of all who could be construed as foreign to a masculine and English authority were made into grotesque spectacles. All the while,
the themes of cultural corruption and of judgment under siege consistently
provided the justification and thus the cover for the genre's not so disinterested
efforts to identify and discredit what was felt to be culturally "out of place."

By exposing the contrivances that support the theatrical illusion of character
on the stage, plays about plays purported to help the audience to learn how to
read the illusions of character in everyday life. Other genres, in contrast, worked
hard to conceal the contrivances, or the epistemological structures, through
which they manufactured the character and character identities of their heroes. In
the chapters on tragedies and comedies that follow, I will endeavor to tease out or
unpack those embedded structures in order to illustrate the critical role they
played in the dialectical fashioning of character and character motivation on the
eighteenth-century stage.

Chapter Three
Tragedy's Tragic Flaw
National Character and Feminine Unruliness

If eighteenth-century plays about plays held the line of defense against foreign invaders, then it was tragedy's task to work the offense in an attempt to "liberate" the English nation. Plays about plays often made this point about the cultural work of this dramatic genre. Drawing an analogy between theater and nation, they figured successful tragedy as the antidote to both a faltering national stagecraft and an ailing national morality.[1] Indeed, they projected tragedy's dignity and authority as an index for the nation's strength and stability. The performance of tragedy was represented as a means to envision and to ensure the future health and prosperity of England as a nation. Projected thus as a metonymic emblem of the country's struggle against foreign attacks and internal moral degeneracy, tragedy was commissioned to resolve the crisis in national confidence by offering a theatricalized, yet sincere, vision of both the English nation and the heroic individuals who would champion and exemplify that nation. Not insignificantly, moreover, the realization of the one was to be accomplished only through the articulation of the other. Tragic heroes were to embody the virtues and principles of the nation, and, reciprocally, the nation's prospects were to be expressed as aggregate functions of those personified virtues. The character of the nation was to be authenticated, paradoxically, through the fictional character of its tragic heroes.

Given such high expectations, it might seem disappointing to find that more than any other dramatic genre of the eighteenth century, tragedy has been accounted, almost unanimously, a "failure." In an influential article titled "The Failure of Eighteenth-Century Tragedy," Eugene Hnatko concluded, for instance, that "Eighteenth-century tragedy failed . . . because of all types of literature it seemed so admirably suited to what the age saw as the purpose of all writing— moral instruction—and the fulfilling of that purpose was inimical to the very nature of tragedy."[2] On a very different note, Allardyce Nicoll offered: "The trouble in the age was lack of orientation. No single tragic dramatist, save Lillo and to a lesser extent Moore, knew precisely at what he would aim . . . everyone felt the want of spirit in the tragedy of the time."[3]

What is interesting about these appraisals, however, is that where Nicoll identifies the highest achievement of eighteenth-century tragedians—the development of domestic tragedy by Lillo and Moore—Hnatko identifies their lowest point. His contempt is only too palpable when he writes, "In a way *George Barnwell* . . . is appropriately the triumph of . . . simplified morality, appropriately because . . . morality has always been associated with the middle classes" (466). In short, Hnatko situates the cause of tragedy's failure precisely where Nicoll locates its only source of success: in the turn to domestic rather than heroic individuals and to particular rather than universal questions about action and morality. For Hnatko, tragedy "failed" because it betrayed its expansive "nature" and pursued questions on a contracted scale. For Nicoll, tragedy lacked spirit because it failed to develop extensive responses to those very questions.

How, we might ask, can this turn to the individual and the particular constitute, at one and the same time, the sign of tragedy's diminishment and its finest achievement? How can we account for the stark contrast in these points of view as well as for Nicoll's and Hnatko's ultimate agreement that tragedy lost its force in the eighteenth century? Moreover, if Nicoll and Hnatko are right in these aesthetic judgments, the question they leave unanswered remains what precisely motivated this timidity or crisis in representation? What was the cause of this "lack of orientation" and why was this uncertainty particularly acute for tragic playwrights?

In the pages below, I will argue that the genre was troubled not so much by a "lack of orientation" or a sense of "failure" as by a historically and culturally specific crisis over the character of tragedy itself. That is, while Hnatko and Nicoll each claim that the entry of the middle classes into tragic representation definitively altered the quality of the genre, neither one takes into consideration either the actual status of the middling classes in the eighteenth century or what that position might have meant in terms of representation on the tragic stage. They argue as if a coherent middle-class ideology were already in place, and they assume that allusions to middle-class morality resonate with self-evident meaning. In doing so, they impose an ahistorical abstraction on such tragedies, reading backward from a twentieth-century model of bourgeois ideology that was firmly instantiated only in the nineteenth century. They fail to recognize, in other words, that the representation of moral principles in eighteenth-century tragedy was complicated at the outset by attempts to adapt the genre to the changing economic and imperial interests of England and by initiatives to adopt the emerging bourgeois individual as the new ideal protagonist of tragic form.

These difficulties were compounded, moreover, by a paradox peculiar to the genre: despite its claim to offer an exemplary hero, tragedy only does so by identifying and giving play to the inherent flaw that will occasion his or her demise. By definition, tragedy seeks to illustrate a tragic fall; that is, the genre inherently prohibits the fulfillment of ideal prescriptions. Put more pointedly, it is the peculiar paradox of tragedy that it both forms itself around an essential ideal and yet discovers the very conditions that either have already made the realization of that ideal impossible or will always render it an ideal rather than a reality.[4] In the case of eighteenth-century tragedy, the prospects of the nation could not be outlined without imagining the means by which those prospects would ultimately be frustrated. Similarly, the stature of heroic character could grow only to the extent that the values embodied by a hero and valorized in the representation were also understood as the cause of the hero's tragic demise. Hence, even as tragic playwrights attempted to produce the character and authority of an emerging middle class, they also had to envision the elements that could undermine any such claims. The fact of this paradox and the indeterminate status of middle-class ideology thus provide keys for understanding the intense ambivalence associated with tragedy both on the eighteenth-century stage and in twentieth-century literary criticism.

Tragedy's Work

Before we turn to readings of specific plays, we need first to come to a fuller understanding of the contours of tragedy and its peculiar orientation in eighteenth-century cultural life. Significantly, the idea of tragedy's patriotic purpose was not limited to the projections of plays about plays. Playwrights who accepted the call of the tragic Muse self-consciously selected fables and themes for tragic interpretation that had allegorical, analogical, or even direct significance for patriotic ends. In prefaces, prologues, and sometimes epilogues, they explicitly invoked service to the state as the primary interest of tragedy and identified the representation of a particular virtue as the means to fulfill this obligation. In the prologue to *The Briton* (1721/1722), for instance, Ambrose Philips proclaims to the "Britons" of the audience, "Love of Freedom is your ancient Glory" and urges:

From the famed Race of our Old Saxon Kings
Remember, then, the Dangers, you have past:–
And, let your Earliest Virtue–be your Last.[5]

Reflecting this patriotic ethic at the turn of the century, John Dennis selected "friendship" as the exemplary virtue of his tragedy *Iphigenia* (1699/1700). In his preface, he explains:

My chief design in writing the following Poem, was to contribute my Mite towards the being serviceable to the publick. And I thought I could not do that more effectually than by endeavouring to enflame the Minds of an Audience with the Love of so noble a Virtue as Friendship. . . . He who is generous enough to love his Friend, has greatness of mind enough to serve his Country: The Virtues have always been inseparable, and never was there an excellent Friend, but he was a good Patriot.[6]

As these examples suggest, playwrights felt compelled to justify their tragic works on the grounds of public service. More significantly, they consistently affirmed that the genre required the skillful representation of virtue and patriotism not merely as compatible claims on heroic character, but rather as inseparable ones.

In an even higher register, many writers claimed a preacherly function for tragedy. Richard Steele pointed out, for instance:

Speeches or Sermons will ever suffer, in some Degree, from the Characters of those that make them. . . . But in the case of the Stage, Envy and Detraction are baffled, and none are offended, but all insensibly won by personated Characters, which they neither look upon as their Rivals or Superiors; every Man that has any Degree of what is laudable in a Theatrical Character, is secretly pleased and encouraged in the Prosecution of that Virtue, without fancying any Man about him has more of it.[7]

Here, as the discussions in Chapters 1 and 2 might anticipate, Steele reminds us of the extent to which the "characters" of individuals were viewed as suspect; in their stead he advances a dramatic genre, tragedy, as a potential moral agent in eighteenth-century culture *precisely because* its "Characters" are admittedly "personated." The genre itself could not be said to have any personal agenda, and it could be held accountable for any failure to meet expectations. At the same time, the surfaces of its "theatrical character[s]" could be viewed as mirrors reflecting virtue, rather than as "rivals" or "superiors" with depth in the marketplace of virtue.

Many writers championed this optimistic view of tragedy, including Aaron Hill, who wrote in the preface to *The Fatal Extravagance* (1720/1721):

In countries, where *Christianity* is received and established, some may, possibly, imagine, there is, now, no longer need of the assistance of *Tragedy*: but experience convinces us, that many frequent the *Stage*, who would harldly [sic] be prevailed upon, to receive counsel from the *Pulpit*. The *Clergy*, therefore, should consider, as auxiliaries and fellow-labourers, those *Poets*, who preach virtue, from . . . the *Theatre*.[8]

Recognizing the increasingly secular orientation of the town, Hill affirms that the stage might reach and teach those who might otherwise disregard church authority. Like Steele, he invests the stage, and tragedy as a generic institution in particular, with the kind of illustrative authority that could transcend the particularities and frailties of human character.

Such claims for tragedy's role as a champion of virtue, patriotism, and national character are all the more striking when we consider that the tragic stage was in a beleaguered state and was perceived to be in need of immediate attention and even resuscitation. As might already be anticipated from the discussion in Chapter 2, many contemporary writers argued that threats of foreign usurpation besieged tragedy on all sides. On one flank, "irrational" entertainments like pantomime and Italian opera were viewed as subversive attacks upon the English stage. On the other flank, French neo-classical rules were attacked for exercising a stranglehold on English genius. John Dennis captures the style of thought associated with the first charge when in the prologue to *Iphigenia* an actor rises to "Warlike Symphony" in the persona of "The Genius of England" and dramatically intones:

Oh is my *Brittain* faln to that degree,
As for effeminate Arts t'abandon me?
I left the enslav'd *Italian* with disdain,
And servile *Gallia*, and dejected *Spain*:

. . . .

But oh, . . .

. . . .

Those Arts now rule that soften'd foreign Braves,
And sunk the Southern Nations into Slaves.
This said the Muse, my *Brittons*, against you:
Oh Supreme *Jove*! And is th'Indictment true?
It is; so wanton are your Stages grown,

. . . .

To see a Bearded more than Female throng
Dissolv'd and dying by an Eunuch's Song.[9]

Here Dennis builds a grid of telling associations between tragedy and gender that we will see played out again and again in the tragedies discussed in the readings that compose this chapter. Placing particular emphasis on the "effeminacy" and "softness" that foreign spectacles supposedly insinuated into the British soul, he expresses the common sentiment that tragedy has strong affinities with and responsibilities to a distinct form of masculinity. In a striking elaboration of generic necessity, Dennis, like so many other writers of the day, identifies femaleness and feminine passions as among the principal causes of tragedy's own recent fall from literary, aesthetic, and cultural preeminence.

On the contiguous front, critics held that English genius was stifled by French neo-classical rule. Echoing sentiments that found expression throughout the century, William Guthrie wrote in 1757, "The dispute between the antients and the moderns, which in itself was idle and immaterial, came over from France and infected our great men . . . [and u]nder the pretext of CORRECTNESS [they] helped to extinguish SPIRIT. England," he continued, "became a party in a French dispute. France by *her* arts avenged *herself* of our arms; our men of wit admitted *her* to be an arbiter."[10] Guthrie's expressions of outrage on behalf of English genius draw an analogy between combat by arts and combat by arms. The French, he suggests, having been defeated by arms on the fields, had found through the arts a more insidious way to infiltrate and enervate English defenses. In this manner, he gives voice to the widespread idea that subjecting the English stage to French rules was tantamount to governing the English state by French law. Law and rule, in his opinion, served merely to cover up defects in genius and to enable the spread of a debilitating form of aesthetic contagion whose country of origin was, not so insignificantly, gendered female.

Envisioning themselves as besieged on all sides, defenders of the English stage thus looked to tragedy as the rational form that could subdue and then drive out those irrational and feminine passions aroused by foreign entertainments. Metadramatic representations of tragedy suggested that if tragedy failed to inspire patriotic virtue, indeed even if it diverged momentarily from that responsibility, the nation itself could be brought to the brink of an invasion by the morally degenerate forces of effeminating foreign spectacles. Similarly, the tyranny of either foreign rules or foreign spectacles was not to be tolerated in any form. Domestic genius, supported alike by critics, writers, and patrons, was to provide the principal means for promoting English liberty on the tragic stage.

It might be a good idea to pause here to consider why tragedy was specifically selected for these tasks. Why, in short, was the imagining of the English nation and its character more focused in tragedy than in any other dramatic genre? One answer might be extrapolated from recent accounts of nationalism and the sociology of cultural meaning. Benedict Anderson argues, for instance, that after the demise of "religious modes of thought" the formidable task of imagining a nation was turned over to historical modes of thought in which the object consisted in the "secular transformation of fatality into continuity, contingency into meaning."[11] Anderson understands this to be the achievement of the "idea of nation" in the eighteenth century, and he designates novels and newspapers as the forms that "provided the technical means for 're-presenting' the *kind* of imagined community that is the nation" (25). Yet his description of the process involved in this imagining might just as well have been a characterization of the course followed by tragic drama, which, more than any other form, has as one of its chief imperatives the epistemological task of assimilating contingency in the form of a singular or "fatal" event or characteristic to the continuous process of human life and thought. Indeed, the particular art of tragic drama inheres in the strategies selected for sustaining the effect of continuous narrative meaning despite the practically exceptional, even aberrant circumstances of its action. By convention, tragedy performs the function of mediation, working to negate the signifying differences between its contingent form and the authoritative meanings it conveys. Hence, if Anderson theorizes correctly that nations come into representation through narratives that erase contradictions, defuse paradoxes, and fill in discursive gaps, then the very conventions of tragedy mark it as a narrative form that corresponds, more than other dramatic genres, to the "technical" needs of nation making.

In contrast to the emphasis on the contingency of character in plays about plays, tragedy thus brackets the episodic and the random as much as possible in order to situate identity within a stable and seamless pattern of social life and social thought. Character in tragic representations was not designed to offer depth so much as it was deployed to present impregnable figures of emulation; play with character was meant to be minimal. In this manner, eighteenth-century dramatists could take advantage of the structural affinities between tragic form and the requisites of narrativizing a nation to reorient the genre into imagining the eighteenth-century English nation as it stumbled toward the colonial empire that it would eventually become. In effect, tragedy provided the means to represent that contingent movement as naturally fated, indeed, as logically inevitable.[12]

This project could not move ahead, however, without experiencing a number of complications and crises, for as James William Johnson has pointed out, "In the eighteenth century, the problem of correlating historical fact with the requirements of dramatic tragedy continued to demand attention."[13] Although Johnson refers here to the particular obstacles faced by the writers of neo-classical tragedies, his commentary holds true as well for those who were trying to move away from classical models to develop modern tales. Across the period, these types of tragedy have in common what Johnson has identified as the "critical assumption that tragedy was dramatized history" (174). Yet questions still remain as to the significance of this "dramatized history." First, what kinds of histories were these tragedies producing? Second, what types of characters were represented as agents in these particular versions not only of the past, but of the present and the future as well? Third, what was the relation of these agents to the ideas of virtue and liberty, and how did their representations transform the very meaning of those terms? Obviously, the declarations for liberty, virtue, and nation that feature so prominently in prologues, epilogues, and prefaces must be viewed with a skeptical eye, as much for their rhetorical as for their literal effect. Yet given that they constitute at least the announced intent of playwrights and critics, it only seems fair to ask what in fact *was represented* in tragedy as both the ideal and pragmatic "essence" of English character and thus as the foundation of certitude for the English nation?

A first step in addressing such large questions is to note that like the epics and the history plays that laid claim to the narrative place of history in earlier eras, tragedy was similarly associated with the expansive vision and nobility of spirit inhering in the idea of the "nation." Addison invoked this very convention when he praised tragedy as, "the Noblest Production of Human Nature."[14] Yet, despite the frequency of such accolades, the source and the significance of tragedy's nobility in the eighteenth century was much debated. Whereas seventeenth-century theorists maintained that tragedy's eminence derived from the great and powerful persons it represented, many early eighteenth-century critics, theorists, and dramatists issued a call for a new kind of tragic hero: the domestic or common man.[15] As Eric Rothstein notes in his account of tragedy during the Restoration, "Universalized or moralized characters of high degree began, very slowly, to be supplanted by more particularized characters conceived psychologically."[16] This was especially the case in the latter part of the period as tragedians like Banks, Lee, and Otway chose to emphasize pathetic rather than heroic passions. Yet the cultivation of a more common and domestic type of hero occurred with increasing variety and vehemence only during the eighteenth century, and, thus the period marks a major departure from the already diminished, but still standard, heroic and aristocratic protagonist of the Restoration stage.[17] Indeed, even in those eighteenth-century tragedies in which the convention of elite heroism was retained, the ethics and sentiments articulated bear greater resemblance to the values associated with the ascendance of the middling classes than to those of an elite culture.[18]

This shift can be seen in the discursive confluence of arguments for domestic heroes with discussions of tragedy's national interests and provides strong evidence that the great and powerful no longer functioned as the most meaningful emblems of national destiny. Instead, the middling classes increasingly shouldered that burden, and with it came the necessity of producing "heroic" narratives that could effectively convey the logic of apportioned, rather than exclusive, nobility. The need to legitimate these new classes as actors on the public stage of the nation accounts, moreover, for the fact that the agenda for tragedy became increasingly domestic in at least two different senses of the term. First, England, a "domestic" rather than foreign place, was taken as the scene for tragedy, and English figures appeared as the actors in, or subjects of, tragedy with greater frequency than in earlier periods. Second, the day-to-day private, or "domestic," circumstances of thought and action exerted a heavier influence upon the concerns of tragic plots.

This is not to say that the hero of title was entirely abandoned or that the hero of merit received universal support. Many tragedians continued to favor aristocratic protagonists, and distinguished critics like Samuel Johnson argued for superior personages as models for tragic heroes as late as the 1750s.[19] In much the same spirit, plays about plays often lamented the displacement of the great hero from the stage and persistently represented that event as a travesty of tragic form.[20] Indeed, many of these metadramas went so far as to dramatize that transgression as both a symptom and a cause of a national tragedy in which Shakespeare, as the apotheosis of English stagecraft, emerges as the hero whose actions, that is, playwrighting, could restore the national conscience.[21]

It would not be fair, however, to dismiss such reactions merely as conservative judgments; these concerns were neither wholly unwarranted nor limited to those who condemned the new protagonists. Indeed, as I have observed above, the middling classes were only just in the process of forming the narratives that would legitimate their new, central place in the culture, and this was a process that was drawn out across the span of the eighteenth century and into the nineteenth. In the meantime, and as part of this legitimation process, tragedians who did attempt to integrate the interests of the middling classes into their work confronted a number of difficulties. First, the new emphasis on the particularities of individual action conflicted with traditional expectations that tragic action results in submission to universal principles. It seemed paradoxical that the expansive properties of tragedy and the expanding ambitions of imagining a nation were to be realized through the diminished and more parochial figure of the common man. Tragedians thus faced the challenge of either resolving that paradox or at least providing a sophisticated rationalization in their plays for both the appearance of that figure and the imposition of its values on more elite characters.

Second, the "interests" of the middling classes in early eighteenth-century England had not yet been coherently formulated or clearly established. While there may have been a growing faith in the shift from the great public man to the common private individual as the foundation for public good, there was also uncertainty and ambivalence about the "character" of this rising class. Compared with the sober assets of the landed aristocracy, the market-driven fortunes of the merchant and trading classes appeared particularly unreliable. J. G. A. Pocock notes, for instance, that as the economy came to be driven increasingly by mercantile interests and public credit, old visions of futurity lost their efficacy. Instead this new system "oblig[ed] men to credit one another with [the] capacity to expand and grow and become what they were not."[22] This crediting system among men with a basic currency unit of "becoming" receives a similar reading in Jürgen Habermas's work when he asserts that while the aristocracy embodied authority, the bourgeois were constrained either to attempt to fill the form of authority with substance or, at the very least, to produce representations of the embodiment of authority.[23] With the parameters of the middling classes not yet determined and the focus of their energies unclear, their correlatives in tragic representation—the character of the new tragic hero and the substance of that hero's action—could hardly avoid lapses in coherence.[24]

This uncertainty with respect to the status of the middling classes accounts, in part then, for the particularly vehement expressions of doubt with respect to the figure of the common man as tragic hero. It explains, moreover, the sense of crisis associated with tragic drama as a cultural form in which the future of the nation was to be envisioned. Insofar as eighteenth-century tragedians increasingly placed the fate of the nation in the hands of a class that had yet to define either its character or its authority, tragedy could only produce provisional narratives and suggestive paradigms of action. The stage was thus cited for confirming fears of an identity crisis in the nation, and the visions of tragedies thus appear uneven and ambivalent. Even as genre and nation were imagined as reciprocally constitutive, so too did they appear to be reciprocally, and even dialectically, "disoriented."

This discussion of the cultural imperatives that were directed toward eighteenth-century tragedy provides only a theoretical sketch of the genre. In the readings below, I will turn to how the concerns expressed in these imperatives manifest themselves in practice. My primary texts will be Joseph Addison's *Cato* (1712/1713) and George Lillo's *The London Merchant* (1730/1731) as well as two of Nicholas Rowe's she-tragedies, *The Fair Penitent* (1702/1703) and *The Tragedy of Jane Shore* (1713/1714). I will trace the status of those primary tragic values such as patriotism, virtue, friendship, love, and honor as they converge, diverge, and orbit around one another in each text. More specifically, I will explore both their relationship to the idea of tragedy as a vehicle of moral agency and their contribution to our understanding of tragic characters not only as the moral agents in these dramas but also more generally as the exemplars of national identity in the historical and cultural context of eighteenth-century England. In the process, I will examine the efforts of both the plays and critics of the plays to fix or to de-emphasize the instabilities of character. I will focus in particular on how these efforts took shape as a prejudice against the feminine in tragedy. In doing so, I will demonstrate how gender functioned as a primary signifying category of this genre and how, in this capacity, it mediated the representation of new class imperatives and ideologies for the English nation.

Women, Love, and Addison's Cato?

On the occasion of the first performances of Joseph Addison's *Cato*, Alexander Pope wrote in a now famous letter to John Caryll, "The numerous and violent claps of the Whig party on the one side of the theatre, were echoed back by the Tories on the other" as each side tried to lay claim to the patriotic virtue of liberty on display in the drama.[25] Ever since, the political affinities of Addison's *Cato* have been the subject of popular as well as critical debate, so much so that John Loftis contended in his influential study of the politics of Augustan drama that the "political meaning of *Cato* was and is still an enigma."[26] Yet while so much critical energy has been directed toward solving this "enigma," one that places *Cato* squarely at the center of national political discourse, little or no attention has been paid to the equally, if not more, intriguing controversy that immediately erupted over the love scenes that constitute almost half of Addison's tragedy. This critical omission seems strange, especially when we consider that these love plots provoked some of the most volatile exchanges and virulent attacks on the play in the half-century of critique following its first appearance at Drury Lane.[27] Some readers of *Cato* have offered rationalizations for the love scenes in the larger context of the play's heroic themes.[28] Yet no critic to date has considered why so many of Addison's contemporaries would direct so much energy so persistently not only toward censuring and suppressing the love scenes, but also toward reimagining the very contours of his play. Why, in short, did the love scenes between Portius, Marcus, and Lucia, on the one hand, and between Juba and Marcia, on the other, provoke such a hostile response?

In the section below, I approach the attacks on the love scenes not only as specific discussions of Addison's *Cato*, but as interpretable commentaries that can illuminate the more general question of what kinds of cultural work tragedies were expected to perform in early eighteenth-century England. Addison's *Cato* provides us with an unusually rich opportunity to explore these larger generic concerns because the play gave rise not only to this long and controversial reception history, but also, in 1764, to a wholesale revision of the drama titled *Cato. A Tragedy. By Mr. Addison. Without the Love Scenes.* By analyzing these documents for their characteristic biases, I demonstrate that the resistance to the love scenes in Addison's tragedy was symptomatic of a broader politics of gender and genre that sought to position male characters as the exclusive and impregnable agents of tragedy and its ideological projects.

We can begin with the paradox peculiar to tragedy that I discussed in the previous section. For *Cato*, as well as for neo-classical tragedies more generally, the effects of tragedy's propensity to illustrate the dissolution of heroic values were particularly acute. Addison deliberately drew a parallel in *Cato* between England and the Rome he endeavored to represent. Yet while England could be projected into the glories of an idealized ancient Rome, the complicated and less than ideal politics of Rome's rise to, and more significantly its fall from, power could not be entirely effaced from that representation. As James W. Johnson has noted, Cato's death "marked the end of Republican Rome and the birth of the new imperialistic stage of Roman history." Within the context of an historical consciousness, "Cato served for an example and warning to the individual. . . . In his virtue, Cato perished. From its glory, Rome fell."[29] In other words, if Rome were taken as the analog through which to project the future glory of England not only as a nation but also as a burgeoning empire, the burden of history inexorably required an awareness of that emerging empire's eventual decline. Even more significantly, the very insistence that Cato embodied the last remnants of what could only be termed exceptional virtue (manifested in his inexhaustible commitment to liberty) meant that his death marked not only the irrecoverable loss of Cato in particular, but also, in a more general sense, the loss of the immanence of the qualities he so embodied.

This doubled consciousness of the rise and fall of empires exercised a powerful influence over the neo-classical mind, conscious and unconscious, and, in effect, produced an ironical context for the valorization of even the most virtuous of Rome's republican citizens. Moreover, by projecting Rome, however qualified, as the ideal state whose golden achievements and virtues could never be matched, neo-classicists produced a kind of post-Roman version of the post-lapsarian mythos. In this context, England would always and inevitably be found wanting in its attempts to emulate the ideal figure because the double burden of consciousness signified not only an awareness of an unavoidable decline, following the pattern set by its archetype, but also an inescapable sense of being always already fallen. England could only appear as a diminished imitator of Rome's magnificence, and Cato, the larger-than-life hero of the now apotheosized Rome, could only be regarded as an abstract figure removed from the prospects of eighteenth-century everyday life, a figure to admire rather than to emulate.

Consequently, while neo-classical tragedians endeavored to provide the English audience with exemplary models of patriotic virtue from antiquity, they could only do so with a strained consciousness of that model's inevitable demise. Indeed, a number of twentieth-century interpretations have suggested that Addison recognized these complications and that, for him, the love scenes and the anticipated marriages in *Cato* represented the best possible expectation that could be held in an already fallen world.[30] That is, Addison did not preclude Cato' s status in the play as *exempla virtutis* so much as he conceded that the kind of heroism embodied by Cato no longer obtained either as a realistic expectation or as a desirable model in the context of eighteenth-century culture. The almost tragi-comic conclusion of Addison's *Cato* thus signals a turn away from the larger-than-life aspirations and dreams of empire toward the domestic and private as the grounds for developing the virtue and strength of the nation.

Yet where Addison may have been willing to make such concessions in his tragic representation, it is clear that his contemporaries were not only unwilling to make the same kinds of adjustments but viewed such accommodations as a form of compromise that could taint the ideal vision of tragedy. In attacks that echoed already powerful themes in discourses of national interests, eighteenth-century critics denounced the love scenes, transforming them into scapegoats for the tragedy's failed vision. The commentaries on Addison's *Cato* can thus be read both for the ways they reinforce our sense of tragedy as the genre responsible for articulating national interests in the eighteenth century and for the ways they attempt to fix the type of character upon which those interests could depend. As I will demonstrate below, those elements that were identified as threats to the integrity of that ideal tragic character, and thus to the prolonged posterity of the nation, were almost uniformly construed as agents of effeminating passions. More often than not, moreover, the force of this animosity was extended to women either as characters or as agents in tragedy.

By almost all accounts, the love scenes constituted an unwonted complication in what could have been a more straightforward tragedy of the death of Cato. Even Addison's defenders attempted to focus attention exclusively on Cato or, if a broader view were called for, to locate the tragedy in relation to its generic responsibilities both as a narrative of virtue and liberty and as proof of English superiority.[31] Indeed, the favored alternative to an all-out attack on Addison has been simply to dismiss the scenes as unfortunate, but nevertheless irrelevant to the meaning of *Cato*.[32] This tactic as well as its ties to a gendered discourse of national interest can be found in what might be termed the first public response to Addison's *Cato*, Pope's original prologue for the tragedy's Drury Lane premiere.

Pope's prologue opens with a conventional declaration of the tragedy's patriotic intentions as well as with a first attempt to distinguish the play's heroism from feminine or "weak" passions:

Our author shuns by vulgar springs to move
The hero's glory, or the virgin's love;
In pitying love we but our weakness show,
And wild ambition well deserves its woe.
Here tears shall flow from a more gen'rous cause,

Such tears as patriots shed for dying laws:
He bids your breasts with ancient ardour rise,
And calls forth Roman Drops from British eyes.[33]

Pope proclaims *Cato* a new kind of play, one in which the conflict between love and honor so typical of Restoration heroic tragedy is dismissed in favor of "a more gen'rous cause." As the prologue proceeds, however, it becomes clear that only the second part of this formula—sexual, erotic, or passionate love—seems to require eradication for tragedy to fulfill its patriotic mandate.[34] Indeed, in the figure of Cato, the exempla virtutis of Addison's tragedy, we are instructed to see the figure of the great public man, unencumbered by private concerns such as love and thus unshackled, free to think only of the honor and liberty of his country. In other words, Cato's status as an ideal tragic hero depends on the extent to which he can be dissociated from the "weakness" of "pitying love."

Having grounded the patriotic intentions of the play in its rejection of "pitying love," Pope articulates the second cultural imperative of tragedy by offering *Cato* as a tragedy dedicated to restoring taste and vigor to the British stage. In particular, he presents *Cato* as a challenge to the British audience to rouse themselves out of a dangerous dullness induced by exposure to too many foreign entertainments:

Britons, attend; be worth like this approved,
And show you have the virtue to be moved.
With honest scorn the first famed Cato viewed
Rome learning arts from Greece, whom she subdued;
Our scene precariously subsists too long
On French translation, and Italian song.
Dare to have sense yourselves; assert the stage,
Be justly warmed with your own native rage.
Such plays alone should please a British ear,
As Cato's self had not disdained to hear. (Prologue)

Conjuring the specter of the inevitable fall of empires, Pope implies that the Greek empire crumbled precisely because it was saturated by "arts" and that Cato, upon seeing Rome take up these arts, could only view them scornfully with the knowledge that they would also be the eventual cause of Rome's fall. He then explicitly extends this sentiment as a warning to the English nation, characterizing it as a nation on the brink of its own folly in its absorption by those French and Italian arts that were so powerfully and ubiquitously associated in eighteenth-century English discourse with an effeminating softness.[35] Pope's invocation of "native rage" as an ideal tragic effect is thus mingled with and set against the alternative of the "natives" going soft, and we find once again that Cato's status as a tragic hero depends on Pope's ability to dissociate him from potential sources of effeminacy.[36]

In short, this formulation of the tragedy's status is predicated not so much upon the success of the masculine protagonist as upon the extent to which it insists that the representation successfully avoids and precludes the introduction of "soft" elements. It is no coincidence then that Pope's argument for *Cato* as an exemplary tragedy omits any reference to the love scenes. For only by doing so can he represent *Cato* as a remedy to the persistent problem of the effeminizing influences that precipitate falls from eminence both on the stage and in the political life of the nation. Pope's prologue thus draws together and draws upon the most persistent undercurrents in tragedy and tragic theory in the eighteenth century. On the one hand, it illustrates how the representations of tragedy were understood to act both as registers indicating the nation's current strength and as agents for maintaining and furthering that nation's claims to posterity. On the other hand, it intimates an aversion to all things feminine by associating both the "weakness" incited by love and the effeminating qualities of foreign entertainments with the kind of enflamed passions that distract from, and thus threaten, tragedy's designed purpose: the inspiration of "native rage" and the inculcation of patriotic virtue.

If the tactic of Addison's defenders was merely to gloss over the presence of the love scenes, that of his antagonists was to represent the love scenes and, in particular, the female characters who participated in those scenes, as the very source of the tragedy's aesthetic and ideological failures. Indeed, when we begin to take a critical look at the works devoted to admonishing Addison for what Francis Gentleman termed strange "triflings" with the plot, a pattern quickly emerges that makes it all too clear that the so-called problem arises not so much from the love scenes per se as from the fact that those love scenes include women.[37]

Dennis inaugurated this critical tradition with a vicious polemic against the intrusion of "amorous passions" in the tragedy, and his *Remarks upon Cato* (1713) provides us with one of the most telling examples of this systemic attitude.[38] In an examination of the scene in which Lucia and Portius grapple with their mutual love and the menacing effect its discovery might have on the high-spirited Marcus, who is also in love with Lucia, Dennis inveighs:

And now I desire to ask the Reader, whether *Lucia's* Swooning upon *Portius's* resolving to comply with her Desire, does not shew more of an Histerical fit, than of the magnanimous Spirit of a *Roman* Lady.

Finding Portius's response to Lucia's "Swooning" equally absurd, he continues:

This is the first time that ever I knew that a Fit of the Mother was catching. . . . Now the common Accidents of Life, which we have seen him meet *unruffled and serene*, are, the Destruction of his Country, the Ruin of Liberty, and the probable Approach of his Father's Death. And the *Storm of Ills that beats down all his Strength* is this Histerical Fancy of *Lucia*, that *Marcus* will be forc'd, by the resistless Power of her Beauty, to lay dead-doing Hands upon himself. (35–36)

Dennis's attribution of "histeria" to Lucia obviously relies upon a long and controversial history of attacks on women that cast the female as well as the feminine as the breeding grounds for irrationality. Indeed, his stroke is practically overdetermined by this discourse as he deploys it to critique a play in which the tragic hero, Cato, stands precisely for the Stoic ideal of reason, the subordination of all emotions and desires to the rational will. Reduced thus to a misogynist caricature of the "essentially" female, Lucia's presence comes to stand in Dennis's gender-ridden critique for values that are anathema to what he positions as masculine ideals.

Yet Dennis not only equates Lucia with the intrusion of "feminine" passions unfit for tragedy, he also discovers in her presence a malignant contaminant. Indeed what distinguishes Dennis's attack is the extent to which he seems to believe that women incite "amorous passions" in men. Like a form of contagion, they distract and then deform, or effeminate, the natural, masculine passions of tragedy and direct those energies instead into a "Fit of the Mother." For Dennis, this "tragic" displacement of a purely masculine discourse facilitates the very deformation of the genre, transforming it from an exceptional figure of pathos into a mundane form of bathos. As a matter of course, the ideals that tragedy is given to represent—virtue, honor, and patriotism—are irreducibly tainted.

Dennis's argument suggests that if tragic representations could be distilled, with the impurities of the effeminating presence of women removed, then tragic ideals could be attained not just on the stage but in real life as well. This appears to be the strange project behind the 1764 revision of Addison's tragedy titled *Cato. A Tragedy. By Mr. Addison. Without the Love Scenes*, for it takes the critical trajectory of Dennis's argument to its obvious conclusion by conspicuously eliminating all of the female roles from the tragedy. Where Addison may be said to have responded pragmatically to the conditions of a world already fallen by turning to the domestic and private spheres, *Cato Without the Love Scenes* seems to cling to the view of the great in public life as absolute models of conduct and seeks to eliminate any elements in the representation that might distract from that focus.[39] In an extended reading, I will illustrate how this alternative version of *Cato* deliberately focuses its energies on bonds between men, especially those of brotherhood. I will demonstrate further how reflecting on *Cato* in this way promotes the view that if women and effeminating elements could be completely purged from the public sphere of tragedy, a standard of virtue and honor could be attained among men that not only would ensure the stability and prosperity of the nation, but, more importantly, would endlessly defer what otherwise appeared as an inevitable fall from glory.

Ironically, the first and most salient point to make about *Cato Without the Love Scenes* is that, despite what the play's title page might have us believe, the love scenes do not in fact altogether disappear from the tragedy. Indeed, one of the strangest aspects of this revision of *Cato* is that almost all the language of the love scenes remains in the play.[40] The author meticulously insisted on preserving as much of Addison's original text as possible and did so by moving whole portions of dialogue from one place in the text to another to produce what might be termed a radical cut-and-paste version of *Cato*. With the female roles completely cut from the revision, bits and pieces of the love scenes appear instead at alternative points in the play as verbal exchanges between male characters. The context of these utterances is thus materially transformed, especially insofar as the characters to which they are attributed are changed. Yet the erotically charged energies that one might associate with the love scenes remain, only to be channeled into exchanges between men as expressions of admiration and love either for each other or for Cato.

This "new and improved" *Cato* concerns itself first and foremost, then, with the generation of impassioned bonds between men that are based solely on, and triangulated by, an emotionally charged admiration and affection for Cato. As opposed to the standard model of homosocial relations in which emotionally charged energies and desires for relations between men are channeled through the bodies of women, *Cato Without the Love Scenes* eliminates that female factor as a mediating point and substitutes for it not only the body but also the soul of Cato.[41] This alternative affective structure both secures and intensifies Cato's absolute command of the tragedy. No emotional energy is expended, no action takes place, no expression is uttered without reference to Cato. His is meant to be both the controlling and infallible vision of the play.

The most obvious effect of this rerouting of emotional energies in *Cato Without the Love Scenes* is the elimination of one of the most troubling ironies with respect to Cato's "vision." When Marcus's death is announced by his brother Portius in Act IV of Addison's *Cato*, Cato first confirms that Marcus died fighting "obstinately brave" and then, with great economy of words, pronounces, "I'm satisfied." Cato's composure in this moment of grief and subsequently in his speech over his son's corpse has been interpreted by many as one of the singularly emblematic moments of the tragedy. It has been taken as the very sign of Cato's absolute conviction that there are no higher principles than those of virtuous patriotism and service to country.[42] Not insignificantly, such critical judgments depend almost entirely on Cato's own interpretation of his son's death. When Cato pronounces, "What pity is it, / That we can die but once to serve our country," we are meant to take the speech at face value as a perfect example of Cato's unremitting ability to put public concerns before private ones. By his own avowal, we are not to mourn the loss of his son so much as we should lament the destruction of virtue and liberty in Rome. We are meant to cry along with Cato: "Oh, liberty! Oh, virtue! Oh, my country!" (IV.i, pp. 43–44).

Yet, in a play where motive, cause, and principle account for and control so much of the meaning, Cato's complete assurance that Marcus died serving no other purposes than those of "Rome," "liberty," and "virtue" appears especially ironic. The scene may very well confirm Cato's "natural virtue," but it also reveals the extent to which that assurance or conceit in the power and clarity of his vision produces inadequacies and blind spots. In point of fact, Marcus's supposed bravery is undercut throughout the text by his characterization as an impassioned, intemperate, and, finally, rejected lover of Lucia. Indeed, the last words he utters in the play are: "Oh, for some glorious cause to fall in battle! / Lucia, thou hast undone me: thy disdain / Has broke my heart; 'tis death must give me ease" (III.i, p. 34). Here the cause of Rome is clearly secondary to, a by-product of, this intemperate despondency; it is the "glorious cause" for which to "fall" only insofar as his heart "has broke." In effect, then, there is an ironical disjunction in Addison's *Cato* between our knowledge of Marcus's motives and the motives Cato attributes to him in death, a disjunction that severely undermines Cato's self-assured "satisfaction."

That Marcus's honor could in fact be perceived as "compromised" by love is evidenced by the extent to which *Cato Without the Love Scenes* revises his character and these scenes. In fact, it works almost line by line to eliminate the sense of irony that threatens the authority of Cato's Stoic interpretation of his son's death. In Addison's original text, Marcus appears as a major speaker in just two scenes, the first scene of both Acts I and III. In the opening scene, he interrupts his brother Portius's solemn ruminations on the "great, the important day, big with the fate / Of Cato and of Rome" to confess the "[p]assion unpitied, and successless love" that "plant[s] daggers in my heart." He balks at Portius's exhortation to "quell the tyrant Love," for though he avows the quickness of his courage, he also insists that "Love is not to be reasoned down, or lost / In high ambition" (I.i, pp. 7–8). Marcus continues to vacillate between "high ambition" and "love" and finally works himself into such a frenzy that he feels compelled to leave the scene for fear that Sempronius will see the shameful "softness hanging on me" (I.i, p. 9). Love for a woman has "softened" Marcus in Addison's *Cato*, and it distracts him here, as well as in Act III, from what ought to be his duty. As the text tells us, it "melts" all manly strength and reason; his disappointment in love "dooms" him, by his own admission, to death (I.i, p. 8; III.i, p. 34).

Cato Without the Love Scenes rewrites these scenes to minimize Marcus's exposure. Indeed, Marcus appears as a major speaker only once in this revision (in the first scene of the first act), and in this scene all allusions to despairing love are replaced by references to faltering courage. For instance, Marcus's tormented outburst over "Passion unpitied, and successless love" is replaced with his testimony to "an unlook'd-for storm of ills" that "beats down all my strength," lines plundered ironically from the tortuous love scene in the third act of the original in which Lucia vows to part with Portius rather than risk the possibility of causing the unstable Marcus to commit suicide (I.i, p. 7).[43] In Cato Without the Love Scenes, all traces of original reference are purged from these lines. Consequently, while they convey all of the intensity of fraught passions, of a conscience in conflict with itself, they nevertheless produce a different set of meanings. Although the source of Marcus's "ills" is never clearly defined, insofar as it succeeds his statement that "our father's fortune / Would almost tempt us to renounce his precepts," the most obvious implication is that Marcus suffers from wavering principles (I.i, p. 7). This revision thus allows for a narrative in which it would appear that Marcus finally overcomes these immoderate passions to embrace true principle and courage. We are to believe that Marcus's death offers proof of his virtue, proof, that is, of his triumph over doubt and his harkening to his brother's admonition to "call up thy father in thy soul: / To quell thy fears"—the term "fear" substituted here for "tyrant love" from the original text—and that with clear conscience he thus "for honour plunge[s] . . . into a war" (I.i, p. 9). Marcus is no longer made "soft" by an effeminating love for a woman, but rather by an understandable fear and sense of awe for Caesar, a man of compelling distinction. The son shines out as an effect of the greatness of his father's soul in its capacity to master even the charismatic attractions of Caesar's powerful personality. The glorious clamor of Cato Without the Love Scenes thus drowns out the ironical undertones that dog Cato's speech over his son's body, and the emotional energies now circulate narrowly and exclusively through male channels.

Through the complete excision of Marcus's other main scene in Addison's Cato and the dispersal of many of that scene's most passionate lines to other sections of the play, Cato Without the Love Scenes also manages to gloss over the disturbing theme of concealment between brothers that haunted the original. For by removing the women from the play as well as all references to Marcus's "successless love," the revision eliminates any need for Portius to conceal the truth that not only is he his own brother's rival, but that Lucia prefers him to Marcus. The brotherly bond between Marcus and Portius is thus purified by identifying and eliminating the sources of that bond's corruption, that is, by excising not just love but also the conventional objects of that love: women.

Yet the rehabilitation of Marcus's character also raises new difficulties for the central status of unadulterated brotherhood in *Cato Without the Love Scenes* because it requires his marginalization as a figure in the text. Without further intervention, the ethos of brotherhood, a paradigmatic emblem of all relations among men and the guarantee of a father's continuing legacy, would have been reduced similarly to a mere sideline in the revised text.[44] In order to prevent this consequence, *Cato Without the Love Scenes* amplifies the already brotherly bond between Portius and Juba and places it closer to the center of the play. Ironically, this shift in emphasis is effected by reinterpolating many of the lines from exchanges between Marcus and Portius and between Portius and Lucia from Addison's *Cato*, III.i into exchanges between Portius and Juba. These bits and pieces of dialogue are fleshed out, moreover, both with lines that had formerly composed the more emotional exchanges between Lucia and Marcia concerning their respective loves and with portions from Juba and Marcia's ecstatic love-revelation scene. They lend to what were otherwise passionless scenes an emotional intensity that threatens to overwhelm the figure of Cato through whom these passionate energies and desires are triangulated.

The first of these significant revisions is the transformation of Juba and Marcia's love-revelation scene into a love-revelation scene between Juba and Portius. In Addison's narrative, Marcia's confession of her love for Juba is incidentally triggered when, after hearing the clash of swords, she and Lucia come upon a dead body, dressed in Numidian garb, which she mistakes for Juba. The corpse is actually that of Sempronius, who, while attempting to kidnap Marcia so that he might ravish her, had been discovered and slain by Juba. Shocked by the sight and unaware that she is being overheard by the living Juba, Marcia launches into a wild lament in which she frantically expresses the grief of her "virgin's heart," offers her regret that he "never knew how much I loved him," and ultimately confesses: "Marcia's whole soul was full of love and Juba!" (IV.i, pp. 39–40). Anguished, but gratified by what he has just heard, Juba reveals himself, and the scene continues at an even higher pitch as Juba and Marcia declare their "mutual warmth" and the "eagerness of [a] love" that "burns in its full lustre." Overflowing with happiness, Juba declares his a "life worth preserving," and he brings the scene to a close with an oddly unheroic heroic couplet: "Juba will never at his fate repine: / Let Caesar have the world, if Marcia's mine" (IV.i, pp. 40–41). Clearly, Juba's placement of love over honor and patriotic duty presents much work for the "love" censor's hand.

To begin, then, *Cato Without the Love Scenes* alters the premise that brings Sempronius to his death (see Figure 6a–c). Instead of tracking Marcia like a "deer" in "her covert" (*Cato*, IV.i, p. 38), Sempronius is discovered while attempting to kidnap Cato and is killed by Juba.⁴⁵ This time, moreover, Portius, rather than Lucia and Marcia, enters worrying over the clash of swords he has just heard and mistakes the Numidian-garbed Sempronius for Juba. Thus jettisoning Lucia's intimations that the clash of swords was that of Portius and Marcus battling over her, *Cato Without the Love Scenes* (IV.iii) cuts Marcia's allusions to her "warmed . . . virgin's heart" and substitutes a description of the crumpled body, "Stabb'd at his heart, and all besmear'd with blood" (IV.iii, p. 117).⁴⁶

Portius then proceeds with his protestations, substituting "virtue" for "love" in his catalogue of Juba's admirable qualities and concluding with the familiar outburst: "Why do I think on what he was! he's dead! / He's dead, and never knew how much I lov'd him." This is the cry of anguish that, without further ado, provokes Juba to reveal himself and clasp now with Portius:

JUBA: See, Porcius, see,
The happy Juba lives! he lives to catch
Thy dear embrace, and to return it too.
PORCIUS: With pleasure and amaze, I stand transported!
. . . .
My joy! my best friend! all is bliss round me.
This, this is life, indeed! life worth preserving.
JUBA: How shall I speak the transport of my soul!
I'm lost in extasy! O my dear Porcius!
PORCIUS: Believe me, prince, before I thought thee dead,
I did not know myself, how much I lov'd thee.
JUBA: O fortunate mistake! O happy Juba!
Fortune thou now hast made me amends for all
Thy past unkindness; I absolve my stars. (*Without Love*, IV.iii, pp. 119–21)

The scene ends with a few auspicious lines, borrowed again from the original III.i, though with the substitution of a reference to Marcus's life hanging in the balance rather than Cato's.

This alteration follows, of course, from the crucial fact that in *Cato Without the Love Scenes* Juba has just saved Cato's life by discovering, challenging, and killing the duplicitous Sempronius. Indeed, the revisions of this scene have an at least doubled effect upon Juba's character and his status in the representation. First, he risks his life for Cato and in so doing becomes worthy of a reward of kinship. Second, if there were any doubts about his "worthiness" prior to this event, and here Juba's apostrophe to fortune indicates that perhaps there were, Portius seals the bond both by reiterating his love and by pronouncing Juba's a "life worth preserving," a significant designation that had been one of self-attribution in the original. The displacement of those lines in the revision from Juba to Portius authorizes Juba's character with an external sanction of greater objective validity.

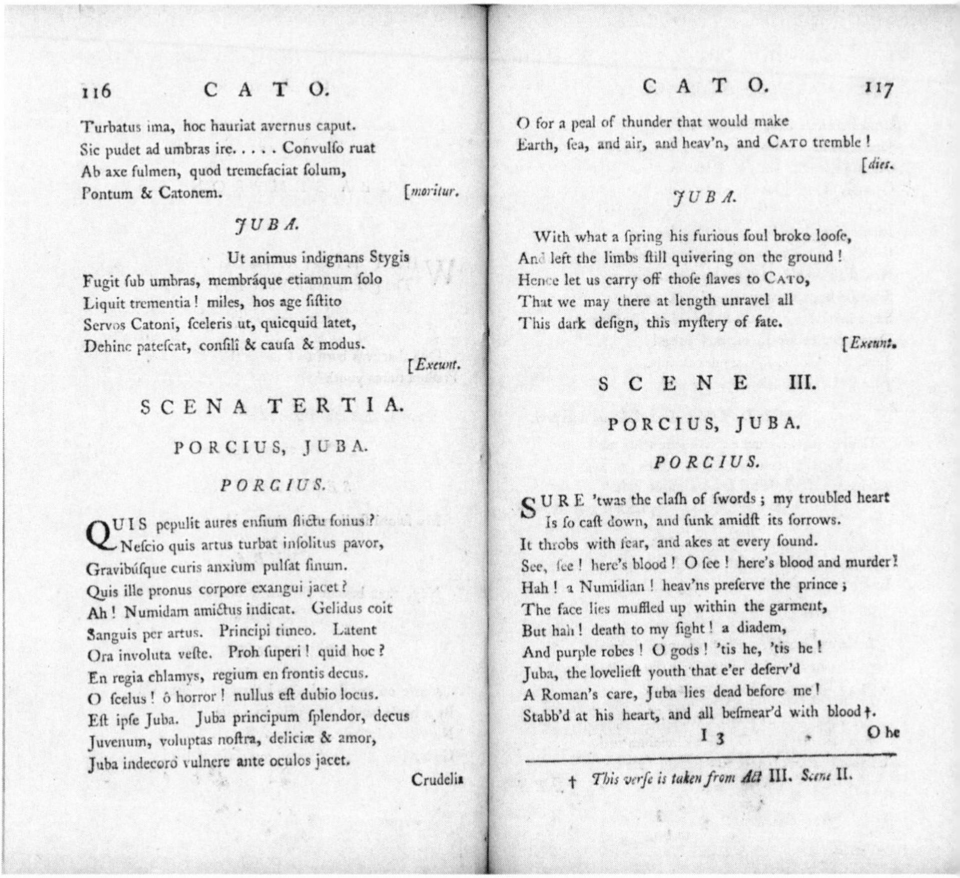

Turbatus ima, hoc hauriat avernus caput.
Sic pudet ad umbras ire. . . . . Convulfo ruat
Ab axe fulmen, quod tremefaciat folum,
Pontum & Catonem.   [*moritur.*

J U B A.

Ut animus indignans Stygis
Fugit fub umbras, membráque etiamnum folo
Liquit trementia ! miles, hos age fiftito
Servos Catoni, fceleris ut, quicquid latet,
Dehinc patefcat, confili & caufa & modus.
                                            [*Exeunt.*

SCENA TERTIA.

PORCIUS, JUBA.

P O R C I U S.

QUIS pepulit aures enfium flictu fonus ?
Nefcio quis artus turbat infolitus pavor,
Gravibúfque curis anxium pulfat finum.
Quis ille pronus corpore exangui jacet ?
Ah ! Numidam amictus indicat. Gelidus coit
Sanguis per artus. Principi timeo. Latent
Ora involuta vefte. Proh fuperi ! quid hoc ?
En regia chlamys, regium en frontis decus.
O fcelus ! ô horror ! nullus eft dubio locus.
Eft ipfe Juba. Juba principum fplendor, decus
Juvenum, voluptas noftra, deliciæ & amor,
Juba indecorö vulnere ante oculos jacet.
                                            Crudelis

O for a peal of thunder that would make
Earth, fea, and air, and heav'n, and CATO tremble !
                                            [*dies.*

J U B A.

With what a fpring his furious foul broke loofe,
And left the limbs ftill quivering on the ground !
Hence let us carry off thofe flaves to CATO,
That we may there at length unravel all
This dark defign, this myftery of fate.
                                            [*Exeunt.*

SCENE III.

PORCIUS, JUBA.

P O R C I U S.

SURE 'twas the clafh of fwords ; my troubled heart
Is fo caft down, and funk amidft its forrows.
It throbs with fear, and akes at every found.
See, fee ! here's blood ! O fee ! here's blood and murder!
Hah ! a Numidian ! heav'ns preferve the prince ;
The face lies muffled up within the garment,
But hah ! death to my fight ! a diadem,
And purple robes ! O gods ! 'tis he, 'tis he !
Juba, the lovelieft youth that e'er deferv'd
A Roman's care, Juba lies dead before me !
Stabb'd at his heart, and all befmear'd with blood †.
            I 3   O he

† *This verfe is taken from Act* III. *Scene* II.

Figure 6a–c. *Cato. A Tragedy. By Mr. Addison. Without the Love Scenes.* 1764. Act IV, scene iii. By permission of the British Library. Shelfmark 1344.i.58.

In fact, each line from the original is carefully vetted to modify or simply to eliminate any phrase, clause, or statement that might be understood as unflattering to Juba's honor and virtue. The unqualified deletion of Juba's concluding exaltation: "Let Caesar have the world, if Marcia's mine" constitutes only the most obvious example of this method. Juba's surging self-absorption had not only to be curbed but to be wholly effaced because the sentiments he expresses in this frenzy fall well below all strictures of honorable conduct. In principle, they represent a betrayal of Cato and of his Stoic ethos of country before self. Virtue, as an earlier substitution reveals, must take priority over love, even if, paradoxically, virtue itself is expressed as love for other men and, as I will demonstrate in my final example, especially as love for Cato.

Although *Cato Without the Love Scenes* executes the substitution of Portius

Crudelia nimis fata, crudeles deos !
Jacet cruore membra concreto rigens,
Cujus ubi vultus enituit, ibat dies
Gratior, & orbis luce fplendebat nová.
Heu vana fpes mortalium ! ut Stygius color
Infecit artus ! capitis ambrofii decor
Cecidit, nigranti vividum oculorum jubar
Nox texit umbrá : frigore æterno algida
Silet illa lingua, cujus eloquium CATO
Sæpe ipfe ftupuit. . . . . Sed quid ego fruftra pio
Dolore fluxas repeto virtutes Jubæ ?
Juba Pyladeá me fide amplexus fuit,
Juba Pyladeá me fide amplexus perit.

      J U B A.   [*derepentè in theatrum erumpens.*

Define queri : coram ecce quem defles adeft.
Et incolumis & vivus en adeft. Juba
Accipere amicum lætus amplexum & dare.
               [*Inter fe complectuntur.*

      P O R C I U S.

Superi ! quid hoc eft ? Vivis ? An fallax fubit
Imago ? Si vivit Juba, quis ibi jacet ?

      J U B A.

Scelerum magifter, regio affumpto Jubam
Mentitus habitu, dum impia oppreffo parat
Vincula Catoni, audaciæ pœnas luit.

      P O R C I U S.

Benè eft, revixi. O dulce dimidium mei,
Ut voce, ut ore, ut me tuo afpectu beas !

                  J U B A.

O he was all made up of charms and virtue !
Whatever maid cou'd wifh, or man admire :
Delight of ev'ry eye ! when he appear'd,
A fecret pleafure gladned all that faw him ;
But when he talk'd, the proudeft Roman blufh'd
To hear his virtues, and old age grew wife.
Why do I think on what he was ! he's dead !
He's dead, and never knew how much I lov'd him.

      J U B A.
                 [*rufhing haftily in.*

  See, Porcius, fee,
The happy Juba lives ! he lives to catch
Thy dear embrace, and to return it too.

      P O R C I U S.

  With pleafure and amaze, I ftand tranfported !
Sure 'tis a dream ! dead and alive at once !
If thou art Juba, who lies there ?

      J U B A.

             A wretch,
Difguis'd like Juba on a curs'd defign.

      P O R C I U S.

  My joy ! my beft friend ! all is blifs round me.
This, this is life, indeed ! life worth preferving.

         I 4   *J U B A.*

for Marcia with great skill, this alternative revelation scene also raises a number of perplexing issues. The fact that Juba and Portius's protestations appear to be unmotivated by any prior event in the text presents only the most prominent difficulty produced by this modification. The text has to work hard in the final act to iron out all of the wrinkles it creates through the process of revision, and it does so by redirecting, and then subsuming, all emotional energies under the figure of Cato. While love for Cato may have constituted only the peripheral motive in this earlier scene between Juba and Portius, in the fifth act it forms the central fact anchoring the production of meaning. In particular, Cato comes to mediate and cement the brotherly relationship established between Juba and Portius, even as Juba comes to play a predominant role in an act in which he had formerly uttered no more than eight lines. By cutting and splicing lines from

J U B A.

Dilecte Porci, ut tua mihi placet fides !
Vix credidissem sacrum adeò tecum mihi
Interfuisse vinclum amicitiæ, nisi
Luctûs fuissem testis oculatus tui.

P O R C I U S.

Neque ipse nôram, quàm penitus animo, Juba,
Meo insideres, antequam afflixit tuæ
Me mortis error.

J U B A.

Error is felix fuit.
Fortuna ludum ludere levem pertinax
Jam vetera versâ damna compensat vice.

P O R C I U S.

Nos hinc ad arma buccinæ clangor vocat.
                        [Tuba canit.
Nimis est morarum : fortè jam Marco imminet
Inimicus ensis. Roma, libertas, salus
Nos vocat ad arma. O sacra libertas, manu
Hâc te tueri liceat ; adverso æthere
Sin ista voveo, fortiter in armis mori.   *[Exeunt.*

S C E N A   Q U A R T A.

L U C I U S, C A T O.

L U C I U S.

ATTONITUS hæreo. Quid ?....Hoc Sempronius ?
    Hoc acer ille patriæ assertor suæ ?
Huc omnis ille in Cæsarem effluxit furor ?
                      C A T O.

J U B A.

How shall I speak the transport of my soul !
I'm lost in extasy ! O my dear Porcius !

P O R C I U S.

Believe me, prince, before I thought thee dead,
I did not know myself, how much I lov'd thee.

J U B A.

O fortunate mistake ! O happy Juba !
Fortune thou now hast made amends for all
Thy past unkindness ; I absolve my stars.

P O R C I U S.

Quick ! let us hence ; who knows if Marcus's life
                     [Trumpet sounds.
Stand sure ? O Juba ! I'm warm'd, my heart
Leaps at the trumpet's voice, and burns for glory *.
                        [Exeunt.

S C E N E   IV.

L U C I U S, C A T O.

L U C I U S.

I Stand astonish'd ! What, the bold Sempronius !
    That still broke foremost thro' the crowd of patriots,
As with a hurricane of zeal transported,
And virtuous ev'n to madness. . . . . . .

                      C A T O.

---

   * *Almost all this Scene, changing the names and some few things, is in Scene III. Act IV. The three last verses are spoken by* Porcius *in Scene* III. *Act* III. *with this alteration,* Marcus's *life, instead of* Cato's *life.*

---

various points in the original (especially Act III) and by reassigning dialogue from the fifth act belonging to Marcia and Lucia to Portius and Juba, *Cato Without the Love Scenes* purposefully marks the two men as essential witnesses to Cato's noble spirit and as mutual heirs to his legacy of public virtue.[47] Hence, when Juba suddenly starts with the outburst: "My blood runs cold; my frighted thoughts fly back, / And startle into madness" (V.v, p. 157, a set of line fragments taken from Lucia and Portius's interview about Marcus), we accept his premonition as further evidence of his being party to that kind of specialized knowledge associated, however speciously, with kinship relations.

    Subsequently, in the ensuing moments prior to Cato's entrance for his death scene, Portius and Juba anxiously erupt into excessive displays of emotion in which they appear to vie for title to who feels the most for Cato's fate:

PORCIUS: O Juba, Juba,
Have I not cause to rave and beat my breast.
To rend my heart with grief and run distracted.

. . . .

        Now tell me, Juba tell me from thy soul
If thou believst, 'tis possible for man
To suffer greater ills than Porcius suffers?
JUBA: O Porcius, Porcius! might my big swoll'n heart
Vent all its griefs and give a loose to sorrow,
Juba could answer thee in sighs, keep pace
With all thy woes, and count out tear for tear. (*Without Love*, V.vi, pp. 161–63)

As in earlier revised scenes, most of these lines are taken from other sections in
the original and inserted here to produce an effect of heightened emotional
intensity. The materials, extracted both from Marcia's anguished cries over Juba
and from Portius and Lucia's frantic exchange, thus form a scene of passions that,
to borrow a phrase from the original, seems completely "out of season" with the
pains formerly taken to suppress emotional energies. In contrast to Cato's heroic
Stoicism and his subordination of private woe to public concern at the death of
his son, we find Juba and Portius indulging repeatedly in declamatory and solip-
sistic expressions of sentiment. Are these, then, the *same* "histerical" rantings as
those in the original scenes from which these lines were taken and for which
Addison's *Cato* was censured?

    The answer is both yes and no. Insofar as the parameters of the tragedy have
been modified by the removal of the female characters and the recontextualiza-
tion of the love scenes, so too are the meanings the play text is capable of
producing. To the extent that the alterations shift the focus of the text exclusively
onto Cato as the embodiment or center of the public soul, it could be argued, for
instance, that Portius's and Juba's private suffering constitute concrete expressions of universal loss. The grief expressed in *Cato Without the Love Scenes* could
be said to be thoroughly masculine. As Juba and Portius match each other in a
crescendo of "tear for tear" over Cato, they complete a circuit of emotional energy
that flows explicitly through exclusively masculine channels. Their heated expressions have Cato as their object, even as the idea of Cato forms the mediating
point through which the bond between Juba and Portius is produced, distilled,
and secured. Cato's legacy is preserved, redeemed, and extended into the next
generation through the intensified bond of brotherhood.[48]

    Yet in borrowing so heavily from the materials of the anguished love scenes
to produce a scene of grief over Cato, the text also preserves an emphasis on
excessive passion that contradicts its earlier efforts both to suppress copious
expressions of sentiment and to define all such excess as the province of the

feminine. The cascading exclamations "O Porcius" and "O Juba" erupt across the text to undercut the ideal of masculine emotional reserve articulated through the character of Cato. The difference between *Cato* and *Cato Without the Love Scenes* is thus one of inflection: in the former effeminating passions are expressed over a woman; in the latter they are expressed over a man.

Despite these differences, however, both versions of the tragedy portray Cato as an exceptional figure—remote, dispassionate, yet unimpeachable. Removed from the consequences of his own actions, his character stands apart from those of the other figures in the tragedy in such a way as to signal a falling away from the ideal he so singularly embodied. His death inaugurates the succession of a new kind of order symbolized by Caesar, in which the appetites and ambitions of empire corrupt virtue by transforming it from an absolute into a relative principle of conduct, that is, into the contrived expedient of charismatic, rather than sincere, character.

Cato and *Cato Without the Love Scenes* each grapple with this tension as a condition of tragedy. For Addison's *Cato*, the gravity of this fall away from great, public virtue is mitigated to a certain extent by the display in the love scenes of an alternative location for the articulation of virtue. Here the day-to-day concerns of the private, domestic, and emotional spheres take precedence. If Cato leaves any enduring legacy in this tragedy, it can be found in the emphasis on individual consciousness and private conscience. Those values acquire new importance and influence in *Cato* as a resource for opposing the naked aggression of imperial ambition and thus for ensuring virtue and posterity beyond the fall into empire.

For *Cato Without the Love Scenes*, these shifts in emphasis—from great to diminished, from public to private, and from masculine to masculine joined with feminine—represented precisely the error that had brought English tragedy, indeed English posterity, to this historical point of crisis. Rather than accept the idea of a world already fallen, it turns enthusiastically to the project of building and sustaining the idea of empire by trying to recapture or reconstruct the very conditions that would allow for the realization of an ideal and perpetual state. As a kind of case history, then, it illustrates both the extent to which it was believed that male tragic heroes ought to act as the sole agents in tragedy, embodying the virtues and principles of the nation, and the lengths to which some were willing to go in order to prove that point. In sum, *Cato Without the Love Scenes* attempted to deny the paradox of tragic representation by displacing the anxiety it occasioned, especially in relation to Cato as symbolic hero, onto the love scenes and, more specifically, onto women. Although in some respects the text only carries out what would logically follow from the complaints lodged against the love scenes, it also amplifies and sanctions the view implicit in these critiques that women and the effects of the feminine were responsible for that fall away from a golden world. The excision of women from discourse is thus constituted in *Cato Without the Love Scenes* as the essential condition for recapturing that ideal.

Gender and the Ideology of Class Interests: George Lillo's The London Merchant

The phenomenon of Addison's *Cato* and *Cato Without the Love Scenes* provides an example of tragedy's ambivalent intersection with the historiography of nations and the myths of empire and also of the ways this ambivalence was displaced into and articulated through the category of gender. Yet these plays touch only obliquely on the connections between tragedy's involvement in producing a national identity and the specific economic and class concerns of the early eighteenth century. They do not attempt to demonstrate how private concerns might translate into new class interests, nor do they attempt to provide a rationalization for the gross incongruities between the affairs of empire and the ethics of domestic virtue. In stark contrast, George Lillo explicitly involves his tragedy *The London Merchant; or, The History of George Barnwell* (1730/1731) in these cultural conflicts of interest.

In this section, then, I turn to *The London Merchant* not as an epiphenomenon of an entrenched bourgeois ideological program, but rather as an effect of the ongoing series of class transformations that occurred across English culture in the early eighteenth century. By taking *The London Merchant* as my text, I will be able to illustrate more particularly the problems tragedy confronted in this period, both in shouldering the burden of representing the nation and in turning to middle-class protagonists and plots to fulfill that mandate. For while Lillo's play clearly anticipates much of what was to become recognizable as bourgeois ideology, it also betrays an acute awareness of the troubling gaps in that ideological discourse and the ambivalent strains felt within the culture toward the grounding of that ideological discourse in middle-class "character." In my reading of *The London Merchant*, I demonstrate how this particular tragedy proceeded to resolve these tensions in a typical fashion by deploying the category of gender not only to deflect attention away from the inconsistencies of its ideological project, but also to mediate the very articulation of class as nation.

George Lillo's *The London Merchant; or, The History of George Barnwell* represents one of the earliest and most coherent examples of the form conventionally referred to as domestic or bourgeois drama and is deeply inflected by the cultural tensions I described in the earlier portions of this chapter. The tragedy relates the tale of a London merchant's apprentice, George Barnwell, who is seduced by a viragolike prostitute named Millwood and then convinced by her to embezzle funds from his master Thorowgood and to rob and murder his Uncle Barnwell. Although the narrative concerns private individuals, Lillo makes it clear from the outset that his interest lies in addressing the middling classes on a broad scale by outlining their public role in securing the prosperity and future of England. In the published dedication to the play, Lillo defends his choice of a mercantile apprentice as tragic hero by arguing that the excellence of any drama can and must be determined by how effectively it shapes morality. He writes, "What I would infer is this . . . evident truth: that tragedy is so far from losing its dignity, by being accommodated to the circumstances of the generality of mankind that it is more truly august in proportion to the extent of its influence and the numbers that are properly affected by it."[49] Invoking a logic of what might be termed reasoned proportion, Lillo suggests that if tragedy adopts a hero who bears a lateral rather than hierarchical relation to a large part of the populace, it will be more likely to obtain sustained influence over their actions and moral sentiments in real life. Whereas earlier tragedies had rehearsed the public sorrows of the great because of a belief in singularly embodied moral authority, Lillo believed that new tragedies should operate on the premise that the expansion of public virtue can be achieved only through the efforts of the private many in concert with one another. In effect, tragedy was to be accounted effective by its "numbers." An analysis of Lillo's moral tale in relation to figures of accounting can thus reveal a great deal about the formation and emerging status of bourgeois character in early eighteenth-century England.

The first figure offered to us by this tragedy comes in the form of the play's titular equation: "The London Merchant; *or*, The History of George Barnwell" (emphasis mine). While in practice the play itself came to be advertised almost immediately on playbills as simply *George Barnwell*, the conventional "or" of eighteenth-century play titles provided Lillo with a formal opportunity to gloss his narrative and direct our attention to a relationship he considered vital: the relationship between a master, "The London Merchant," and an apprentice, "George Barnwell."[50] This titular equation immediately raises the problem of identifying how or even whether these two narratives are commensurate. That is, in order to understand *The London Merchant* as a tragedy, we need to explain how the tragedy of the London Merchant is signified in the life and death of George Barnwell. Are the stories of the London Merchant and George Barnwell coextensive or interchangeable? To which protagonist does this tragedy belong? As I will demonstrate below, the responses we give to such questions depend on how we choose to read the self-declared lessons of the text.

Lillo's prologue gloss provides us with our first and perhaps most obvious directive for apprehending the lessons of *The London Merchant*. We are instructed to condemn Millwood for her "dreadful guilt" and to forgive George Barnwell for his "thoughtless youth" (Prologue 31, 27). Before the first scene even begins, we are meant to assume that the drama will present a straightforward, perhaps even allegorical, tale of good and evil. Indeed, throughout the play we are bluntly informed that Millwood is a voracious villainess who seduces Barnwell, a young and innocent apprentice, and draws him away from the reasoned life of Christian mercantile economy into a profane life of irrational depravity, appetite, and crime. In case we don't know what to make of Millwood's agonizing yet unrepentant death, Trueman, a merchant's apprentice who repeatedly acts as our moral interpreter, pronounces, "May she prove a warning to others, a monument of mercy in herself" (V.xi.8–9). Thus from prologue to closing scene, the text attempts to contain Millwood "in herself" as an emblem against which to measure and delineate proper bourgeois morality, with the implied assurance that her demonized essence will not extend beyond herself. These would appear to be the self-evident "facts" of the drama—an unbiased "account" of the events. The pattern of morality appears to have been cleanly drawn, the spheres of good and evil clearly separated, the "fatal flaw" of dissolute or irrational desire identified as the contingency that must be folded and then assimilated into a continuous moral narrative of posterity.

For the most part, critical studies to date have left this project intact. Focusing on Barnwell and the significance of his tragedy in relation to the value system of the London merchant Thorowgood, these readings consistently frame the tragedy as a moral exemplum, its meaning self-evident in Barnwell's contrition at the end of the play.[51] Yet if we shift our focus even slightly, if we begin to read the self-proclaimed lessons of the text somewhat more skeptically, it becomes immediately apparent that although it would be difficult to deny that Lillo's text valorizes ideals such as "Christian sympathy" and "faith in reason," it is equally true that none of these standards emerges in the text untroubled by contradiction. This becomes most clear when we begin to consider Millwood. For in point of fact, Millwood never repents and never speaks on behalf of bourgeois moral values.[52] As noted above, her final actions have "moral" meaning only to the extent that they are reported and glossed by Trueman. This observation raises a series of related and compelling questions. First, if Barnwell's "meaning" in the text is so clear, why must the text work so hard to produce an authorized version of Millwood? Second, why has criticism focused so much attention on Barnwell to the exclusion of Millwood? Third, and perhaps most significant, where Millwood has been discussed at all, why have critics barely acknowledged or merely rationalized the fact that her status in the text depends upon her sex?[53]

With these more skeptical questions in mind, I focus, in the reading below, on Millwood and the ways in which both she and the very fact of her sex trouble the text's—and the critics'—efforts to impose "self-evident" interpretations that purport to exhaust the meaning of Barnwell's story. I demonstrate that while Millwood is positioned in *The London Merchant* as the site for concealing the contradictions of a bourgeois ideology, she ultimately remains unassimilated to that narrative project. I argue that, she thus functions as the figure through which the less self-evident meanings of the text may be deciphered.

In order to ground this reading, I will scrutinize *The London Merchant* for the ambivalent tensions associated with questions of class, desire, and self-evidence in eighteenth-century culture. As Neil McKendrick points out, in the first half of the eighteenth century, "The unleashing of the acquisitive instincts of all classes still posed too great a threat . . . the 'democratization of consumption' threatened to undermine a class discipline and a system of social control previously bolstered up by the patriotic and ascetic elements in orthodox mercantilist theory."[54] Eventually this program of consumption found what McKendrick terms its "theoretical justification," as well as, I would argue, an interpretive gloss that deemphasized desire. Yet until those new modes of thought and action, what we now term bourgeois capitalism and imperialism, were reconciled with older mercantilist orthodoxy as part of a national program and rationalized as something other than gross consumption or raw appetite, English society continued to register tremendous ambivalence over the transformation of its economic culture. This tension was particularly acute insofar as that orthodoxy was forced to confront the elements of desire inherent, but concealed, in its own doctrine, the elements, that is, which enabled mercantilism to develop into capitalism. As a number of cultural theorists have recently demonstrated, and as we shall see in the case of *The London Merchant*, these tensions over appetite and desire were often displaced into and articulated through misogynist representations of sexual difference.[55]

In Lillo's play, Thorowgood can be understood as a nostalgic representative of the old system of orthodox mercantilism attempting to accommodate the new project of imperial expansion. Millwood, in turn, appears as the ostensible site of displacement for any desire that could detract from the moral probity of the project. In order to produce this dichotomous relation between Thorowgood's and Millwood's spheres of economic activity, Lillo's text borrows what in a comedy might be termed a gray world/green world motif.[56] Within this frame, arguments are presented to distinguish the mode of acquisition in Thorowgood's realm from that in Millwood's. Thorowgood's house is projected as a green world in which benevolence, virtue, and reason motivate the pursuit of bourgeois capitalism and imperialism, while, in supposedly self-evident contrast, excess, self-interest, and avarice inform the spirit of criminal opportunism in the gray world over which Millwood presides. This ordering structure carries a certain interpretive risk, however, for the successful deployment of this principle of difference depends on the extent to which the text can consistently rationalize this separation and defend these characterizations. In order for the text to "succeed," Thorowgood's mercantile programs for expansion and acquisition must emerge unambiguously as disinterested projects marked only by their moral integrity; the latent avarice that motivated this transformation must remain concealed.

The argument for mercantile development is thus initiated aggressively in the opening scene of the play with an emotional appeal to patriotism and an assertion that the merchant's first priority is the happiness of his country. We find the merchant Thorowgood with his apprentice Trueman didactically extolling the virtues of mercantile interest and influence and their complementary relation to England as a nation of liberty and law. Puffed with pride, Thorowgood explains how the merchants of London managed to prevent or at least forestall the imminent invasion of English seas by the Spanish Armada by convincing Genoese bankers not to extend a loan to the Spanish. He exhorts, "from thence you may learn how honest merchants, as such, may sometimes contribute to the safety of their country as they do at all times to its happiness" (I.i.16–18). Setting *The London Merchant* in Elizabethan England, Lillo thus lays the foundation for a genealogy of mercantile patriotism, casting its point of origin in England's epic victory over the Spanish Armada and by association lending legitimacy and authority to the merchant's role in the more recent confrontations with eighteenth-century Spain.

This first scene thus articulates the ideological rationale for what Linda Colley has termed the emergent eighteenth-century "cult of trade." Under the sway of this discourse, the interests of commerce and empire were represented as inextricably linked and mutually beneficial; "Abundant trade," as Colley points out, "was not just materially desirable: for Britons . . . it was also proof positive of their status as the freest and most distinctively Protestant of nations."[57] The title of merchant was esteemed a badge of liberty and honor, and, as Trueman avows, those who "bring any imputation on that honorable name . . . must be left without excuse" (I.i.24–25). In this respect, a merchant's most valuable source of capital, as Thorowgood informs us, is his "sincerity" (I.i.30). He makes it quite clear, moreover, that because the merchant's sincerity is the key to his reputation, and thus his business interests, it must be maintained as scrupulously and as openly as his account books.

Significantly, all of these declarations occur without reference to the material desirability of this arrangement. Such a notable silence occurs once again when Thorowgood presents a second explanation of the "method of merchandise" in the opening scene of the third act. Representing his profession as a "science" that is "founded in reason and the nature of things," Thorowgood moralizes that trade "has promoted humanity . . . by mutual benefits diffusing mutual love from pole to pole" (III.i.1–9). Picking up on this imperial rhetoric of benevolence, Trueman affirms:

I have observed those countries where trade is promoted and encouraged do not make discoveries to destroy but to improve mankind—by love and friendship to tame the fierce and polish the most savage; to teach them the advantages of honest traffic by taking from them, with their own consent, their useless superfluities, and giving them in return what, from their ignorance in manual arts, their situation, or some other accident, they stand in most need of. (III.i.11–19)

"Honest traffic" under the aegis of tradesmen like Thorowgood thus consists in relieving colonial lands of *unnecessary* raw materials and selling those materials back to the native populace in the form of *necessary* manufactured goods. Historically, this reported "accident" provided England with enormous markets in which to sell its goods at great economic advantage.[58] Yet up to this point Thorowgood's reflections suggest only that merchants had nothing to gain other than the pleasure of spreading "love and friendship" throughout the world. The single indication that there may be some other motive for pursuing these markets occurs when Thorowgood concludes the lesson by reminding Trueman that "It is the industrious merchant's business to collect the various blessings of each soil and climate and, with the product of the whole, to enrich his native country" (III.i.25–28). This subtle allusion to "enrichment" obliquely illustrates the extent to which the rhetorics of nationhood and enlightened reason served as umbrella terms shading the profits of what might otherwise be termed the "spoils of empire."

The larger context within which to read this shading is provided by Millwood. For although her ostensible role in the tragedy is to act as the object of ritual vilification through which bourgeois discourse may be justified, if we examine the terms under which she is vilified more critically we find that she actually problematizes Thorowgood's representation of mercantile integrity and benevolence by providing alternative meanings for those very terms. At first, the distinction seems clear-cut. In contrast to Thorowgood's musings on liberty, Millwood lingers over the motif of enslavement and consistently renders an account of society in which human behavior is governed by oppressive power relations and greedy desire.[59] In an early conversation with her attendant, Millwood resolves, "I would have my conquests complete, like those of the Spaniards in the New World, who first plundered the natives of all the wealth they had and then condemned the wretches to the mines for life to work for more" (I.iii.24–27). Millwood's method of governance seems to present a startling antithesis to Thorowgood's avowed attitude of benevolence toward the conquered territories and peoples. It appears, moreover, to ally her both with Catholic Spain, the despised enemy of England, and with the practice of human exploitation. Yet, in the context of early eighteenth-century England, this apparent contrast was apt to summon more ambiguous and troubling connotations. For through its most recent wars and settlements with Spain, England had acquired the *asiento* and gained the right to "traffic honestly" in slaves.[60] From this perspective, even the initial effort to position Millwood as the antithesis to English liberty and morality casts suspicion on the very practices of imperial commerce that were valorized by Thorowgood for their efficacy in promoting English values. Where Millwood's association with slavery is only metaphorical and discursive, the merchants of London maintained an active and actual interest in the slave trade. Thus signaling the hypocrisy in Thorowgood's meticulous excision of power and material gain from his rehearsal of mercantile interests and moral integrity, the text prepares us for Millwood's discursively volatile and theatrically climactic confrontation with that merchant representative at the end of the fourth act.

By this time, however, "sincerity," the critical term in Thorowgood's discourse, has been literally displaced by its semantic opposite: "concealment." For soon after committing his first crime, Barnwell meets his best friend Trueman and mutters in an aside, "By my face he will discover all I would *conceal*." In turn, Trueman pleads with Barnwell to divulge the source of his distress, imploring, "Have I a thought I would *conceal* from you?" (II.ii.15, 62–63, emphasis added). The significance of the exchanges in this scene lies in their emphasis on the loosening of a bond of trust between men. As part of Thorowgood's household, Barnwell and Trueman are both expected to honor sincerity as the principal term of engagement, and, indeed, Trueman invokes this authority in his confrontation with Barnwell. Barnwell's refusal to respond with proper candor coincides with the introduction and repetition of the term "conceal" in the text. His turn to deceit thus marks the scene as a turning point in the tragedy. The conventions of tragedy require that the drama's highest ideal also represent its greatest vulnerability, and Barnwell's tragic fall can be said to consist not so much in the actual crimes he commits as in his betrayal of the merchant's ideal of sincerity. In short, he destabilizes the crucial value of a man's word. Once that occurs, the tragedy is set irreversibly in motion, and the events play themselves out around the fated figure of concealment.

This, of course, returns us to the figure of Millwood; for she *is* the figure that comes between Trueman and Barnwell and between Barnwell and his master. As Barnwell cries out in a passion, she is his "*fate*, Heaven or Hell" (II.xiii.18, emphasis added). Yet if Millwood is positioned as the figure of fate and the occasion for concealment in *The London Merchant*, what precisely does she hide from our view and what, if anything, does it have to do with the fact that she is a woman?

This last question originates in the text itself and demands explanation. For once Barnwell's crimes are discovered and Millwood is captured as his accomplice, she is charged above all else with going against the nature of "woman." First, Trueman ventures to execrate her, inveighing, "To call thee woman were to wrong the sex, thou devil!" (IV.xviii.4). Barely flinching, Millwood sharply retorts, "That imaginary being is an emblem of thy cursed sex collected, a mirror wherein each particular man may see his own likeness, and that of all mankind!" (IV.xviii.5–7). Millwood defiantly rejects the title "woman" in Trueman's usage, pointing to it as the site of concealment for what men wish not to see in themselves and thus turning that displaced reflection back upon Trueman. Baffled by Millwood's contemptuous responses, Trueman yields the interrogation to Thorowgood. Yet this pious master fails as well, for in response to his attempts to mollify her with his religious condescension, Millwood resolutely replies,"War, plague, and famine has not destroyed so many of the human race as this pretended piety has done, and with such barbarous cruelty as if the way to honor Heaven were to turn the present world into Hell" (IV.xviii.53–56). Millwood consistently maintains her attitude of disgust for the hypocrisy of Christian mercantilism and other state institutions. She refuses, moreover, to construe the fact of her sex as the proof of her crimes. Ironically, in fact, it is her "sincerity" under fire that brings about the collapse of Thorowgood's system of distinctions and reveals the truths he works so hard to conceal beneath the figures of his account books. Rather than confirming Thorowgood's claim to sincerity, her responses lay bare his "method of merchandise" as a system of complicated rationalizations by and for men in pursuit of their own material interests, a system in which women are made to absorb the negative moral implications of that pursuit. Indeed, her scathing counterattack renders Thorowgood almost speechless; he can only weakly reply, "Truth is truth, though from an enemy and spoke in malice" (IV.xviii.57). With this feeble answer, Thorowgood indicates that his attempts to assimilate Millwood to a frame of Christian piety have resulted only in a crushing indictment of the mercantile system he so devoutly and so desirously defends.

On an analytical level, what Millwood resists in this confrontation and throughout *The London Merchant* is the process through which the proximate comes to be reinscribed as the opposite.[61] That is, in order to represent bourgeois capitalism and imperialism as irreducibly benevolent and virtuous modes of acquisition, the text must work to recast as diametrically opposed all similarities or "proximate" appearances between that mode of acquisition and Millwood's. Indeed, the problem with Millwood is not so much that she is so different from Thorowgood in her business practices, but rather that she is so similar. Consequently, the text strains noticeably to position Millwood as a cipher through which to filter those proximate signs and thus produce a pure vision of a new economic order. The more the text extends itself in that direction, the more it collapses under the weight of its own artificiality as Millwood emerges as the text's cipher in more than one sense of the word.

On the narrative level, she is figured as "nought," a self-evident symbol of evil passion to be read and written off much like the figures in Thorowgood's account book. On the level of interpretation, however, Millwood's function as cipher to the text also positions her, paradoxically, as the figure for concealed meanings. Deciphering Millwood results in the understanding that desire drives the balanced accounts of the merchant's ledger book as much as it supports the economy of Millwood's household. Indeed, Barnwell unwittingly anticipates this concealed reality when he compares his imminent fall to the entrepreneurial ventures of a merchant, declaring, "Reluctant thus, the merchant quits his ease, / And trusts to rocks and sands and stormy seas" (I.viii.25–26). As the concluding, almost choric, assessment of events in the first act, Barnwell's woeful testimony likens his fall to Millwood to a merchant's pursuit of trade—motivated by desire and equally dangerous, with the return on investment uncertain. Rather than glorify the mercantile institution, Barnwell's fall envisions the doomed fortunes of capitalism resulting from its own hazardous investment in material desires.[62] At the same time, Millwood resists claims that fashion criminal opportunism and bourgeois capitalism as opposites and instead affirms their proximity as both take their form from a desire to profit from the labors of others.

Millwood's final allegation bring us back to the question of her sex and provides us with one of our last clues for deciphering meaning in *The London Merchant*. She swears: "What are your laws . . . but . . . the instrument and screen of all your villainies by which you punish in others what you act yourselves. . . . Thus, you go on deceiving and being deceived, harassing, plaguing, and destroying one another, but women are your universal prey" (IV.xviii.60–68). Millwood's charge registers the fact that the text has programatically associated the term "woman" and the female sex in general with excess, passion, excessive passion, concealment, and concealed evil. Indeed, it is the sign under which Millwood is cast as a demonic and demonized other.

By play's end, in fact, the issues of mercantile economy have been almost completely displaced by the question of gender. The tragedy has come into focus not as a direct examination of the moral integrity of imperial mercantilism, but as an illustration of the problem of female seductiveness and its supposedly inexhaustible capacity to divide men. Symptomatically, Barnwell's redemption in the final scenes is emblematized by a return, as it were, to the homosocial fold. He lies down on the cold, bare stone, embracing his dear friend Trueman in a masque of renewed sincerity and devotion to the tenets of a Christian economy (V.v).[63] The text would have us believe that Barnwell has not committed crimes so much as he has been improperly diverted from the pursuit of mercantile conquest—seduced by the lure of conquest in the female bed.

In the final act, as throughout the play, Millwood comes to be projected as the embodiment of voracious lusts alongside of which the bodies of men in pursuit of material interests may appear chaste. Yet her resounding defiance in the previous act casts a pall of doubt over these purification rituals; they appear forced and mechanically recuperative. Ironically, and despite all attempts by the text to turn her into a "monument of mercy," Millwood persists as the example of the "woman" who, in her words, "prove[s], to plague mankind," precisely because she embodies the merchants' own denied and displaced desire for empire (IV.xviii.78). Hence her presence in the drama signals, rather than conceals, English discomfort with empire because she conflates, and then embodies the conflation of, the very terms that were to be held apart in that vision of the nation. Millwood cannot be fully reduced to a subjected emblem within a bourgeois economy because, as the tragic form bears out, the cultural project of mercantile expansion remained too self-consciously implicated in and complicit with the very characteristics designated to signify her demonic difference. Millwood is not so different from the merchant in her desire to accumulate material goods, but the text works rhetorically to transform sexual difference into the appearance of absolute difference. In sum, the fact of her gender comes to be construed as the fatal obstacle to the realization of what is, in turn, marked off as an ideal, because essentially masculine, mercantile nation and empire.

Historian Kathleen Wilson has written that *The London Merchant* "is clearly the ultimate mercantilist fantasy and morality tale, in which commerce, empire, and their agents, the merchants, are admired and supported as the founts of national wealth and the conduits of civilization."[64] If this is so, then it is also the case that *The London Merchant* represents the worst nightmare of that emerging class. For by virtue of its generic status, *The London Merchant* had not only to envision its ideal but also to represent the tragic violation of that ideal.[65] From this perspective, we can begin to understand why the "History of George Barnwell" is also the tragedy of "The London Merchant," for in his fall away from the path of virtue and into the way of duplicity, George Barnwell signals the very failure of mercantile rhetoric to have the disciplinary effects it sought in eighteenth-century culture. In his dependent, and symbolically representative, relation to the merchant, the apprentice Barnwell illustrated not only the potential benefits but also the liabilities of the heroic status so doggedly pursued by the mercantile classes. In short, the "history" of George Barnwell is the "tragedy" of the London merchant because the certainty of that history only underscores the uncertainty of both the merchant's ideology and the genre enlisted to support that ideology.

What About She-Tragedy?: Masculine Ideals in Nicholas Rowe's
The Fair Penitent *and* The Tragedy of Jane Shore

By now it should be clear not only that tragedy functioned in the eighteenth century as a vehicle for nation building, but that the figures in tragedy who were to embody that nation were meant to be exclusively male and to evince purely "masculine" values. Conspicuously absent from my account of tragedy to this point, however, has been any discussion of she-tragedy. How, one might inquire, can the heightened displays of "feminine" power, realized through the bodies of powerful female actresses, be reconciled with such an account? In the discussion that follows, I argue that despite the dramatically powerful position occupied by female protagonists in she-tragedies, this subgenre of tragedy was devoted, as was the genre in general, to promoting masculine ideals from which women were actively excluded. I thus maintain that while the heightened, histrionic pathos of she-tragedies positioned the *female actress* as dramatically central, the narratives of those tragedies, with their attending web of motifs, themes, and allusions, consistently attempted to position the *female characters* as ideologically marginal.[66] In so doing, I shall demonstrate both how the different aspects of character were played against one another even in tragedy, where play was meant to be kept to a minimum, and how the interests of the genre functioned here, as they did in all dramatic productions in the eighteenth century, as the imperative source for controlling that conflict.

There is no doubt that the rise of the first female actresses during the Restoration period acted as a critical element in the development, and, one might even argue, the rise of she-tragedy in the late seventeenth century.[67] Dramatists such as John Banks, Thomas Southerne, Nathaniel Lee, and Thomas Otway could write with the strengths and weaknesses of the preeminent actresses of the day in mind. Elizabeth Barry and Anne Bracegirdle dominated the boards, and their acting skills, as well as their public reputations, figured significantly in the calculations and plots of the affective or pathetic tragedies that ultimately came to be known as she-tragedies.[68] In what amounted to a kind of typecasting that capitalized on competing aspects of character, Elizabeth Barry, the notorious mistress of, among others, the earl of Rochester and George Etherege, was almost inevitably cast in these very successful tragedies as an emotionally high-strung fallen woman, while Anne Bracegirdle, who fastidiously maintained a reputation for strict chastity, was cast as her gentle and chaste counterpart.[69] Yet the presence of women acting on the stage was fraught with as many liabilities as potentialities. As observed in Chapter 1, female bodies on the stage raised troubling questions about the control and containment of female sexuality.[70] These concerns were

Figure 7. Anne Oldfield. By permission of the V & A Picture
Library.

exploited not only by the playwrights who produced astonishing parts for the
actresses but also, and for different ends, by the authors of antitheatrical discourse and contemporary criticism. Indeed, it would not be beyond the speculative pale to surmise that the violent reactions to the love scenes in Addison's *Cato*
were triggered at least in part by what must have seemed to some a disturbing and
unavoidable reminder of female sexuality: the nine-month-pregnant Anne Oldfield playing the part of Cato's virgin daughter Marcia (see Figure 7).[71] This
extreme case, in which the character of the actress's body put into question the
character of the role she played, suggests clearly that the presence of female
actresses was as seductive to some as it was disturbing to others.

Yet whether one was attracted to or repulsed by the presence of dramatically
powerful female actresses was ultimately beside the point. The main tension that

the performance of she-tragedy presented to the audience, I would submit, was the tension between the spectacle of women in emotionally compelling roles and the narratives that were devoted to taming the characters they portrayed. Indeed, the very same pairings that made actresses such as Barry and Bracegirdle so popular and so powerful in their own right were also the vehicles for developing and carrying forward moral dichotomies of virtue and vice in the delineation of female sexuality and of masculine activity and feminine passivity in the delineation of gender roles.[72] The bulk of recent criticism has been devoted to foregrounding this project, often in the context of developing an analogy between the shift in tragic representation from aristocratic, heroic dramas to sentimental bourgeois tragedies, on the one hand, and the emerging vision of ideal womanhood on the other.[73]

But what of the ideal of manhood in these tragedies? In focusing our attention exclusively on the construction of female identities, have we missed something critical about the ways she-tragedies carried out the imperatives of tragic discourse in the eighteenth century? In the readings below, I demonstrate that, as in tragedy more generally, an ideal of manhood, or an ethos of masculine virtue, rather than one of womanhood or feminine virtue, constitutes the controlling interest in the narratives of she-tragedies. That is, what other critics have situated as the background against which the production of female identity takes place, I highlight as the foregrounded ideological project that marks the narratives of these dramas from beginning to end. I will take as my cases in point Nicholas Rowe's *The Fair Penitent* (1702/1703) and *The Tragedy of Jane Shore* (1713/1714) because they represent two of the best examples of she-tragedy written in the eighteenth century proper and reflect, at least obliquely, an evolving sense of the place of the female protagonist on the tragic landscape.[74]

In the prologue to *The Fair Penitent*, Nicholas Rowe tells us that he has chosen a "humbler theme" for his tragedy, a tale not of "ambition" but of "love," a narrative of "private woes" rather than of public sorrows.[75] With these pronouncements, he deliberately marks a turn away from the soaring rhetoric and expansive vision of heroic dramas toward the more contracted register and realm of so-called domestic affairs, a turn that we have already seen in Lillo's *The London Merchant*. Yet where Lillo, at an almost thirty-year's remove from Rowe, feels comfortable situating these "domestic" concerns against the backdrop of a nation voyaging out and contending with other countries in pursuit of empire, Rowe remains preoccupied with the threat of faction within the nation. In this sense, Rowe's drama is very much a vestige of Restoration culture, where issues of sovereignty, succession, patriarchal authority, and patriarchal inheritance haunted a nation that had recently experienced civil war as well as, in the later Restoration, a

Glorious Revolution that radically altered the lines of succession.[76] These interests, in fact, constitute the controlling concerns of this tragedy.

The plot of Rowe's *The Fair Penitent* relates the story of Calista, our purported "fair" one, who in defiance of her father Sciolto and without his knowledge engages in a sexual affair with Lothario, a libertine villain. The play opens on Calista's wedding day to Altamont, a young man adopted and supported by Sciolto after the death of his father. While much critical attention has been devoted to determining whether Calista is penitent for her affair with Lothario, the reading below will concentrate on an aspect of Calista's "penitence" that has long been ignored.[77] Ultimately the crime for which Calista is condemned and, even more significantly, for which she condemns herself, is not that of adultery or sexual wantonness, but rather that of parricide. By attending to the emphasis on patriarchal inheritance and filial piety that preoccupies the play, we will be better able to apprehend Calista's "crime." We will be able to understand, moreover, how and why the text comes to construe her conduct not just as a crime against the patriarchal system but also as a crime against the state.

There is no theme more pervasive in the first scene of *The Fair Penitent* than that of the reciprocity owed to patriarchal benevolence in the form of a son's filial piety. The agenda of this tragedy is set as conversation between Altamont and Horatio turns almost immediately from the happy day that brings Altamont's marriage to Calista to the course of events leading up to this day. Apparently, it was "Sciolto's noble hand" that had raised Altamont "[h]alf dead and drooping" from his father's grave, after "ungrateful Genoa had forgot / The merit of [his] godlike father's arms / . . . / And made their court to faction by his ruin." In offering Calista's hand to Altamont, Sciolto "completes" his bounty and gives Altamont the chance to "[restore his] name / To that high rank and luster which it boasted" (I.i.9–18). Altamont thus owes his loyalty to more than one "father," and at this recollection of Sciolto's generosity, he bursts out:

O great Sciolto! O my more than father!
Let me not live but at thy very name
My eager heart springs up and leaps with joy.
When I forget the vast, vast debt I owe thee,
Forget! (but 'tis impossible) then let me
Forget the use and privilege of reason,
Be driven from the commerce of mankind
To wander in the desert among the brutes (I.i.19–26).

Significantly, Altamont is not the only one to claim Sciolto as a father; his best friend, Horatio, also testifies:

When that great man I loved, thy noble father,
Bequeathed thy gentle sister [Lavinia] to my arms,
His last dear pledge and legacy of friendship,
That happy tie made me Sciolto's son;
He called us his, and with a parent's fondness
Indulged us in his wealth, blessed us with plenty,
Healed all our cares, and sweetened love itself. (I.i.32–38)

In the first thirty-eight lines of the play, Sciolto's influence as father figure is felt everywhere. Indeed, the gestures are so obtrusive and overdetermined that they attracted the censorious attention of Richard Cumberland when he wrote in *The Observer* (1785):

If Rowe would have his audience credit Altamont for that filial piety which marks the character he copied from, it was a small oversight to put the following expression into his mouth:
Oh great Sciolto! Oh my more than father!
A closer attention to character would have reminded him that it was possible for Altamont to express his gratitude to Sciolto without setting him above a father to whose memory he had paid such devotion.[78]

Cumberland's account provides us with evidence that audiences and readers in the eighteenth century recognized the extent to which Rowe worked so hard to foreground the themes of fatherhood and patriarchy in the opening scene. The question that remains is: to what end? What does patriarchy come to stand for in these first thirty-eight lines and in the remainder of the scene and how does that category signify throughout the play?

What we discover first and foremost in these opening lines is that the realm of the patriarch constitutes a kind of Eden, an ideal place where reason and benevolence reign. To be exiled from this realm, from the "commerce of mankind," would be to experience a tragic fall into a world of unreason, that is, into a realm dominated by brutes, disorder, and as we shall later see, by violent faction.[79] But there are conditions that govern status in the ideal realm of the patriarch. In this golden realm, sons owe their duty to their "godlike" fathers; indeed they are designed not merely to succeed their fathers but to exemplify and, in a typological sense, to complete the father. Altamont had already proved himself worthy of Sciolto's bounty by his act of filial piety towards his own father; he had offered himself as a bond to ensure his father's burial and still seeks to "restore" his father's name. Following the logic of reciprocity, he now appears to owe Sciolto, his "more than father," a "vast, vast debt." We are thus made to understand that any turn away from this obligation or from the values that Sciolto represents will also mark a tragic fall away from the patriarchal ideals projected in this opening scene.

When Sciolto finally appears, the rhetoric of patriarchal invocation, what Vaska Tumir refers to as the "notion of father-sanctity," only intensifies (423). Sciolto enters exclaiming his joy at a day that "makes me father of a son" like Altamont. Altamont hails Sciolto as his "father." Sciolto praises Altamont for his "[g]oodness innate and worth hereditary" and declares, "thy noble father's virtues / Spring freshly forth in thy youth." In response, Altamont likens himself to that "fair creation" that "heav'n from nothing raised . . . / And then with wond'rous joy beheld its beauty, / Well pleased to see the excellence he gave." Sciolto then recalls the day when he first saw Altamont: "Adorned and lovely in thy filial tears, / The mourner and redeemer of thy father, / I set thee down and sealed thee for my own; / Thou art my son, ev'n near me as Calista." Finally, embracing Horatio too, he declares, "Horatio and Lavinia too are mine; / All are my children, and shall share my heart" (I.i.64–88). Once again the motif of the creation of man is invoked. Altamont is the image of his father, as Adam was the image of heaven formed in the garden of Eden. The son shines out as an effect of his father "adorned and lovely," and Sciolto presides over all as his "own." Thus the agenda for this tragedy is set. Subsequently and throughout the play, the spectre and name of the father and the son's obligation to his sire will be repeatedly invoked, guiding the plot, motivating almost all of the characters' actions, and controlling the meaning of the tragedy.

This condition becomes all the more apparent when we consider that in a play that critics have championed for its moral dichotomies of good and bad, virtue and vice, the authority of the father and the imperative of exemplification in the son extends not just to cases of virtue, but also to cases of vice. For just as Altamont shines out as an effect of his father's virtue, Lothario inherits and sustains his father's proclivity for vice. As the dominant principle of male character formation in this tragedy, patriarchal transmission and succession transcend the usual differentiation between virtue and vice. Cast as the serpent-fiend who invades Sciolto's garden paradise to seduce Calista, Lothario, like his father who led the factions of Genoa against Altamont's sire, may "laugh at human nature and forgiveness" and function as a "[factor] for destruction," but he is no less dedicated to his "name"—a mark of his patrimony—than Altamont is to his (I.i. 54–56). The sons are thus locked into a hereditary rivalry, and the plot takes its cues from this structurally overdetermined and irrefragable controlling interest. Indeed, when Altamont finally confronts and kills Lothario in Act IV, he cries out, "this for thy father, / This for Sciolto, and this last for Altamont" (IV.107–8). In other words, he thrusts first at Lothario's "father," as if to avenge the cruel treatment of his own. The son thus honors and completes the father. With his second stroke he invokes a second father, Sciolto; only with his last lunge does Altamont name himself.

The invocation of the "father" as a kind of totemic figure reaches its highest pitch when Horatio confronts Altamont with Calista's treachery. When Altamont disclaims his friendship, Horatio responds with this horrified burst:

Canst thou so soon forget what I've been to thee?
I shared the task of nature with thy father,
And formed with care thy unexperienced youth
To virtue and to arms.
Thy noble father, O thou light young man!
Would he have used me thus? One fortune fed us,
For his was ever mine, mine his, and both
Together flourished, and together fell.
He called me friend, like thee; would he have left me
Thus, for a woman, nay, a vile one too? (III.266–75)

In this volatile confrontation, Horatio displays his faith in the signifying power of the "father" not only by invoking the memory of Altamont's father but also by claiming for himself the status of father figure to Altamont. His emphasis here is on patriarchy as the sign under which what ought to be inviolable bonds of friendship between men are cemented. His faith, however, is not so well placed because it underestimates the sway such an ideal might have when challenged by the more immediate desires aroused by the possibility of female friendship. Indeed, as we have seen in *The London Merchant*, Altamont's tragic fall is signaled when he betrays this bond of friendship—and in this case the homosocial bond of patriarchal inheritance—and chooses instead the "panting breast" of Calista (III.352). Plagued by what is portrayed as a naive and irrational desire, Altamont refuses to follow the "father" in Horatio and estranges himself both from his honor and from Sciolto's Eden.[80]

This does not mean that the "father" as totem has no protective value at all. Altamont and Horatio each desist from fighting when they see the "father" in the other. Altamont pronounces:

Thou wert my father's friend, he loved thee well;
A kind of venerable mark of him
Hangs round thee, and protects thee from my vengeance;
I cannot, dare not life my sword against thee. (III.281–84)

And Horatio, in turn, stops himself:

Yet hold!—By heav'n, his father's in his face.
Spite of my wrong, my heart runs o'er with tenderness,
And I could rather die myself than hurt him. (III.301–3)

The "father" leaves an indelible trace on both of these men that prevents them
from lifting their swords in violence against one another. The mystique of patriarchal succession and the son's inheritance is thus reinforced, even as its ideals
are violated.[81] In short, we are able to comprehend the tragic turn of events
signified in the fracture of this male friendship because of the power exercised
over the text by a patriarchal narrative in which sons sustain the ideal of a
homosocial Eden by succeeding and completing the father.

But what about daughters? Where are they supposed to "fit" in this patriarchal narrative? According to the narrative scheme presented in the first act,
daughters are supposed to act as passive pawns in transactions and rivalries
between men. Just as Calista represents the tender that "completes" Sciolto's
bounty to Altamont, so too does she represent the medium by which Lothario
takes his revenge on Sciolto for refusing his proposal of marriage. In the first case,
she constitutes the means by which Altamont can restore his father's name; in the
second case, she constitutes the means by which Lothario can ensure that "the
shame / [He] mean[s] to brand [Sciolto's] name with" will not stick on his own
(I.133–34). Like property, a daughter is supposed to be at the sole disposal of her
father. Thus there is no better way to avenge oneself against the father than by
consummating the "theft" of his daughter.

Despite the force of this rhetoric, Rowe also intimates that there is something inherently dangerous about daughters that puts the ideal patriarchal vision
in jeopardy, and he implies that daughters might constitute both the greatest
potentiality and the greatest liability of that ideological project. Indeed, even
before we see Calista, we learn that she resists her place in this narrative. She has
asserted, as Altamont reports, "sorrows" that "were her own, / Nor in a father's
pow'r to dispose of" (I.112–13). Laying claim to a kind of ownership in herself,
she exceeds her father and denies him full rights of dispensation. Not insignificantly, moreover, Calista explicitly frames her desire for autonomy as resistance
to narrative incorporation. She vows:

... 'tis the solemn counsel of my soul
Never to live with public loss of honor;
'Tis fixed to die, rather than bear the insolence
Of each affected she that tells my story,
And blesses her good stars that she is virtuous.
To be a tale for fools! Scorned by the women,
And pitied by the men! (II.i.32–38)

Calista's pride disdains the standard patriarchal narrative that divides all women into either virgins or whores, transforming them from individuals into types and emblems. She seeks a way to elude this form of narrative control and the containment of female desire that it dictates. Indeed, she reserves her strongest expressions of defiance and indignation for this narrative and the double standards it entails. Bristling, for instance, both at Sciolto's admonishment that she be happy on her marriage day and at his threat that if she "stain[s] the honor of [her] name," he will cast her out of his house, Calista delivers this stunning critique:

How hard is the condition of our sex,
Through ev'ry state of life the slaves of man!
In all the dear, delightful days of youth
A rigid father dictates to our wills,
And deals out pleasure with a scanty hand;
To his, the tyrant husband's reign succeeds;
Proud with opinion of superior reason,
He holds domestic business and devotion
All we are capable to know, and shuts us,
Like cloistered idiots, from the world's acquaintance
And all the joys of freedom. (III.32–33, 39–49)

For Calista, the most difficult thing to bear is the oppression of her "will." She wants not only to tell, but to live, an alternative tale in which women exercise an "equal empire o'er the world" (III.52). Rowe can be appreciated here for giving voice, at least momentarily, to protofeminist concerns. Indeed, when we imagine this soliloquy as delivered by a skillful actress, Calista grows in dramatic stature and gains considerable audience sympathy as she achieves the status of victim.

At the same time, however, it is patently clear that Calista's greatest expressions of resistance are also her greatest expressions of fear. Fear, that is, that inevitably and despite all of her defiant efforts, she will be made into an emblem in a moral tale of virtue and vice. Indeed, we see this fear turn to panic and a momentary loss of composure when Horatio informs her that she and Lothario have become the talk of the town, "A shameful tale to tell for public sport / Of an unhappy beauty, a false fair one" (III.119–20). The nagging question that arises for us, as readers and as audience members, is whether in terms of both the narrative and the performance, Calista is already contained and her assertions of narrative autonomy already illusory? While we might cheer for Calista, and the actress who plays her, as she critiques the construction of female identity, we already know, as audience members would have known at the first performances when they saw that Calista and Lavinia would be played by Barry and Bracegirdle, that Calista stands as the doomed figure of sexual excess. Indeed, we can read the play itself as a rehearsal of that moment envisioned by Lavinia when:

We'll sit all day and tell sad tales of love,
And when we light upon some faithless woman,
Some beauty, like Calista, false and fair,
We'll fix our grief and our complaining there;
We'll curse the nymph that drew ruin on,
And mourn the youth that was like [Altamont] undone (IV.420–25)

Ironically, then, even as Calista acts out her resistance, she merely performs the part that her audience expects. The narrative works against the performative in this she-tragedy to contain the dangerous daughter, as the imperatives of the genre "fix" the aspects of character that are intelligible.

Still, we have yet to identify the nature of a daughters danger, that is, why daughter's are resistant and why they have to be "fix[ed]." We have yet to explain, in other words, how the narrative of this play "fix[es]" Calista so that the complaint that is ultimately lodged against her is not that of whore but rather that of parricide. To answer these questions, we need to recall the ideals of Sciolto's patriarchal realm and to follow through on the logic of this Edenic narrative of patriarchal succession: if sons are the Adams of this tragedy, then daughters are the Eves who precipitate their tragic fall. Indeed, Horatio makes this parallel explicit when he laments Calista's guilt and anticipates Altamont's ruin:

With such smooth looks and many a gentle word
The first fair she beguiled her easy lord;
Too blind with love and beauty to beware,
He fell unthinking in the fatal snare;
Nor could believe that such a heav'nly face
Had bargained with the devil to damn her wretched race (II.i.167–72)

Daughters are a liability for fathers; they are unpredictable Eves, deceivers who blind and beguile men of reason. Indeed, their "smooth looks" and "fatal snare[s]" extend beyond the bounds of their immediate families to the generality of mankind, that is, to the state. As Sciolto instructs us, Calista is like "Helen," that other great "[s]pectatress of the mischief which she made," when she stands "[a]midst the general wreck" as the city of Genoa erupts into factional violence and civil unrest, "distraction and tumultuous jars" (V.45–54).

Still, our understanding of why this is the case and how it is related to the patriarchal narrative that has guided our understanding throughout the play comes fully into focus only when Sciolto asks Calista why she has cursed him and destroyed his posterity. She explains:

Because my soul was rudely drawn from yours,
A poor imperfect copy of my father,
Where goodness and the strength of manly virtue
Was thinly planted, and the idle void
Filled up with light belief and easy fondness;
It was because I loved, and was a woman (V.68–73)

In short, where sons are the perfect copies of the fathers, as Adam was created in the image of heaven, daughters, like Eve, are "imperfect copies," created out of the rib of man. As a woman, Calista can only have "something of Sciolto's virtue" and only "somewhat" of his "great spirit" (IV.161 ; V.58). The rest is left indeterminate and unformed. Daughters, and that category includes all women, thus lack the firm imprint of the father, a condition that, as Pope presents it, leaves them with "no Character at all."[82] That is, where the character of sons is fully determined according to the lines of succession, daughters present an "idle void" that still needs to be filled. Ironically, and here we can locate the inevitable potential for tragedy, they have more freedom to shape themselves and their fates than their male counterparts. In order to restore the ideal of patriarchal succession from its fallen condition, the daughter needs to be made to submit to its narrative authority. The daughter needs to learn how to complete the father.

Thus in the final act of *The Fair Penitent*, the rhetoric of "father-sanctity" returns in full force. Despite Calista's many transgressions and the tragic consequences for the state, Sciolto benevolently relents and claims her as his "daughter still" (V.124). At this concession, Calista falls weeping at his feet and, for the first time, confesses herself a "parricide" (V.128). She asks for a "father's pity and forgiveness" (V.139), and though in this initial scene of parting, Sciolto makes no explicit statement of forgiveness, he quits the scene by naming her "my daughter!" (V.147). As if to reinforce and extend the significance of this turnabout in the narrative, Rowe provides us with a second scene of farewell between father and daughter. This second scene follows the news that Sciolto has been wounded in his fight against Lothario's followers and is probably dying. At this, Calista charges herself for the second time as a "parricide" and immediately stabs herself (V.234). Like a son, she finally completes the father by accomplishing what "nature and the father" could not carry out on its own: her death (V.107). Calista's labeling of herself a parricide not once but twice in this final act signals that she has finally accepted the authority of the patriarchal narrative in which she has played such a crucial role. She is a parricide, in effect, not only because Sciolto is killed by Lothario's followers, but also and more significantly so, because she has destroyed the possibility of her father's posterity in subsequent generations.

Given her submission, it is ironic that when Sciolto is brought in and explicitly forgives and blesses Calista in this second scene of farewell, he does so by pronouncing:

Let silence and oblivion hide thy name,
And save thee from the malice of posterity
And may'st thou find with heav'n the same forgiveness
As with thy father here. (V.243–56)

The father's final dispensation is to grant his daughter amnesty from narrative incorporation. The benevolent father as individual is thus allowed the performative gesture of embracing a daughter who has already submitted herself to the narrative authority of patriarchal ideology. Indeed, Calista's narrative has been before us all the while; despite her performance she has ever been subject to the "malice of posterity."

While the daughter is thus sacrificed to restore the father's authority, the play turns to the final business of restoring the posterity of patriarchal succession. With his last breaths of life, Sciolto names Altamont and Horatio as his coheirs and, ensuring his place as patriarch, asks to be buried alongside Altamont's father. Avowing that Altamont "hast been my son," Sciolto implores heaven for the "blessings still in store / For virtue and for filial piety" (V.276–77). Peace and tranquillity are thus restored to the state of Genoa, and though Altamont mourns, a bright horizon of possibility for a new Eden opens up once again on the tragic landscape.

While the ties between private affairs and the state are kept relatively implicit in *The Fair Penitent* and are mediated by a thematic preoccupation with issues of succession, Rowe concerns himself directly in *Jane Shore* with the problems of succession and usurpation in the state and draws an unmistakable connection between private actions and those very public concerns. In the prologue, Rowe explicitly marks this tragedy as an "English" tragedy. He takes his plot from the events surrounding the duke of Gloucester's usurpation of the throne, including his elimination of the sons of the deceased Edward IV and his removal of any potential figures of opposition to his ascendancy as Richard III. In taking this episode as his subject, Rowe positions himself not only to reflect on what was already a well-known tale both in "official" English history and in popular lore but also to make a statement, through a series of implicit and explicit comparisons and analogies, about the current and future state of the nation.[83] Perhaps the most important analogy Rowe draws in this tragedy, however, is one between the governance of the state and the governance of the passions. In this respect, the tragedy is both a moral tale and a political tale that in each case warns against "the fatal rashness of ungoverned love."[84] In the reading below, I will explore how Rowe construes three of the main figures in his tragedy in relation to this "fatal" breach: Jane Shore, the former mistress of Edward IV and now an abject penitent for betraying the vows of marriage; Lord Hastings, a nobleman who potentially has at least some power to block Gloucester; and Matthew Shore, Jane Shore's long-in-exile husband, who, under the name Dumont, returns to redeem his wife. My aim will be to trace how Rowe marks a distinction between an England of a past moment and an England in an eighteenth-century present and to indicate how in each case he holds out the potential for political and moral ascendancy at the same time that he marks the politics of sex as the inevitable cause of a tragic descent into a moral fall.

Jane Shore, of course, is the figure on whom the vast majority of critical attention has been lavished. Just as her pathos repeatedly takes center stage in the tragedy, whether through verbal description or through her physical appearance and speech, so too does it make a central figure in criticism. She is, in Rowe's representation, living proof of "the fatal rashness of ungoverned love." While she may once have lived the good life as the mistress of Edward IV, the Jane Shore we see in Rowe's tragedy is an abject, weeping penitent who, when referring to her husband, wishes only, "That I had lived within his guiltless arms, / And dying slept in innocence beside him!" (I.ii, p. 67). Unlike Calista, Jane Shore is duly penitent. The moral of Jane's tragic descent seems clear, as she herself recounts the cry of the people against her: "Behold the harlot and her end!" (V.i, p. 100).

Significantly, however, while a great deal of critical attention has been devoted to demonstrating how Jane's guilt is mitigated by the lengths to which Rowe goes to elicit audience sympathy, with extended descriptions and repeated representations of her suffering and her self-abnegation, little or no attention has been paid to the fact that her guilt is moderated as well by the dramatically compelling role she plays in a political tale of patriotism.[85] In point of fact, the audience comes to admire Jane not just for her endurance of misery but for her staunch defense of the lives of Edward's doomed boys and the principles of rightful succession and rule. When Gloucester connives to force Jane to use her sexual wiles on Hastings and "make him yield obedience to my will" in the matter of a usurped throne or else to suffer "woe upon thy harlot's head," Jane refuses to "[s]tand by and see [Edward's] children robbed of right." Instead, she defiantly avows:

Let me be branded for the public scorn,
Turned forth, and driven to wander like a vagabond,
Be friendless and forsaken, seek my bread

Upon the barren, wild and desolate waters,
Feed on my sighs, and drink my falling tears;
Ere I consent to teach my lips injustice,
Or wrong the orphan, who has none to save him (IV.i, pp. 87–88)

In a scene that is at least as powerful and compelling as those that feature Jane at the height of an emotive pathos, the political stakes of the drama are made crystal clear. One is either a patriot who defends the principles of right rule or one is a sycophant to tyranny, willing to sacrifice the interests of the country to "bring yourself advantage" (IV.i, p. 86). Jane Shore proves herself a patriot in this instance, and we come to see her fate as determined not only by her loss of virtue but also by her fierce stand against political injustice and the usurpation of right rule.

Yet here the sexual politics begin to complicate the politics, and the moral of our political tale becomes less transparent. For while Jane may stand against one form of usurpation, she has, as Alicia points out, already accomplished a usurpation of another kind. Recalling the days before the death of Edward IV, Alicia numbers Jane among those women who

delight in empire,
Whose beauty is our sovereign good, and gives us
Our reasons to rebel, and power to reign.
What could we more than to behold a monarch,
Lovely, renowned, a conqueror, and young,
Bound in our chains, and sighing at our feet (I.ii, p. 67)

Through this image, we are reminded early on in the tragedy that while Jane may reject these ways now, in the past she exercised a kind of sovereignty that was disruptive to right rule. With her "beauty" she had conquered the conqueror; a monarch had been made into a slave to sexual passions. Hence, while Rowe carefully hedges the question of whether Jane was an active or a passive agent in a monarch's enthrallment, the text nevertheless points to female beauty as the cause of a kind of usurpation of the natural order of things. Once unleashed, moreover, the "fatal rashness of ungoverned love" has more than merely personal repercussions. The consequences of Jane's "fatal beauty" (IV.i, p. 93) and her compromised patriotism extend beyond her personal suffering and shame to endanger the very posterity of the political state.

These consequences become more clear when we examine the role of Lord Hastings. While our view of the political stakes in this drama may have been obscured by the pathos of Jane Shore, when we turn to Hastings it becomes abundantly clear that the fate of the state hangs in the balance throughout this tragedy. Indeed, the play opens not with a view or speech of Jane Shore, but rather with Gloucester and his cronies as they plot to take over the "sceptre and the golden wreath" of the throne of England (I.i, p. 63). Significantly, they express concern over Hastings as one who is "amongst the foremost in his power" and may be able to thwart their plot (I.i, p. 63). He is acknowledged a man of great patriotic spirit with a "religious reverence / To his dead master Edward's royal memory" (I.i, p. 64). These qualities would appear to give us hope that Hastings may act as an obstacle to Gloucester's plan. Yet we soon discover what from historical accounts we might already know, which is that he also has an Achilles heel of a sort that we have seen in other tragedies, a weakness that the ma-chiavellian Gloucester will be only too happy to exploit. He is, as Gloucester puts it, "governed by a dainty-fingered girl / . . . / A laughing, toying, wheedling, whimpering she, / Shall make him amble on a gossip's message, / And take the distaff" (I.i, p. 64). Although Gloucester initially mistakes the "she" on whose word Hastings waits (he has grown tired of his mistress Alicia and is now enam-ored of Jane Shore), the implications of his observations are clear. Confirming the popular prejudice that concupiscence effeminates a man or depletes his mas-culine essence, Gloucester estimates that Hastings will be easily disarmed be-cause he is unmanned. In the very first scene of the tragedy, then, we discover that Hastings is politically vulnerable because he has given into the "fatal rashness of ungoverned love." We know, too, that the fate of the nation will hang through-out the tragedy on the management and manipulation of Hastings's lustful heart.

In a tense exchange between Gloucester and Hastings in Act III, the high stakes in this struggle were brought home to an eighteenth-century English au-dience that was still haunted by the traumas of civil war and the cruel memory of bloodshed in the land. Gloucester, cool and calculating, attempts to draw the guileless Hastings out in order to better assess his potential enemy's commitments. In the hope of gaining Hastings's support in altering the line of succession, Gloucester insinuates that others, not himself, have raised the question of whether England can ever be secure from civil unrest "when the crown sits upon a baby's brow" (III.i, p. 81). Although Hastings fails to recognize the manipulating agent in Gloucester's repeated thrusts, he at least apprehends the ominous portent they represent. Pulling up in alarm, he holds forth in a manner that recalls in sentiment, if not in eloquence, John of Gaunt's prescient prognostications of civil strife in Shakespeare's *Richard II*:

Have we so soon forgot those days of ruin,
When York and Lancaster drew forth the battles;
. . . .
Our groaning country bled at every vein,
When murders, rapes, and massacres prevailed;

When churches, palaces, and cities blazed;
When insolence and barbarism triumphed,
And swept away distinction; peasants trod
Upon the necks of nobles; low were laid
The reverend crosier and the holy mitre,
And desolation covered all the land:
Who can remember this, and not, like me,
Here vow to sheathe a dagger in his heart,
Whose damn'd ambition would renew those horrors,
And set, once more, that scene of blood before us? (III.i, pp. 82–83)

In this stirring speech, Hastings gives full vent to his patriotic feelings and draws a vividly bleak portrait of the devastation of civil war. He describes a world in which what was then understood as the natural order of things was turned upside-down, with the "distinction" of rank "swept away." Gloucester's treachery in wanting to reopen these wounds and pursue his "damn'd ambition" looms large in this scene, and Hastings's fierce patriotism proves itself admirable. In this moment of theatrical suspension, he appears as a figure worthy of emulation.

Yet this moment of suspension cannot last; Hastings's sexual politics undermine his politics, as was the case for Jane Shore. Indeed, the audience already knows that Hastings has fatally compromised that honor of which he speaks so passionately in this scene because though he condemns the violence of rape in his harangue, he himself attempted to rape Jane Shore in the previous act and was stopped only by the intervention of her servant Dumont, her husband in disguise. Hastings enters the scene with Gloucester distracted by thoughts of Jane Shore, muttering to himself about how he "must possess her" (III.i, p. 81). As one contemporary reviewer of Rowe's play observed of Hastings, "His plainness and unwary Conduct betray him to the Arts of the Protector, and his passionate Love helps one of his Mistresses to destroy him. His natural Temper, warm and sanguine, breaks out on all Occasions, and over-rules him both in his Politicks and his Love, as is plain by the Scene between him and the Protector."[86] Hence, while Hastings might vow at the end of this scene that "Beyond or love's or friendship's sacred band, / Beyond myself, I prize my native land; / . . . / Think England's peace bought cheaply with my blood, / And die with pleasure for my country's good" (III.i, p. 84), we know that he has fatally compromised his ability to serve his "country's good."

In an ironic but telling turn of events, then, we find that Gloucester, the villain of the tragedy, is best equipped not only to grasp the peril Hastings has put himself in and to exploit that weakness, but also to articulate the moral of this political tale. Having assessed Hastings's loyalties and having received an anonymous letter from the jealous Alicia, which falsely alleges that Hastings would be for Gloucester if his heart were not mislead by "Shore's bewitching wife" (III.i, p. 80), Gloucester forms a plan to remove his opposition. Gloucester clearly understands the advantage he holds over Hastings once he discovers his weakness for Jane Shore. As he muses:

How poor a thing is he, how worthy scorn,
Who leaves the guidance of imperial manhood
To such a paltry piece of stuff as this is!
. . . .
Now shame upon it! Was our reason given
For such a use? To be thus puffed about
Like a dry leaf, an idle straw, a feather,
The sport of every whistling blast that blows?
Beshrew my heart, but it is wondrous strange;
Sure there is something more than witchcraft in them,
That masters even the wisest of us all. (IV.i, p. 85)

No matter how contrived or cynical this misogynist assessment may appear to a modern eye, Gloucester's assessment—that women are dangerous to men because they have bewitching powers that drain men of strength and reason—provides the moral for this political tragedy.[87] Hastings falls in this tragedy because he allows the attractions of a "puling, whining harlot [to rule] his reason" (IV.i, p. 84). He allows himself to be made into a conquest, losing an empire in himself, that is, his "imperial manhood," and thus effeminized creates an opening for Gloucester to exploit. Tyranny and usurpation appear to triumph because of the "fatal rashness of ungoverned love."[88]

So far *Jane Shore* appears to read as a subtle variation on the themes we have already seen in *The Fair Penitent*. Yet there is still one important figure, Dumont/Shore, whose role in the tragedy we have yet to take into account and whose significance we ought not to underestimate. For while Rowe could refer to, and to some extent was constrained by, both official and popular histories in developing the characters and motives of Jane Shore and Lord Hastings, very little was known about Matthew Shore and Rowe was thus free to construe this character to suit his own ends.[89] If we are to apprehend what those ends might be, we ought to consider the significance of at least two major circumstances in Rowe's tragedy. First, while the tragedy takes as its subject Gloucester's unlawful and ambitious pursuit of the crown, our understanding of that tragic event and the characters who figure in it is shaped largely by Shore's perspective. Second, while "there is no evidence that [Jane and Matthew Shore] ever met again," Rowe followed Thomas Heywood's lead in providing his audience with a "sentimental reunion" of the estranged couple.[90] Let us then consider the following questions in turn:

What perspective on English history does Rowe offer us through the figure of Matthew Shore? And why, in this tragedy, does he offer us the glimmer of a comic ending?

While in his time the real Shore could do nothing to alter the political landscape, as a character in Rowe's tragedy he is able to shape the ways the audience understands those events. Indeed, Rowe positions Shore as a privileged observer throughout the play. His return in the guise of Dumont justifies an exposition of the circumstances of Jane Shore's fall from favor. His anguish as an abandoned husband provides the occasion for a recollection of the duress she suffered in being forced to leave him. His disguise as a servant to Jane Shore explains his constant attention to and description of her misery and her penitence.[91] In sum, Matthew Shore presents a view on the events that reflects eighteenth-century moral and political values; he offers the audience the ideals of both a modern sense of right and a model of masculinity that stresses the governance of the passions.

This modern sense of right emerges during Matthew Shore's fight with Hastings following the latter's attempted rape of Jane Shore. Hastings becomes enraged that a "base groom," who ought to know his "office better," would dare to attack or challenge him. Against this claim of rank, Shore urges "[t]he common ties of manhood" that "bid me thus stand up in the defence / Of an oppressed, unhappy, helpless woman" (II.i, p. 76). He berates Hastings for "stain[ing]" the honour that had been his solely by the advantage of birth and for "blot[ting] a long illustrious line of ancestry" with such "unmanly . . . violence." When Hastings persists in threatening Jane Shore and assailing her character, Matthew Shore holds forth, warning:

I have as daring spirits in my blood
As thou, or any of thy race e'er boasted;
And though no gaudy titles graced my birth,
Titles, the servile courtier's lean reward,
Sometimes the pay of virtue, but more oft
The hire which greatness gives to slaves and sycophants,
Yet Heaven that made me honest, made me more
Than ever king did, when he made a lord. (II.i, p. 76)

At this "insolence," Hastings draws and strikes Shore. But the master is mastered here. Shore disarms and defeats Hastings and, in yielding him his life, nobly instructs, "know, a lord / Opposed against a man is but a man" (II.i, pp. 76–77).

Staged as a scene of class struggle, with almost every line laden with notice of the claims of rank, the contest between Hastings and Matthew Shore takes on a wider significance. Shore assails systems of patronage that are more likely to benefit the flattery of "slaves and sycophants" than honesty and worth. In effect, he performs a kind of class leveling that promotes a modern sense of right and justice based not on rank, status, or birth but on the virtue, merit, and good sense of individual men. Shore thus articulates ideals that were held not in fifteenth-century England but rather in post-1688 England, where the monarchy was no longer "divine," potentially tyrannical powers had been abrogated, and the commonwealth of men was devoted to liberty, not blind loyalty. In this new England, as Rowe would have it, the equality of men serves not as an emblem of a world upside-down, as in Hastings's visions of civil war, but rather as an emblem of hope for domestic tranquillity and peace in the state.[92]

Hence it follows that Matthew Shore punctuates his momentary defeat of Hastings with an invitation to Jane Shore to abandon this scene of strife and retreat to an idyllic setting. He urges her to "Fly from the Court's pernicious neighborhood; / Where innocence is shamed" and to come to "a little peaceful refuge / Far from the Court and the tumultuous city. / Within an ancient forest's ample verge." Characterizing the realm of the court as a fallen world, where innocence is no more, Matthew Shore, still in the guise of Dumont, offers Jane a new Eden:

> . . . a healthful dwelling,
> Built for convenience, and the use of life:
> Around it fallows, meads, and pastures fair,
> A little garden, and a limpid brook
> . . . .
> No faction, or domestic fury's rage,
> Did e'er disturb the quiet of that place. (II.i, p. 77)

Matthew Shore holds out a place of new possibilities to Jane, a place that hasn't been marked by the passions and ambitions of men. Here the term "domestic" has at least two connotations, referring both to the state or nation and to the individual "healthful dwelling" or household, as the private emblem of the public state. In this home there is no "fury," no "contention"; there is only peace and quiet. Matthew Shore thus emerges in Rowe's tragedy as a representative of an emerging middle-class ideology and the domestic ideals promoted by that ideology. As we are subsequently made to understand, the model of conduct that will reign in this new domestic Eden is one marked not by tyranny and passion, but rather by mercy and compassion.

We discover, and are instructed in, this new ethos when Bellmour tests both Matthew Shore's resolve to reveal himself to his wife and his ability, in doing so, to govern his passions. Bellmour begins his inquiry:

Have you examined
Into your inmost heart, and tried at leisure
The several secret springs that move the passions?
Has mercy fixed her empire there so sure,
That wrath and vengeance never may return?
Can you resume a husband's name, and bid
That wakeful dragon, fierce resentment, sleep? (V.i, p. 95)

At first, Shore is resentful and responds by asking Bellmour why he would bring up such things. But Bellmour's strategy is one of cathartic expedience. His inquiries awaken Shore's passionate resentments, his pride, and his jealousies, all of which he had "long laboured to forget" (V.i, p. 95). Yet unlike Alicia, who is driven to madness by her jealousies, Shore, guided by Bellmour through a process of remembrance and observation, is able to master his. He recalls how he doted on Jane early in their marriage and comes to see that she suffered as well when Edward IV carried her away. Before our eyes and Matthew Shore's, Bellmour conjures a vision of Jane Shore "possessed" by force, whose "unconsenting heart dwelt still" with her husband. Finally, we are presented with a portrait of Jane's current miserable state, "Hunted to death, distressed on every side." She, too, is a victim of the class tyranny, and realizing this, Matthew Shore is gradually moved from jealousy and resentment to pity and compassion, exclaiming, "Hence with her past offences, / They are atoned at full" (V.i, p. 96)

Matthew Shore's middle-class sentiments and his compassion are thus set in stark contrast to the sexual tyranny exercised by both Lord Hastings and Edward IV. With his passions guided by reason and his "[governed] love," he comes to represent a new masculine ideal of restraint. On this basis, moreover, Rowe grants us a moment of relief amid the despairing inevitability of tragedy. Shore, now revealed, beckons to Jane and implores:

Cast every black and guilty thought behind thee,
And let 'em never vex thy quiet more.
My arms, my heart are open to receive thee,
To bring thee back to thy forsaken home,
With tender joy, with fond forgiving love,
And all the longings of my first desires. (V.i, p. 101)

Here Shore sounds as much like an adoring suitor as a forgiving husband. In this moment, we are tempted by the possibility of the kind of ending seen in a comedy, as the horizon of romantic love opens out into an imagined scene of domestic tranquillity restored.[93]

This vision of a domestic idyll is the ideal that Rowe finally offers us in this tragedy. Although it cannot be sustained in the fallen world of fifteenth-century England, where "charity [has] grown treason," Rowe intimates through this moment that this ideal might be sustained in an eighteenth-century world in which merit outweighs rank, a husband's authority is restored, and the bonds of marriage are honored. Distinguished, then, both by his modern sense of right and by his capacity for mastering, rather than abandoning himself to, the passions, Matthew Shore emerges as the hero, that is, as the new male exemplar in a bourgeois tragedy. The tragedy of a state brought down by the distractions of a faithless woman becomes emblematized in the domestic tragedy of a husband brought low by a faithless wife. The fate of the nation becomes beholden to the fate of the domestic couple. Indeed, by the end of *Jane Shore*, Gloucester's ambition has faded into the background as all emotional energies become concentrated on the tragedy of a goldsmith and his estranged wife. At the same time, the pathos of Jane Shore is subsumed by the pathos of the domestic couple. Finally, when Bellmour peers out to deliver the closing moral on "[w]hat fate attends the broken marriage-vow," he addresses an eighteenth-century audience that represents the "children in succeeding times" to which he refers. Perhaps in this new age of liberty, that is, in the age of the rise of the middling classes, they might learn from the example of England's past. By containing female passions within the bonds of marriage, moreover, they might avoid the "[un]common vengeance" of civil war and enjoy the fruits of an Edenic posterity (V.i, p. 104)

Rowe's *The Fair Penitent* and *Jane Shore* thus illustrate that she-tragedy too was dedicated to, and informed by, the project of nation building and represented male agents and masculine virtue as the keys to ensuring the future and posterity of the nation. To this end, the pathetic displays that characterize the genre served at one and the same time not only to rouse audience sympathy but also to underline the tragic consequences of female interference in state affairs and matters of governance. Hence, while it is significant that in the later tragedy Rowe ties the future of the nation to the emergence of a hero from the middling classes, it is perhaps even more telling that in both plays the future and posterity of that state could be put in jeopardy only when the male heroes, noble or middling, were handicapped by female agents or feminine passions.

Tragedy's Future

In his article "The Failure of Eighteenth-Century Tragedy," Eugene Hnatko complains: "Against the fascinating backdrop of Richard's drive for the crown, of political intrigue, of grand ambition and grand villainy, to point to infidelity and seduction as the follies or vices meriting punishment by death seems woefully inadequate and short-sighted." As the readings above suggest, however, it is Hnatko who fails to apprehend just how "far-sighted" Rowe and the other authors discussed in this chapter were in their estimation of tragedy and its role in eighteenth-century culture. While Hnatko argues that Rowe's turn to "the 'passions' involved in sexual misbehavior" constituted "an oversimplification of morality, . . . [that] is inadequate for tragedy, where the audience looks for cosmic questioning," we find Rowe and these other authors engaged in attempts to move the genre forward to meet the representational needs of their period.[94] In short, they departed from the genre's past role as a medium for posing either ontological or universal questions and positioned the genre pragmatically to confront the social and economic transformations of English culture. Their plays took up the challenge of finding ways to represent the new middling classes as moral agents in the public sphere. Abiding by the imperatives of the form in theory, they sought in practice to represent the interests of this new class as inseparable from those of the nation.

As the example of *Jane Shore* intimates, the fate of the heroic homosocial would gradually be displaced over the course of the latter part of the century by that of the middling domestic couple as the focus of tragic pathos and tragic ideals. Significantly, however, this shift would only sharpen the divisions between public and private spheres that were already incipient in the earlier dramas. Hence, while female characters would begin to figure more prominently in plots as wives and mothers, they would also continue to be regulated by the bias of the form against female agency. Women and female passions would continue to be cast as dangerous forces, indeed as the very causes of tragic error. And female characters would continue to be proscribed from, or at the very least, somehow marginalized in tragic representations in order better and more efficiently to produce and preserve the authority of male characters as virtuous agents in the public sphere, the nation, and the emerging empire.

Chapter Four

Constituting Parodies of Identity
Manners, Humours, and
Intrigue on the Comic Stage

In this chapter, I turn to comedy as the genre most intimately associated with the representation of social relations. In contrast to tragedy, which, as demonstrated in the previous chapter, works toward the articulation of public virtue through the suppression of the private, we will see that eighteenth-century comedy works to investigate and expose the private social relations that made public life possible. Indeed, where eighteenth-century tragedies either pass over or subordinate the family to the imagined communities they project and publicize, we will see that comedies represent both the private negotiations among individuals and the public conditions that govern and naturalize those negotiations.

Before we proceed with the particulars of these arguments, however, it is important to note that comedy was called upon to carry out this kind of cultural work during a time of considerable change both in the social order reflected in the drama and in the very nature of comedy and its generic distinctions. In 1698, Jeremy Collier had launched his infamous attack on the theater, *A Short View of the Immorality and Profaneness of the English Stage*. Directed primarily against the "lewdness" and "debauchery" of the heated sex comedies that had commanded the stage in the Restoration period, this tract and the pamphlet exchanges that followed cast a sharp pall over the pursuits of comedy.[1] Significantly, moreover, this decidedly moral turn against the comic stage was not an isolated event. Rather, as Robert D. Hume has pointed out, a change in attitude toward the comic stage had been afoot since the early 1690s. Collier's voice was only one among many to call for a reform not only of "lewd" stage representations but also of the prevalent attitude of harsh cynicism that had held the comic stage in thrall for so long.[2]

This moral turn had at least two effects on comic representation: first, a new comedic genre, sentimental comedy, emerged; and second, a kind of laughter developed in the laughing strain that was not so much satirical and cynical as it was amiable and skeptical.[3] At least in part, this split in comedy between the "laughing" and the "sentimental" kind was an artificial one, a division historically sustained at least as much by rhetoric and personal interest as by substance.[4] The spirit of laughter never abandoned the stage to sentimentality in the ways that Oliver Goldsmith might have us believe, and elements of laughter and sentiment mingled freely in plays in ways that often prevented sharp distinctions from being drawn.[5] Nevertheless, the fact remains that two distinct strains in comedy did emerge in this period, enough so to be taken up and reflected upon by eighteenth-century playwrights, critics, and theorists. And in this, the first of two chapters to discuss comedies, I focus on those of the laughing kind—the comedies of manners, humours, and intrigue—in order to explore what happened to comedy and to comic character when "Success in . . . Debauchery" no longer constituted the primary impetus of plot structures.[6]

With respect to this transformation in the laughing strain, a number of useful and insightful observations have been offered. Shirley Strum Kenny has gone so far as to classify this much overlooked body of comic works as "humane comedy," a comedy in which good nature prevails and characterization and action take precedent over displays of wit and cruelty.[7] Robert Hume has also adopted this appellation and in extending Kenny's account points to the "increasing predominance of intrigue" as the engine of action in these comedies. Indeed, he goes so far as to argue that "Where once sex, cuckoldry, the love game, satire on cits and fops, social display, humours, and conversation occupied a major place, now authors rel[ied] on plot for plot's sake"[8] Significantly, however, neither Kenny nor Hume situates these changes in the context of broader historical change. In other words, they fail to note that what is significant about the timing of this shift in tone is that it also intersected with a series of fundamental transformations in the political, economic, and financial orientation of English culture. Indeed, the 1690s were marked not only by the transition to the Whiggish reign of William and Mary, but also by the establishment of laws and institutions of finance that would provide the basis for England's rise as a center of capital, commerce, and trade. In this light, what is striking about a play such as George Farquhar's *The Twin Rivals* (1702/1703), a play specifically written to appease those like Collier, is not just that it represents a direct response to such diatribes, but that, as John Bull writes, it suggests the "ways in which Farquhar was moving comedy away from the world of the privileged and leisured classes, and somewhat nearer the day-to-day concerns of the newer, civic members of the audience."[9] In short, as was the case with eighteenth-century tragedy, comedy too left behind the preoccupations with Stuart authority and aristocratic privilege that had so consumed the Restoration stage and turned instead toward the work of socializing the newly mobile middling classes for their role in an emerging public order.[10]

The moral turn, then, may not be the only reason for the shift in tone in comedy, and the turn to intrigue may not just have been, as Robert Hume would hold, an "end in itself."[11] Rather, as I will argue in the readings below, the turn to intrigue constituted a means by which comedy could carry out a process of negotiation, valuation, and exchange among its characters that mirrored the changes in the social and economic circumstances of the culture at large. In this respect, the genre of manners, humours, and intrigue could reflect upon and participate in the kinds of "structural transformations" of the public and private spheres that Jürgen Habermas has so elegantly described. For while these plays focused their attention on the articulation of the relations that composed the private sphere, or that "interior domain" known as the family, they could also demonstrate how those private persons engaged in the forms of "commodity exchange" and "social labor" that sustained the public sphere.[12] In short, as the discussion and readings below will demonstrate, the shift to humane comedy can be viewed not just as the moment when "Lewdness" was abandoned as the source of "Diversion" on the comic stage, but also, and more significantly so, as the moment when the "diversion" became a display of the social labor necessary to bring about a comic ending of marital exchange.[13]

The Contours of Comedy

Before we can begin to trace the specific forms of social labor and commodity exchange that mark the intrigues of eighteenth-century comedies, we ought first to have a better sense of the general contours and concerns that regulated the genre in this period and the impact of these contours on the representation of character. For many theorists in the eighteenth century the main issue at hand when considering comedy was how to direct it toward making the audience "fitter for society."[14] In the majority of cases, they alighted on the drawing of character as the main instrument in this socialization process, and it is in the articulation of this principle of representation that we can begin to detect the tensions that regulate comic meaning on the eighteenth-century stage.

John Dennis argued, for instance, that while "Tragedy answers to History-Painting . . . Comedy [does so] to drawing Portraits."[15] To fill out this claim, he first insists that the characters set before the audience ought to be "allegorical and universal one[s]," if they are to yield a moral (2:247). Yet only a page or so later, he asserts that the "Business of a Comick Poet . . . must be with the reigning

Follies and Vices. . . . The Comick Poet therefore must take Characters from such Persons as are his Contemporaries, and are infected with the foresaid Follies and Vices." Extending the comparison between comedy and tragedy, he contends, "The violent Passions, which are the Subjects of Tragedy, are the same in every Age, and appear with the same Face; but those Vices and Follies, which are the Subjects of Comedy, are seen to vary continually" (2:248). Dennis thus describes two separate, though not necessarily mutually exclusive, criteria in the drawing of comic characters—one general and one particular. On the one hand, he supports the creation of a representation that will have coherence over time. On the other hand, he advocates the creation of portraits that are discrete and timely. In this manner, Dennis unwittingly provides us with our first intimation that the laughter of eighteenth-century comedy arises not from the degree of stability or coherence in the drawing of characters, but rather from the irregular oscillation between the general and the particular. That is, his description raises the possibility that comedy does not inhere in the type, but rather, as anticipated in Chapter 1, in the deviations from the type and in the dialectical process of attempting to reconcile the incongruities between general types and particular manifestations.

In a related fashion, we could say that this tension between the general and the particular with respect to character finds a working analog at the level of plot. Comedies, we know, are supposed to end in marriage; and in the case of eighteenth-century comedy, they often conclude with the promise of not just one, but multiple marriages. In a paradoxical sense, then, each comedy generates its own momentum at the same time that it actualizes the principle of inertia. For almost from the outset of any comedy, we know how the play will end. We know which couples will come together, and the play thus ends precisely where our apprehension of its plot began—there is almost no movement in our expectations from beginning to end.

As a consequence the play must offer a series of imaginative contrivances to capture the interest of the audience, to gain credit as it were, even as it brings the two individuals together to form what constitutes an already overdetermined union. This series of devices or intrigues displaces a sense of stasis and provisionally replaces it with what appear to be dynamic transformations of the plot. Designed to create the illusion that the union is somehow in doubt, these diversions precipitate what can be termed the point of crisis in eighteenth-century comedy. A more dramatic, complicated contrivance must then be generated to bring about the resolution of this crisis and to reaffirm our initial conceit that the union was at all times logically inevitable.

Yet by the time we reach this formal resolution, the problem of comedy's meaning has already begun to arise. The marriages with which the plays conclude appear more as dissonant contrivances deployed to fulfill generic demands than as the natural outcome of the represented events. Indeed, marriage appears incongruous and almost beside the point—a view dramatized, as in Gay's *The What D'Ye Call It?* by the fact that with few exceptions in eighteenth-century comedy we either never see the marriage ceremony performed or are asked to imagine that the marriage will take place at some indeterminate time in the near future, beyond the bounds of the representation. The "logical" conclusion thus fails to ensure a sense that the union will be entirely satisfactory, precisely because the particularities of the contrivances generate more seams or gaps in character motivation than they do explanations of it. In short, our conceit may be substantiated in form, but it is not satisfied by the content. We are caught between taking pleasure from the intervening events with the assurance that we know how the play will end and the disturbing final knowledge that the ending itself hardly coincides with the events we have witnessed. Hence, while we may be willing to suspend disbelief and take pleasure from the scenes of the comedy, the concluding events test our willingness to believe and make that act of suspension visible precisely as an act of willfulness.

This pattern follows from the privilege that Froma Zeitlin has identified as so particular to comedy, that of "exposing those parts and functions of the body which decorum keeps hidden."[16] For eighteenth-century comedy, what this meant is that where tragedy worked to conceal its fictions and plays about plays exuberantly exploded the conventions of theatrical representation, comedy exposed them just enough to make us aware of our own complicity in maintaining the "decorum" or integrity of the representation. The predictable ending of comedy thus constitutes, at one and the same time, both the affirmation and the parody of the form.

Returning full circle to where this discussion began, we find that this unsettling consequence of comedic plotting has a reciprocal impact upon the not-unrelated project of elaborating character, that is, on the bodies that are assembled through the process of the comedy. For when we speak of plot motivation, we need to understand that each ingenious contrivance requires the assignment of certain forms of motive, agency, gesture, and language to particular characters. This necessity is complicated by the fact that the motives ascribed to a character for the sake of carrying out a stratagem often seem out of character in terms of the type we are given to understand as ultimately definitive once the formal union has been announced. While our laughter may be motivated throughout the representation by a continual stream of dramatic ironies—the incongruities between what we take to be our knowledge of the characters and what the characters appear to know of each other—the final moments force us to question and reorganize our own assignments of value and motive to the characters. Hence, just as the plot plays upon our conceit that we know how it will all end, the drawing of characters plays upon our conceit that, as the omniscient monitors of actions and words, we "know" the characters. The discrete knowledges we have derived from each gesture, word, and action conflict not only with each other, but with the type with which they are supposed to form an identity. And our inability to reconcile the parts with the whole motivates an ambivalent form of laughter as we experience the discomfort of willfully sustaining the tension between what we know we are supposed to believe and what we think we know. Indeed, our laughter is uneasy at the realization that the only clear knowledge that has been produced by the end of the comedy is that we have lost the ability to discriminate the provisional from the permanent realities of the representation; that is, we cannot necessarily distinguish the parody from the mimetic real. In short, as the readings below will illustrate, what eighteenth-century comedies revealed to their audiences was that character itself was no more and no less than a constitutional parody of identity—performances of historically situated identities that mimic and mark the provisional contours of their counterparts in everyday life.

As we trace these "constitutional parodies" through a series of comedies, it will be important to keep in mind that marriage is not merely a romantic institution but also a social one. Indeed, it could be said that comedies and characters oscillate about a baseline called marriage, where marriage, as a social institution, is itself embedded in and regulated by a series of economic ideologies. Saturated by linguistic exchanges that rely heavily on socioeconomic metaphors, eighteenth-century comedies conspicuously advertise the active role they play, that is, the social labor they perform, in articulating the mutually constitutive relationships both within and between the public and private spheres. In particular, they consistently make visible the class and gender interests that govern negotiations in what otherwise appear to be the strictly disengaged spheres of love and matrimony. In this manner, as I have already suggested above, the contrivances that shape the plot of comedy also administer a process of character valuation whereby the economic and social status of each character come to be identified and the couple's interests aligned and secured. On the one hand, then, this process appears to ensure parity in the pairings with which the comedy concludes. On the other hand, it reflects ironically on the ideal of romantic love by dramatizing the social labor required to produce that appearance of motivated disinterest. The incongruities that emerge at the level of plot in comedy must thus be considered as a function of a complex dialectic between the general rhetoric of comedy and the particularities of the socioeconomic conditions reflected within comedy. In short, as Hume and Judith Milhous suggest in a case study of Farquhar's *The Beaux' Stratagem*, the issue that emerges when considering comedy in this period is how "determined" the members of the audience must be "to take the happy ending straight," that is, to read it as an ending without irony.[17] In our examination of the plays below, we will have to consider whether part of our discomfort at the end of each comedy arises out of our recognition of the paradoxical disjunction between the general celebration of marriage, in which its status as a social institution is suppressed, and our particular knowledge of the social and economic contingencies that have been negotiated to situate those marriages as viable dramatic options. We will have to consider how far exposed is the very institution to which we are supposed to look for final assurances in our attribution of character identities.[18]

In the pages that follow, I will trace the impact that these socioeconomic concerns had on the intricate process of articulating plot and character in eighteenth-century comedy, first in a series of two paired readings: Susanna Centlivre's *A Bold Stroke for a Wife* (1717/1718) with Hannah Cowley's *A Bold Stroke for a Husband* (1782/1783), and George Farquhar's *The Beaux' Stratagem* (1706/1707) with Hannah Cowley's *The Belle's Stratagem* (1779/1780); and second in a concluding reading of Richard Brinsley Sheridan's *The Rivals* (1774/1775).[19] Insofar as each pairing involves one play from the beginning and one from the end of the century, I will use the pairings to demonstrate how a more complex understanding of character—its contradictions, mutabilities, and cultural embeddedness—came to be reflected in comedy over the course of the period.

Bold Strokes

In the case of Centlivre's *A Bold Stroke for a Wife* and Cowley's *A Bold Stroke for a Husband*, the tension between social economics and romance is signaled immediately by the titular use of the pivotal term "for" to introduce the plots of the plays. "For" can indicate an object, aim, or purpose of action, a desired object that an individual wishes to obtain. At the same time, it may also point to an action taken by one party to benefit another, that is, "for the sake of" some other person. Finally, it can indicate a relation of equivalence in which, for example, a service rendered is assigned a barter or a monetary exchange value.[20] While this brief enumeration does not exhaust the term "for," it does collate those meanings that are most relevant to these particular comedies and to the thematics of eighteenth-century comedy more generally. The first instance of the term invokes a rhetoric of desire and possession that finds resonance in a narrative of economic interest; the second cultivates an image of the kind of selfless or even disinterested action most often associated with romance narratives. The types of narrative initiated through the titular use of this pivotal term thus appear to be diametrically opposed. Yet if we bring the third meaning into play, we find that it offers us a way not only to describe the relationship between the two narratives but also, as anticipated in the overview of the genre's mechanics, to apprehend the source of comedy in the representations. For insofar as this last meaning indicates a relationship of equivalence, we can begin to understand both of the comedies as a series of structured contrivances through which the primary agent ostensibly gains value and thus the character of worthiness with respect to the desired romantic object.

In *A Wife* and *A Husband* respectively, Centlivre and Cowley both deploy at least one narrative in which either a potential or a wayward spouse is figured as imperiled so that it would appear the primary agent must act on his or her behalf. Yet it is precisely the imperiled status of the object that offers the agent an opportunity both to further his or her interests and gain or regain title to the desired object. As the comedies progress with the two general narratives competing in constant tension with one another, the particularities of the contrivances, devices, and ploys offer the means to negotiate a relationship of equivalence, to close the gap between romance and economic interest. Yet the critical question we must ask as the comedies progress and finally draw to a conclusion is whether that gap is ever satisfactorily closed. Do the "bold strokes" taken in these comedies to demonstrate a character's merit actually accord with the final identity under which that central character's worthiness is ultimately pronounced? Have the various debits and credits of character been brought into balance, or has the accounting merely been fudged for comedy's sake?

Performed for the first time on February 3, 1718, at Lincoln's Inn Fields, Susanna Centlivre's *A Bold Stroke for a Wife* features Ann Lovely, a young woman under the care of four male guardians without each of whose written consent she may not marry. Conceived as a variation on the comedy of humours, the four guardians are Sir Philip Modelove, Periwinkle, Tradelove, and Obadiah Prim, characters drawn by Centlivre from popular eighteenth-century satires and sketches of beaux, virtuosos, tradesmen, and Quakers, who in turn represent foppery, folly, avarice, and hypocrisy.[21] Noted for the metaphor of humours that unites this intrigue plot, Centlivre's play has also been praised as a kind of fairy-tale romance in which the male protagonist, Colonel Fainwell, cycles through a complicated series of individually tailored contrivances to win the consent of guardians who appear constitutionally predisposed to disagree with one another.[22] Yet to call this a fairy-tale romance is only to confirm what, as I have already indicated in the introductory portions of this chapter, we already know from the outset: Fainwell and Ann Lovely will emerge from the comedy on the threshold of marriage. Further, such a simplistic characterization occludes what is of interest to us here, that is, the kinds of social labor and commodity exchange that must occur in the drama to bring it to this point of comedic closure. In particular, it obscures the fact that the main conflict in the drama does not consist in the hero's wooing of his beloved, that is, in heterosexual romance, but rather in successive contests of wit between men, that is, in the forms of homosocial labor and exchange that underwrite heterosexual romance. Fainwell's love for Ann Lovely does not occupy the focal point of this narrative. Rather, Fainwell, the man who "feigns well" to outwit or to gain the advantage over other men, occupies the center of the drama.[23] The plot follows Fainwell as he seduces each of Mrs. Lovely's four male guardians by appealing to their particular humours and thereby gains their contractual consent to possess Mrs. Lovely as his wife. In this respect, Centlivre's comedy could be said to provide a sharp illustration of what Eve Sedgwick has identified as homosocial desire and commerce passing under the sign of heterosexual narrative.[24] Indeed, to the extent that Mrs. Lovely remains a disengaged party in those transactions, this reading will show how her body serves as a conduit for the consummation of bonds between men.[25] More specifically, it will explore and delineate the complicated dynamic whereby the fairy tale of a hero coming to the aid of a damsel in distress operates as the ideal, rhetorical discourse of affection under which Fainwell implements a master narrative of gaining possession.[26]

An early conversation between Ann Lovely and her servant Betty reveals this dynamic as the mode of operation in the drama:

MRS. LOVELY: He promised to set me free, and I, on that condition, promised to make him master of that freedom.
BETTY: Well, I have read of enchanted castles, ladies delivered from the chains of magic, giants killed, and monsters overcome; so that I shall be the less surprised if the Colonel should conjure you out of the power of your guardians. If he does, I am sure he deserves your fortune. (I.ii.43–50)

Framing the comedy as a fairy tale romance, Betty privileges the masculine quest and clearly marks Fainwell as the active agent and Mrs. Lovely as the passive one. Thus early on in the comedy, Centlivre articulates the necessary conditions of homosocial exchange in which, as Luce Irigaray points out, "The work force is . . . always assumed to be masculine, and 'products' are objects to be used, objects of transaction among men alone" (171). Although Lovely has herself contracted for the marriage with Fainwell, her freedom remains dependent on Fainwell's ability to "work" or to "conjure [her] out of the power of [her] guardians."

Lovely's status in the drama begs the question as to who or what has set the conditions for her apparent powerlessness and consequently her need for Fainwell's heroic "work." Again Betty's remarks prove revealing, for in spite of the play's rhetorical gesture to conceal the discursive relationship between power, possession, and romantic love, her commentary testifies to power's practical continuity with and control over romantic play. Her practical regard for the guardians' proprietary power over Ann Lovely recalls the otherwise displaced, though inescapable, fact that the action is literally dictated, driven, and controlled by the "will" of Lovely's otherwise absent, because deceased, father. His will states first that she may marry only with the express consent of each of her four guardians and second that she may not be removed from their guardianship unless she gets married. Clearly, the misanthropic Mr. Lovely did not want his daughter to marry at all, and he selected the disagreeable guardians described above to guarantee his desire. In this sense, *A Wife* maps the constraints of eighteenth-century marriage law on women; its action is both scripted and circumscribed by the prerogatives of patriarchal power to dictate the terms of a daughter's dispensation. Thus the manner in which Ann Lovely negotiates for her own desire, and the elaborate schemes through which Fainwell satisfies his, provide what Sedgwick terms a "sensitive register precisely for delineating relationships of power and meaning" in the period (27). With marriage as the exclusive option for escape from the stranglehold of her guardians, Ann Lovely could only, like many of Centlivre's other heroines, "negotiate for a better contract and greater individual choice."[27]

Indeed, the stakes and opportunities in these negotiations differ dramatically for Fainwell and Ann Lovely. As Centlivre makes clear, the society within which this play is enacted rewards Fainwell's desire even as it barely, if at all, acknowledges Lovely's. Mrs. Lovely may not be an entirely hapless female protagonist—she does exercise a limited authority in the comedy by having selected Fainwell to gain her freedom—but the fact remains that she cannot enter into a marriage contract because that can only be a contract between men. Moreover, the freedom Lovely negotiates for with Fainwell entails, and even assumes, a subsequent loss of independence. As Fainwell himself anticipates, "Were the lady her own mistress I have some reason to believe I should soon command in chief" (I.i.67–68).

From this perspective and in terms of the discursive economy of the tale more generally, Lovely's act of autonomy in selecting Fainwell could be interpreted ironically as the very act or sign under which the play text conceals a chiasmatic crossover from a narrative of heterosexual affection to a narrative of homosocial possession. That is, Lovely's consent to wed Fainwell, an action that could be read as an assertion of desire, also serves rhetorically as a means both to de-emphasize the influence of patriarchal power on that decision and to justify Fainwell's actions. It is not insignificant, then, that, as in most comedies, her consent has been obtained prior to our entry into the representation. Thus it can never occupy a site of dramatic tension that could betray the grosser claims of a narrative in which the "beloved" functions as a token of exchange.

Indeed, for Fainwell the "production" of Lovely's freedom constitutes the means to a second, though by no means secondary, end. In accordance with eighteenth-century marriage laws, which defined couples as one person commanded by the husband, Fainwell could fully expect his marriage to Lovely to result in the transfer of title to her and her property from her guardians to himself. He reveals this motive when he boasts, "What would not a man attempt for a fine woman and thirty thousand pounds?" (I.i.127–28), a veritable fortune for a soldier who has just received a reduction in pay. As Betty's remarks indicate, the reward for all of Fainwell's work will be not Mrs. Lovely, but rather her fortune. While Fainwell may very well love Mrs. Lovely, his conquest of her guardians promises to result not only in his acquisition of her as his wife, but also in the institutional consolidation of his authority and power over her person, her property, and her fortune. Like the territory fought over and exchanged for peace between men, Ann Lovely to Fainwell is literally "a city *worth* taking" (II.ii.150–52, emphasis added). Thus worthy and "worth" much, her patriarchally conditioned consent secures the narrative as our attention comes to be directed exclusively toward Fainwell's wit and stratagem in what may be aptly construed as a peculiar war of cuckoldry.

Eve Sedgwick has pointed out that cuckoldry involves a struggle between men that is "necessarily hierarchical in structure, with an 'active' participant who is clearly in the ascendancy over the 'passive' one." "Characteristically," she adds, "the difference of power occurs in the form of a difference of knowledge: the cuckold is not even supposed to know that he is in such a relationship" (50). In the "battles" fought over Ann Lovely as possessible territory, Fainwell gains the advantage over each of the four guardians by enlisting allies who can provide him with the most intimate knowledge of his "enemies." Tapping the exclusively male taverns and coffeehouses, which functioned during the eighteenth century as sites both for traffic in material goods and for trade in public and private information, Fainwell enlists Sackbut, a local tavern keeper, and Freeman, a local merchant, to serve as his vital sources of information. Each unabashedly reveals that the remuneration for his labor will be the pleasurable sense of superiority gained from making dupes of other men. Their enthusiasm for exploiting knowledge in order to confound arrogant, but unwitting men informs the mode of operation for Fainwell's concealed, though no less enthusiastic, desire to "overpower" each guardian and force the surrender of title to Ann Lovely as a token of their submission. The concept of "cuckoldry" understood in a figurative, rather than explicitly sexual, sense thus suggests an apt description for the stock trade or economy of information through which Fainwell actively lays siege to, gains the advantage over, and consequently the consent of, the passive, because unknowing, guardians. It suggests an apt form for the kinds of social labor and exchange in which he engages to gain his desired end.

The extent to which such an economy of information operates to transform Mrs. Lovely into a token of exchange and Colonel Fainwell into her new owner becomes most apparent in the schemes engineered to gain the consent of Tradelove and Obadiah Prim. In the first case, Freeman and Fainwell devise a scheme to play on Tradelove's avarice. They provide him with what we might today call false "insider" information—that Spain has laid siege to Cagliari. As doubts are raised on the trading floor about the "truth" of this matter, Freeman reassures Tradelove as to the reliability of his source and prompts him to make the "Dutchman" Jan van Timtamtirelireletta Heer van Fainwell, or Fainwell in disguise, his mark in a wager of £2000 on the actuality of the siege. Believing himself to have gained the upper hand in a play on knowledge, Tradelove gleefully celebrates aside, "I have snapped the Dutchman" (IV.i.105). As soon as Tradelove departs, Fainwell in turn celebrates what he assumes to be his as good as accomplished victory, declaring, "if he would keep his money, he must part with the lady" (IV.ii.4–5).

Using language in a manner that bears a striking resemblance to Tradelove's hardened syntax of exchange, Fainwell's outburst explicitly marks Ann Lovely as potentially convertible property. More significantly, it reflects and articulates the foundational assumptions of a social culture that regards women as secured value in a trade economy. The fact that Fainwell can assume Lovely's potential exchange value as proprietary property secures the success of this particular ruse. Subsequently, when Tradelove finally realizes that he traded in false information and lost, Freeman offers him the option of negotiating with the "Dutchman" for the trade of his bond in exchange for his ward Mrs. Lovely. Where before Mrs. Lovely had represented a potential burden to Tradelove, he now comes to view her, per his legal right, as an unrealized asset upon which he can stake a trade, exclaiming:

Who the devil would be a guardian,
If when cash runs low, our coffers t'enlarge,
We can't like other stocks, transfer our charge? (IV.ii.144–47)

As anticipated by Fainwell, Tradelove literally converts Ann Lovely into an exchange value of £2000 and closes the transaction by giving his consent to Fainwell's marriage with Mrs. Lovely for the return of his bond. Realizing that his consent signifies nothing without the agreement of the three other guardians, Tradelove still believes that he can claim the superior ground of knowledge and sings to himself, "mynheer, ha, ha, we have bit you" (IV.iv.80). What he does not realize is that, like all of the other guardians, he has been mastered or cuckolded out of his consent by Fainwell's informed "masterpiece of contrivance" (IV.iv.83).

Obadiah Prim, the hypocritical Quaker, suffers a similar, unwitting loss of control over the circulation of knowledge in his encounter with the masquerading Fainwell (see Figure 8). Posing this time as Simon Pure, a Quaker friend, Fainwell convinces Prim to give him the opportunity to "convert" the impudent Mrs. Lovely. In so doing, Fainwell aspires to take advantage of Prim's conceit that he can discern the difference between parody and sincere Christian discourse. Fainwell acts swiftly, transforming the point of marriage into a crisis of religious faith. As Prim proudly looks on, unaware that he is being cozened, Fainwell engages Mrs. Lovely in a duplicitous play on the language and form of religious discourse:

MRS. LOVELY: Something whispers in my ears, methinks, that I must be subject to the will of this good man and from him only must hope for consolation . . . it also telleth me that I am a chosen vessel to raise up seed to the faithful and that thou must consent that we two be one flesh according to the Word. . . (V.360–65)

. . . .

FAINWELL: And I will take thee in all spiritual love for an helpmeet, yea, for the wife of my bosom.—And now, methinks, I feel a longing—yea, a longing, I say, for the consummation of thy love, hum—yea, I do long exceedingly. (V.384–88)

Working not only themselves but also the voyeuristic Obadiah into a frenzy, Fainwell and Lovely make it quite clear that even as they invoke the socially permissible rhetoric of spiritual love, sexual desire constitutes the substance of their exchange. Significantly, Ann Lovely's eager participation in this dialogue enables her, if only briefly, to act as an agent in the alienation of her own goods. Her command of the language of desire suggests that she understands how best to manipulate her status as symbolic capital, for she constitutes herself as an object for consumption in order to reconstitute herself in what for her represent the more desirable identity positions of wife and mother.[28] Yet for Prim, as earlier for Tradelove, Lovely's worth consists in her convertibility to an exchange value, and it is in this sense that her desire acts as a register or mirror for that of her guardians. Driven by his own desire to be allied with a man of Fainwell's apparent spiritual skill, Prim immediately converts Lovely into property and signs her over to Fainwell.

The final scene of A Bold Stroke for a Wife makes it even more clear that the play's fundamental dramatic material consists in the negotiation and celebration of relationships between male figures of authority. As the details of Fainwell's masterful contrivances come to light, the guardians alternately "take hold" of Mrs. Lovely until she is ultimately and finally taken hold of by Fainwell, her new

Isaac Taylor ad viv. del: *Walker Sculp:*

Mr SHUTER in the Character of OBADIAH PRIM.
She talketh unintelligibly Sarah,
Verily it troubleth me.

Publish'd June 8th 1776. by T. Lowndes & Partners.

Figure 8. Mr. Shuter as Obadiah Prim, in Susanna Centlivre's *A Bold Stroke for a Wife*. Courtesy of the Lewis Walpole Library.

rightful owner. We watch, then, as ownership of Mrs. Lovely literally changes hands, even as our attention remains focused on Fainwell and the expressions of mutual admiration among the men. Each guardian in turn laughs at himself and his fellows and justifies his consent on the basis of his respect for Fainwell's ingenuity. As Richard Cumberland notes, though with different intent than my own, the scene thus "naturalizes" the exchange that is being effected.[29] To save face, the guardians convert Fainwell's acts of cuckoldry into successful acts of seduction.

In this play on cuckoldry, in which potency of knowledge stands in as the discursive metaphor for sexual potency, Fainwell maintains what Sedgwick designates "cognitive control of the symbolic system that presides over sexual exchange . . . [to achieve] a relation of mastery to other men" (50–51). With a romantic narrative as his alibi, he earns the right to assume the mantle of proprietary authority over Ann Lovely and thereby consummates the homosocial bonds he has worked so hard to build. Ann Lovely may fulfill her desire for Fainwell, but she does so only insofar as the presentation of *A Bold Stroke for a Wife* remains constrained by what Helen Burke has termed the "old play" that takes place in a "domain where the Law of the Father governs" (228).

By the end of the play, then, the intrigues of the plot seem to have assured that Fainwell has passed through a process of character valuation whereby he has gained enough "value" to be worthy of Mrs. Lovely. Significantly, however, he has gained this value only through his capacity to adapt the linguistic register of each guardian and to play the role demanded by each situation. He projects himself into the space of performance from a place external to it. Indeed, as Fainwell passes through each subplot, he reveals a protean capacity to perform rather than inhabit each type. Despite his appearance of worthiness, he appears to have no center in himself, no particular identity that would secure our confidence in the play's happy ending. The specificity of the comic contrivances of plot thus results in uncertainty at the level of generality. As if aware of this problem and its threat to the generic ending, Centlivre attempts to instill Fainwell with a reliable solidity when he avers in the closing moments:

Look ye, gentlemen, I am the person who can give the best account of myself, and I must beg Sir Philip's pardon when I tell him that I have as much aversion to what he calls dress and breeding as I have to the enemies of my religion. I have had the honor to serve his Majesty and headed a regiment of the bravest fellows that ever pushed bayonet in the throat of a Frenchman; and notwithstanding the fortune this lady brings me, whenever my country wants my aid, this sword and arm are at her service. (V.545–54)

Here Fainwell's worthiness appears to be signified by a declaration of Whiggish patriotism, his authenticity symbolized in a commitment to country that transcends even the bonds of marriage. The passage works subtly, moreover, to support this claim; for through his expressions of disgust for the proclivities of the guardians, Fainwell implicitly repudiates that which is not officially sanctioned as English: dissenting Quakers, French foppery, etc. Fainwell thus represents himself as being a stalwart defender of the nation and the faith on both the foreign and the domestic fronts, and this claim is supported by the fact that, with the exception of the scenes in which Fainwell accommodates his speech to that of each of the guardians, he consistently speaks in a military idiom.

Yet Fainwell's adeptness in being able to command language and rhetoric is precisely what gives the lie not just to his critical testimony here but also to the romantic narrative that has loomed so large in the play. Fainwell's speech is designed to authenticate his integrity and loyalty, but his choice of words, particularly with respect to Ann Lovely, brings that sense of selfless sacrifice into question. On the one hand we are to believe that Fainwell is no mercenary, for, as he testifies, he would willingly leave the lap of luxury to serve his country. Yet when he refers to Ann Lovely in this "account," he alludes not to her love but rather to the "fortune this lady brings me." Oddly enough, the only language this fairy-tale hero cannot seem to speak is the language of love. Indeed the only role we have actually seen Fainwell play is that of a soldier of fortune, a fact that suggests that perhaps he is not the best witness for his own character. In the final analysis his "account" of himself just doesn't seem to add up, and though in keeping with Centlivre's Whiggish sentiments, his closing proclamation of "liberty of choice" as the moral of the comedy hardly seems adequate to account for the complicated negotiations needed to bring about this comic marriage (V.563).

Although Centlivre's bow to "liberty of choice" in the final couplet of *A Bold Stroke for a Wife* rings a hollow chord as the closing comment of her play, it seems to have echoed loudly in the ears of Hannah Cowley because she transforms it into one of the central themes explored in her comedy *A Bold Stroke for a Husband*. For Cowley, moreover, the issue of free will *within* marriage was every bit as critical as liberty of choice *prior to* it; in her plays spousal tyranny and parental tyranny are represented as equally abhorrent abuses of power. Significantly, then, and in marked contrast to Centlivre's plot for *A Wife*, Cowley directs the action of *A Bold Stroke for a Husband* through her female rather than her male characters. Indeed, she dramatizes the comic disparities between the general ideal of marriage "as a loving partnership rather than a union of a ruler and a subject" and the particularities of what a woman might have to do to bring about such a balance of power in a society in which they were defined and treated as less than equal to men.[30] In one plot Victoria cross-dresses as Florio in order to seduce Laura, her husband Carlos's mistress, and regain possession of both her husband and the dowry property he has gifted away to Laura. In the parallel plot, Victoria's cousin Olivia devises a series of ingenious strategies both to repulse every suitor introduced by her father Caesar and to seduce Julio, the man whom she has loved from afar for over three years.

According to the first editor of Cowley's *Works*, "It was intended that VICTORIA, amiably employed in reclaiming her Husband, and CARLOS should be the Leading Characters in this Drama, the vivacious adventures of JULIO and OLIVIA enlivening the serious business in which the Moral of the Play is enforced." The editor then goes on to complain that in practice the clarity of the play's moral was often obscured because the roles of Carlos, Victoria, and Laura were assigned to inferior actors as compared to those assigned to play Julio, Olivia, and her plot-enabling servant, Minette. Yet a close examination of the text suggests that perhaps the managers of the English stage were not mistaken in their reading of Cowley's play text when they cast strong players in those comic roles. Indeed, Olivia's actions and words are manifest examples of some of Cowley's wittiest and sharpest writing. Even the commenting editor concedes in the final sentence of the headnote that "the adventures of OLIVIA and her Lovers proceed . . . in one unbroken current of Vivacity."[31] Such enthusiastic approval intimates that Olivia's plot may be much more than a merely "enlivening" distraction from the more "serious business" conducted in Victoria's plot. Indeed, the obvious disparity between the complaint and the final comment suggests that we should take a closer look at the kinds of energies and tensions generated in the play through Olivia's "vivacity" and the impact those energies have on the production of a moral in the other marriage plot.

In the pages that follow, I offer a multilevel analysis of the relationship between the two marriage plots in order to demonstrate how each takes part in the making and unmaking of dramatic meaning. I argue that Victoria's plot does not succeed in presenting a clear-cut moral. Rather, and even more so than in Centlivre's *A Wife*, it is continually marked by an internal division between its formal rhetoric and its performative implications. This division leaves the audience suspended between the meaning of what it hears and the significance of what it sees. While the critical tendency from the very first has been to highlight the former and repress the latter, such readings only contribute to the sentimentalization, rather than elucidation, of Cowley's comic genius. Moreover, they can appear compelling only when Olivia's role in the drama is either completely effaced or at least marginalized as not serious. For, as I will demonstrate, it is Olivia's energy that illuminates the dark recesses or gaps that occur in the logic of Victoria's character, and it is through Cowley's insistent and, for the most part, consistent articulation of Olivia's character that we can learn how to recognize and interpret the ironic distinctions she draws between the sentimental and the real. As the rhetorical and the performative aspects of the drama compete for the upper hand, particularly in the representation of female character, we must attend not only to the meanings produced by each component part but also to the meanings generated through the interplay of those parts.

Cowley signals her reorientation of the thematics of Centlivre's *A Wife* with a prologue that introduces her play as a battleground in the war over the character of women in which women, rather than men, act to prove their worth.[32] Championing the "female pen" and "one Bold Hit of female virtuous art," or female wit, as her weapons of choice, Cowley enters into the lists of what Felicity Nussbaum terms "the conquest over meaning and the contest over the power to name the real."[33] In the last four lines of the prologue, moreover, she uses her authority to stage a coy challenge to the complacency of patriarchy, proclaiming:

Husbands, beware! from Satire not exempt,
You'll find exposed your vices to contempt;
Our sanction'd aim, to rectify the age
By bringing rising folly on the stage.

In the first two lines, Cowley threatens husbands with a satire of their "vices." Yet she follows this threat with a canny sleight of hand, cloaking this attack on patriarchal self-satisfaction as merely an effort to "rectify" its authority. In this manner, Cowley crosses a subversive narrative, a narrative of critique, with a conventional one, a narrative of improvement, and sets up a contest for control over dramatic meaning in the comedy that ultimately puts into question the possibility of a seamless reading of the performance and its representational content.

The issue of reading is further complicated in *A Husband* by the almost ubiquitous use of cross-dressing and masquerade as a narrative device. Terry Castle has explained how "travesty had [a] . . . subversive function in eighteenth-century life" because "It posed an intimate challenge to the ordering patterns of culture itself."[34] Indeed, in an age that both featured and censored cross-dressers like Charlotte Charke, transvestism came to constitute a particularly provocative site for the expression of cultural anxieties over the stability of gender hierarchies.[35] Female theatrical cross-dressing, as Kristina Straub points out, "[opened] possibilities for challenging the stability and authority of that sexuality" because the "cross-dressed actress point[ed] to a feminine desire in excess" of her role as "man's commensurate and oppositional other"; in this case that desire [was] explicitly sexual."[36] Thus playing upon the most disturbing aspect of female transvestism and female desire in the eighteenth century—that "masquerading granted women the essential masculine privilege of erotic object-choice,"[37] as well as the freedom to pursue such a choice—Cowley's *A Bold Stroke for a Husband* makes a spectacle of one woman having fallen in love, albeit unwittingly, with another woman, as Victoria exchanges her garments and then pursues and fulfills her desire of "bewitching" Laura.

Cowley's representation of the seduction of a woman by a woman in order to gain title to property constitutes a strategic play on and rewriting of the "invisible" relationship between men in Centlivre's *A Bold Stroke for a Wife*. Where Centlivre's comedy conformed for the most part to a discourse of homosocial mastery in which "only the man" may manipulate the sex/gender system, Cowley's *A Bold Stroke for a Husband* strategically performs what Sedgwick describes as "the particular ambiguity of [women] being at the same time objects of symbolic exchange and also, at least potentially, users of symbols and subjects in themselves" (50). For insofar as Victoria appears to have assumed a "male" sexual role, the action represents a subversive play on the prerogatives of masculine desire. Manipulating the sign system that regulates the correlative relationship between sex and gender, Victoria subverts the discourse of homosocial desire when she seduces her own husband's mistress and carries out what was figuratively represented in *A Wife* as the privileged, masculine act of cuckoldry.

Olivia directs our attention to this form of cultural transgression when she teases Victoria: "As a Cavaleiro, it seems you are striking. So suddenly to have robbed your husband of his Charmer's heart you must have used some Witchery!" At first, Victoria responds cheerily to this taunt by offering "knowledge of [her] sex" as her most effective bewitching power (II.ii). But when Olivia continues to question her as to the efficacy of her stratagem, Victoria moves, just as the prologue offered to mitigate its own challenge, to circumvent the kind of moral censure and sexual ambiguity implied by Olivia's use of the term "witchery." In broadly conventional and recuperative strokes, Victoria defends her actions:

Merely to defeat him was not my first motive. As the Portuguese robbed me of his heart, I concluded her mind had fascinations which were unpossessed by me. It was impossible to visit her as a Woman; I have therefore assumed the character of a Cavalier . . . that, in my visits I may so study her as to imitate the perfections he found in her, and lure him from the degrading situation of remaining within the power of such a being—seeking for happiness where there is the absence of all Principle. (II.ii)

Victoria strives to contain the volatile threat associated with her use of sexuality as a weapon "where there is the absence of all Principle" by bringing it within the legitimate or authorized realm of the marriage bed. She insists that her purpose in gaining the acquaintance of Laura was not to gain sexual favors, but rather to gain an education in sexual wiles and make herself a better lover for her husband Carlos. Yet this attempt to quell our suspicions raises a number of particularly nagging questions: what did she learn from Laura that would make her a more alluring sexual partner and how did she acquire those new skills? Her explanation, which allows reference only to the "fascinations" of Laura's "mind," leaves some question as to precisely what kind of knowledge we ought to take away from her protestations.[38]

Significantly, our curiosity finds a voice for its lurid skepticism in Olivia, who continually inserts herself into Victoria's anxious declarations with heavily punctuated expressions of sardonic shock and ironic sympathy. Highlighting all that Victoria appears to feel most self-conscious about, Olivia forces Victoria to explain herself over and over again for fear that her actions are being mis-construed. Finally, Olivia crosses the line of propriety to point directly at the sexual nature of Victoria's activities, inquiring slyly, "But pray how, under all circumstances, can you be thus passive? having assumed the Man, I dont know whether I should not make him feel a man's resentment" (II.ii). In response to these insinuations that she make a cuckold of Carlos by indulging in sexual relations with Laura, Victoria alludes weakly to duty and honor. But when Olivia rejects even these terms as the "*arcana* of married life," Victoria's protestations rise to an almost feverish pitch. In perhaps her most dramatically compelling address, Victoria vehemently appeals both to Olivia's knowledge and to her already well-established reputation as a judge of character in the play:

You, who know me, can judge how I have suffered in prosecuting my plan! I have discarded, for a season, the natural reserve of my sex, and have worn the mask of love—to the destroyer of my Felicity! But, the Object is too great to be abandoned—nothing less than to save my Husband from Ruin, and to restore him to me and to his Children. (II.ii)

Victoria's anxious address relies strategically upon the representational power of requesting and receiving independent confirmation of her character. She portrays her actions as sacrifices made for the sake of her family and tries to position herself as a paragon of virtue. Ironically, however, to confirm this portrait she turns to Olivia, who constantly reminds us of the very fluidity of character by affecting a series of repugnant personae to repulse all of the suitors presented by her father. Indeed, Olivia celebrates the fact that, unlike Ann Lovely in *A Wife*, in this comedy the women do the work and their work is the work of masquerade and seduction. She makes no secret of her admiration for Victoria's cross-dressed ruse as a visible sign of female initiative in sexual matters. In response, then, to Victoria's impassioned plea, she offers only an equivocal: "Well Victoria, I hardly know whether most to blame or praise you; but, with the rest of the world—I suppose the *Result* will determine me" (II.ii).

Olivia's muted and pointedly noncommittal reply resists Victoria's attempt to vitiate the subversive implications of the alternative gender ideology offered in the image of a cross-dressed woman. Indeed, through her almost mocking sigh of resignation, she leaves open the possibility of what Helen Burke has termed "the presence of [female] desire, women's own love of the sport" (234).[39] Even more significantly, while Olivia claims she will suspend judgment, she does so by pointing to the judgment of "the world" and therefore to the audience's willingness to acquiesce in the convention of comedy whereby the end is retroactively understood to fix the limits of meaning for the preceding action. Through the unusual emphasis on the "*Result*" in Olivia's speech, in other words, Cowley lets us know that our judgment of the characters depends on the extent to which we choose to submit ourselves to the overdetermined rhetoric of the genre, that is, on how "straight," in every sense of that word, we decide to take the ending.

The choice we have to make between sentimental rhetoric and dramatic realism when we offer an account of the play's moral is again put on display one act later when Cowley literally stages the tension between Victoria's and Olivia's conflicting representations of the play's events (III.ii). Taking full advantage of the dimensions of the stage, Cowley juxtaposes the marriage plots by bringing the two couples onstage at the same time and alternating the focus of the dramatic action from one to the other. As the exchanges between the pairs shadow each other, we are forced by Cowley's staging to engage with the disturbing disjunctions between what we have seen and what we have heard throughout the play.

This intricately orchestrated scene at the Prado opens as Victoria and Olivia enter the stage veiled in anticipation of Olivia's assignation as Incognita with her beloved Julio. There they discover Victoria's husband, Carlos, alone and drunk. Eventually Julio arrives, and Carlos and Victoria move upstage, with Carlos trying to seduce the veiled Victoria, as the exchange between Julio and Olivia moves forward to take center stage. Olivia and Julio first spar over the issue of her veil. Julio wants it removed, and when Olivia refuses he taunts her with an ugly "picture" of that which she veils. Provoked by her own pride, Olivia throws off the veil, whereupon an astonished Julio immediately sinks to one knee and launches into a courtly blazon of her features. Olivia, however, is not interested in being either pacified or seduced by such rhetoric and calls Julio to account: "Is that extemporaneous, or ready cut for every woman that takes off her veil?" By directing our attention to the trite quality of this set piece, that is, to the ways in which it merely follows convention, Olivia brings into question the truth value not only of Julio's words, but of the forms that structure the meanings we attribute to words. Once again her refusal to submit to convention places before the audience the issue of their own submission to the rhetoric of form in conceiving the moral of the comedy.

The essentially irrational persistence of such structures comes to be figured subsequently in Julio's inability to recognize the import of Olivia's ironic jab. Indeed, it almost seems as if he cannot even begin to imagine speaking in any register other than that of courtly love in his exchanges with women. When he continues to invoke this rhetoric, protesting that it was simply Olivia's beauty that called the "Sentiment . . . into Words," she grows impatient with his foolishness and moves to draw the conversation toward more serious considerations. Demonstrating an acute awareness of her situation and the most effective strategies of engagement in that context, she involves Julio in a flirtatious, yet pointed debate about the meaning of love and the obligations implied by the marital bond:

OLIV.: Suppose I were to understand, from all this, that you have a mind to fall in Love with me; wouldn't you at last be finely caught?
JULIO: Charmingly caught! if you'll let me understand, at the same time, that you have a mind to fall in love with me.
OLIV.: In love with a man! I never loved any thing but a Squirrel!
JULIO: Let me be your Squirrel! I'll put on your Chain—and gambol and play for ever around you!
OLIV.: But suppose you should have a mind to break the chain?
JULIO: Then loosen it; if once that humour seizes me restraint wont banish it. Let me spring and bound at liberty, and, when I return to my lovely rightful owner, tired of all but her, fasten me again to my chain, and kiss me whilst you chide!
OLIV.: By way of Reward, I suppose, for playing Truant.
(Carlos is seen struggling for Victoria's veil in the background—she unveils)
JULIO: Why so silent?
OLIV.: I am debating whether to be pleased, or displeased, at what you have said.
JULIO: Well?

Despite his avowed desire for a woman of "spirit," Julio rallies for the same prerogatives that Carlos assumes in his marriage to Victoria. Yet Cowley's insertion of a silent pause in the play text at precisely the same point as the italicized stage directions provides a clear indication that we are meant to read the spectacle of the action in the rear of the stage against the content of the verbal exchange that takes up the center. The silent pause allows us to focus, at least momentarily, on the struggle between Victoria and Carlos that has in fact been going on and shadowing the central action throughout the scene. That struggle, though still pantomimically silent, thus registers an explicit comment on the performance downstage, where before its significance was only implicit. In other words, while we may have been entertained by the boisterous banter, the silence reminds the audience of the high stakes involved in this rapid-fire verbal sparring between Olivia and Julio: the distribution of power, authority, and liberty under the institution of marriage. With no answer provided to Julio's impatient "Well?" the question hovers over the remainder of the scene as a disturbing interrogative mediating and informing our response to the pathetic spectacle that follows when Carlos and Victoria move forward to center stage.

Carlos recoils in horror when he realizes he has been making love to his own wife and cries out at the deception; like the squirrel, he chafes at being "caught in this snare." We watch then as he berates and then cruelly dismisses his wife:

CAR.: Do not expostulate; your first vow'd duty is Obedience—that word so grating to your sex.
VICT.: To me, it was never grating—to obey has been my Joy; even now I will not dispute your Will, though I feel, for the first time, obedience hateful.

Carlos's posturing as the injured party in this episode is undercut by the fact that he has already informed us in a series of asides that his indignation is motivated by a perverse combination of his own shame and pride. Hence, as he deflects his guilt onto Victoria and we watch her submit with almost no resistance, the scene becomes a parody, that is, an unveiling, of the status of masculine authority. We come to understand Carlos's posture as a performative gesture that gains its credence from a particular social structure of gender. Ironically, then, this dramatic gesture undermines, rather than reifies, the authority of its own rhetoric. For Carlos's invocation of obedience as a "word" that should carry moral force in itself proves to be as sentimental and as empty a gesture as Julio's appeal to the force of sentiment in bringing forth the "Words" to describe Olivia's beauty. Masculine authority is unveiled as a sham without substance.

These disjunctions between words and meanings, between what we hear and what we see, and between masculine authority and its parodic double, prepare us for our first encounter with the cross-dressed Victoria. We watch as she transforms herself from a woman to a man, and we overhear her anxiously consoling herself:

Now must I, with a mind torn by Anxieties, once more assume the character of the Lover of my husband's mistress—of the woman who has robbed me of his heart, his Children of their Fortune. . . . There! I have hid my Griefs within my heart; and now, for all the Boldness of an accomplished Cavalier? (IV.i)

In a poignant scene that plays the rhetorical power of language against the compelling image of the performance, the audience is given the intimate privilege of witnessing Victoria's performative "transformation" into "an accomplished Cavalier." We are thus enlisted as accomplices in her bold and "unfeminine" stratagem, even as she reassures us of her feminine fragility and vulnerability. As we witness Victoria's transformation into Florio, her alter ego comes to be constituted as artifice in such a way, presumably, as to preclude the same consideration for the position she assumes as a woman. Yet this metadramatic twist on "reality" represents only the rhetorical thrust of the scene. Indeed it is complicated and even contradicted by the performative ambiguity of the female actress who is presented to the audience as a woman playing a woman playing a man. That is, not only does Victoria's performance make a spectacle of masculinity, it also betrays the performativity inherent in assuming the role of a woman. In short, Cowley plays comic contrivances against the conventions of comic plotting to produce a new, more ambiguous, kind of character identity. Masculinity and femininity both emerge as performances that can be put on and taken off at will by either men or women.

This conflict between narratives comes to be enacted in the final scenes of *A Husband* as a discursive gap in the representation that cannot be wholly resolved or concealed by the insistent demands of comedic closure. That is, while Carlos attempts to recover his sense of masculinity once he realizes that his rival—the man who has made him into a cuckold—is not just a woman but also his own wife, he can only do so insofar as he subscribes to a cultural ideology that either cannot imagine or must suppress the image of sexual relations between women. Operating within the framework of a social economy that oxymoronically renders inconceivable "any interplay among women's bodies," without the intervention of the phallus, or what Irigaray terms the "symbolic token" of exchange, Carlos's confident response to Victoria's cross-dressed activities works to corroborate her insistent denials of sexual misconduct and recuperates her travesty (196). Yet the circumstances suggest that some form of exchange has been effected between women as Victoria regains "possession" of her husband. And it is this possibility that actively insinuates the challenge of sexual interplay between women, where women are themselves active agents in the discourse of desire. Thus recasting the distribution of gender roles in Centlivre's *A Bold Stroke for a Wife*, Cowley's *A Bold Stroke for a Husband* offers a comedy in which both the cross-dressed actress and the cross-dressed character present a challenge to the prerogatives of masculinity that cannot be wholly suppressed. Consequently, when Victoria slides into apparent acquiescence and reassumes her socially determined role as a subordinate subject in marriage, her consent functions only partially to conceal the chiasmatic return to a discourse of homosocial power and authority. For insofar as it is juxtaposed with Olivia's sudden conversion to obedience, Victoria's consent can also be read as constituting an ironic signal that disrupts that return by revealing the gap between the excessive rhetoric of masculine authority and the performative movements of female character. The final scene thus points toward a stable ground of signification for character even as it interrogates the very credibility of that conventional ground.

This is precisely the predicament captured by Olivia when she closes the comedy with an utterance that poses at once as imperative and interrogative: "Shall we venture now to make a bold claim—on the Approbation of our Judges!" (V.iv). Olivia's mischievous remarks punctuate the play with a final emphasis on the dissonance between rhetoric and action—in this case between the conventional rhetoric of comedic submission and the defiant tone of that submission's delivery. Ultimately, this last line licenses the audience to speculate upon the appearances of comedic closure. In effect, the audience is explicitly invited to play the final role in the drama—that of interpreter and judge.

That eighteenth-century audiences were not insensitive to, indeed that they may even have been disturbed by, the seductions and challenges offered by Cowley's play can be seen in the complicated rationalizations they generated to stabilize the ground of character. Elizabeth Inchbald, for example, tried to play Olivia against Victoria, commenting on the former:

In the delineation of this lady, it is implied that she is no termagant, although she so frequently counterfeits the character. This insinuation, the reader, if he pleases, may trust—but the man who would venture to marry a good impostor of this kind, could not excite much pity, if his helpmate was often induced to act the part which she had heretofore, with so much spirit assumed.[40]

What seems to trouble Inchbald about Olivia is her constant refusal to submit to male authority. Indeed, she suggests that Olivia has not merely counterfeited the character of a shrew; the fact that she is such a "good impostor" proves she is one. Yet while Inchbald suspects Olivia's transformation from a termagant to a wife, she insists that Victoria's "good impostor" of Florio does not represent her real and virtuous self. Thus, betraying a cultural anxiety about the orientation of female sexuality, Inchbald writes:

Plays, where the scene is placed in a foreign country, particularly when that country is Spain, have a license to present certain improbabilities to the audience, without incurring the danger of having them called such; and the authoress, by the skill with which she has used this dramatic permittance, in making the wife of Don Carlos pass for a man, has formed a most interesting plot, and embellished it with lively humorous, and affecting incident.

Inchbald identifies Victoria's "passing" as a plot contrivance that would be credible only in "licentious" and Catholic countries like Spain. In England, she insists, such an act would constitute a gross improbability.[41] Yet, by attempting to situate sexual behavior between women outside the boundaries of England, Inchbald exposes her commentary as part of a cultural discourse that sought to consolidate gender and sex categories either by displacing so-called aberrant behaviors to foreign sites or, more simply, by attributing them to dangerous foreign influences. Rather than engage the critique of gender categories offered by Cowley's drama, Inchbald merely slips the knot through a discourse of national chauvinism.

Cowley's *A Bold Stroke for a Husband* breaks down the authority of masculine sexuality, acknowledges female desire, and finally confronts the audience with the instability of these supposedly natural and stable categories by making a spectacle of what theorist Judith Butler terms the constitutive acts of gender and sexuality.[42] Mapping parallel intrigues that repudiate the public prerogatives traditionally granted fathers and husbands with respect to desire and marriage, Cowley's comedy presents a plurality of meanings about the private nature and value of female character. Her representation suggests, moreover, that where characters acted in singular capacities as foils for one another in the earlier part of the century, by the end of the century they increasingly acted in multiple capacities as foils both to themselves and to the appearance of meanings about themselves. Hence, where Centlivre's Fainwell only played at various roles, Cowley's Olivia and Victoria seem almost to inhabit each of the multiple roles they play. The more Cowley explores the masks women adopt in their relationships with men, the more difficult it becomes to distinguish between when the characters are merely playing roles and when the characters are actually performing "in character." It becomes difficult, in sum, to distinguish between the parody and the mimetic real. In the end, our ability to claim a definitive knowledge of character begs the question of how willing we are to allow the general "whole," which is the comic plot ending in marriage, to "straighten" the meaning of the particular parts of the plot we have witnessed.

From Strokes to Stratagems

The contest between the parodic and the mimetic also drives the plots of both George Farquhar's *The Beaux' Stratagem* and Hannah Cowley's *The Belle's Stratagem*. In these comedies, both authors dramatize the overdetermined relationship between legible identities and readable narrative forms with an acute level of awareness. Bringing a metadramatic sensibility to bear on, respectively, the ideals of gentility and femininity, Farquhar and Cowley cast those ideals as excessive representations rather than as simple truths. Beyond the obvious contiguities of title and plot, their comedies share an ironically pragmatic tone that at once signals a yielding to the demands of the comedic form and yet casts doubt on both the probity and probative value of that form. Each "strategically" establishes this tone by targeting the artifice of idealized comic romance as a cause for ridicule, even as they form their own narratives around such conventions. In short, as the readings below demonstrate, Farquhar and Cowley each deploy a strategy not unlike the antitheatrical theatricalism we saw in plays about plays; that is, they deploy the metadramatic against the dramatic in order to unmask the nature of identity in performance.

The titular plot of Farquhar's *The Beaux' Stratagem* follows two London gentlemen, Aimwell and Archer, each of whom are younger sons of aristocratic families; they are of rank but do not have the wherewithal to pursue the lifestyle associated with that rank. Their business in the town of Lichfield, where the play is set, consists of searching out eligible daughters of country gentry whom they might seduce into marriage, thereby gaining access to the substantial financial settlements these daughters would bring to the altar. In Lichfield, it is Aimwell's turn to play the gentleman and Archer's to play his footman, making the former appear more rich and thus worthy of a wealthy man's daughter. If they fail here, they plan to move on to the next town, where they will switch roles and try their luck once again. Of course, this is a comedy, and from the outset we know that they will not have to move on. By the end of the play, Aimwell, as his name indicates, has "aimed well" and successfully secured Dorinda, daughter of the wealthy Lady Bountiful, to be his wife. Yet Farquhar also offers us a surprise in this comedy through a parallel plot that ends in the dissolution of the marriage of Squire and Mrs. Sullen. As Archer, the primary mover and foil of the comedy, exuberantly exclaims by the end of the comedy, " 'Twould be hard to guess which of these parties is the better pleased, the couple joined, or the couple parted."[43]

Farquhar's comedy was an instant success, but it was also besieged by negative commentary that focused on the play's apparent celebration of divorce.[44] Although I do not wish in any way to diminish the dramatic shock of representing either divorce or separation on the early eighteenth-century stage, I would like to suggest that to overemphasize this event necessarily foreshortens our view of the discourses that structure Farquhar's comedy. Indeed, in focusing so many of their judgments on Mrs. Sullen's conduct, critics have often diverted attention away from the conflict that informs the entire play: Aimwell and Archer's social and economic status. By taking aim instead at this conflict and at the self-conscious reflections on the comic apparatus that permeate *The Beaux' Stratagem*, we may gain a better understanding of what otherwise appears to constitute a gross violation of one of the cardinal principles of comedy.

Farquhar's deployment of comic structures finds its sharpest elaboration in the play's interrogation of class categories and their meanings. Like the other comedies discussed in this chapter, Farquhar's *The Beaux' Stratagem* exhibits a vested interest in articulating the value of its characters, that is, in producing a measure of their worthiness for marriage. In this case, that end is achieved through a complicated calculus of both rank and wealth, appearance and reality. These calculations appear to provide the basic materials for the identification of gentility throughout the comedy. In the end, however, Farquhar's metadramatic reflections on these calculations result instead in epistemological uncertainty with respect not only to character value but also to the value of comedy as a form that conveys meaning. We are forced by Farquhar's maneuvers to recognize that our own consent to comic resolution is grounded more upon the rhetorical persuasiveness of the conventions embedded in the comedy than upon any empirical evidence or knowledge that the comedy provides.

These tensions are established and dramatized in the comedy's opening act, in which we are first introduced to Aimwell and Archer and to the debate over rank and wealth as determinants of character and character value. Archer and Aimwell arrive in disguise at the inn owned by Boniface, a loquacious innkeeper and associate of highwaymen, from whom Aimwell immediately extracts information about the most eligible young woman in Lichfield: Dorinda, daughter of the generous and charitable Lady Bountiful. When Archer returns from the stables where, as footman to Aimwell, he has dutifully seen to the horses, he and Aimwell engage in a discussion that reveals their current situation and their mercenary motives. Greeting Aimwell as his "brother in iniquity," Archer articulates his creed: "there is no scandal like rags, nor any crime so shameful as poverty" (I.i.126–28). The cases in point that Archer and Aimwell cite to support this principle suggest, however, that the appearance of wealth overrides actual considerations of poverty. In other words, the crime, as viewed from their position of rank without wealth, is not poverty per se, but rather the appearance of poverty. Indeed, if the semblance of wealth can be maintained, then, at the very least, access to actual wealth will be more readily attained and appearances may never have to be betrayed. In this respect, as Archer affirms, "men of sense are left to their industry" to ensure this outcome (I.i.151–52). Theatricality, or the deliberate cultivation of appearances, is thus represented in this specular economy as a form of labor even as the principle of playing the role in order to become the part forms the basis of the play's plot. The principal protagonists thus rely upon the comic ethos that appearance and reality can be brought into a relation not only of equivalence, but more importantly, of identity.

Indeed, Aimwell and Archer had left London only after their money began to run low and they could no longer afford to maintain a veneer of wealth and ease. They have come to Lichfield with £200 and the "horses, clothes, rings, etc." that signify wealth (I.i.168). Yet, as is made clear in the following exchange, the plot itself remains suspended between at least two different systems for evaluating actual class or worth:

AIMWELL: Would not any man swear now that I am a man of quality, and you my servant, when if our intrinsic value were known.—
ARCHER: Come, come, we are the men of intrinsic value, who can strike our fortunes out of ourselves, whose worth is independent of accidents of life, or revolutions in government: we have heads to get money and hearts to spend it. (I.i.154–59)

Aimwell's comments refer to an older system of identity under which intrinsic value was defined by birth or what Archer terms the "accidents of life" and "revolutions in government." At the same time, however, they also recognize the transformation of this exclusive society into a culture in which at least the appearance of intrinsic value could be purchased and worn. Archer's emphasis on "accident" and "revolution" highlights the arbitrariness of this old system of valuation and marks the critique through which he seeks to redefine the very meaning of intrinsic value. His view is of a piece with the emerging contemporary discourse of commercial individualism in that it agitates for an understanding of intrinsic value as the capacity to recognize opportunity, to generate capital, and to capitalize in order to create worth.[45] Amid the "bewildering and exhilarating mobility and ambiguity of social role and identity" that these economic transformations have brought, Aimwell and Archer are joined together in their pursuit of both wealth and pleasure.[46]

Most discussions of *The Beaux' Stratagem* tend to concentrate on this tension between birth and merit in the determination of value. Yet in this opening act of exposition, Farquhar also attempts to offer us an anchor on which we may secure our expectations of the comedy and dismiss any misgivings we may have as a result of those economic tensions. It turns out that Aimwell has what Archer considers to be a tragic flaw that will "spoil [the] sport": "[he] can't counterfeit the passion without feeling it" (I.i.227–28). In other words, despite all of his mercenary motives, Aimwell appears to possess a quality that guarantees his gentility. Indeed, this humane or sentimental streak is reinforced structurally through a series of juxtapositions with the behavior and attitude of his foil Archer. As Archer is consistently more rakish, mercenary, and appetitive in his approach, Aimwell consistently appears more moderate and sincere.

Yet it is precisely this attempt on Farquhar's part to secure his comedy that ultimately gives the lie to it. For Aimwell's inability to sustain a "counterfeit" does not merely underwrite his show as sincere, rather it introduces a theatrical economy in which an extrinsic and strategically adopted pose collapses into what is represented as an intrinsic and romantic reality. Rather than secure his comedy, Farquhar actually sets up a complicated play in which conventional, mimetic realities will not only mirror, but will also be implicated in, parodic fictions.

Indeed, throughout the play Farquhar continually reminds us of the tension between mimetic realities and scripted discourse. In the second act, he prepares us almost motion by motion for Aimwell's "execution in a country church" of his "business" with respect to Dorinda (II.ii.16–18). Plotting out not only his actions, but also the results of those actions even before they occur, Aimwell proves that he knows his part well when he narrates:

The appearance of a stranger in a country church draws as many gazers as a blazing star; no sooner he comes into the cathedral, but a train of whispers runs buzzing round the congregation in a moment:—Who is he? Whence comes he? Do you know him—Then I, sir, tips me the verger with half a crown; he pockets the simony, and inducts me into the best pew in the church; I pull out my snuff-box, turn myself round, bow to the bishop, or the dean, if he be the commanding officer; single out a beauty, rivet both my eyes to hers, set my nose a-bleeding by the strength of imagination, and show the whole church my concern endeavouring to hide it; after the sermon, the whole town gives me to her for a lover, and by persuading the lady that I am a-dying for her, the tables are turned, and she in good earnest falls in love with me. (II.ii.21–35)

This entire scenario would be absurd if it were not the case that it produces precisely the results it anticipates. In the ensuing act, we find Dorinda sequestered with Mrs. Sullen and engaged in giddy conversation about their encounter with a mysterious "gentleman" at church. Dorinda protests at first that she is not so apt to "fall in love with a fellow at first sight" (III.i.5–6). Yet with continuous prompting from Mrs. Sullen, she is finally brought to confess that "with an air he shone, methought, like rays about his person. . . . No forward coquette behaviour, no airs to set him off, no studied looks nor artful posture—but nature did it all—" (III.26–30). Finally, she rhapsodizes over his eyes, "Sprightly, but not wandering, they seemed to view, but never gazed on anything but me.—And then his looks so humble were, and yet so noble, that they aimed to tell me that he could with pride die at my feet, though he scorned slavery everywhere else" (III.i.34–38).

It would appear that Aimwell has hit his mark; he has performed so well that Dorinda perceives his actions as free of all artifice. Yet Aimwell's prolonged speech highlights the premeditated "nature" of the "artful posture[s]" he assumes in the church. Significantly, moreover, with all the emphasis on "riveted" eyes, we never actually see the scene enacted; we engage only with the scenario outline and the report of its effects. In this way, Farquhar parodies the comic, for even as he incorporates conventional plots into his own narrative and brings the marriage of Dorinda and Aimwell forward, he also puts those structures on display as irrational contrivances. In other words, Farquhar produces a comedy, but it is a comedy with what Froma Zeitlin might term a "difference" (141). That is, the very structures that are meant to mark the genre's progress form the basis for an ongoing critique of that movement.

In fact, Aimwell is not the only one who lays out and predicts the plot. Mrs. Sullen is equally attuned to what she refers to as the "mathematics" of comic relations, and she assures Dorinda that even as she confesses her passion, the mysterious gentleman "has got to his confidant already, has avowed his passion, toasted your health, called you ten thousand angels, has run over your lips, eyes, neck, shape, air, and everything, in a description that warms their mirth to a second enjoyment" (III.i.85, 8–12). Again these kinds of immediate effects seem absurd, unless of course we recall first that this is a comedy and second that the play holds a trump card: Aimwell cannot counterfeit passion without feeling it. When we next come upon Aimwell, we find him celebrating his marksmanship as well as his passion as he scans a blazon of Dorinda in precisely the manner predicted. Later, Mrs. Sullen no sooner suggests to Dorinda that if Aimwell "loves you or deserves you, he'll find a way to see you" than we find Aimwell at Lady Bountiful's doorstep feigning sickness and delirium (III.iii.262–63, IV.i). Farquhar punctuates this result when Mrs. Sullen nods to Dorinda and with satisfaction declares, "Did not I tell you that my lord would find a way to come at you?" (IV.i.92–93). In the parodic scene that follows, Aimwell swoons and Archer explains that he was "of a sudden touched with something in his eyes" that "by degrees . . . grew and mounted to his brain . . . that his transported appetite seized the fair idea, and straight conveyed it to his heart" (IV.i.129–36). When Aimwell recovers, he looks to Dorinda, pretends to see her as a goddess, kneels, and kisses her hand. At this point, it is difficult to tell whether this passion is sincere or entirely feigned, a command performance that has been carefully planned and orchestrated to provoke a series of effects. Given Farquhar's constant promptings, however, what we can do is recognize these moves as conventional contrivances of the comic.

Under Farquhar's hand, in other words, the comic is emptied out of all substance and parodied as a series of forms, a process that finally receives its most absurd and complete illustration when Mr. Sullen's servant Scrub rushes in to report a plot between the fake French preacher Foigard and Gipsy, a maid to Mrs. Sullen. For a guinea he exclaims:

First, it must be a plot, because there's a woman in't; secondly, it must be a plot, because there's a priest in't; thirdly, it must be a plot, because there's French gold in't; and fourthly, it must be a plot, because I don't know what to make on't. (IV.i.330–34)

Scrub has assembled all the elements of a standard comedic plot: a woman, a preacher, and a touch of French venality, but the plot itself remains obscure to him, suggesting that the pieces in and of themselves hold no particular meaning. Plots are assembled, then, from a series of unrelated and in many ways arbitrary parts, and they acquire meaning only when a skilled craftsman, like Archer, steps in to contrive the relations of cause and effect. In this case, Archer figures out that Gipsy and Foigard have conspired to hide the French Count Bellair in Mrs. Sullen's chamber, and he vows to find a way for himself "to be included in the treaty" (IV.i.355).

Indeed, very little occurs in this comedy that Archer does not have a hand in or at least knowledge of. His role is a rather complicated one, for it is Archer rather than Aimwell who seems most concerned and is most deeply associated with class anxieties. Whether he is arguing with Aimwell on the basis of the proper "sphere" for his rights as a footman to enjoy Boniface's daughter Cherry (II.ii) or disciplining Aimwell to focus on the "business" at hand, the acquisition of money for the purpose of enabling future genteel pleasure (II.ii), Archer proves himself to be a consummate guardian of class interests. When Cherry offers herself in marriage to Archer along with the £2000 she has managed to squirrel away, he quickly calculates that her money would last only a "year or two, and the wife may live–Lord knows how long!" (II.ii.232–33). Money is certainly one of Archer's primary considerations, yet his next remarks suggest that he has a vested interest in rank as well. He concludes the act exclaiming to himself, "an innkeeper's daughter! ay, that's the devil—there my pride brings me off . . . / Pride saves man oft, and woman too, from falling" (II.ii.232–38). Archer refers here to the prospect of "falling" in class status; his pride assures that decorum in rank will be maintained in the comedy.

Nevertheless, Archer is also the major focal point for a series of comic misprisions that bear on the relationship between class and language. From the very outset, Cherry suspects that Archer only plays the footman, for his linguistic register does not match his liveried status. Eventually Cherry calls Archer on the "contradiction" between his "discourse" and his "habit," but not before airing her suspicions to her father that Archer and Aimwell might be highwaymen from a rival gang. This rough calculus of language and rank thus produces the analogy between Archer and Aimwell and the gang of highwaymen led by Gibbet; after all, like highwaymen, Archer and Aimwell have taken to the country roads to seek their fortune. While this parallel between gentlemen and thieves produces much of the comedy in The Beaux' Stratagem, as well as much of the material for critical commentaries on the play, in the end class order is not only maintained but reinforced by linguistic register. Ultimately, in other words, such thematics constitute the busy contrivances and distractions that fill out the comedy while the negotiations of value reinforce an overdetermined form of gentility.

What I am suggesting here is that the critique of class in Farquhar's The Beaux' Stratagem does not occur through the direct examination of class itself.

Rather, Farquhar forms his critique through the less direct, but I think more effective strategy of taking a parodically critical approach to comedy as one of the cultural forms that perpetuates class structures. For instance, one trait of comedy that has been discussed often is the motif of "the world upside-down" in which the social order is temporarily subverted but ultimately reinstated. One device of this motif has been termed "levelling," a situation in which the "artificiality of all social distinctions" are demonstrated and the comedy "eyes ironically the proposition that our social superiors are also our moral superiors."[47] In this case, it could easily be argued that Archer and Aimwell are placed on a level with Gibbet's gang of thieves. Yet Farquhar does not so much "demolish the entire artificial structure of contrasts" within his comedy as he exposes the artificiality of the very structure of comedy itself.[48] That is, he exposes and indicts comedy as an institution that produces and sustains rigid hierarchical structures such as class. The critique of class is thus articulated through the critique or parody of comedy. The "re-mark" on genre betrays the social categories that comedy was meant to support.[49]

Returning to the main plot, then, we once again find a prepared script. Aimwell has fallen in love "to distraction" with Dorinda, and Archer must constantly coach him to keep his eye on the business at hand—securing the bride so that they no longer have to suffer the indignity of poverty among their peers in London (IV.ii). Archer and Aimwell take on swashbuckling roles as they subdue the gang of thieves who have broken into Lady Bountiful's home. Amid the excitement, Archer presses Aimwell to take advantage of moment:

[N]ow while she's hurried between the palpitation of her fear and the joy of her deliverance, now while the tide of her spirits are at high-flood—throw yourself at her feet, speak some romantic nonsense or other—address her like Alexander in the height of his victory, confound her senses, bear down her reason, and away with her. (V.iii.33–39)

Archer's high rhetorical register again points to the overdetermined status of his utterance with respect to generic expectations because it ironically resembles the speech of heroic tragedy more than that of genteel comedy. Indeed, comically enough, it foreshadows Aimwell's surrender to his "tragic flaw." Rather than follow the romantic script offered by Archer, the guilt-torn Aimwell confesses himself an impostor even as he and Dorinda stand before Foigard to be married:

I'm all a lie, nor dare I give a fiction to your arms; I'm all counterfeit, except my passion. . . . I am no lord, but a poor, needy man, come with a mean, a scandalous design to prey upon your fortune; but the beauties of your mind and person have so won me from myself that, like a trusty servant, I prefer the interest of my mistress to my own. (V.iv.23–30)

Dorinda's response to this romantic confession is one of relief because now she can marry him for love and with a clear conscience, where before she had suspected herself of being attracted to his title. Farquhar appears to present us with a moment of truth and sincerity that can secure comedic closure. Yet no sooner do we receive these heart-wrenching confessions of love than the ceremony is once again interrupted by a message, the contents and timing of which undermine and parody this display of comic truth as too weak to secure the ending. Dorinda departs and returns, and the ceremony begins again only for Dorinda to interrupt with another startling confession: she has just been informed that Aimwell's older brother has died and that in fact he is now truly Lord Viscount Aimwell. Deus ex machina! "Thanks to the pregnant stars that formed this accident!" Aimwell exclaims, only to be seconded by Archer, "Thanks to the womb of time that brought it forth" (V.iv.106–8). All would seem to be both right *and* wrong in this comedy: passion and fate have come together to secure true love but fate has exposed just how tenuous and arbitrary that security is.

As if to make this point all the more clear, the play does not end here with the auguries and blessings of love. There are still other matters that need to be settled: Archer and Aimwell's business relationship and the Sullen's divorce, as orchestrated by her brother, Sir Charles Freeman, who was also the one to bring the news of the first Lord Aimwell's death. The play thus closes not only with a series of financial and contractual negotiations but with the separation of marital parties. Moreover, though we have witnessed numerous disruptions of the wedding, we never actually see the marriage ceremony performed. Although celebrated, the marriage between Aimwell and Dorinda is itself left in a state of suspension while the separation is settled.

Through the contrast between the excessive style of language lavished on love and the hard-hitting language used in the negotiations, Farquhar strikes his last blow at comedy. The separation underlines just how contrived and illusory are these comic marriages. It does not constitute a gross violation of the laws of comedy so much as it signifies the extent to which Farquhar has undone the social and economic function of comedy altogether. The rhetoric of comedy makes us want to believe that the plot has concluded as an affair of the heart despite the fact that it was set in motion as a theatrical ploy. Yet when Aimwell's fiction collapses into his reality a gap opens up between the comedy and its contrivances, and we are compelled to echo Dorinda's confession, "I hardly dare affirm I know myself in anything except my love" (V.iv.15–17). In other words, we "hardly dare affirm" that we "know" anything but love in this play, precisely because we do know so much more about the characters and their performances. Is it "all a lie . . . all counterfeit?" If we dare to look at Farquhar's intervention in comedy, we see that on the surface class has been preserved; the play on class has been a counterfeit and the world is now "right-side-up." But we must also acknowledge at a deeper level that the comic center of that world's axis has been left hollow and exposed and is well on its way to a thorough collapse. Either way, Farquhar's persistent parody of comic contrivances makes it difficult to read this comedy as a "straight" whole.

Where George Farquhar relied on comic structures to produce a critique of class in *The Beaux' Stratagem*, in *The Belle's Stratagem* Hannah Cowley directs these structures toward the dominant gender ideology they support. Cowley once again contests the conventional idea of "woman" and situates it as an assumption under interrogation. As her comments in a letter of dedication to Queen Charlotte indicate, she proposes to draw an ideal English female character from the competing and contradictory discourses on female modesty and spiritedness circulating in English culture at the time.[50] While this project appears conservative at first, a closer look reveals that it resonates with the same dissenting tone that marks Cowley's self-presentations. In fact, her announced intent of incorporating spiritedness in her production of female character publicly resists what Ellen Pollak has termed the dominant myth of passive womanhood.[51] As the reading below will illustrate, Cowley works within the frame of comedy to posit a conventional English female character even as she subverts the very frame of that representation by self-consciously staging that character as no more and no less than a performative identity.

The Belle's Stratagem refers to the plan that Letitia Hardy puts in motion to win the affections, rather than merely the duty, of her fiancé Doricourt when she finds herself disappointed by his rather indifferent reaction to her upon their first meeting. Letitia had expected Doricourt to "have look'd as if a sudden ray had pierced him! he should have been breathless, speechless!" even as she had been at the sight of him (I.iv). Instead, Doricourt finds Letitia to be merely adequate, a "fine girl" to whom it would be worth pledging his honor to gain control over an estate worth £80,000. When his close friend Saville inquires as to what Doricourt found lacking in Letitia, he responds that "she should have spirit! fire! *l'air enjoué!* that something, that nothing, which every body feels and which no body can describe, in the resistless charmers of Italy and France." Saville, in turn, faults Doricourt's taste, exclaiming, "I would not have lost my relish for true unaffected English beauty" (I.iii).

If we pause here and consider the sentiments expressed by Letitia as compared with those offered by Doricourt, we can discover the very point of disjunction that, like the one in *A Husband*, enables the simultaneous drive of the play toward both the rhetorical recuperation of, and the performative resistance to, the dominant ideology of gender. At the same time, we can begin to trace the one discourse that appears to secure the comedy: the discourse of Englishness. With respect to the first issue, we find that Doricourt views the encounter as a trial of essence. Apparently, he finds Letitia lacking in a certain Continental *je ne sais quoi* which Saville sets in opposition to "true unaffected English beauty." While Saville and Doricourt's disagreement comes to be expressed as a matter of taste, the fact remains that each posits woman in terms of an essential core.

Moments earlier in the same exchange, Doricourt had offered a similarly essentialist, but more flattering, view of Englishmen. When Saville scolds Doricourt for having French rather than English servants, Doricourt explains that where a Frenchman is constitutionally obedient, an Englishman "reasons, forms opinions, cogitates, and disputes; he is a mere creature of your will: the other, a being, conscious of equal importance in the universal scale with yourself." At the end of the conversation, he affirms, moreover, "I have never yet found any man whom I could cordially take to my heart, and call Friend, who was not born beneath a British sky, and whose heart and manners were not truly English" (I.iii). Suppressing the deep class division among Englishmen, Doricourt transforms the issue of national identity into a relation of gender. In Doricourt's opinion, what makes the Frenchmen good servants is their willingness to act as subordinates in relation to a "real" male presence. He thus attributes a distinct femininity to men who are not English and posits "Englishman" as an almost transcendent category of masculinity. In contrast, he finds that the value of English beauty goes down when compared to beauties of the Continent. These propositions persevere throughout the comedy and seem to secure it. Yet insofar as the essentialist category "woman" comes under heavy fire, the stability of the category of Englishness, defined as the opposite to the feminine, also experiences heavy questioning as an illustrative and productive category of value.

In stark contrast to Doricourt's rather essentialist perception of identity, Letitia models herself as a principal player and reads her meeting with Doricourt as a scene in which he deviates from his scripted role in the romantic comedy she wants to produce. As she plays the "true unaffected English beauty" exemplified by her pretensions to "beauty, modesty, and merit," she expects that Doricourt will play the ideal suitor. Thus, while Saville locates "true unaffected English beauty" as an essential value in crisis that can and must be redeemed through the restoration of Doricourt's adulterated sight, Letitia performs, or should we say "affects," "true unaffected English beauty" as just one role in a vast repertoire that she can offer to the masculine gaze. Cowley thus sets her drama to work rhetorically to redeem and to ratify that female essence, even as the comedy plays upon that conceit and works performatively to subvert its authority in the representation and constitution of female character.

Capitalizing, then, on the doubled ironic perspective that subtends the theatrical space, Cowley takes up the myth of passive womanhood as it came to be articulated in the positionalities of spectacle and spectatorship. As the myth reduced woman to a site of stability in an economy defined and circumscribed by the production and satisfaction of masculine desire, so too did the emergent eighteenth-century ideology of spectatorship privilege an active masculine gaze upon passive feminine objects. Yet these discourses were neither seamless nor completely totalizing. As Patricia Spacks argues, "it is far too simplistic . . . to claim that the myth of eighteenth-century womanhood is one of passivity. . . . Myths declare wishes and reveal fears; the fantasized compliant woman expresses fear of alternative possibility."[52] The ideological disjunction through which this alternative possibility is staged in *The Belle's Stratagem* occurs, then, precisely at that point where the masculine gaze insists on an ideal essence and where, at the same time, the female character produces and displays that "essence" as mere masquerade.

Indeed, Letitia plays upon Doricourt's presumption that there is an essence behind every mask to produce herself both as an object of his desire and as an active agent in fulfilling her own desire. After having secured Doricourt's absolute contempt by playing the idiot at their second meeting, Letitia disguises herself with a mask and seduces him at the masquerade ball. To distract Doricourt when he desperately attempts to discover the identity of the figure beneath the mask, Letitia engages him in a witty repartee on the subject of matrimony that prompts him to ask the mask: "But what will you be when a Wife?" Letitia responds: "A Woman—If my Husband should prove a Churl, a Fool, or a Tyrant, I'd break his heart, ruin his fortune." Amazed by her wit, Doricourt asks in turn, "What if you lov'd him, and he were worthy of your love?" to which Letitia answers, "Why, then I'd be any thing—and all!" (IV). Going on to provide an exotic register of what that "all" might be comprised of, Letitia includes that at such a husband's desire she would go so far as to "change my country, [and] my sex." Coupled with the alluring appearance of the mask, this claim to changefulness resonates with a doubled meaning that repeats the earlier split in levels of signification. On the one hand, Letitia's claim can be read precisely as what Spacks has identified as a "vision of a woman powerfully, continuously, herself, yet unfailingly adjusted to male desire" (281). Such an interpretation would be commensurate with the myth of passive womanhood, for even as it allows for fluctuations in female character, it insists that all such movements and indeed, the category woman itself, are changelessly directed, shaped, and circumscribed by masculine desire. Doricourt's desperate attempt to seize Letitia's mask enacts this very conceit as it presumes to penetrate to the "thing itself" that exists behind the mask, waiting only to be brought under his spectatorial control. Yet Letitia's successful resistance to such seizure indicates her elusiveness, even as her ability to wear an infinite number of masks reminds us of, indeed, makes a spectacle of, the alternative possibility that the "thing itself" that Doricourt desires does not exist except as another mask. More significantly, the masquerade scene subverts Doricourt's spectatorial authority by denying his gaze the privilege of determining desire; that privilege is reallocated to Letitia, who controls the site of specular production. The scene thus suggests that the critical question should be not *who* is watching, but what is there to see at all and who is producing that spectacle?

As the drama moves toward the perfunctory conclusion demanded by the genre, this question provides the basis for the contradictory effects of the rhetorical claims of comedy and the performative resistance to comedic closure. Letitia reveals herself as the mask only after Doricourt has been forced to marry her as the insipid Letitia Hardy. As he rejoices at the discovery, she boldly confesses:

The timidity of the English character threw a veil over me, you could not penetrate. You have forced me to emerge in some measure from my natural reserve, and to throw off the veil that hid me. . . . You see I *can* be any thing; chuse then my character—your Taste shall fix it. Shall I be an *English* Wife?—or; breaking from the bonds of Nature and Education, step forth to the world in all the captivating glare of Foreign Manners? (V.v)

Ironically, even as Letitia offers herself to Doricourt's sight, she reveals only that there is nothing that cannot be affected, including the so-called "natural" role of English Wife. Thus playing upon and resisting the social reality that a woman's will becomes legally subordinated to that of her husband, Letitia allows only that Doricourt shall fix her character, that is to say, not her self. Moreover, insofar as "character" itself is constituted through the dynamic chiasmus between performance and categorical identity, Letitia offers Doricourt only a transient opportunity to fix her value and the value of English character.

Nevertheless, Doricourt's conceit remains intact, and he arrogantly presumes to pronounce:

You shall be nothing but yourself. . . . It was a strange perversion of Taste, that led me to consider the delicate timidity of your deportment, as the mark of an uninform'd mind. . . . I feel now it is to that innate modesty, English Husbands owe a felicity the Married Men of other nations are strangers to: it is a sacred veil to your own charms . . . the surest bulwark to your Husband's honour; and cursed be the hour . . . in which British Ladies shall sacrifice to foreign Graces the Grace of Modesty! (V.v)

This passage raises the question as to what, precisely, Doricourt "sees." That is, in response to Letitia's confession, what does he now claim to know? The carefully stylized rhetoric of this final declaration reveals ironically that what Doricourt claims to see is something that by the end of the production can hardly be said to exist, except as either a performative contrivance or an unproductive ideal. Doricourt's exhortation works to recuperate "timidity" and "modesty" and to identify Letitia as a natural exemplar of those English qualities that an English husband values, even as her bold performance demonstrates that her husband's desire and his promised felicity derive from anything but the effects of innate modesty on her part.

Working against the dominant mode of spectatorial authority, Cowley's comedy thus privileges the spectacle over the spectator by dramatizing the rhetorically feminized object of the gaze as a performative identity that is irreducibly in process and never fixed. The stratagem belongs to the Belle, as she maintains control of the script and the spectacle produced for the gaze. The very theatricality of the identities she stages breaks down the absolute distinction between the conventionally gendered positionalities of spectacle and spectator to intimate that the spectatorial pose itself is already and only a performative role for the gaze of another spectator. Thus, even as the drama offers a fixed economy of gender in accordance with the comedic genre's insistence on marriage, the Belle directs the theater audience to the alternative possibility of a speculative economy of gender. Working within the frame of eighteenth-century gender ideology, Cowley posits conventional eighteenth-century English female character, even as she subverts the very frame of that representation by self-consciously staging character as no more or less than a performative, or constitutional parody of, identity.

While both *The Beaux' Stratagem* and *The Belle's Stratagem* work to negotiate and to sustain a balance in the domestic economy, the plays differ in terms of the register they adopt for securing that economy. Farquhar offers us a comedy in which both visual and linguistic registers play a critical role in organizing identity, but where the latter is privileged and operates as the source of comedic misprisions and revelations. Cowley's comedy, on the other hand, eschews linguistic play and relies almost exclusively on visual idioms to carry the comedy and to produce evidence of identity. In the end, however, Farquhar and Cowley both raise powerful questions about what counts as evidence of character not only in the fictional world of their comedies, but, more pointedly, on the stage of the so-called real world. They suggest that the knowledges we form and act upon might just as likely be the illusory products of stratagem.

Generic Rivalries

I want to turn in this concluding section to a focused consideration of Richard Brinsley Sheridan's *The Rivals* because more than other comedies of its time, this play takes as its very subject the status of comedy and comedic conventions. I want to demonstrate how Sheridan draws on the generic clichés of popular forms in his time not only to produce the imaginative contrivances of his comic plot but also to render an argument for the merits of laughing comedy. In the process, I hope to provide one final illustration of the ways in which comedy exposes character as a performative vehicle that must be viewed skeptically under the evaluative eye of genre.

Performed for the first time in January 1775 at Covent Garden Theatre, Sheridan's first play has been classified and read in standard accounts as a comedy of character.[53] In these accounts, plot is viewed as subordinate and even incidental to episodic displays of character absurdities and eccentricities.[54] The play is found to lack a "sophisticated overall informing aesthetic design," and the commentators turn away from an analysis of the play's meaning to trace the individual literary genealogies of the character types represented.[55]

It is true that *The Rivals* features a cast of exaggerated characters, each of whom represents a particular literary type and takes up a corresponding linguistic register. Yet, as I will argue in the discussion below, we miss something critical about *The Rivals* and about Sheridan's concerns in writing this comedy when we read the play only for the isolated moments of "pleasure" afforded us by the comic absurdities of the individual characters and ignore the ways in which the plot of the play carries forward a program of generic rivalry, argumentation, and intervention.[56] This position is supported not only by the fact that Sheridan directs us to such concerns in the prologue for the tenth night's performance, which takes up Goldsmith's line and opposes laughing comedies to sentimental comedies, but also by the fact that the characters in their exaggerated states do not represent individuals per se, but rather particular generic interests and values that comment upon and compete against one another in the action of the comedy as a whole. This will become more apparent not only when we look at the roles played in the comedy by such legendary characters as Lydia Languish and Mrs. Malaprop, but also when we look at the role played in the comedy by our putative hero Jack Absolute. While most accounts of *The Rivals* take Jack as a normative and natural voice of reason, freed from typical interests and clichés, the reading below will demonstrate that Jack Absolute is no more "natural," that is, no less a literary type, than any of the other exaggerated types represented in this play. Indeed, Jack Absolute's "natural" appearance emerges only when measured, as Sheridan so deliberately allows, against the rampant eccentricities of the characters who surround him. When viewed from another perspective, however—one which I suggest Sheridan provided for with equal, though more subtle deliberation—we can begin to recognize him as the type for comedy itself, akin to the Fainwells, Aimwells, and Archers we have already seen, who sets the intrigues in motion and attempts to carry out the forms of social labor required to bring the comedic plot to closure. How we come to read Jack Absolute thus also determines how we come to understand Sheridan's perspective on comedy as a dramatic genre. That determination will depend, as I have contended throughout this chapter, on whether we choose to read the comedy "straight" or to take up the subtle cues to the ironic perspective that Sheridan offers both as the reason for laughter's triumph in its rivalry against sentiment and as the key to understanding the operations of eighteenth-century comedies of manners, humours, and intrigue.

The plot of *The Rivals* concerns the fate of two romantic couples that act, in varying capacities, as foils for one another: Lydia Languish and Captain Jack Absolute and Julia Melville and Faulkland. Lydia Languish and Faulkland serve as parallel humours characters who play out the consequences of particular literary forms—a female and male version respectively of two distinct fictional strands: that of romance narrative and that of the sentimental man of feeling. In contrast, their lovers, Jack Absolute and Julia Melville, are set up as rational foils, that is, as the "straight character[s] who [help] the audience see what is wrong with the comic character's language and, therefore, with his [or her] character."[57] In the first plot, Captain Absolute masquerades as the lowly Ensign Beverley in order to seduce Lydia Languish, who, in keeping with the romance narratives she so avidly consumes, is petulantly determined to lose her vast portion by marrying beneath her and without her aunt's consent. In the second plot, Julia responds to Faulkland's churlish displays of jealousy and capricious sensibility by adopting a pose of patient resignation and by holding out hope that her sincerity and consistency will effect a cure of his at once lugubrious and overwrought condition. The two plots develop in parallel with one another and then dovetail and are resolved in an anticlimactic scene of averted dueling. As we shall see in the reading below, the invention of a duel averted to bring about the resolution of the plots, a stock element not of laughing but of sentimental comedy, only punctuates Sheridan's argument for an ironic perspective as the informing ethos of comedy.

Sheridan lays the groundwork for this campaign in the very first scene of the play in an encounter on the streets of Bath between Absolute's man Fag and Thomas, the coachman of Jack's violently temperamental father, Sir Anthony Absolute. There Fag informs Thomas, and by implication the audience, that "Captain Absolute and Ensign Beverley are one and the same person" and that the cause is "L, O, V, E—love . . . who . . . has been a masquerader ever since the days of Jupiter."[58] As Fag explains, Absolute's masquerade has been contrived because "my master is in love with a lady of a very singular taste: a lady who likes him better as a half-pay Ensign than if she knew he was son and heir to Sir Anthony Absolute, a baronet with three thousand a year!" (I.i.42–46). Here we learn that while "love" may be idealized as a sincere emotion in comedy, the resolution of a comic love plot, by long tradition, requires not only "masquerade" or deceit, but the transformation of the supposedly beloved into a kind of dupe, into the object, that is, of dramatic irony. As we have already seen in other comedies, such intrigues involve a power play that relies on one character having more knowledge than another. Indeed, the intrigues of Captain Absolute are not meant simply as ends in themselves, rather they are meant to have an instrumental value. They are the means to an end that is decidedly unromantic and unsentimental: the acquisition not only of Lydia's person but of her large fortune as well. In this manner, Sheridan sets the wit of comic plotting against the fantasies of romance narrative—Absolute's plots and motives against those of Lydia Languish. By letting the audience in on the joke from the outset, moreover, he sets the scene, and the argument, for one display of dramatic irony after another when, under the guise of his several characters, Absolute/Beverley takes on the other characters in the play.

We first encounter Lydia Languish and her plots in the second scene of Act I when she engages in an interrogation of her maid Lucy, who has just returned from an excursion to the circulating libraries of Bath in search of reading materials conducive to Lydia's peculiar temperament. The titles enumerated in this exchange signal her singular absorption in romance narrative of a particularly tragic variety. Lydia asks for *The Rewards of Constancy*, *The Fatal Connection*, *The Mistakes of the Heart*, and *The Delicate Distress*, only to be disappointed when she finds that they had already been borrowed and all that was left for her were fictions more suitable to a strictly sentimental taste such as *Tears of Sensibility*, *Humphrey Clinker*, and the second volume of *The Sentimental Journey*. These she roundly rejects as undesirable reading matter. Indeed, we soon discover that Lydia's exclusive generic fixation extends so far as to make her determined to play the fateful protagonist in a romance narrative of her own design. As she explains to Julia:

you know I lose most of my fortune, if I marry without my aunt's consent, till of age; and that is what I have determined to do, ever since I knew the penalty. Nor could I love the man, who would wish to wait a day for the alternative. (I.ii.93–97)

Following one of the generic motifs of romance narratives, Lydia has determined to forfeit her fortune of £30,000 in order to live out her fantasy of a pastoral life of love in poverty. Indeed, she is so scrupulous in her planning that she contrives miniplots to mirror the fictional experiences of her heroines. Her distress at this particular moment in the play, for instance, has been brought on by her contrivance of a break with her lover, Beverley, who she believes is an impecunious ensign. Concerned that they have never had a quarrel, a usual and necessary marker of momentary crisis in romance narratives, she explains:

I wrote a letter to myself, to inform myself that Beverley was at that time paying his addresses to another woman. I signed it *your Friend unknown*, showed it to Beverley, charged him with his falsehood, put myself in a violent passion, and vowed I'd never see him more. (I.ii.79–84)

Lydia's contrivances are obviously absurd. Yet they do make an odd kind of mad, strategic sense. Indeed, if we take a closer look at what interests motivate her clichéd actions, we might find, as Mrs. Malaprop suggests, that Lydia Languish is "an object not altogether illegible" (I.ii.287–88).

The method behind Lydia's madness becomes "legible" to us once she discovers that Ensign Beverley is in fact Captain Jack Absolute, the son of Sir Anthony, and the man for whom Mrs. Malaprop has entered into contractual negotiations for a marriage to Lydia. In response to Captain Absolute's pleadings on his knees that Lydia "lay aside some of our romance," submitting that "a little wealth and comfort may be endured after all," Lydia astutely cries out, "what signifies kneeling, when you know I *must* have you?" (IV.ii.169–70). She accuses Absolute, moreover, of having committed an act of "fraud," for as she puts it:

while I fondly imagined we were deceiving my relations, and flattered myself that I should outwit and incense them all—behold! my hopes are to be crushed at once, by my aunt's consent and approbation!—and I am myself the only dupe at last! (IV.ii.190–94)

Lydia's outrage here is triggered not only because she discovers she is the dupe in another person's plot, but because Absolute's plot has succeeded in foiling the ends of her own. In a world where marriages could be contracted and executed under the signature of guardians or parents, Lydia Languish employs the clichés of romance fiction in order to authenticate her own experiences and passions. With their narratives of love triumphing over poverty, the contrivances of romance fiction provide a way to verify and ensure the sincerity of her lover's affections. How else could a young woman of such a large fortune be sure that her charms were being sought not for the sake of her money, but rather for the sake of "her affections"? Indeed, Lydia's concerns are neither trivial nor unfounded. As she observes in this scene, "once your tricks have made you secure of my fortune, you are little solicitous about my affections" (IV.ii.198–99). In an earlier scene, moreover, Absolute in fact averred that he had no intention of losing Lydia's fortune (II.i). Despite the romantic rhetoric of comedy, then, it is not clear to us which is his primary and which his secondary aim—Lydia's heart or her fortune. What we do know is that Absolute intends to prey on Lydia's romance proclivities, to pander to her eccentricities in order to "prepare her gradually for the discovery, and make myself necessary to her, before I risk it" (II.i.75–76). In this light, Lydia's desire to separate her fortune from her person makes perfect sense. What is ridiculed in this comedy, then, is not her aim, but rather her generic method.

The problem with Lydia's method is that it calls upon a genre and a series of conventions that demand total absorption by its characters. Indeed, what makes romance heroines so disturbing and intriguing is that they lack any sense of ironic distance from the role they play in the narrative.[59] Moreover, they lack a pragmatic sense of what is identified in the second prologue to *The Rivals* as the "flesh and blood" of life. Lydia's quixotic absorption in generic clichés is precisely what enables Absolute to exploit her so effectively, that is, what enables him to make himself so "necessary" to her. Thus the contrivances of romance narratives become ends in themselves rather than a means to an end. Where Lydia thought she was in control of the plot, she finds instead that she has become the dupe in someone else's play. Despite all of her efforts to separate her person from her fortune and to bring herself and Beverley into the "prettiest distress imaginable," she finds that she has nevertheless become the coin of exchange in a "mere Smithfield bargain" (V.i.149–50). Lydia's failure to effect her end is thus marked as a generic failure, and it is set against the apparent success of the comic mode, exemplified by the ironic forms of manipulation and mimicry employed by Captain Jack Absolute.

Not insignificantly, Lydia's is not the only plot in this play to fail for lack of an ironic perspective; the ineffectiveness of genres other than the comic receives equal attention and ridicule in the sentimental love plot of Julia Melville and Faulkland. Here we find that Faulkland is driven by the same kinds of passions and insecurities as Lydia Languish. His petty jealousies and captious temperament are motivated by his concern that Julia's interest in him derives not from any genuine affection for him but rather from her sense of obligation to him, first, because she was contracted to him before her father's death (presumably by her father), and second, because Faulkland had once saved her from drowning (I.ii). Further, he is a capricious man of sentiment who one moment can rhapsodize over his apprehensions for Julia's well-being and in the next moment can descend into a raving tizzy upon discovering that rather than falling into a morose indisposition, Julia has been smiling, laughing, and even dancing in his absence (II.i.95–96, 103–6). Haunted, as Jack Absolute mocks, by "a confounded farrago of doubts, fears, hopes, wishes, and all the flimsy furniture of a country miss's brain," Faulkland lays a plot to test Julia's affections and assure himself of her "sympathetic heart" (II.i.84–86, 222). With the same naive self-absorption that marks Lydia Languish's plot, he rushes to Julia, claims he has become caught up in a quarrel that will force him to flee the country, and waits for her to declare herself willing to take flight with him.

Up to this point in the play, we have viewed Julia as a "straight" character, as sincere, earnest, patient, and rational in her dealings with Faulkland. Yet Sheridan has her respond impulsively to Faulkland's announcement with a vow to "fly together" (V.i.22). Remarkably, and in a matter of moments, our only earnest and rational character is transformed into an echo of Lydia Languish, extolling the virtues of a pastoral exile and the irrelevance of financial necessity. Viewing the situation romantically as an opportunity to prove the "warm sincerity of my love," Julia first envisions a time in exile when, "on the bosom of your wedded Julia, you may lull your keen regret to slumbering; while virtuous love, with a cherub's hand, shall smooth the brow of upbraiding thought, and pluck the thorn from compunction" (V.i.20, 25–29). She then extends this image of simplicity in exile by affirming that even Faulkland's loss of fortune "can never make us unhappy. The little I have will be sufficient to support us; and exile never should be splendid" (V.i.45–47). We watch, then, as Julia's sincerity and earnestness compel her, ironically, to fall into a parodically sentimental scene of lovers' vows that could just as easily have appeared in one of Lydia's romance narratives.[60] As James S. Malek points out, moreover, "Sheridan uses dramatic irony to undercut the seriousness of his episode. . . . The audience knows that Faulkland is lying and that there is no real threat; hence it also sees that Julia's response is not only excessive, but comically unnecessary."[61] In short, while Absolute's derision makes obvious the satire on Faulkland's peculiarly overwrought brand of sensibility, Sheridan renders a more profound and subtle critique of sentiment and of the sentimental plot when he turns the joke on Julia and makes her the dupe of Faulkland's scheme. Her "excessive" response to Faulkland derives from her sentimentally styled sincerity, precisely, that is, from her lack of an ironic perspective in relation to Faulkland's behavior. Once she discovers his duplicity, she breaks off relations with him altogether, citing as the cause his "trif[ling]" with her "sincerity" (V.i. 88) and vowing, moreover, never to enter into an engagement with any other man. Finally, she exits the scene with a histrionic flourish that scales the heights of sentimental rhetoric, as she charges Faulkland to lament the loss of "one—who would have followed you in beggary through the world!" (V.i.110–11). Sentiment, thus constituted either as sincerity or as overwrought sensibility, becomes an end in itself, and the resolution of this plot is suspended for the moment, waiting for a comic, that is, for an ironic, final gesture to bring about the happy illusion of a sentimental and romantic ending.

In the figure of Captain Jack Absolute, Sheridan appears to present us with the comic alternative to romance and sentimental narrative, that is, with a figure of irony who can bring the comic plot to closure. Employing the standard comic

ruse of masquerade or obscured identity, Jack Absolute plays the comic protagonist who is aware of the roles he plays. He is adept in adapting his linguistic
register to his part, and the stratagems he adopts have long-range instrumental
value. We see these skills on display once Absolute realizes with relish that "my
father wants to force me to marry the very girl I am plotting to run away with!"
and decides to put on the "penitential face" of submission (III.i.2–3, 20). Knowing that Sir Anthony is working toward Jack Absolute's own ends, we enjoy the
dramatic irony when Jack offers to his father "to sacrifice every inclination of my
own to your satisfaction" (III.i.36–37). We laugh as Sir Anthony deems Jack's
sham acquiescence a manifestation of "absolute sense," and we savor the paradox
of performative reversal when Sir Anthony pronounces Jack "shall be *Jack* again"
at the precise moment when Jack postures in the role of consummate actor
(III.i.40). Perhaps the most ironic and telling moment is reserved, however, for
when the dupe, Sir Anthony, penetrates unwittingly to the truth of the matter,
that is, that what makes Jack Absolute the "*Jack*" of our comedy is his facility at
"playing the hypocrite" (III.i.107).

These qualities have led a number of critics to look upon Jack Absolute as
the unequivocal hero of the drama. A. N. Kaul writes, for instance, "Lydia's lover,
Captain Absolute, is what might be called the positive hero of this culture. He
knows what he wants and also knows how to get it all." Kaul praises Absolute,
moreover, as the "embodiment of manly confidence and good sense," especially
insofar as he "accepts from the outset the play's thesis that financial interest and
filial duty are not opposed to love but are rather its necessary supports."[62] The
problem, however, is that Absolute does not come by his "success" in the way
Kaul and others might have us believe.

In comparison to Lydia's romantic contrivances that merely entertain us,
Jack Absolute's comic contrivances do appear to move the plot. He makes a dupe
not only of his father, but also of almost every other character in the play.
Through Jack Absolute's "hypocritical" intrigues, moreover, we come to see the
ways in which irony surpasses both romance and sentiment as the productive
engine of comedy. Ultimately and rather ironically, however, Absolute's intrigues
fail to bring about the kind of comic resolution or "fine purpose" at which he aims
(IV.iii.13). Instead, Lydia's lament exposes Jack Absolute to us as a type for the
comic agent who through his social labor tries to reconcile or bring into balance
the imperatives of economic pragmatism and romantic ideals. While our awareness of his comic contrivances may have been dulled by the distracting and
heightened satire of the contrivances of other genres, Lydia's response to Absolute
makes it clear that we have been cheering for a character whose "interest" in her
heart has been "acquired by a mean, unmanly imposition," that is, by the fraud of
hypocritical performance (IV.ii.184–85). In short, Absolute's performance has

appeared natural and commonsensical to this point only by comparison to the extravagances of the other characters.[63] Under these circumstances, his scheme to capture the heart and fortune of Lydia Languish has appeared rational, even judicious, rather than a madcap comic escapade. Yet once his plots are foiled and exposed, Absolute can no longer function in the play as the "natural" author of dramatic ironies. Ironically, indeed, in order for the plot to arrive at its prescribed conclusion, Absolute must himself become the object or dupe of comedy's ironic contrivances.

One way to conceive of *The Rivals*, in other words, is as a comic struggle for authority and control between a character and an author in which the author holds the final, ironic trump card. If Absolute acts as the author of plots in the first three acts, by the end of the fourth act he has been exposed as a comic intriguer and stripped of his plotting powers. In the fifth act, he submits abjectly and sentimentally to fate, as symbolized by his engagement to enter into a duel, and thus becomes the ironic dupe of what the audience can easily recognize as Sheridan's highly artificial contrivance of a duel averted. Inured to the conventional endings of comedy, the audience observes Absolute's anguish and at the same time anticipates, with a full sense of dramatic irony, how the plot will be brought to a swift conclusion. And, indeed, our expectations are quickly fulfilled when Lydia and Julia, horrified by the dangers their lovers may be facing, rush to the duel scene and, after Sir Anthony puts a stop to the dueling, allow the pleas of Absolute and Faulkland for their hands.

Anne Parker has also observed how the averted duel "proves more successful in winning [Absolute] the hand of Lydia than all his tricks," and she has characterized this final move as "an apparent concession to pathos" (18). Viewed from the perspective developed in this reading, however, we might better say that Sheridan's invention of a duel averted does not constitute a "concession to pathos," that is, to sentiment, so much as it mocks the kind of perfunctory and absurd conclusion of sentimental plots with their reliance on sudden reformations. Indeed, Parker herself has noted the ways in which Sheridan transforms the duel from a point of serious crisis into an "effective comic device," with Sir Lucius O'Trigger swaggering about and Bob Acres cowering (18). The duel averted thus constitutes a final ironic swipe, for through this device Jack Absolute is made to submit unawares to the role he has been playing all along in someone else's comically ironic plot. He becomes "not altogether illegible" as a comic character in a comic play, who serves as a means to someone else's end—ours and Sheridan's. As Julia struggles to articulate some plausible rationale for her surrender to Faulkland, and as Faulkland arrogantly pronounces a series of morals on the reformation of character, we can choose either to read this ending "straight" or to read it as a response to the rhetorical demands of a genre that makes us laugh.

As the readings above have borne out, the paradox of eighteenth-century comedy is that even as it carries out the social labor and commodity exchanges that are necessary for sustaining the posterity of the social body, it also offers us an ironic perspective on that labor and on the romance ideology that makes those exchanges seem so natural. The endings of comedies of manners, humours, and intrigue are thus both predictable and ironical. They are predictable because they provide for a kind of comic "poetical justice" that "to heighten that resemblance," as Lord Townly informs us in the closing scene of John Vanbrugh and Colley Cibber's *The Provoked Husband* (1727/1728), "wants" only that the heroine "[re-ward] the hero of the fable by naming the day of his happiness."[64] Yet as the comedies persistently mark their own contours, that is, their "heighten[ed] . . . resemblance" to the anticipated generic conventions, they also produce a kind of comic irony that leaves us "wanting," that is, with only the "heighten[ed] . . . resemblance" of closure. The general rhetoric of the genre is confounded by the particularities of the intervening intrigues, and the end of comedy appears to stand emphatically apart from the rest of the action. The incongruities and disso-nances between the final event and the intervening plot episodes cast shadows over the institution of marriage and consequently over the gender and class ideologies it sanctioned and sustained in eighteenth-century English culture. This process is carried out, moreover, not only at the level of plot, but also at the level of character through what I have described in this chapter as constitutional parodies of identity. That is, to the extent that eighteenth-century comedies conventionally employ masquerade, deception, and the effects of spectacle, they also put into question the ability to distinguish the kinds of real, stable, or essential identities upon which the class and gender ideologies associated with marriage rely. The comedies thus offer us an ironical perspective on the norma-tive values enforced by comic ideology, and they enable us to cast a skeptical eye over the social labor they perform. In sum, the "heighten[ed] . . . resemblance[s]" generated by comedy are not so much paradigmatic as they are parodic. And, as readers and as spectators, we can choose, on the one hand, to read these come-dies "straight," that is, we can choose to engage willfully in selective acts of disbelief, collapsing all the contradictory values we discern in the movements of the plots and characters into the face values offered in the play's final moments. Or, we can choose, on the other hand, to hold the contradictory elements of plot and character in tension with one another and thus discern the ways in which comedies of this period were designed both to produce the relations that sus-tained the private sphere and to question the public status of the terms under which those relations were produced. We can choose, in other words, as I have done in this chapter and as Sheridan submits in his epilogue, to shine "the lamp of knowledge at the torch of love" (Epilogue, 57).

Chapter Five
Sentimental Comedy: Or,
The Comedy of Good Breeding

While the last chapter explored what happened to comedies of manners, humours, and intrigue when comedy turned away from "Success in . . . Debauchery" as its primary end, this chapter will examine what happened to comedy when it forswore the ironic perspective that had dominated the comic tradition for so long.[1] For if sentimental comedies marked a departure on the English stage, it was a departure, as I shall contend, away from that ironic perspective and towards a rhetorical posture of sincerity. In this chapter, I want to explore what it meant for comedy to lay claim to sincerity in an eighteenth-century context and to look in particular at what kinds of motives and interests lay behind the sentimental strain of comedy that first emerged in this period and would continue to confound and perplex comic taxonomies for years to come.

It has become almost conventional to begin discussions of sentimental comedy with a nod to *Spectator* No. 65, Steele's famous attack on George Etherege's *Man of Mode*.[2] In my examination of the genre, I would like to open instead with an overview of *Spectator* No. 51, which offers not only a more extensive essay on the differences between laughing and sentimental comedy, but also, I would argue, a far more revealing one. The essay begins with a pseudo-letter from a "Young Woman in Town" who finds that from a "very careful Education" she has contracted a "great Aversion to the forward Air and Fashion which is practised in all Publick Places and Assemblies" and which she attributes "very much to the Stile and Manners of our Plays." The focus of her particular complaint is a line from Steele's *The Funeral* (1702), in which the mildly rakish Campley anticipates the moment when he will "*fold* these Arms about the Waste of that Beauteous strugling, and at last yielding Fair!"[3] Our young woman protests, "Such an Image as this ought, by no means, to be presented to a Chaste and Regular Audience"; she solicits the Spectator's "Opinion of this Sentence" and recommends in general that the "SPECTATOR" consider "the conduct of the Stage at Present, with Relation to Chastity and Modesty."[4]

Allowing the justice of the young woman's criticism, the *Spectator*, in this case Richard Steele, moves with characteristic alacrity to respond to the challenge of what he too censures as the "Smuttiness" of the stage.[5] Steele contends that all "Bawdry," all "Luscious Expressions," arise on stage for no other reason than the poverty of poetic invention. When an author exhausts his store of refined wit, he or she will turn more often than not, Steele claims, to the expedient of "Description which gratifies a sensual Appetite."[6] This being the common case, he knows of one "who has professedly writ a Play [solely] upon the Basis of the Desire of Multiplying our Species, and that is the Polite Sir George Etherege; if [he] understand[s] what the Lady would be at in the Play called *She Would if She Could*." While "Other poets have, here and there, given an Intimation that there is this Design, under all the Disguises and Affectations which a Lady may put on," Etherege, claims Steele, "has made sure Work of it; and put the Imaginations of the Audience upon this one Purpose, from the Beginning to the End of the Comedy. . . . [F]or whether it be, that all who go to this Piece would if they could, or that the Innocents go to it, to guess only what *She would if she could*, the Play has always been well received" (1: 216–17). Deploying an astounding and tantalizing array of elaborate and playful circumlocutions for sexual intercourse, Steele takes issue with what he considers an excessive concern in Restoration and early eighteenth-century comedies with "the Desire of Multiplying our Species." While this concern is expressed bluntly enough, it acquires even greater resonance when set against the criteria that Steele offers for those who had a "mind to be new in [their] way of writing." For the hero of such writings, Steele enjoins, would be one who is, "Temperate, Generous, Valiant, Chaste, Faithful, and Honest," in short, a man *of* "good Breeding" rather than a man who thinks of *nothing but breeding* (1: 219–20).

I take this distinction to be a definitive one both in drawing comparisons between laughing and sentimental comedies and in providing an extensive historical and interpretive account of the latter. It will form the focal point of my discussion in this chapter. At first this may seem like a rather unusual way to characterize the difference between sentimental comedy and comedies of manners, humours, and intrigue, especially when critical discussions of this distinction have been focused almost exclusively for over two centuries on whether serious emotion, or what Steele calls "a joy too exquisite for laughter," ought to have a place in comedy.[7] Yet what seems to have gone unremarked in almost every one of these discussions is the obvious formal attribute that, in the most simplistic fashion, makes each type a genre of comedy: the signature ending in which a marriage or series of marriages are arranged and settled. In other words, what sentimental comedies have in common with comedies of manners, humours, and intrigue is a concern with the relations that sustain the public and private spheres, that is, with who will breed with whom, on what basis, and with what prospects ensured for future offspring. Hence Steele's argument against "smuttiness" in comedy does not preclude an interest in "the desire of multiplying our species"—indeed the retention of the conventional comedic marriage ending, like Steele's playful circumlocutions, ensures our focus on precisely this matter from beginning to end in every sentimental comedy. Rather, Steele signals a desire to reform the manner in which those multiplications are conceived and represented. He signals, in short, the transition toward what Horace Walpole would later call the "first instance of good breeding in the world," that is, the "substituting [of] the word *love* for *lust*," a substitution realized in sentimental comedies by a turn away from the titillations of mutual intrigue in sexual pursuit and toward the measured establishment of mutual affection in marriage.[8]

Like the comedies of manners, humours, and intrigue discussed in the previous chapter, sentimental comedies also carry out a process of character valuation through the contrivances of their marriage plots. Yet they are distinguished from these other types of comedy by the basis upon which this process of valuation is carried out, that is, by the standards against which a character's worth is measured. At least rhetorically though not always in practice, sentimental comedies advance the ideologies of sentiment and sensibility as they were articulated in philosophical, aesthetic, psychological, and economic thought across the eighteenth century. In the most general sense, sentiment and sensibility were associated with a philosophical discourse of confidence in the goodness of human nature and with a tearful pathos that petitions for the ascendance of right over wrong in the resolution of social and moral problems. Such a grounding perspective departs radically from the more cynical and ironical ethos driving laughing comedies, and its effects are most apparent in the governing tone and forms of conflict resolution that distinguish the sentimental comedies.[9]

To illustrate this point let us consider in broad outline a plot structure common to both sentimental and laughing comedies: the forced marriage plot. Typically in these story lines, a parent or guardian motivated either by callousness or by venality conspires to force a child into marriage with someone he or she has little affection for or, in the most extreme cases, actively despises. In most cases, the young person has already formed an affectionate attachment to another and seeks a way to consummate that attachment. The plot thus focuses on the conflict between the mutually exclusive desires of the parent and the child. At stake in these plots are not only parental, and in particular patriarchal, authority proper, but also, by analogy, the authority to rule, distribute property, and determine posterity.

In a laughing comedy, as we have seen in the previous chapter, the young persons in question engage in intrigues that not only circumvent parental authority but actively undermine it along with the distinctions of sexual difference that support that authority. A happy ending is achieved only when the parental figure concedes that he or she (usually he) has been outwitted and that what has been done cannot be undone. All recourse to the law is abandoned, and the parties are reconciled to one another.

In sentimental comedies, however, the process whereby the young lovers come together in marriage requires a more complex series of social negotiations and depends fundamentally on reconciling the interests of parents and children before the marriage union takes place. Conflicts over marital choice are not so much to be relished as to be pathetically lamented in sentimental comedies because the moral precept of duty to parents assumes the status of an inviolable and therefore insurmountable obstacle.[10] From the outset, then, the oppositional sides are softened. Patriarchal figures are portrayed as benevolent authorities rather than tyrannical powers, as in laughing comedies. Their authority grows from the wise restraint they exhibit in exercising their prerogatives and from the extent to which they ultimately countenance a child's liberty of choice in marital matters. On the other side of the equation, our young protagonists spurn the dissembling necessities of intrigue and strive instead to achieve a kind of sincere rapprochement with their elders, one that preserves the prerogatives of patri-archal authority even as the child's desire is satisfied. This happy resolution is made possible in sentimental comedies when the parent's benevolent indulgence is rewarded by proof of both the child's and the potential suitor's "good breeding" —their filial piety, their chaste deportment, their refinement of taste, their deli-cacy of sentiment, and their overall good nature. In this manner, sentimental comedies reform comedic plots, taming intrigue and transforming generational conflict into generational respect by substituting displays of "good breeding" for contests of wit.

Another way to describe this shift would be to characterize it as a move away from an investment in sexual intercourse and towards an interest in social inter-course. For if wit, a symbol of sexual potency, was the currency in Restoration laughing comedies, then good breeding, a symbol of sociability, was the currency in eighteenth-century sentimental comedies. The main project of this chapter will be to examine this shift in emphasis from sexual to social intercourse, from breeding to good breeding in eighteenth-century sentimental comedies. Such an approach to sentimental comedy will draw on its relation to, and implication in, many of the larger social, economic, and philosophical debates of the eighteenth century in which the discourses of sociability, politeness, and manners played a central role. Hence at least part of the task of this chapter will be to elucidate the conditions and discourses from which this reorientation of comedy arose and to read sentimental comedies not only for the ways they reflected these discourses but also for the ways they participated in them. For if the purpose of Addison and

Steele's *Spectator* was to "[bring] Philosophy out of Closets and Libraries . . . to dwell in Clubs and Assemblies, at Tea-Tables, and in Coffee-Houses," then, this chapter contends, it was the cultural work of sentimental comedies to bring that philosophy, moral and polite, into the theater.[11]

The Discourse of Good Breeding

To begin, then, a discussion not only of the idea of "good breeding" but also of the cultural, moral, and philosophical politics that gave that concept currency in eighteenth-century England is in order. In its oldest sense, "breeding" indicated genealogical descent or extraction, a criterion of social standing associated more with the lineages of aristocratic families than with the obscure origins of the emerging commercial classes. By the eighteenth century, however, the concept of "breeding" was increasingly tied to notions of education and training and to the quality of a person's skills and manners in conducting the business of commercial and social life. While the residual traces and influences of "breeding" as an inherited trait, an attribute of birthright and rank, remained significant, "breeding" as an acquired quality of person that could be demonstrated in social exchanges gained in importance and came to be recognized, as an aspect of character, under the denomination of "good breeding." Most importantly, "good breeding" was understood as a quality that could be attributed to persons of any class or rank; it was understood as a distinction of merit rather than of inheritance.

That this last consideration was of the utmost significance to eighteenth-century cultural observers can be gleaned from the care that Henry Fielding takes to conclude his "An Essay on Conversation," which is a guide to "good breeding," with this point: "That whoever, from the Goodness of his Disposition or Understanding, endeavours to his utmost to cultivate the Good-humour and Happiness of others, and to contribute to the Ease and Comfort of all his Acquaintance, *however low in Rank Fortune may have placed him* . . . hath in the truest Sense of the Word, a Claim to Good-Breeding."[12] A closer examination of Fielding's essay affords us the opportunity to gain insight into the status of "good breeding" and its function both as a marker of class and as an instrument of class mobility in eighteenth-century England. It can also provide an important guide to the premises upon which the ethos of "good breeding" was built.

Fielding opens this essay with a clear mandate in the sentimental tradition, adding his voice to those of Locke and Shaftesbury to confirm the premise that formed the central corollary of English sentimental theory: man is fundamentally a "social animal" (119).[13] With this premise as his point of departure, Fielding goes on to reason that "Man's being a social Animal . . . presupposes a natural

Desire or Tendency" toward the "Art of pleasing or doing Good to one another," which is "the Art of Conversation." "Ignorance only in the Means," according to Fielding, is the only conceivable pitfall in "attaining this truly desirable End" (123). The design of his essay, then, is to offer a "Guide to conduct . . . in the proper exerting of those Talents, which are the noblest Privilege of human Nature, and productive of all rational Happiness" (121). In his view, "Good Breeding" constitutes the best "word" to describe those forms of "proper" exertion, where by "Good Breeding (notwithstanding the corrupt Use of the Word in a very different Sense) [he] mean[s] the Art of pleasing or contributing as much as possible to the Ease and Happiness of those with whom you converse" (123).

Taking care, like Steele, to distinguish "good breeding" from its sexual and necessarily lineal connotations and limitations, Fielding reveals the extent to which "good breeding" was understood in the eighteenth century to be the social and behavioral correlative to "good nature," that is, to "the natural Desire or Tendency" to "Contribute to the Ease and Comfort of all." To be a man "of good breeding" was by definition to be a man "of good nature." Yet while man, in theory, may have been understood to have a natural tendency toward "doing Good to one another," in practice he was thought to lack a "natural" means by which to express this tendency. From Fielding's essay we learn that that means was encapsulated by the term "good breeding" and that it necessarily involved an accommodation of those natural tendencies to man-made, that is, social, forms. In this manner, Fielding articulates a view of the natural affections that has much in common with that of other English sentimentalists such as Shaftesbury, Hume, and Smith because it immediately and inextricably implicates the natural affections not only in the social affections but in the social order itself.

Accordingly, the first and foremost consideration that Fielding enumerates in the exercise of good breeding is an ever-vigilant attention to the "Degree of the Person," that is, to the status in the social order of the addressee in conversation (124). And while he concedes that "ceremony" is of "Form only" and not of "substance," he still insists that since such forms are "imposed by Laws of Custom, [they] become essential to Good Breeding" (127). Ironically, then, we learn that while "good breeding" may be laid claim to by persons of any class or rank, the actual exercise or expression of "good breeding" requires the development of a finely tuned social intelligence, a social sensitivity capable of calibrating the finest distinctions among ranks of persons.

In this respect, Fielding asserts that the "Business" of good breeding "is no more than to convey to others an Idea of your Esteem of them" and that in order to do so effectively one must calculate not only the esteem one actually has for another, but also the esteem the other person expects from you. Anticipating Adam Smith's *Theory of Moral Sentiments*, Fielding cites as the golden rule of "good breeding" that you "*do* unto Men what you would they, IF THEY WERE IN YOUR SITUATION AND CIRCUMSTANCES, AND YOU IN THEIRS, should do unto you" (124). Fielding counsels his readers that most men tend to be elevated in their own opinion and that since such expectations are grounded most often in the laws and customs of a nation, in England judgments of the esteem owed to "superiors" ought, accordingly, to be rendered "by Title, by Birth, by Rank in Profession, and by Age" (133). While Fielding explicitly excludes "Fortune" from this list of criteria, he makes it clear earlier on that those who have succeeded by fortune "[bear] a Degradation with more secret Comfort and Ease than the former, as being more inwardly satisfied with itself, and less apprehensive of Neglect or Contempt" (128–29). In this formulation, then, good breeding preserves the outward forms customary for an aristocratic society, even as it locates substance and meaning elsewhere, in the "inward satisfaction" of earned rewards. Indeed, the key to the concept of "good breeding" was that it at once respected class distinctions even as it leveled the playing field of merit. Calculated to flatter and to please, good breeding as an aspect of character called for a performance of esteem and for the preservation of "external Difference between Men and Men," even as in theory it provided a mechanism of exchange among persons of all ranks and classes (127). In short, it provided a source of social mobility even as it preserved the general form of the social order.

Good breeding thus played a crucial role in providing a social and behavioral code that could smoothly negotiate the dramatic shifts in class status that occurred in the eighteenth century. Indeed, an estimation of "good breeding" indicated the culminating achievement of a larger movement dedicated to the cultivation of sentiment, manners, and politeness that historians as various as J. G. A. Pocock, G. J. Barker-Benfield, Paul Langford, and Lawrence E. Klein have all linked to the complicated social demands of an expanding commercial economy.[14] It was, as Paul Langford notes, "a logical consequence of commerce" because "a society in which the most vigorous and growing element was a commercial middle class, involved in both production and consumption, required a more sophisticated means of regulating manners" (4). In this sense, good breeding allowed as much for the maintenance of class demarcations as for the class fluidity and mobility generated by a burgeoning commercial culture. It was not only a mode of character, but also the very means of economic and social intercourse.

To the extent, then, that sentimental comedies made their business the business of "good breeding," they both participated in and reflected an eighteenth-century interest in elaborating a code of conduct that would bring the unruly behaviors of individuals, or characters, in a market culture under some form of social regulation. At its core, this "sentimental" project, elaborated not only on stage but also in the essays of the *Spectator* and in the works of Hume and Smith among others, involved the articulation of a theory of entry into the social realm and the "naturalization" as well as the "de-naturalization" of particular social identities and practices within that realm. As we shall see in later portions of this chapter, these social and economic considerations resulted in dramatic exemplars who were neither emotionally extravagant nor economically guileless, but rather exhibited social, emotional, and fiscal prudence. Indeed, despite a thoroughgoing rhetoric of concern for moral and spiritual advancement, these plays describe a social realm governed by property relations and fiscal considerations.[15]

That these concerns form the basis of English sentimental comedy was made explicit in a series of scenes in James Miller's sentimental comedy *Art and Nature* (1737/1738).[16] For the purpose of illustrating this point, I will concentrate on just two of the scenes (the opening scenes of Acts II and III) in which the conditions governing the social realm in sentimental comedy are articulated. The two scenes involve the play's proto-Rousseauian protagonist Julio, a "noble savage" who has been transported to England from the West Indies by Truemore, the hero of the play, and is taken about London as an observer of English "culture."[17] In keeping with the efforts made in sentimental comedies toward the refinement of eighteenth-century taste, Julio's displays of good nature and ignorance provide ample opportunity for conventional critiques of the pretensions, excesses, and absurdities of contemporary English life. Like Truemore, the audience is meant to "take great Pleasure in seeing pure simple Nature in [Julio] oppos'd to Laws, Art and Sciences amongst us."[18] Yet these scenes also have a far more serious end in that they articulate the very basis of the social order that gives cultural forms value.

In the first of these scenes, Julio opens a dialogue with a sharp-tongued maid named Violetta by commenting:

What a Strange Country this is? Some are carry'd about in Cages, others are help'd to their very Victuals and Drink, and a great many don't know how to put on their Cloaths; one wou'd think they had neither Arms nor Legs to help themselves. . . . I find that here are a parcel of haughty big-looking Savages, that domineer over their Fellow-Creatures, most of whom seem to be better than themselves; I don't understand it—I'll be a Slave to none of 'em, nor won't live where there are Slaves. (II.i)

What Julio notices, but doesn't seem to have the experience to comprehend (despite his recent arrival from the West Indies), is the division of society into different economic classes. From his idealized perspective as the noble savage, he is shocked to find that some persons appear to live at a remove from the obligations of basic necessity. Rather than transport, feed, or clothe themselves, they have others perform those tasks for them. Those others who serve appear to him as no more than slaves whose labor and persons have been completely alienated. Yet as Violetta explains to him, this is the way of the "civiliz'd part of the World," where "Men . . . are governed by Laws, and are skill'd in Arts and Sciences." When Julio misunderstands the word "Laws," taking it to indicate actual persons in power, Violetta obligingly offers that laws are only "Rules and Orders to make men wise and honest." Sounding like an apostle of Shaftesbury, she intimates that they are what give rise to the "Beauty of Order and Politeness in others."[19] Finally, to conclude this lesson, Violetta provides a demonstration of politeness in inviting a guest to dinner that bears a striking resemblance to the entertainment guide that Fielding offers in his "Essay on Conversation."[20] At the very least, she attests, the purpose of politeness is "to shew the Regard I have for the Friends I invite." At its best, she affirms, it is what "makes us humain [sic] and good-natured" and "it teaches us to assist our Neighbours in Misfortune, and relieve 'em in their Necessities" (II.i).

Violetta's explanations provide a kind of flow chart for the complex web of discourses that supported and sustained the structure of English society in the eighteenth century. They also belie, however, the most powerful rhetorical claim made for that structure, that is, that it is natural rather than naturalized. Indeed, what Julio picks up on in his unwitting commentaries is the extent to which coercion, rather than natural inclination, shapes English society under the imposing signs of "law" and "order." He is baffled by the idea that "good nature" and compassion are qualities that must be taught or made. As he explains to Sir Simon Dupe in a later portion of the extended scene, he is "from the Country of Woods and Forests, where there is not a Mortal of us that know one Word of the Laws, but we are all naturally wise and honest enough; we have no need of being *forc'd* to do our Duty; we are so very ignorant, that meer natural Reason is enough for us" (II.i, emphasis added). What prevents Julio from apprehending either the division of classes or the need for coercion to maintain the harmony of a society is his lack of any notion of what lies behind those divisions: the ownership of private property and the system of money exchange. Those concepts are supplied in his next lesson, and they mark his climactic point of entry into the socioeconomic order of sentimental comedy.

The occasion for his full initiation into this symbolic material order is provided when Julio takes a picture from a bookseller's shop and is threatened with immediate arrest. Truemore steps in and pays for the picture; Julio, of course, does not understand that he has committed a crime because he is untutored in the concept of property. An extended exchange then ensues as Truemore offers Julio a tutorial in exchange relations as they pertain to a moneyed economy:

TREMORE: [W]e don't here live in common as you do in your Woods; ev'ry one has a Property of his own, and no body must take what does not belong to him, without giving Money for it.

JULIO: What is this Money?

TREMORE: Here's some of it.

JULIO: Is this Money? Oh la! What is to be done with this Money now?

TREMORE: It is to purchase what we want, and may in some sort be call'd a Surety, which engages ev'ry Man's Honesty that has it.

JULIO: What Rogues are those from whom a Man must take such Surety as this? (III.i)

In this exchange, Truemore makes it clear that private property constitutes one of the founding conditions of human relations in English society; it defines the status both of individuals and of objects in relation to individuals. More importantly, he immediately collapses the question of property into the question of property exchange. In the form of "money," the "civilized" world has instituted a system of symbolic exchange to facilitate material exchange. Further complicating matters, he acknowledges that in an expanding commodity culture in which even identities can be manufactured, money has come to stand not just for credit but for credibility as well. In this sense money, like good breeding, is both the end and the means of social intercourse because it underwrites all transactions and exchanges. Indeed, it provides the "surety" that makes them possible.[21]

Immediately, Julio asks how he might get some money and is distressed when he finds out that it isn't given away, he can't take it, nor can he make it (unless he wants to risk his life). Perplexed, he exclaims: "why what a parcel of Stuff is this? I must have a thing, and yet I must not get it" (III.i). This exclamation functions as a cue for Truemore to explain the class-labor system, reiterating the earlier lesson offered by Violetta, in its relation to money. He begins, "there are amongst us two sorts of People, the Rich and the Poor; the Rich have all the Money, and the Poor none. . . . They are under a Necessity of working for the Rich, who give them Money in proportion to their Labour." Acting simultaneously as a tutor and an apologist for the system of political economy that took shape in the eighteenth century, a system that Marx would later critique in the nineteenth century, Truemore presents the alienation of labor as an inevitable and incontrovertible fact in the life of the poor, even as he goes on to evoke sympathy for the rich for suffering the temptations of luxury in the laborious management of their wealth.[22] While Julio plays true to character and offers a full-blown critique of the rhetorical pretensions and self-deceits endemic to this economic system, Truemore only throws up his hands and protests: "What wouldst thou have us do, *Julio*? There's no living here without Money, and those that han't it got ready to their Hands, must submit to take pains for it, for the Poor can have nothing for nothing" (III.i). From this assertion, we learn that entry into the social order of sentimental comedy requires an act of "submission" to the economic system that gives that social order its shape. Social status in this realm is governed by economic status as money, property, and exchange relations shape the "reality" of sentimental comedies, circumscribing characters and motivating plots.

That money functions not only as the fundamental currency of exchange, but also as the surety of a man's status signals a significant shift from an earlier era in which status, power, and property relations derived almost exclusively from land-based wealth. As J. G. A. Pocock has observed, this shift, following the political settlement of 1688 and the financial revolution of the 1690s, marked the emergence of "an ideology and perception of history which depicted political society and social personality as founded upon commerce: upon the exchange of forms of mobile property and upon modes of consciousness suited to a world of moving objects."[23] This new commercial society featured a burgeoning middling class that rapidly gained economic and political influence and sought, in turn, to acquire a commensurate measure of social and cultural capital.[24] Members of these middling classes did so by adopting and then substantially modifying notions of aristocratic gentility to suit their own middling class agenda, joining, as Lawrence E. Klein has demonstrated, a commercial idiom to a gentlemanly metaphor to produce the discourse of politeness and good breeding.[25] In short, good breeding was not only, as we have already discussed, a way of "enhancing [and regulating] sociability among diverse individuals," it was also "a way of reconstructing gentility for an age perceived to be novel."[26] It was a way for persons of the middling classes to acquire the outward forms and status of aristocratic refinement even as they adapted those forms to, and directed them toward, the pursuit of material advancement in a commercial society.[27]

This transformation of both the economic and social order was reflected as well in the changing tone and content of cultural forms such as the drama. Sentimental comedies could be said to have participated in this movement in a most literal way, working at the level of plot to join aristocratic and commercial interests in marriage unions. In this manner, as Robert Markley points out, they became "literary manifestations of an ongoing attempt to reconcile aristocratic systems of value based on innate worth and patrilinear inheritance to middle-class conceptions of value based on individual merit and worthy deeds."[28] Reading sentimental comedies from this perspective, we can begin to develop a better understanding of how sentimental dramatists worked in the eighteenth century to retain the cachet of ancient inheritance, even as they redefined "breeding" and sought to claim "good breeding" as the moral ground and outward form of middle-class ascendance.

The main task of the subsequent portions of this chapter will be to demonstrate how sentimental comedies worked under the auspices of presenting "moral actions" to shift the focus of comedy from a concern with "breeding" per se—a discourse associated with the inherited genealogies of the aristocratic classes—to the more subtle and far-reaching issue of concern for "good breeding" as it was understood in relation to both the reproductive behavior and the social and economic merits of the middling classes in eighteenth-century cultural discourse. I will do so, first, by exploring the discourses surrounding the "breeding" of the genre itself and, second, by offering a series of individual readings of sentimental comedies from the period. In particular, I will illustrate how sentimental comedies staged conflicts over the nature of class intercourse—social, economic, and marital—as arguments over class-specific definitions of good and bad breeding. I will contend, moreover, that through this emphasis on "good breeding" the genre actively participated in the larger eighteenth-century project of rendering distinctions—between "natural" and "unnatural" affections and between "moral" and "immoral" actions—that would both support and validate new social and economic motives. In this respect, I will argue, the main rhetorical and cultural work of sentimental comedies was to demonstrate how "good breeding" was commensurate with an interest in breeding well.

Good Breeding and the Breeding of a Genre: The Cultural Politics of Sentimental Comedy

Among the dramatic genres explored in this study, only sentimental comedy could be said to have been "bred" in the eighteenth century. The product of an awkward coupling of comic form with the social and emotional strains of moral philosophy, sentimental comedies came into what John Brewer and Roy Porter have christened the "brave new world of goods" and faced a market economy brimming with all kinds of new consumer commodities, each competing for custom and for status.[29] Amid this restive marketplace where consumer taste moved fleetingly from one fashion or novelty to the next, sentimental comedies were billed self-consciously in prologues and epilogues as a new kind of drama that could offer something of more enduring value than the transitory laughter and passions of laughing comedies: an education in polite values, polite behavior, and polite feeling. The explicit promise of these plays was that such an education would raise one's social status and ensure entry into what Susan Staves once termed the "class of the polite" or "the class of the refined."[30] This strategy, which involved cultivating a taste for the very product it provided, was effective because it appealed, as did periodicals such as the *Spectator*, to "the new and growing middle-class audience, an audience which longed to be modish, to be aware of the fashion yet wary of its excess, to participate in the world of the great yet be free from its anxieties, to feel smug and superior to provincial rusticity and old world manners, above all to be deeply respectful of the world of commerce."[31] Drawing deliberately on the discourses of sentiment, sentimental philosophy, and sentimental reform, which ostensibly eschewed material interests, authors of sentimental comedies could advertise themselves as the purveyors of a genteel, rather than a vulgar, product. So long as the cultivation of "good breeding" appeared to be the end of their efforts, they could create a taste in the market for this new "breed" of comedy and at the same time disclaim any commercial motive.[32]

While advocates of sentimental comedy thus argued that their plays promoted both "good breeding" and the public good by providing models of virtue for imitation, those critics who opposed sentimental comedy sought to undercut such claims by demonstrating that the very form was itself a species of bad generic breeding, a corrupt and corrupting example of the damage that could be done when authors and audiences were allowed to indulge in the specious belief that "honest dissimulation" was anything other than an oxymoron.[33] In a culture in which one's tastes in entertainments were treated as a gauge of one's "breeding," whether good or bad, this strategy depended on the critic's ability to cast sentimental comedy as a kind of illegitimate breed, a "bastard" genre that, like bastardy in a legal or moral context, heralded a kind of abstract threat to the social order. To approve of sentimental comedy under these circumstances was tantamount to giving the nod to "bad breeding"; to applaud sentimental comedy in public was only to display one's bad taste and therefore one's poor breeding.

In the pages that follow, I will review these kinds of claims against sentimental comedies and then turn to a more focused examination of the terms in which this attack was formulated. By doing so, I hope to develop, in a manner not yet done before, a deeper understanding of what cultural values were perceived to be at stake in this transformation of comedy and how those values resonated with and were indicative of a larger and more complex cultural politics. I will show first how the language of "breeding" played an important part not only in the comedies themselves, but in the ways that the genres of comedy were conceived and discussed. Second, and more significantly, I will demonstrate that the disputes over the "breeding" of sentimental comedy were more than just taxonomical disputes of limited formal scope. Rather, they formed a part of a much larger and more fraught debate over the very nature of English liberty and its expression in theatrical representation. Finally, as part of the project that has formed a focal point in this book, I will suggest that the resistance to sentimental comedy in the eighteenth century can be read as a form of resistance to the formation of what we now generally term a middle-class consciousness and in particular to the kinds of tacit behavioral discipline that gave shape to and still regulate that mode of consciousness, identity, and being. The play readings following this discussion will trace how sentimental comedy participated in the emergence of this mode of consciousness through a shift in emphasis from breeding to good breeding.

The main attack on sentimental comedy was initiated by John Dennis in 1722 with his "A Defence of Sir Fopling Flutter." Not satisfied with the results of this essay, which was written in anticipation of Steele's *The Conscious Lovers* and positioned rhetorically as a long-deferred response (by eleven years at least) to Steele's attack on George Etherege's *Man of Mode* (1676) in *Spectator* No. 65 (1711), Dennis then took a more direct approach to critique with his "Remarks on . . . *The Conscious Lovers*" (1723). What stands out in this second essay, and what I want to highlight here, is Dennis's accusation that Steele was palming off a "double Cheat . . . [upon] the town," the first "upon their Pockets" and the second "upon their Understandings."[34] For Dennis's vehement outcry against sentimental comedy in general and against *The Conscious Lovers* in particular arose not just from his perception that Steele pandered to audiences by offering them a flattering, rather than a realistic, portrait of themselves, but also, and more consequentially, from his judgment that Steele had committed a kind of aesthetic "Fraud" (2: 251). In this respect, he directs his outrage toward what he identifies as the series of improbabilities that Steele tries to pass off as probable, the greatest one of all being Steele's attempt to pass off what is clearly a "Species of Tragedy" as comedy (2: 259).

With its appeal to a language and a logic of breeding, this kind of argument appears to have reached a kind of critical mass in the 1770s, when a perception that sentimental comedy had conquered the English stage was spreading and a polemical counteroffensive was launched.[35] Oliver Goldsmith, for example, incorporated this line of reasoning in the arguments of his influential "Essay on the Theatre; Or, a Comparison Between Laughing and Sentimental Comedy" (1773). Goldsmith opens this essay by noting that "The Theatre, like all other amusements, has its Fashions and its Prejudices; and when satiated with its excellence, Mankind begin to mistake Change for Improvement."[36] As an example of this kind of misprision, a kind of false taste that has its origin in novelty, he offers the example of a "new species of Dramatic Composition," that is, sentimental comedy. Although he concedes that "these Sentimental Pieces do often amuse us," Goldsmith goes on to speculate whether, if given a fair hearing, "True Comedy would not amuse us more? . . . Whether a Character supported throughout a Piece with its Ridicule still attending would not give us more delight than this *species of Bastard Tragedy*, which only is applauded because it is new?" (3: 211–12, emphasis added). Goldsmith then heightens the effect of his polemic by following this charge with an enunciation of dark foreboding. He warns that the consequence of countenancing this kind of illegitimate speciation on the stage would be a complete fall into aesthetic and, we are to infer, social and moral anarchy (3: 213). Dolefully, he intones, "it would be a just punishment that when, by our being too fastidious, we have banished Humour from the Stage, we should ourselves be deprived of the art of Laughing" (3: 213).

While Goldsmith's comments on the consequences of "bastardy" among the dramatic genres may seem strangely apocalyptic to us, they sound almost prosaic when compared to William Cooke's colorful condemnation of the genre in his *Elements of Dramatic Criticism* (1775). Cooke sets the tone for his chapter "Of Sentimental Comedy" by preemptively enjoining that the "laws of the drama know no species of comedy under this title."[37] While he thus appears to desire the eradication of the sentimental from comedy's evolutionary tree, he nevertheless bows to popular taste and makes it his business to trace the genealogy of a form that features instead of "wit and humour, (the very essence of comedy) a driveling species of morality, which . . . from being falsely applied to comedy (however it may excite the *piety* of the crowd) must nauseate men of sense and education" (141–42). Subsequently, in his attempt to trace the genealogy of this "false taste," Cooke cites Steele's *The Conscious Lovers* as the first instance of the genre and laments the fact that so "elegant and judicious" a writer in all other respects should have been responsible for giving the "stamp of fashion" to such an egregious form (143). In Cooke's view, from this one poorly considered act of licensing by a cultural eminence, all else followed: "Comedy being thus debauched, like an unhappy female, began to be viewed in the light of *common game*, by those poets who dare not look up to her in the days of her chastity; such finding the intercourse easy, and the profits great, immediately hired themselves in her service" (143–44). Thus, he concludes, the "success of one fool drew many," the *vis comica* was exchanged for the "pathetic," and "an art originally invented to lash the follies, and imperfections of mankind, through the vehicle of ridicule . . . is changed into what is vulgarly called a moral kind of entertainment" (144).

Cooke presents an account of sentimental comedy that is laced with sexual innuendo. According to him, the genre's descent is one that is besmirched by indiscriminate breeding, debauchery, and prostitution. The dramatic family tree has been sullied, and comedy in particular has been not only cheapened but made altogether too "common." These comments are designed rhetorically to position sentimental comedy as an immoral rather than as a moral genre. Further, Cooke's references to the "end" of comedy and to the "prospect of improvement" make it clear that his goal in providing this genealogy is not only to impugn the "legitimacy" of the dramatic genre, but to question the legitimacy of the genre's claims upon its audience. Indeed, behind Dennis's, Goldsmith's, and Cooke's charges against the speciation of the genre lies an idea of comedy that entails a series of arguments not only about what meanings a genre can or ought to carry, but about the role comedy ought to play in relation to its audience.

That idea of comedy is evident in the abundant references they each make to ridicule and humour as the essence of the genre; it was widely thought, as Dennis indicates, that "The Subject . . . of every Comedy ought to be ridiculous by its Constitution; the Ridicule ought to be of the very Nature and Essence of it. Where there is none of that, there can be no Comedy."[38] Ridicule was considered the means to the end of comedy: the exposure of vice and folly. Humorous individuals, characters invested with temperamental imbalances, idiosyncrasies and ruling passions, provided the catalysts of action and the illustrative objects of that ridicule.[39] Drawing on a view of human nature that owed much to the cynicism of Hobbes, this theory of comedy persisted in eighteenth-century commentaries despite the softening that, as discussed in the previous chapter, was occurring in the actual practice.[40] With its satirical emphasis on ridicule and humours, this theory of comedy opposed the good-natured approach to human character favored by sentimentalism.

Most commentators have stopped here and characterized this conflict precisely as a clash between competing accounts of human nature. Yet such an abstract and philosophical explanation does very little to explain why the attacks on sentimental comedy were so vituperative and the defense of ridicule and humour so vehement. Only something more concrete, something that raised more than merely the specter of harmful repercussions could give rise to the level of passion evident in these essays. We would do better, then, to determine what was thought to be at stake when Goldsmith trembled at the prospect of a stage from which all humour had been banished. We need to ask, in short, what were the cultural politics of ridicule and humour?

Goldsmith provides us with a first clue to an answer in the preface to his sentimental comedy, *The Good Natur'd Man* (1768). Here Goldsmith expresses the same fear, writing that he "hopes that too much refinement will not banish humour and character from our's, as it has already done from the French theatre."[41] Goldsmith's comment reflects the fact not only that evaluations of the English stage were obsessively filled with comparisons to the state of the stage in other nations, but that "humour" functioned in these comparisons as the very proof and emblem of English superiority.[42]

Humour assumed this position as early as the seventeenth century, but in the period following the political settlements of the Glorious Revolution and the commercial settlements of the Financial Revolution, it began to take on even greater symbolic weight. The nature of this change in status was captured best by William Congreve in a letter to John Dennis. Agreeing with Dennis that "there is more of Humour in our English Comick Writers than in any others," he continues:

I do not at all wonder at it, for I look upon Humour to be almost of English Growth; at least, it does not seem to have found such Encrease on any other Soil. And what appears to me to be the reason of it, is the great Freedom, Privilege, and Liberty which the Common People of *England* enjoy. Any Man that has a Humour, is under no restraint, or fear of giving it Vent.[43]

From this statement we learn that the abundance and variety of humours were understood to be the natural effects of political conditions in England, conditions that supported the "Freedom, Privilege, and Liberty" of individuals to express themselves "under no restraint." In tyrannical nations like France, by contrast, humours were "banished" from the stage and individual expression was suppressed. Humour thus came to be perceived not only as the product of these conditions, but as the very emblem of liberty and the freedom of individual expression that such liberty ensured.

This distinction continued throughout the eighteenth century as persistent hostilities between the English and French inflated contrasts between the cultural effects of Protestant liberty and those of Catholic tyranny.[44] Again we find, as we did in our discussions of plays about plays and tragedy, that the stage functioned as a kind of flashpoint for the expression of anxiety and concern over national interests. Cultural invasions seemed to be almost as feared as actual invasions; they were figured as an underhanded way to weaken the populous and open them up to successful attack. At midcentury, for instance, Samuel Foote took great pride in explaining that in contrast to the submissions of the French, the "Bonds" of neo-classical rule "[did] not hit the Taste and the Genius of the free-born luxuriant Inhabitants of this Isle" because "They will no more bear a Yoke in Poetry than Religion" (20). Maintaining, moreover, that the English "will not be indebted to any other Country for what they can obtain without its Assistance," he attributes the fact that "no Nation has more Comedies, no Comedies more diversified humourous Characters" to the "Nature of our Constitution, and the Complection of our Inhabitants" (22). Like Congreve, Foote believes humour to be a home-grown product, a unique resource of English soil and the English nation. At the same time, he extends this account of humour by attributing its proliferation on English soil not just to political equality but also to economic equality:

In *France*, one Coxcomb is the Representative of the whole Kingdom. In *England* scarce any two are alike. I don't know but this Variety of Humour may, in a great Measure, derive its Source from Vanity. Property, with us, is so equally diffused, that the Distinctions arising from it are very trifling. In order then to procure a Pre-eminence, we have recourse to particular Singularities, which, though at first affected, are at last by Habit so closely rivited [sic] to the Mind, as to make it impossible for the Possessor ever to divest himself of it. (22)

In Foote's account, the variety of humour derives from the fact that property is so equally distributed in England that it would be difficult to form distinctions among persons on the basis of class. Consequently, individuals take advantage of the liberty of expression allowed them in a free nation to shape "singular" habits of mind and characters of humour. While Foote's contentions about the equal distribution of property are clearly implausible, they do bring humour into relation with commercial as well as political interests. England's economic prosperity was linked to English liberty, and humour both on and off the stage functioned as the representational emblem of their health. As Stuart Tave points out, humour was discovered not only to have been of "English breeding," but of a "land of rich and free men" (95). Indeed, by the last quarter of the century, we find Thomas Davies counseling, in an eerie echo of Goldsmith's apocalyptic strain: "At length Commerce, and her companion Freedom, ushered into the world their genuine offspring, True Humour. To these she owed her birth; and when they expire, it will require no great sagacity to prophesy that she will follow her parents to the same grave."[45] "True Humour" thus was the legitimate "offspring" of a coupling between freedom and free trade; its "parents" sustained the environment in which it could be bred and nurtured.

The objections raised to sentimental comedy thus emerged out of a cultural politics that viewed the transformation of humour into good humour not only as a turn away from comic honesty, but as an ideological turn toward the abridgment of English liberties. On the one hand, the promotion, proliferation, and production of humours was viewed as a patriotic duty. On the other hand, any attempt to curb, censure, or censor humour on the stage was viewed as a direct assault on English liberty and on the prosperity of the English nation.[46] Above all, the objections to sentimental comedy were aimed at the extent to which the culture of politeness was thought to enforce a kind of behavioral uniformity that implicitly, yet effectively, curbed the kinds of idiosyncratic and passionate expression that were the signs of those liberties.

One expression of precisely this concern can be found in Horace Walpole's "Thoughts on Comedy." Here Walpole propounds the usual associations of humour with English liberty, alleging that "In this nation we have certainly more characters than are seen in any other" and attributing that remarkable singularity to "our liberty and the uncertainty of our climate." Yet as Walpole laments, in a culture of politeness, "this does not help the comic writer." For in order "to be tasted" in such a culture, Walpole reports, the humours must be reduced to something "common enough," that is, to the least common denominator. In his opinion, the "inundation of politeness . . . softened [English] features as well as weakened [the English] constitution," and he looks back, almost nostalgically, to an age when "Englishmen used to exert their independence by a certain brutality, that was *not* honesty, but often produced it" (2: 319). In short, Walpole supports the view that while the man of humours resisted and indeed was constitutionally (in every sense of that word) incapable of conforming his behavior to the conventions and demands of a social culture, the man of sentiment and good breeding, by definition, took his cues from that social culture and adapted his behavior to its normative codes. As he observes, "the attentions exacted by society . . . confines man to an uniformity of behaviour, that is composed to the standard of not shocking, alarming, or offending those who profess the same rule of exterior conduct" (2: 317).

What was ultimately at issue in the controversy over sentimental comedy, then, was whether this new genre (bastard or not), with its discourse of politeness and good breeding, restrained the humours, abridged the variety of individual expression, and thereby undermined the very basis of liberty in the English nation. Walpole's commentary makes clear the extent to which sentimental comedies were understood to have called into being a kind of homogeneous economy of persons in which the expression of individual humours was severely curtailed. And indeed, while theorists of the sentimental, like the third earl of Shaftesbury, would have claimed to have been promoting liberty in their own way, the evidence suggests that the desired effect of liberty for these theorists was not the multiplication or amplification of humours, but rather their diminution and their conformation to the normative demands of sociability.[47] As Lawrence E. Klein puts it, "politeness was a standard of behaviour at the same time that it summed up the fulfilment of right behaviour"; it aimed at nothing less than making the gentlemanly, that is, good breeding, "normative over a wide range of expressive forms."[48] To the extent, then, that sentimental comedy emerged in the eighteenth century as one of these "expressive forms," what remains to be done in this chapter is to elucidate through readings of particular plays how the argument for good breeding was articulated and how the form of that argument promoted the kinds of conventional behavior and affect that we have come to associate with the rising middling classes of eighteenth-century England. To do so, I will turn first to the sentimental comedy that is so often cited for being exemplary: Richard Steele's *The Conscious Lovers* (1722/1723).

Setting the Example: Richard Steele's
The Conscious Lovers (1722/1723)

Steele opened his dual campaign for "good breeding" and the role sentimental comedy could play in its cultivation with a prologue written by Leonard Welsted for *The Conscious Lovers*.[49] "By new and desp'rate rules resolved to write," our author, we are told, will eschew the methods of one who "smuts his scene" and attempt instead to gain that "Praise" which "from worthier Motives springs" (Prologue, 16, 11, 19). Steele's play is thus situated as an occasion for moral exchange and enrichment. The sentimental author, we are to believe, rejects self-interest and the financial rewards he could reap if he were inclined to "smut" his scene. His generosity in accepting the role of "champion of [our] Virtues" ought to be reciprocated by the audience with equally generous praise both for his motives and for the chaste contents of his play (Prologue, 11, 30). In this manner, members of the audience are presented with an opportunity to display their good breeding by performing an act of generosity not just toward the author, but in the interests of society at large. Indeed the prologue specifically enjoins: " 'Tis yours with breeding to refine the age, / To chasten wit, and moralize the stage" (Pro-logue, 27–28). The author, in other words, enjoys only the limited pleasure of acting as the "champion" to the audience's virtue; the audience, by contrast, could multiply the effects of sentimental comedy by becoming the champions of "good breeding."

Steele's desire to be the champion of good breeding on the stage and to produce a kind of exemplary drama was long-standing, and we can trace the bent of his reformist impulse in some of his earliest writings.[50] In *Tatler* No. 8, for instance, Steele had portrayed "a gentleman of taste" named Eugenio who was scandalized by a 1709 performance of Ravenscroft's play *The London Cuckolds* (1682). He concluded this ventriloquistic diatribe by having Eugenio issue a call for "the apt use of a theatre, as the most agreeable and easy method of making a polite and moral gentry, which would end in rendering the rest of the people regular in their behaviour, and ambitious of laudable undertakings."[51] Whether we concur or not with the rather simplistic model of cause and effect represented here, this commentary does, at the very least, reveal the extent to which Steele sought early on to shape an image of a "polite and moral gentry" that not only would influence behavior but, as Walpole so astutely surmised, would "regulate" it as well. Steele's use of the term "gentry" also suggests the class inflection that he sought to bring to this set of behaviors. For while his affinities were for the social and material interests of the rising middling classes, his aim was to elevate that class by cultivating in them the forms of refinement and social grace that were associated with the upper classes. Aristocratic caprice and wit would, of course, be tempered by what we now term bourgeois sense. At the same time, bourgeois consumption would be refined by aristocratic taste to form an "exemplary" class of persons on stage. Hence, as the reading below works toward illustrating my claims about good breeding and sentimental comedy, it will do so, in part, by demonstrating how, in modeling this new kind of exemplary drama, Steele sought to reform the aristocratic characters and plots that were so pervasive in Restoration comedies and to elaborate the "regular" behaviors that would distinguish a "polite and moral gentry."

While the prologue pronounces the altruistic and moral incentives for good breeding, the play itself takes up the less honorable, but perhaps more pragmatic and consequential, task of demonstrating how "good breeding" could support the audience's material interest in breeding well. This, of course, is the main concern of Mr. Sealand, "a great India Merchant" whose daughter Lucinda is betrothed to Bevil Jr., son of Sir John Bevil (I.i.50). In this forced marriage plot, neither Lucinda nor Bevil Jr. are interested in their match. Lucinda is in love with Bevil Jr.'s best friend Myrtle, and Bevil Jr. is in love with Indiana, a young maiden whom he has rescued from a lecherous guardian in France. We will later find out in a tearful discovery scene that she is the long-lost daughter of Mr. Sealand. Sir John is determined to make the match for his son and gain thereby the rather lucrative marriage settlement that Lucinda's hand conveys. Bevil Jr. has too much "delicacy" to disobey his father's commands but believes he will be able to convince Lucinda to release him from any obligation because of her prior attachment to Myrtle. At the same time, Bevil Jr. has been spotted at a masquerade in the company of a mysterious young woman (Indiana), leading to speculation that he might already be married or "worse," have a mistress. This development provokes Sealand to break off the match until he can be sure his daughter will marry a man of good character (I.i.98).

In a frank exchange of views with Sir John Bevil, Sealand reveals precisely what is at stake in the plot as well as in their negotiations: "projecting races that are to be made out of both sides of the comparisons," in other words, breeding stock (IV.ii.59–60). Significantly, the debate between Bevil and Sealand focuses on what constitutes capital on each side of the "comparison" and on whether a common denominator of exchange value can be established. On his side, Sir John Bevil, representing the interests of landed wealth, feels compelled to assert "the business of an ancient house," that is, "[g]enealogy and descent" as the fundamental denomination for marital exchange (IV.ii.2–3). This declaration holds little weight with Sealand, who represents the interests of prosperous merchants; from his point of view "the business of an ancient house" is no business at all, as he asserts:

Sir, as much a cit as you take me for, I know the town, and the world. And give me leave to say that we merchants are a species of gentry, that have grown into the world this last century, and are as honorable, and almost as useful, as you landed folks that have always thought yourselves so much above us. For your trading, forsooth, is extended no farther than a load of hay or a fat ox. You are pleasant people, indeed, because you are generally bred up to be lazy; therefore, I warrant you, industry is dishonourable. (IV.ii.46–54)

With this critique, Sealand discredits not only the basis for "breeding" championed by Sir John, that is, a claim to high rank, but also the form of "breeding" or training that offspring of such families are subsequently given. In place of this older set of values, Sealand presents the claims of the ascendant commercial classes whose "industry" was now leading and sustaining the national economy and whose trade was extending English power into international markets. In this capacity, Sealand implies, merchants have transcended the pretensions to rule that once supported the aristocracy and have evolved into a new "species of gentry."

What is significant about this claim and others that Sealand makes is that he preserves the language of aristocratic status even as he imbues that vocabulary with different values. And it is in this nominal register that Sealand and Sir John can find common ground for transacting a marital exchange. While they may dispute the contents of a "gentleman's honor," with Sir John requiring only that his son be a "gentleman of merit" "in the eye of the world" and Sealand calling for a more substantial proof of moral fiber, what they can agree upon is that Bevil Jr. ought to be a "gentleman" (IV.ii.28, 61–62). We are to understand, then, that like the title his offspring will bring to any marriage, Sir John's claims for a "gentleman" are only titular or nominal rather than substantive. By contrast, Sealand demands that a title, a product of breeding only, be accompanied as well by good breeding. What he is determined to discover is whether Bevil Jr. will be the kind of husband who "soils with his wife for a month" before returning to his dalliances with mistresses, that is, a man who thinks only *of breeding*, or whether Bevil Jr. is a man of good breeding who will not only honor and respect his wife, but will "value" her properly (IV.ii.81).

Steele draws this distinction through the hyperbolic, negative example of Cimberton and makes it clear that a man who values a wife only for her "breeding" capacities is a man who underestimates her value. Cimberton is Mrs. Sealand's suitor of choice for Lucinda, and as we are told early on by Lucinda's eventual match, Myrtle, he is a "formal, philosophical, pedantic coxcomb" who "pays no more compliment to her personal charms than if she were a mere breeding animal" (II.i.41–48). This account of Cimberton is crudely confirmed in the next act when he shows up to settle the details of the match. He declares: "I have considered it as a most brutal custom that persons of the first character in the world should go as ordinarily and with as little shame to Bed as to dinner with one another. They proceed to the propagation of the species as openly as to the preservation of the individual" (III.231–35). At first one might think that Cimberton shares both Steele's and Mr. Sealand's view of marriage as first and foremost a bond of affection rather than as an expedient for fleshly desires. But we soon discover that his interests are quite vulgar and mercenary; indeed we might say he protests too much. Cimberton goes on to examine Lucinda part by part, "considering her, on this occasion, but as one that is to be pregnant," or as Lucinda puts it, he surveys her "like a steed at sale" (III.292–93, 299). Cimberton's desire for marriage derives from an interest in "breeding" in its most crude and calculating form. Sizing her up for her reproductive potential, he lasciviously estimates that "pregnant undoubtedly she will be yearly" for he "shan't, for many years, have discretion enough to give her one fallow season" (III.295–97). Yet "breeding" for Cimberton is not merely an end in itself; it is also a means to an end. By estimating Lucinda's reproductive potential at a high rate, he aims to increase the size of her settlement portion and thus of his own fortune. As he so bluntly informs Mrs. Sealand, "This young woman's beauty and constitution will demand provision for a tenth child at least" (III.315–17). Cimberton's single-minded obsession with "breeding" is thus linked to his covetous attitude toward material goods; together these attributes illustrate the character of a man of bad breeding.

It has long been understood that Cimberton's exaggerated priggishness and his callous cupidity identify him with the hypocritical sensualists found in Restoration comedies. Elizabeth Inchbald specifically begged pardon on Steele's behalf for this Restoration holdover if "in the character of Cimberton, the author has at times degraded his muse, to comply with the degraded taste of the auditors of that period."[52] In the twentieth century, Shirley Strum Kenny has identified Cimberton as one of the characters whose presence in Steele's drama leads her to argue that the play consists of a "fusion of Restoration conventions of characterization and plot with Steele's own dramatic concepts rather than a totally new kind of comedy."[53] I would argue, however, that Cimberton's presence in the comedy, along with that of other Restoration figures, derives neither from a critical lapse in judgment, as Inchbald would have it, nor from an attempt to "fuse" a new form with an old one. Rather these figures were drawn quite deliberately to function as foils not only to elaborate the contours of the new kind of hero Steele sought to promote, but also to distinguish his comedy from those in the Restoration tradition.[54]

The evidence to support this claim can be found not only in the play text, as I have argued to this point, but also in the materials that make up Steele's preparatory writings for this play.[55] Although we have credible evidence that the love plot between the servants Tom and Phillis was in fact either suggested or added by Colley Cibber in order to satisfy a taste for low romance that had been cultivated by Restoration comedies, the characters of Cimberton as well as Sir John Bevil and Mrs. Sealand appear to have been created early and deliberately by Steele as Restoration figures whose behavior and motives, by way of contrast to those of Mr. Sealand and Bevil Jr., he sought to display and to correct in his exemplary comedy.[56] As John Loftis has shown, Steele began to plan for *The Conscious Lovers* at least as early as 1714; by 1720 it appears that much of the play had been written. In Nos. 1–3 of his periodical *The Theatre* (1720), Steele introduced his audience to the main characters of his projected comedy, and in the concluding essay of this series (No. 28), he promised his readership that he would soon publish this "new Comedy, call'd *Sir John Edgar.*"[57]

Significantly, the most extended character portrait that Steele supplies in his series of introductions is that of Mr. Sealand:

This Gentleman was formerly what is call'd a Man of Pleasure about the Town; and having, when young lavish'd a small Estate, retir'd to *India*, where by Marriage, and falling into the Knowledge of Trade, he laid the Foundation of the great Fortune, of which he is now Master. . . . He is a true Pattern of that kind of third Gentry, which arose in the World this last Century: I mean the great, and rich Families of Merchants, and eminent Traders, who in their Furniture, their Equipage, their Manner of Living, and especially their Oeconomy, are so far from being below the Gentry, that many of them are now the best Representatives of the ancient ones, and deserve the Imitation of the modern Nobility.[58]

Here Steele takes great pains to underline the idea that while Sealand may have fallen into the dissipated and spendthrift ways of a Restoration rake in his earlier years, he has subsequently undergone a kind of reformation and is now distinguished by a fastidious sense of industry, economy, and perhaps most tellingly, of taste. In this manner, Steele allies Sealand with the values and semantics of sentimental discourse even as he elevates the class of merchants to the level of "nobility." Sealand was meant to function deliberately in *The Conscious Lovers* as a representative of the kind of "polite and moral gentry" that Steele sought to shape and promote. His reformation stands out as an exemplary emblem of a desirable shift from an old set of values to a new one, from a comedy of breeding to a comedy of good breeding.

Additional evidence about the qualities that Steele sought to vest in his exemplary characters and the old values from which he sought to distinguish them comes to us in the form of a memorandum in Steele's handwriting about *The Conscious Lovers*. In this document we find an extended directive on the characters of Sir John Edgar/Sir John Bevil and Mrs. Coeland/Mrs. Sealand. Steele prescribes:

That the Character of Sr. John Edgar be Enlivened with a Secret vanity about Family, [And let Mrs. Coeland, the March', Wife have the Same Sort of Pride, rejoicing in her own high Blood, Dispising her husbands Pedigree, and Effecting to Marry her Daughter to a Relation of her Own, to take of the Stain of the lowe Birth of her husbands Side. . .].[59]

Like Cimberton, and in contrast to Mr. Sealand, both Sir John Bevil and Mrs. Sealand are characterized by an overdeveloped fixation on status as determined by the fleshly indicators of birth and blood. This gross materiality emerges in the play as a function of their passions and their humours. Their visceral affect is thus conveyed as firmly fixed in the body and stands in stark contrast to the tempered and apparently even and more cerebral affect of Mr. Sealand.

This contrast in character and in particular the association of Cimberton, Sir John Bevil, and Mrs. Sealand with the base desires and needs of the body produces at least two consequences for our understanding of the play's narrative and the socioeconomic transformations it maps. First, insofar as each of these characters either belongs to or has pretensions to membership in the aristocracy, they stand for an older order in which birth rather than merit accounted for status. Not insignificantly, this is the value system that underwrote the plots of Restoration comedies where cits, merchants, and men of the city were routinely caricatured and held in contempt as greedy, covetous, and self-interested. In this "new" kind of comedy, however, we find that these attributes have been reassigned to the "aristocratic" protagonists. Their fixation on the purity of "high Blood" and on the size of a settlement marks them as self-interested and self-absorbed; they cannot think beyond the appetites, humours, and passions of their own bodies. This old species of gentry is degraded by their sensual self-absorption and by their failure consequently to acclimatize themselves to the new conditions of sentiment and sociability.

On the other side of this reversal, we find Sealand, whose humours and passions have been tempered by experience and industry. Paradoxically, the merchant whose wealth derives from the exchange of material goods emerges in Steele's play, as in sentimental discourse more generally, as if he were unconcerned with status, wealth, and the accumulation of things as the measures of true worth. Indeed, to the extent that their motives and concerns appear to be elevated beyond the passions and humours of the body, this "new species of gentry" is that much more ennobled. Steele thus takes great pains to distinguish Mr. Sealand from his generational peers. They may try to shape the plot to the conventions of Restoration comedies, but Mr. Sealand's probity curbs the force of the passions and the humours and brings the comedy to an end based instead on good breeding.

Returning to the play, then, we find that Cimberton, with his mercenary motives and his exaggerated obsessions with money and breeding, acts the foil for Bevil, Jr. as much as do Sir John Bevil and Mrs. Sealand for Mr. Sealand. In contrast to Cimberton's lecherous proclivities, Bevil, Jr. supports Indiana in a private house but has asked no sexual favors of her. He has been scrupulous, moreover, to avoid any declarations of his intentions toward her because he believes he cannot make such commitments without his father's consent.[60] Goaded by her aunt's suspicions of his motives, Indiana enters into a hypothetical exchange with Bevil, Jr. and asks him whether he agrees that "no man ever does any extraordinary kindness or service for a Woman, but for his own sake" (II.ii.232–34).[61] At first, much to Indiana's surprise, Bevil, Jr. agrees with this assessment, but he then goes on to redefine self-interest in a manner that demonstrates his merit as a man of good breeding. Rejecting one of the fundamental premises of male heroism in Restoration comedies, Bevil, Jr. denies that "making an expense in the service of a valuable woman" is "heroic business" (II.ii.238–42). Rather, he asserts, it is only "a better taste in expense" (II.ii.245–46). Far from being disinterested, moreover, he finds that such a man "is no more than what every gentleman ought to be. . . . He is only one who takes more delight in reflections, than in sensations" (II.ii.256–59). Matching Indiana's earlier rejection of sensation in favor of reflection in a discussion of taste and the variety of entertainments, Bevil, Jr. marks the sentimental hero as one who places a high value on the still-dominant meaning of "sentiment" as a function of thought rather than of feeling.[62] Finally, when Indiana presses him again, insisting that "his having no private interest in the action makes it prodigious, almost incredible," Bevil, Jr. replies:

Dear madam, I never knew you more mistaken. Why, who can be more an usurer than he who lays out his money in such valuable purchases? If pleasure be worth purchasing, how great a pleasure is it to him who has a true taste of life to ease an aching heart, to see the human countenance lighted up. . . . What could a man do better with his cash? This is the effect of an humane disposition, where there is only a general tie of nature and common necessity. What then must it be when we serve an object of merit, of admiration! (II.ii.279–91)

What Bevil, Jr. offers in his sentimental response is an alternative model of economic return, a form of "usury" that does not result in the "breeding" of money, but rather in the increase of fellow feeling. His language retains the idiom of purchase, value, interest, and worth, even as he transforms the meaning of those terms to signify generosity, beneficence, selflessness, and humanity. His "good breeding" is thus demonstrated not only in the self-restraint he exhibits in his relations with Indiana, but in his unwillingness to assign a monetary value to human feeling and in his belief that merely witnessing the pleasure his generosity can bestow on others is more than a good return on his investment. In sum, as this exemplary text seeks to show us and as Indiana testifies in the fifth act, a man of good breeding is one who "bestow[s], without a prospect of return" (V.iii. 122–23).

Here, however, we must recall that this is the pretense rather than the reality of the genre. For just as our earlier examination of the economic grounds of sentimental comedy would predict, the play turns immediately after the revelation of Indiana's identity to the business of compensating Bevil, Jr. for his "good breeding." Indeed, this matter is so crucial to the didactic demands of the genre that Sealand announces not once, but twice, that "a fortune" will be "the reward of all [Bevil, Jr.'s] virtue" (V.iii.195–98).[63] While the text is careful in each case to characterize such rewards as the "merit which his father seeks," rather than as a condition of Bevil Jr.'s affections, the security of a fortune acts as a crucial element in the resolution of the marriage plot (V.iii.197). It not only provides "the means to reconcile the best of fathers to [Bevil, Jr.'s] love" (V.iii.227–28), it also provides the illustrative basis for the play's final couplet, intoned by Sir John Bevil: "Whate'er the generous mind itself denies / The secret care of Providence supplies" (V.iii.289–90). We learn, in effect, that while it may be unseemly to display an interest in material goods, good breeding does not go unrewarded; on the contrary it can prove a profitable instrument in the quest to breed well.

Finally, just as Bevil, Jr. is rewarded for his good breeding, so too is the audience invited in the epilogue of the first night's performance "to make your Profit your Delight" (34). The value explicitly offered in sentimental entertainments, then, is the benefit of an opportunity to display good breeding by demonstrating one's approval of virtuous action, ostensibly without "Prospect of Return." Implicitly, however, the promise is held out that displays of good breeding will be rewarded with opportunities to breed well—that displays of good breeding will result in such a superfluity of wealth that we all have "much more than we want" (V.iii.277).[64]

"A Link, torn off from the general Chain":
Edward Moore's The Foundling (1747/1748)

What is significant about the ending of *The Conscious Lovers* is that following the revelation of Indiana's identity the play turns immediately not just to the exchange of property, but to the dispensation of a daughter *as* property. Indiana is a long-lost daughter, and in this sense she is a property that awaits reclamation and dispensation by her rightful owner, that is, by her father. As the century wore on, the figure of the long-lost daughter would make repeated appearances in senti- mental comedies, with plot elements drawn more or less from the model offered by Steele's exemplary text. Each of these daughters, as Edward Moore put it in *The Foundling*, is meant to represent "A Link, torn off from the general Chain," and the plots circulate around the issue of how to resituate these "unlinked" females in the "chain" or social order of the drama.[65] In an insightful essay, James Thompson has explored the ideological trajectories of such "incognita" plots and has framed them precisely as illustrative cases in which the question of character can be read as an epiphenomenon of a more general crisis over value in the circulating economies of eighteenth-century English life.[66] Thompson is interested in "how the incognita plot comes to serve a peculiarly bourgeois form of the traffic in women," and he explores the ways such plots depended, as did the current crisis over coin, upon the question of how—whether "'by weight or by tale'"—to determine the value of these circulating figures.[67] He concludes that in all of these plays, "it is the female character whose value is subject to fluctuation and must be verified by one method or another, and so fixed. In each of these works, the method of valuation shifts from extrinsic to intrinsic, from name to face," where "face"—as the negation of the negation, that is, the tale of the "name"—has been reconstituted as the intrinsic and therefore privileged tale of the form (301). Significantly, Thompson is able to reach these conclusions only by insisting that the plays represent a strict separation of the public, civil sphere from the private, domestic sphere. Yet, as I have already demonstrated earlier in my discussion of *Art and Nature*, the domestic negotiations of the sentimental genre are not cut off from the political economies of the public sphere; indeed these plays represent precisely the ways in which those political economies infiltrate and then regulate the private sphere as well. Each sentimental comedy, in effect, illustrates the conditions of entry into the public sphere from the space of the private as well as the conditions of entry into the private sphere from the space of the public. In this manner, as we have seen in the previous reading, they produce a dialectic in which breeding meets good breeding to produce a new species of gentry.

In these narratives, then, not only is the tale of the daughter significant, but so too is the tale of the father. If the tale of the father is meant to represent a tale of the external imprimatur of the public sphere and that of the daughter the internal value of the private, then it is also the case that those tales are interactive and indeed mutually constitutive. Hence the "value" of the female character is not the only character "value" "subject to fluctuation . . . [that] must be verified by one method or another, and so fixed" in the course of the drama. Rather, in order for these plays to attain a comic ending, that is, an ending in marriage, the value of male character, and in particular that of the father, must also be rhetorically verified and fixed. In the reading that follows, I will trace how in Edward Moore's *The Foundling* the father's "tale" offers the external imprimatur or "weight" that legitimates the daughter's tale, even as the daughter's "tale" provides the external imprimatur or "weight" that authorizes the tale of the father. What we will discover is that ultimately these plays are not in fact directed toward the recognition of the daughter's internal or intrinsic value, but rather toward the restoration of the father's external, which is to say patriarchal, authority, as signified by the culminating exchange of the daughter *as* property.

Moore's *The Foundling* was first performed at Drury Lane during the 1747/ 1748 season. It was a successful play with an initial run of eleven performances, followed by intermittent appearances through the rest of the season. It was, as Allardyce Nicoll and Ernest Bernbaum note, the only sentimental comedy of its period, and it featured a plot that greatly resembled that of Steele's *The Conscious Lovers*.[68] Like Steele, moreover, Moore took great care, in a prologue written by Mr. Brooke, to style his play as being a new kind in which the author "forms a Model of a virtuous Sort, / And gives you more of Moral than of Sport." Aiming in the sentimental fashion at drawing the "melting Sigh" and the "pitying Tear," the play offers to "charm, to polish, and to bless Mankind" by exposing the audience to the example of "female Virtue" (Prologue). Our paragon of "female Virtue" in this play is the aptly named Fidelia, who, like Indiana in *The Conscious Lovers*, was rescued from the clutches of a lecherous keeper, here named Villiard, and brought to England by her rescuer, in this case the Young Belmont. However, unlike Bevil Jr., Young Belmont is a bit of a rake, and he seeks to separate Fidelia from his family household, where he had in haste installed her, so that he can take advantage of her person. As anticipated, the text circulates around the issue of how to place Fidelia in the social order of the drama. Her origins or "weight" are unknown, even to herself, and her fate thus depends on which version of her "tale" will prevail as the legitimate text from which her value can be read. Indeed, over the course of the performance, we encounter a number of different narratives about Fidelia, each of which has been put into circulation by a different character in order to further his or her own interests. This dramatic situation only highlights the kinds of instabilities associated with the assessment of character in the context of a burgeoning print culture of publication and publicity. Even more significantly, it underlines the particular vulnerabilities of an "unlinked" young woman whose value in this culture derives solely from her reputation, that is, from the qualities associated with her name in circulation.

In the first scene of the play, we are introduced to the cover story or "tale" under which Young Belmont has brought Fidelia to his family home. Apparently he has informed his family that Fidelia is "the Sister of a dead Friend of mine at

College, bequeath'd to my Guardianship." His family seems to have taken this story in whole. Believing everything Young Belmont has told her about Fidelia's "Family and Fortune," his sister Rosetta has, for instance, gone so far as to suggest a marriage for Young Belmont to Fidelia on the basis of "Equality of Birth . . . of Virtue, Prudence and Good Sense." At this point in the play, however, Young Belmont has no intention of playing Mr. B to Fidelia's Pamela. Resisting what his friend and confidante Colonel Raymond suggests would be "the Merit of raising her to a Rank, which she was meant to adorn," Young Belmont vows instead, "As I brought her in by one Lie, I'll take her out by another—I'll swear she's a Whore—that I may get an Opportunity to make her one" (I.i).

Young Belmont's confidence in his future machinations is not unwarranted, for by entering the Belmont household under false pretenses, that is, under the cover of an illegitimate tale, Fidelia has put herself in a compromised position that he can easily exploit. First, in the social/sexual calculus of the day, her acquiescence—no matter that it was extracted under duress and under threat from another ravisher—could be interpreted as a form of active consent that would redound to all future events, circumstances, and challenges. Indeed, Young Belmont is all too aware of and willing to exploit this gendered imbalance in the definition of consent when he observes that Fidelia may have avoided one rape only to be "ravish'd by her own Consent" (I.i.). Second, by associating herself with this false tale, Fidelia has done something that no young woman ought to do; she has put herself in a situation in which she owes an obligation or debt to a man who is neither her father nor her husband. In effect, she has made herself over in trust illegitimately as the potential property of someone who ought to have no sway or authority over her at all. Finally, by entering into a lie, Fidelia creates a situation in which it will be difficult for her to remove herself from taint or suspicion. In a culture in which the mere appearance of impropriety can result in endless speculation, rumor, and loss of reputation for a young woman, Fidelia compromises the integrity of her tale, and thus her value, by keeping one secret and telling one lie.

These are precisely the set of vulnerabilities that Young Belmont seeks to exploit when, for the price of a purse that will buy a "new lac'd coat and a feather," he enlists Faddle to "lie a little" and assist in his plots to secure a "little simple Fornication" (II.vi). To divide Rosetta from Fidelia and thereby facilitate Fidelia's removal from the Belmont household, Young Belmont and Faddle send a letter anonymously to Rosetta warning her against Fidelia as a woman who knows "how to wear the Face of Innocence, when it serves the Purposes of Guilt." To impeach Fidelia's character even further, they close the letter with the following ominous postscript: "There needs no farther Address in this Matter, than a plain Question to Fidelia—Is she the Sister of Mr. Belmont's Friend?" (III.i). This sly form of attack forces Fidelia into the untenable position of having to admit to deceit in order, paradoxically, to defend the honesty and integrity of her character. She is compelled first to plead weakly, "tho' I am not what I seem, I wou'd not be what that Letter calls me to be Mistress of the World," and then to offer cryptically, "What I am, I know not—That I am not what I seem, I know—But why I have seem'd otherwise than I am, again I know not—'Tis a Riddle, that your Brother only can explain—He knows the Story of my Life, and will in Honour reveal it" (III.i).

While Rosetta is at first inclined to believe in Fidelia's innocence, she soon becomes frustrated both by Fidelia's admitted lack of openness and by her obviously misplaced sense of loyalty and obligation to Young Belmont. The former only ensures that Fidelia's claims to ingenuousness will be read as disingenuous; the latter only intimates a form of willingness or consent to enter into a secret relation with a man who is neither her father nor her husband. Hence all Faddle and Young Belmont have left to do is to fan these inflammatory charges into a full-blown fire of suspected scandal. Indeed, their marked insinuations and their studied omissions with respect to Fidelia's "story" complete the second of two conditions for alarm that were offered earlier in the play by Colonel Raymond's father, Sir Charles, to Young Belmont's father, Sir Roger: "If she is what her Behaviour speaks her, and he pretends, a Lady of Birth and Fortune—Why, Secrets are unnecessary—If he declines an Explanation, look upon the whole as a Contrivance, to cover Purposes, which we must guard against" (II.i). Confronted with Fidelia's continued resistance to full disclosure and Faddle's and Young Belmont's refusal to offer any satisfactory explanation of Fidelia's "story," Rosetta is thus finally moved to go on her guard and to admonish: "When you incline to be a Friend to yourself, *Fidelia*—you may find one in me—But while Explanations are avoided, I must be allow'd to act from my own Opinion, and agreeable to the Character I am to support" (III.iii).

Rosetta's exiting line indicates her all too real concern that, by association, her character might catch the odor of impropriety. Her first consideration, as she makes perfectly clear to Fidelia, must be to protect the value of her own reputation. At the same time, she also makes plain that insofar as Fidelia remains unwilling to take the necessary precautions to protect her own character, she makes herself into the object of rampant speculation where "opinion" takes the place of truth in the articulation of her tale. This lesson is subsequently reiterated in an exchange between Fidelia and Colonel Raymond's father, Sir Charles. Here Fidelia explains her failure to take Rosetta into her confidence by protesting, "Alas, Sir!—if it concern'd me only, I shou'd have no Concealment." To this declaration, Sir Charles offers the following sharp corrective: "It concerns you most, Madam. . . . You have deceiv'd your Friend; and tho' I believe it not, a severer Reproach rests upon you—And shall an idle Promise, an extorted one too—and that from a Man, who solicits your Undoing, forbid your Vindication? You must think better of it" (III.vi). Sir Charles's admonition calls for Fidelia to take greater care for her reputation by exercising better judgment in bestowing her secrets. By failing to take Rosetta into her confidence, she has cost herself a potential ally against the intrigues of Young Belmont. More importantly, while Sir Charles's commentary acknowledges Young Belmont's use of coercion, it also underlines the extent to which Fidelia's willingness to countenance "conceal-ment" of her tale might ultimately be taken as a form of consent in her own ruin. Indeed, her lack of discretion, and thus the extent of her peril, is displayed in her reply to Sir Charles: " 'Tis not an extorted Promise, Sir, that seals my Lips—But I love him—And tho' he pursues my Ruin, I will obey him in this, whatever happen—He may desert me, but never shall have Reason to upbraid me" (III.vi). By sealing her lips and refusing to tell her tale, Fidelia risks her honesty. More significantly, by empowering Young Belmont to act as the guardian not only of her person but also of her tale, Fidelia effectively makes herself over as his property, subject to his claims of authority.

That authority over Fidelia's tale constitutes the basis for lodging a property claim in her person becomes all the more clear when Villiard appears on the scene to reclaim his charge. He lays his claim in the form of a threatening letter to Sir Roger: "I Am Guardian to that Fidelia, whom your Son has stolen from me, and you unjustly detain. If you deny her to me, the Law shall right me." Here Villiard construes Fidelia as a kind of property and accuses Young Belmont of having committed the crime of theft. The difficulty in defending against this charge is that Fidelia has no male relative who can claim her legitimately as property, that is, who can make her value clear by the weight of what Thompson has termed "genealogical credentials" (295). Consequently, any desiring male might produce a tale by which to make her into his property. Thus Young Bel-mont can represent Fidelia as a property "bequeathed" to him by a dying friend, and Villiard can quite literally claim Fidelia as property because he bought her from the nurse in whose charge she had been left as a small child.

By this point in the play, however, Fidelia has finally begun to grasp the appalling consequences of having given over her "tale" into someone else's hands. She has learned that it was Young Belmont who was the "Contriver of that Letter" that maligned her reputation, and in taking her leave of him, she charges him above all with having left her "to the Malice of that Wretch!—To have my sup-pos'd Infamy the Tavern Jest of his licentious Companions!" (V.iii). What Fidelia recognizes in these charges is the extent to which she has allowed herself to be made into an object of speculation in tales on the open market. She finally apprehends that if she is to protect both her value and her virtue, that is, if she is to avoid becoming a "public" property, she must tell her own story. Hence when Villiard appears to stake his claim, Fidelia moves swiftly to plead her own case:

Hear but my Story—and if I deceive you, let your Friendship forsake me—He bought me, Gentlemen—For the worst of Purposes, he bought me of the worst of Women—A thousand Times has he confess'd it, and as often pleaded his Right of Purchase to undo me—Whole Years have I endur'd his brutal Solicitations—'till tir'd with Entreaties, he had Recourse to Violence—The Scene was laid—and I had been ruin'd beyond Redress—had not my Cries brought the generous Mr. *Belmont* to my Relief—He was accidentally passing by—and alarm'd, at Midnight, with a Woman's Shrieks, he forc'd open the Door, and sav'd me from Destruction. (V.v)

By telling her story or tale, Fidelia finally claims a property in herself; in doing so she redeems her virtue and her value. That value is still limited, however, especially insofar as she lacks any male family member who can either claim property in her or endow her with property. Indeed, as Sir Roger makes clear when he forbids a marriage between the now repentant Young Belmont and Fidelia, a woman's claim to property in herself is, at best, a weak one; at worst it is open to challenge in a court of law: "Marry her indeed!—What, without a Shilling!—And be ruin'd by *Villiard* into the Bargain!—If your Story be true, *Fidelia*, you shall be provided for—But no marrying, d'ye hear Child?" (V.v). The extension of sentimental concern, as I have suggested earlier, only goes so far; it stops at the boundary of property and interest. While Fidelia may finally have claimed property in herself, the problem remains that there is apparently no one who can legitimately claim her as *his* property. Without the benefit of "genealogical credentials," there can be no marriage. With no agent of legitimate authority to take an interest in her and thus provide her tale with credit or weight, there can be no exchange.

Such credit or weight, as the play proceeds to illustrate, can only be supplied in the form of a father and in the revelation of paternity. This discovery finally comes about when Sir Charles steps forward to claim Fidelia as his long-lost daughter. When he had to flee England because of his Jacobite sympathies, he had left Fidelia in the care of the nurse who sold her to Villiard. Not insignificantly, this revelation is conveyed to us, quite literally, in the language of interest, where "interest" signifies a claim not only of sentiment but also, and indeed principally, of property. Having first satisfied his concerns about the honor of Young Belmont and the virtue of Fidelia, but before revealing the particular nature of his interest in the case, Sir Charles joins Young Belmont in his suit to his father, offering that "to make *Fidelia* worthy of his Son, a Fortune shall be added, equal to his warmest expectations." Only after he has thus secured his claim in Fidelia as a claim of fortune, as an investment in and of property, does he then proceed to articulate the affective claims of a parent. He does so, moreover, in the form of a response to charges that his "interest" in Fidelia might have been more than paternal: "You have often told me Sir [*To Belmont*] that I had an Interest in this lovely Creature—I have an Interest!—An Interest, that you shall allow me!—My Heart doats upon her!—Oh! I can hold no longer!—My Daughter!—my Daughter!" [*Running to Fidelia, and embracing her*" (V.v). Fidelia's tale is thus secured by a distinction between natural and unnatural affection and between legitimate and illegitimate claims of interest. Affection and interest are thus analogized; sentiment is marked by the bounds of property and property is vested as a function of sentiment.

This analogy is all the more pronounced when we consider the value not just of Fidelia's tale, but of Sir Charles's as well. His tale, too, is one that is fundamentally concerned with the relations between legitimacy, property, and the claims of affection. In this scene of revelation, Sir Charles acknowledges the error of his "mistaken Zeal" that "drove him into banishment" (V.v). Much earlier in the play, in fact, we have learned that it has been only "about three Months, since the King in his Goodness recall'd Sir Charles; and, by restoring the Estate, made the Colonel Heir to a Fortune, more than equal to [Rosetta's] Expectations" (I.ii). When Sir Charles had to flee England, he was also forced to surrender his title and his property. In effect, he had to forfeit all the external privileges and trappings by which to display the authority or weight of his genealogical credentials. In this sense, moreover, he was stripped of the powers, both practical and symbolic, that constituted his authority as patriarch. Most significantly, he lost control of the property that made up his patrimony, that is, his right of inheritance and his right to dispose of his property to his son and heir, Colonel Raymond. Upon his return, the restoration of his status as a subject under the law is articulated explicitly as a restoration of paternal property and property rights. Yet the full restoration of his rights as a subject under the law remains contingent on a far more subtle turn in the comedy, that is, on the reclamation of the right to enter into and to execute contracts and exchanges. That turn, of course, depends on his ability to reclaim the one piece of property still missing from his estate portfolio: his long-lost daughter. In other words, Sir Charles's restored legitimacy is concretized not only in his ability to dispose of his property to his son, but also, and with far greater import, in his ability to dispose of his daughter *as* property. Thus the affective claims of a parent are coupled with the rights of a father to dispose of his daughter in marriage, to make her over to a young suitor as "the richest Gift of Fortune" (V.v).

Fidelia's reentry into the social order thus is also marked as an entry into the order of property and into the order of patriarchal authority with respect to property. Sir Charles had been careful to observe Fidelia's virtue before he revealed himself and in so doing assured himself that her body had not been made the property of any other man. He exalted that he had found her "thus virtuous, in the Midst of Temptations, and thus lovely, in the Midst of Poverty and Distress!" (V.v). In this manner, her virtue becomes the guarantee, or external imprimatur, that secures his restoration to legitimate status, even as he provides her with the external supplement of genealogical credentials that make a marriage to Young Belmont possible. Having secured Fidelia as his property, Sir Charles can contract with Sir Roger for the marriage and reintegrate his familial line into the fabric of English society. Having secured the "weight" that will support her "tale," Fidelia can remove herself from the market as a potentially public good and retreat into the relative safety of the private sphere. The link in the chain has been reforged, and Fidelia's tale, along with that of her father, is brought to a conventional conclusion with external proofs of tears, vows, and sentiment. The tale, the property, and the sentiments have all been brought into a relationship of equal value. Breeding and good breeding have found their proper and propertied balance.

If we turn back to *The Conscious Lovers*, we realize that this narrative of patriarchal redemption has been part of the sentimental project from its beginnings. Mr. Sealand too had been a kind of errant father who, upon losing his small fortune, had had to abandon his wife and daughter and leave the country in search of fortune elsewhere. Like Sir Charles, his fortunes are not entirely restored nor is his redemption complete until he reclaims property in his daughter. This narrative would be repeated again in George Colman the Elder's *The English Merchant* (1766/1767). Here we find Sir William Douglas, a Scottish Jacobite, who has returned surreptitiously in order to find the daughter he had to leave behind when he fled England so many years ago. As he explains to his trusty serving man Owen, he has come now, putting his own life at risk, because "Her sex demands protection; and she is now of an age, in which she is more exposed to misfortunes than even in helpless infancy."[69] Indeed, it is precisely in this respect that each father acts in these sentimental comedies to guide and to secure his daughter and her virtue safely through the most perilous time in a young woman's life—that liminal moment of suspension in the public market that precedes recuperation into the private space of the family, that passage from daughter to wife, from adolescence into adulthood. These plots thus provide a means to articulate patriarchy as a benevolent institution. The forced marriage plot of other types of comedy is rewritten in this sentimental strain as the father emerges as the benevolent conveyor of genealogical credentials or weight rather than as a tyrannical conveyor of property in the daughter's form. In effect, the system of political economy instituted in these comedies enables the father to consolidate his authority over the daughter *as* material property even as he appears to accede affectionately to her wishes and desires. By a subtle process of figuration, moreover, the errant past of these fathers comes to be associated either with the dissipated habits of the aristocracy or with the tyranny of the Stuart monarchy. In contrast, their present moment of recognition and reclamation is marked by a progressive, Whiggish rhetoric extolling the benevolence of bourgeois virtue and exalting the rewards of liberty, merit, and free trade. Indeed, as I will demonstrate in the final reading of this chapter, the redemption of patriarchy in sentimental comedies goes hand in hand with the project of associating trade and empire with a system of benevolent paternalism.

Repatriating the English Other: Richard Cumberland's The West Indian

As the British Empire expanded and more English citizens became colonials, English society sought a way to distinguish its colonial citizens from its colonized and enslaved subjects. This project often took a conflicted discursive form as writers sought to distinguish Englishness as an elevated and indeed a transcendent quality of person and at the same time found themselves drawing distinctions among kinds or classes of English persons that belied this rhetoric of privileged equality. The West Indian Creole and the East Indian Nabob, whose profits derived respectively from the sugar and tea trades, were, for instance, claimed as English citizens abroad and at the same time were deeply resented as nouveau riche upstarts within England itself. In the hierarchy of English citizens, they were ranked as inferior. Discursively they were represented as disruptive and overly passionate people, deformed and tainted by their exposure to the tropical climate of the "torrid zones" and, more consequentially, by their deep and immediate involvement in the brutal practices of slavery.[70] Such distinctions among citizens called into question not only the integrity of Englishness but also the impermeability of whiteness. The great fear was that with too much exposure to the "torrid zone," the darkening of the skin might also result in a darkening, or even a deformation, of English character. Fundamentally, then, and despite its own intentions, this project of recuperation raised the question not only of what, if anything, was irreducibly English about colonial English citizens but also of what was essential about Englishness at all.

Sentimental discourse and sentimental dramas played no small role in this recuperative project and in the debate about Englishness to which it gave rise. One popular eighteenth-century playwright who took an interest in such questions and was sensitive to the implications of distinctions among the English was

Richard Cumberland. By his own account, Cumberland sought in his sentimental comedy *The West Indian* (1770/1771) to introduce

the characters of persons who had been usually exhibited on the stage, as the butts for ridicule and abuse, and [endeavor] to present them in such lights as might tend to reconcile the world to them, and them to the world. I thereupon looked into society for the purpose of discovering such as were victims of its national . . . prejudices . . . to make such favorable and reconciliatory delineations, as might incline the spectators to look upon them with pity, and receive them into their good opinion and esteem.[71]

With this deeply self-conscious and sentimental purpose in mind, Cumberland set out to redeem the much maligned character of the West Indian, that is, to recuperate and to naturalize the West Indian as English citizen. Through the course of the comedy, he attempts to demonstrate that even the most powerful passions of the West Indian can be read as virtues and that the effects of climate and environmental nurture are reversible and, in any case, only distract us from seeing the essentially English goodness beneath the surface of our hero. In this respect, Cumberland seems to follow David Hume's argument that moral causes have more weight in determining national character than do physical ones, that "the same set of manners will follow a nation, and adhere to them over the whole globe, as well as the same laws and language," and that "The SPANISH, ENGLISH, FRENCH, and DUTCH colonies are all distinguishable even between the tropics."[72] Yet, as I will demonstrate in the reading below, Cumberland also follows Hume in more than one respect. Like Hume, it seems that Cumberland ultimately found something unsatisfying and indeed discomfiting about an explanation of national identity that relied on the paradox of naturalizing a "habitual" set of cultivated manners and that he fell back upon a kind of biological determinism to secure the plot of his play as well as the narrative of national identity it produces.[73] That is, under the cover of a sentimental rhetoric, Cumberland firmly grounds his comedy in the promise of paternity. As a result, the process of naturalizing the English Other as English becomes elided and then occluded by the project of repatriating a son. Perhaps even more significantly, as the issue of paternity comes to define the relation of England to the West Indies and its inhabitants, the imperial project of colonial trade and possession comes to be represented as a system of benevolent paternalism.

Cumberland's *The West Indian* seeks rhetorically to represent the process whereby even the tinctures of climatic influence could be expunged from an individual's character as an essentially pedagogical one.[74] In the case of the play's main plot, the moral codes of England are brought to bear on the wild passions of Belcour, a supposed foundling who has just inherited an enormous estate in

Jamaica from his adoptive grandfather and has come to England to enjoy the pleasures that his vast wealth can well afford. While Belcour assumes from the outset that he is a "fellow subject," the text introduces him as a "foreign gentleman" and thus generates the pretense for taking up the task of determining whether Belcour is truly an "Christian Englishman" or alternatively a mere "Creolian" who has, even by his own account, grown too "accustomed to a land of slaves" (I.v.50, 1; I.iii.13, 15, 30–31). Significantly, however, the most interested party in this process is, unbeknownst to Belcour, his real father Stockwell, a once-poor clerk who is now a wealthy London merchant. Indeed, Stockwell takes the text's investigative project as his own. When he reveals his paternity to his close associate Stukely in the opening scene of the play, he also explains:

before I publicly reveal myself, I could wish to make some experiment of my son's disposition: this can only be done by letting his spirit take its course without restraint; by these means, I think I shall discover much more of his real character under the title of his merchant, than I should under that of his father. (I.i.99–105)

In this manner, Stockwell assumes the role of privileged observer in the comedy's study of the "real character" of Belcour. Positioned as a man of reason whose credentials include the fact that he is both a widely respected and wealthy merchant and a member of Parliament, Stockwell, despite his particular interests in the venture, appears as the guide to and interpreter of Belcour's actions. In fact, it is in this capacity that Stockwell agrees to "enter on a course of lectures" to keep Belcour free from the "faults" arising from his "complexion" (I.v.94, 83, 92). The father figure in the role of merchant is thus presented to us as somehow objective and dispassionate, as reasoned and articulate and able to remove himself from his own interests in observing Belcour. "Under the title of . . . merchant," he is construed, moreover, as the figure through whose wisdom Belcour might be redeemed and his essential core, or "real character," revealed. We are meant to view Belcour through Stockwell's eyes and to accept Stockwell's assessments of Belcour's character as the measure of the real. In this manner, the merchant assumes the role of paternal surrogate not just to Belcour but to the audience and reader as well.

The sufficiency of Stockwell's authority and wisdom as paternal surrogate is put to a test in the fourth act of *The West Indian*, when it is discovered that Belcour has made an untoward advance on Louisa Dudley, a virtuous daughter of a good but impoverished family. Stockwell is so "thunderstruck" by the news that he cries out: "What is it you have done[?] . . . If you have done that, Mr. Belcour, I renounce you, I abandon you, I forswear all fellowship or friendship with you forever" (IV.x.101–11). This scene of crisis provides an opportunity for Stockwell to demonstrate his probity and his moral authority in a number of ways. First, the event affords Stockwell the chance to demonstrate his mastery over those natural passions that might cloud judgment; to us he appears willing to repudiate his own son over an egregious breach of honor. Second, we find that an incident that might suggest the irremediable nature of the West Indian's "tropical constitution" (IV.x.6) as well as the insufficiency of Stockwell's program of sentimental pedagogy actually becomes an occasion instead for Stockwell to demonstrate his ability to see beneath the surfaces of things, to shed light on "this dark transaction" (IV.x.124). Indeed, he discerns that Belcour's behavior has been brought about by the perfidy of the Fulmers, who duped Belcour into believing Louisa Dudley was a woman of dubious reputation. Under this set of circumstances, what could be considered vices are now construed by Stockwell as virtues. In Stockwell's view, Belcour may be warm and perhaps overexuberant in his show of affections, but that warmth and openness are precisely what make him vulnerable to the depredations of artifice and graft. Belcour is simply an innocent naif who is "no match for the cunning and contrivances of this intriguing town" (IV.x.125–27). His intentions are honorable, and we learn he would have "died sooner than have insulted a woman of virtue" (IV.x.150–51). The West Indian is not irrecuperable then; he is merely in need of a strong paternal hand to help him steer clear of the "danger of licentious courses" (IV.x.152–53).

Indeed, if there is one thing that we are assured of throughout the comedy, it is the sufficiency of Stockwell's paternal claim. That is, despite all of the pedagogical pretensions to demonstrating the force and sway of English manners, either to us or to Belcour, the fact of Stockwell's paternity consistently underwrites the narrative. We are informed of Stockwell's paternal status in the very first scene, reminded of its peculiar burdens and responsibilities during each of the play's various crises, and finally told that this is the relation that "endear[s]" Belcour and Stockwell to each other in the closing scene (V.viii.118). Further, Stockwell opens the scene of crisis described above by disclosing his anticipated pride in claiming Belcour as his son, and he closes the same scene with a promise of that important "discovery" (IV.x.210). The scene thus functions emblematically as an internal echo of the paternal affirmations that mark the opening and closing scenes of the comedy as a whole. Paternity, in short, holds the key to the text.

Indeed, as Joseph Donohue has already observed, the notion of paternity that supports our sympathetic interest in Belcour even before he appears on stage also provides the loophole through which Belcour has passed at birth from Creole subject to English citizen.[75] His status is more a foregone conclusion than a serious point of contention. In the end Belcour's stereotypically West Indian manners—his florid use of language, his impetuous spirit, and his colorful passions—remain irrepressible, but they are rationalized and reinterpreted as fundamentally irrelevant. His original "stock," provided at conception by Stockwell, overrides all other considerations of character and ensures the blessing of English nativity.

If we read with rather than against the ideological grain of Cumberland's text, we might thus conclude, as has Donohue, that Cumberland's emphasis on paternity "produces an unusual tightness of structure" that makes the audience "reconsider the attributes desirable in a young man, regardless of his origin." We might also consider that "the audience will be forced to acknowledge that, in excluding the West Indian from society, they have proscribed an essential element of its cohesiveness."[76] Viewed more critically, however, it becomes clear that the play does not provide for the general assimilation of all West Indians as citizens, so much as, like an indulgent father, it finds a way to bracket the troubling aspects of West Indian origins and, thereby, to naturalize Belcour in particular as an English son. Even more significantly, by substituting a familial for a political relation, the play allows sentiment to do the work of ideology: paternity supplies the rationale for benevolent paternalism.

Indeed, this characteristic tactic of what might be termed gloss and suppression is illustrated in Stockwell's first lesson to Belcour. When the new arrival speaks with enthusiasm about the prospect of spending his estate on the pleasures of London, Stockwell admonishes: "To use it, not to waste it, I should hope; to treat it, Mr. Belcour, not as a vassal, over whom you have a wanton and a despotic power, but as a subject, which you are bound to govern with a temperate and restrained authority" (I.v.63–67). Stockwell's sentimental exhortation at once implicitly references and suppresses the slave labor that sustains not only Belcour's vast estate but also his own fortune built on trade with the West Indies. It takes for granted and actualizes a perverse dynamic in which wealth comes to be personified as a "subject" worthy of benevolent rule, even as the slaves who produce that wealth are subjected to a "wanton and a despotic power" that dehumanizes and transforms bodies into objects of exchange. In short, the moral worth of good husbandry appears to outweigh, and therefore to justify, tyranny on the sugar plantation. Belcour is thus distanced from any taint that could be associated with slave labor, and the circumstance that poses the greatest threat to a sentimental narrative not only about the West Indian but also about the merchants who have made their fortunes in the West Indies is effectively displaced.

Wearing what Paul Parnell might term the "sentimental mask" of a teacher-father figure, Stockwell thus conflates mercantilism with paternalism and good government.[77] Similarly, an ostensible interest in geographical origin is displaced and replaced by a concentration on genealogical origins. Hence, while Cumberland may have sought to demonstrate unequivocally that national character derives from exposure to, and the internal cultivation of, moral codes, he ultimately resorts, as does Hume, to the external assurances of biological inheritance, in this instance, a case of biological patrimony. Belcour becomes the bearer of an external mark of value as patriarchal imprimatur comes to stand in for "real character." On a broader scale, Cumberland's displacement illustrates the paradigm under which England worked to construe its relationship to its colonies and its colonial peoples. Motivated by powerful political and economic interests at the end of the eighteenth century, England chose to present itself as the paternal source or "fountain head" to its colonies (I.v.58). At the same time, however, it exploited the sentimental strain of that discourse to suppress the fact that under the watchful eyes of this benevolent patriarchy, some offspring would be more equal than others.

In the first scene of Steele's early sentimental comedy *The Tender Husband* (1704/1705), Clerimont Senior issues the following instructions to Lucy, whom he has employed to cross-dress under the alias Fainlove and seduce his gambling-addicted wife into a compromising position so that she may be brought into line before she loses his fortune: "I don't design you to personate a real Man, you are only to be a pretty Gentleman—Not to be of any Use or Consequence in the World . . . but meerly as a property to others, such as you see now and then have a Life in the Intail of a great Estate, that seem to have come into the World only to be Taggs in the Pedigree of a Wealthy House."[78] The distinction Clerimont draws between a "real Man" and a "pretty Gentleman" captures not only the distinction sentimental comedies draw between good breeding and bad breeding, but also the related emphasis these dramas place on the significance of property and the social order. A "real Man," which is to say a man of good breeding, ought not to rely merely on the privileges of birth; rather he ought to be of "use and consequence" in the "world." Moreover, he ought to be a good steward to the property he inherits rather than a burden to, or "property" of, that estate. In this manner, sentimental comedies both imported the logic of an aristocratic society, placing an emphasis on the inheritance of property via a patrilineal line, and at same time eschewed what they characterized as the wastefulness of that logic by joining the idea of inheritance to an emerging bourgeois value system in which breeding had to be supported by good breeding and the cultivation of merit.

These were comedies, then, not of sensibility, where extravagant displays of emotion for its own sake might be privileged, but rather of sentiment in the eighteenth-century sense of that word, as a means to an end. They were comedies directed toward enforcing a kind of behavioral normativity in the form of "good breeding" in which the affections themselves could be produced and bounded by a patriarchal social order. To this end, as I have demonstrated in the readings above, the rhetoric of sentimental comedies may have embraced a general concern for mankind, but ultimately the extension of the affections in this genre was legislated by familial and propertied interests. With respect to a daughter, the father's claim of interest and affection was rendered only once it became clear that she could be claimed as a property with a high exchange value. Before a son could be claimed, his ability to learn to conserve his patrimony had to be assured. In both cases, good breeding provided the necessary capital to recuperate and to re-articulate patriarchy as a benevolent institution vested with the governing author-ity and responsibility for the good stewardship of the nation's wealth and moral virtue. Good breeding thus provided not only the key to character but also the key to breeding well. In this manner, sentimental comedies carried out the same process of character valuation as their laughing counterparts, but in pointed con-trast they did so under the naturalized, because familialized, cover of "sincerity."

Epilogue

If there is an underlying premise that has guided the ideas of this book, it is that articulated by Victor Turner in the course of elucidating his theory of the relationship between performance and society:

For me, the anthropology of performance is an essential part of the anthropology of experience. In a sense, every type of cultural performance . . . is explanation and explication of life itself. . . . [T]hrough the performance process . . . what is normally sealed up, inaccessible to everyday observation and reasoning, in the depth of sociocultural life, is drawn forth.[1]

Turner understands performance as an outlet for social concerns in which various crises and anxieties are not only accessed and reflected but also interpreted and assigned meaning. He places drama not only at the center of human experience, but also at the center of processes for making sense out of that experience. For Turner, drama is no less than "our native way of manifesting ourselves to ourselves and, of declaring where power and meaning lie" (78). The theater is thus a site of cultural ferment, a place where new ways of seeing can be tested and new ways of locating value can be elaborated and explored.

Throughout this study, I have sought to illustrate the ways in which the drama of the eighteenth century can be read not only as text but also as sociocultural phenomenon. I have attempted to delineate the complex dialectical negotiations not only between form and content but also between form and society. I have tried to demonstrate, moreover, that while each genre offers a particular cultural logic with which to engage particular social issues and categories of identity, form itself is not intransigent but rather transformed and rearticulated in relation to the cultural work it is asked to perform. We can look to the theater of the eighteenth century both for the traces it bears of a performative past and for the intimations it offers for a performative future. Through a study that offers a fixed window into this period, moreover, we can discern how eighteenth-century English society represented itself to itself and how theater mediated the oscillations between continuity and change in the self-conception of that society.

I have turned in the final chapter of this study to sentimental comedy because it performs each of these temporal positions simultaneously. As the only dramatic genre in this study that could be said to have been "bred" in the eighteenth century, sentimental comedy bears the traces of the generic tradition from which it evolved and which, to some extent, it still resembles, even as it points toward a new standard of normativity in the dramatic meanings it produces and naturalizes. More immediately, it provides us with a case in point to illustrate the ways in which eighteenth-century society coped with the concerns and anxieties that were raised by the emergence of a burgeoning commercial culture in which new forms of wealth, property, and social mobility had undermined traditional notions of value. Here we find a new political economy aestheticized and draped under an affective canopy that serves as both justification and rationalization for a new dominant class. While the other genres discussed in this study had to be adapted to address these new conditions, in sentimental comedy we find a dramatic genre that was created precisely to serve the interests of the new merchant, trading, and middling classes. Hence, like its counterparts in periodicals such as *The Spectator*, we find sentimental comedy actively engaged in the process of constructing a new ideology, an ideology, that would speak for the moral probity, virtue, stability, and sincerity of the new bourgeois classes.

Nevertheless, that posture of "stability" and "sincerity" could hardly have been sustained or naturalized amid the disorderly conditions of the eighteenth-century playhouse in which the illusory and disciplinary operations of a "fourth wall" had yet to be established and audiences and critics alike thus felt free to intervene in the presentation of theatrical performances. Such a naturalization process had to wait on a series of playhouse reforms and structural alterations that could institute and enforce a space of separation—both physical and psychical—between the audience and the stage. These innovations began in the second half of the eighteenth century when Garrick first attempted to remove theatergoers from their perch on the forestage and continued into the nineteenth century with the gradual withdrawal of the action behind the proscenium and into the recesses of an increasingly deep pictorial stage. By the end of the eighteenth century, moreover, the size of the theaters had grown dramatically, with Drury Lane holding a capacity audience of over 3600 and Covent Garden an audience over 3000. As the size of the theaters grew, so too did the distance between audience and performance, and this physical distance was reinforced on the illusory or psychic level by innovations in lighting and scenic design that created the capacity to spotlight particular performers and generate realistic setting effects. By the mid-nineteenth century, moreover, it was finally possible to darken the playhouse during performances, and with this innovation, the process of detaching and distinguishing the theatrical from the spectatorial space can be said to have been completed. These physical and technical developments fundamentally altered the relation between audience and spectacle; they transformed an audience of participants in the action into an audience of spectators of the action. Most significantly, this form of separation made it possible to produce the effects of consciousness and interiority on the stage behind the stabilizing force of an illusory fourth wall.

For the eighteenth century, however, there was no wall of separation between the theatricality of the stage and the theatricality of the audience. Audience members participated in the performance, and their most compelling point of purchase was not an interest in character development, but rather in the elaboration of the generic form through which meaning could be assigned to character. Instead of focusing on coverage or on an exhaustive survey of the period, I have thus sought in this study to provide a strong interpretive account of the cultural work of each of the major dramatic genres of the eighteenth-century stage. More specifically, I have highlighted the ways in which the representation of character and of categories of identity such as class, gender, and nation followed the social and cultural interests of genre. At the same time, I have sought to elucidate the ways in which these plays engaged contemporary debates over the status of identity and value, and I have demonstrated how, amid a theatrical culture of surfaces, the stage provided a way to apprehend identity and locate value that was not dependent on an illusion of interiority. The theater was thus a critical site for social exchange in eighteenth-century English culture, a site where the all-consuming interest of society in the mobilities of character could be tested and explored and where identity itself could be understood as a public property rather than as the private or privatized concern of the subject. In short, if all the world acted the player in the eighteenth century, then the player and the stages upon which that player appeared acted not as the world, but rather as a vital, rich, and necessary cultural site where, without apology and without the factitiousness of concealment, that world could see itself in action and apprehend itself as acting.

Notes

Introduction

1. See Lannep et al., *The London Stage* and Highfill, Burnim, and Langhans, *Biographical Dictionary of Actors and Actresses*.

2. Hume, "Multifarious Forms of Eighteenth-Century Comedy," 26.

3. Nicoll, *History of English Drama, 1660–1900*, 2: 1–2.

4. I have taken information for this discussion from a variety of sources. For more detailed information, see the general introductions and overviews of eighteenth-century drama in Lannep et al.; Nicoll; Craik and Leech, *The Revels History of Drama in English*, vols. 5 and 6; and Styan, *The English Stage*.

5. Goldsmith, "An Enquiry into the Present State of Polite Learning in Europe," 1: 323. In alluding to a "licenser," Goldsmith refers to the Stage Licensing Act instituted in 1737.

6. In a study whose figures have held up to scrutiny, Harry William Pedicord has fixed regular attendance at the theaters at 1.7 percent of the London population. For this and other statistics related to attendance, see his *Theatrical Public in the Time of Garrick*, 1–18, esp. 17.

7. Klein, *Shaftesbury and the Culture of Politeness*, 11.

8. Worthen, *Idea of the Actor*, 81. For a broader discussion of the semiotics of place, and specifically of the space of the theater as marking a socio-cultural event, see Carlson, *Places of Performance*.

9. See Turner, *From Ritual to Theatre* and *The Anthropology of Performance*; Loftis's two studies, *Politics of Drama* and *Comedy and Society*; and Brown, *English Dramatic Form*.

10. For just a sampling of some of the most recent work in Restoration studies, see Backscheider, *Spectacular Politics;* Canfield, *Tricksters and Estates*; Gill, *Interpreting Ladies*; Markley, *Two-edg'd Weapons*; Peters, *Congreve*; Rosenthal, *Playwrights and Plagiarists*; Staves, *Players' Scepters*. For studies of Shakespeare in the eighteenth century, see Bate, *Shakespearean Constitutions*; Dobson, *The Making of the National Poet*, Marsden, *Re-Imagined Text*.

11. McKeon, "Generic Transformation and Social Change," 161. See also his *Origins of the English Novel*.

12. Watt, *Rise of the Novel*. John Bender and Nancy Armstrong published their groundbreaking studies in the same year as McKeon, and they too looked to the rise of the middle class as the key to understanding the rise of the novel. See Bender, *Imagining the Penitentiary* and Armstrong, *Desire and Domestic Fiction*.

13. McKeon, *Origins of the English Novel*, 22.

14. See Warner, *Licensing Entertainment*, xiv n. 3.

15. Ibid. My emphasis here follows from Warner's emphasis in an earlier phrasing.

16. Lynch, *Economy of Character*, 1, 127–28.

17. In *The Rise of the Novel*, Ian Watt defined formal realism as "the premise, or primary convention, that the novel is a full and authentic report of human experience, and is therefore under an obligation to satisfy its reader with such details of the story as the individuality of the actors concerned, the particulars of the times and places of their actions, details which are presented through a more largely referential use of language than is common in other literary forms" (32).

Chapter One

1. Richard Steele, *Spectator* No. 370, 5 May 1712, Addison and Steele, 3: 393–96.

2. For this phrase see Agnew, *Worlds Apart*, 160.

3. Agnew, 14. For a similar view on the shift to a theatrical perspective in eighteenth-century life, see Paulson, *Popular and Polite Art in the Age of Hogarth and Fielding*, 115–33.

4. Agnew, 161. See Marshall, *The Figure of Theater*.

5. Summarizing the "heart of [his] argument," Michael Fried writes in *Absorption and Theatricality*, that "underlying both the pursuit of absorption and the renewal of interest in the sister doctrines is the demand that the artist bring about a paradoxical relationship between painting and beholder—specifically, that he find a way to neutralize or negate the beholder's presence, to establish the fiction that no one is standing before the canvas" (108).

6. See also, Fried, 93–96, where he discusses Diderot's articulation of the concept of the fourth wall in *Discours de la poésie dramatique*.

7. Watt, *Rise of the Novel*.

8. Bender, *Imagining the Penitentiary*, 253, n. 2.

9. Armstrong, *Desire and Domestic Fiction*, 8.

10. See Braudy, "Penetration and Impenetrability in *Clarissa*," 274.

11. Braudy, 271.

12. Bender, 38.

13. For two recent instances where theorists of the novel have formulated this logic of "compensation" in economic terms see Thompson, *Models of Value* and Lynch, *The Economy of Character*.

14. Gallagher, 171–72.

15. For passing concessions of this kind, see Armstrong, 9 and Thompson, 7. For a significant intervention in this line of thought, see Lynch, 1–20.

16. The cited phrase is taken from Bender, 11.

17. The cited phrase refers back to Agnew, 169.

18. For this phrase, see Thompson, 21.

19. *Remarks on Clarissa, Addressed to the Author*, 35.

20. Steele, Preface to *The Conscious Lovers*, 9–11.

21. While I will demonstrate the ways in which this is specifically the case for the

eighteenth-century stage, Keir Elam has observed in general that, from a semiotic perspective, "the actor's body acquires its mimetic and representational powers by becoming something other than itself, more and less individual." See his *The Semiotics of Theatre and Drama*, 9.

22. For this phrase, see Jameson, *The Political Unconscious*, 48.

23. Among other applications, Steele uses the word as often to speak of general moral quality as to distinguish a particular personality trait. In a completely different register for the term, he intersperses references to "real" people with allusions to fictional personae. Finally, based on the behaviors they represent on the playhouse stage, he elevates the surnames of actors and actresses to emblems for the conduct of life, even as he discredits the conduct of professionals like lawyers and priests as the deceitful impositions of "players" (*Spectator* No. 370).

24. The idea of character has been explicated at various times by a number of critics, and I will draw on those accounts even as I strive to distinguish the particular value character held as the productive model of identity on the eighteenth-century stage. The main difference between my discussion and these is that they all discuss the instability of character as a motive to create discourses of interiority in narrative forms. I, on other hand, concentrate on the relationship of character to a discourse of exteriority as found in dramatic works of the same period. Here I am thinking of the following: Coleman, "The Idea of Character in the *Encylopédie*"; Coleman, "Character in an Eighteenth-Century Context"; Gelley, "Character and Person"; Lynch, "Overloaded Portraits"; Novak, "Sincerity, Delusion, and Character in the Fiction of Defoe and the 'Sincerity Crisis' of His Time"; Nussbaum, "Heteroclites"; Oakleaf, "Marks, Stamps, and Representations." In the following discussion all allusions to, or citations of, definitions for the term "character" are taken from the *Oxford English Dictionary*, 2nd ed.

25. The closest association with human agency among these literal denotations can be located in that designating "the style of writing peculiar to any individual," or "handwriting." Though this meaning adumbrates a notion of individuation, or signature, so critical to theories of the subject, through most of the sixteenth and seventeenth centuries "character" in this literal sense continued to allude only to the physical aspects of penmanship—slant, size of lettering, etc.

26. Pocock, "Authority and Property," 69.

27. See Pocock, "Virtues, Rights, and Manners."

28. Brewer, "Commercialization and Politics," 213.

29. This phrase comes, as mentioned earlier, from Jean-Christophe Agnew, who has argued that the competitive climate of an expanding credit culture and of increasingly speculative commercial markets compelled individuals to adopt masks to "conceal their objects" (*Worlds Apart*, 159–60).

30. As Benedict Anderson suggests in *Imagined Communities*, once faith in an "ontological reality . . . apprehensible only through a single, privileged system of representation" deteriorated, language, that is, the inscription of characters, also lost the authority to claim self-evident referentiality (14).

31. As Lynch has pointed out in *The Economy of Character*, this marks the emergence of character as "the primary designation for imaginary personages in works of imaginative fiction" (27). In the drama, as Randall McLeod has demonstrated, this shift was marked by the formal attribution of dramatis personae in eighteenth-century editions of Shakespeare. See Random Cloud (Randall McLeod), " 'The Very Names of the Persons.' "

32. In "Character in an Eighteenth-Century Context," Patrick Coleman also discusses this loss of immediate recognizability and notes, "Especially for men conditioned by the culture of an earlier era there arises an anxiety that recognizability is an insufficient source of true certainty" (54).

33. The form, as J. W. Smeed explains, generally takes a "typological approach to human personality" where "the subject, although presented to us as an individual person, must also stand for a social, moral, or psychological category." See Smeed, *The Theophrastan "Character"*, 2. The standard study of Theophrastan character is Boyce, *The Theophrastan Character in England to 1642*.

34. Smeed, 34. During this period the most influential works in the genre were Joseph Hall's *Characters of Virtues and Vices* (1608), Sir Thomas Overbury's *Characters* (1614–64), and John Earle's *Microcosmography* (1628–33). The beginning of the eighteenth century was marked by the publication of Abel Boyer's *The English Theophrastus: or, the Manners of the Age* (1702).

35. Smeed, 71.

36. Lynch, "Overloaded Portraits," 125. See also Nussbaum, who writes, "There is at mid-century a disintegration of preexistent categories of gender and character as men and women who wrote their lives were faced with new experiences that could not be subsumed within types and general abstractions" (146).

37. See especially Novak, Nussbaum, and Oakleaf.

38. See Fielding, "An Essay on the Knowledge of the Characters of Men."

39. Fielding writes that in such a culture "deceit must immediately suggest itself as the necessary means; for, as it is impossible that any man endowed with rational faculties, and being in a state of freedom, should willingly agree, without some motive of love or friendship, absolutely to sacrifice his own interest to that of another, it becomes necessary to impose upon him, to persuade him, that his own good is designed, and that he will be a gainer by coming into those schemes, which are, in reality, calculated for his destruction" (282).

40. Holland, *The Ornament of Action*, 19.

41. See Worthen, *The Idea of the Actor*, 71.

42. Worthen, 71.

43. For instance, the Restoration actor Samuel Sandford, whose body was "low and crooked" and who was known for playing villainous parts, was subjected to such an outcry when he attempted to play the part of an "honest Statesman." As Colley Cibber recounts, "so unusual had it been to see Sandford an innocent Man in a Play, that whenever he was so, the Spectators would hardly give him Credit in so gross an Improbability." See Cibber, *An Apology for the Life of Mr. Colley Cibber*, 79.

44. This was reported in a letter written by George Berkeley and recorded in the entry for Anne Oldfield in vol. 11 of Highfill et al., *A Biographical Dictionary of Actors, Actresses, . . .* , 101–11, 109.

45. These points were also referred to as "hits" or "turns."

46. This portion of the chapter heading for Chapter 4 marks the sense in which actors and actresses owned and were viewed as inseparable from their various parts (53).

47. Lichtenberg, *Lichtenberg's Visits to England as described in his Letters and Diaries*, 10.

48. Downer, "Nature to Advantage Dressed: Eighteenth-Century Acting,"1003.

49. Roach, *The Player's Passion*, 87.

50. Stone and Kahrl, *David Garrick, A Critical Biography*, 31.

51. In his perceptive article "Garrick, Iconic Acting, and the Ideologies of Theatrical Portraiture," Wilson reads Garrick's innovations in the context of the painterly arts to argue that Garrick's emphasis on the pictorial passions instituted a "rhetoric of interior life"; yet he also writes that "The subject of Garrick's illustration was not merely dramatic character but, from the *spectator's point of view*, the actor-as-character" (384, emphasis added). For an exhaustive catalog of the gestures which provided this shorthand language for theatrical action and expression, see Barrett, *The Art of Gesture*. As Barrett explains, "The 18th century art of the gesture used a vocabulary of basic gestures, each with an individual meaning known to all in advance, and all performed in accordance with given techniques and precepts of style" (7).

52. See, among others, Stone and Kahrl as well as Woods, *Garrick Claims the Stage*.

53. See Taylor, "'The Just Delineation of the Passions.'" In *The Player's Passion*, Roach echoes this position, writing, "If nature as we define it did not exist in the eighteenth century, the theater historian is bound to ask what Garrick's critics actually meant when they described his acting as natural" (14).

54. This pattern is recorded in Robert Lloyd's *The Actor*, a virtual anatomy of stage practices and a praisesong for Garrick's natural, feeling genius. Of those actors and actresses who fall out of character, Lloyd writes:

THERE is a Fault which stirs the Critic's Rage,
A Want of due Attention on the Stage.
There have been Actors, and admir'd ones too,
Whose tongues wound up set forward from their cue.
In their own Speech who whine, and roar away,
Yet unconcern'd at what the rest may say.
Whose Eyes and Thoughts on diff'rent Objects roam
Until the Prompter's Voice recall them home.
. . . .
Why should the well-bred Actor wish to know
Who sits above To-night, or who below.
So mid th'harmonious Tones of Grief or Rage,
Italian Squallers oft disgrace the Stage.
When with simp'ring Leer, and Bow profound,

The squeaking *Cyrus* greets the Boxes round;
Or proud *Mandane* of imperial Race,
Familiar drops a Curtsie to her Grace (pp. 13–14).

Similarly, after Susannah Cibber curtsied to friends during her performance of Ophelia, a reviewer for the *Theatrical Review* of 1 March 1763 was prompted to query: " 'Pray ask her in what part of the play it is said that the Danish Ophelia is acquainted with so many British Ladies!' " See Stone, *The London Stage, 1660–1800*, 4:2:948. For other references to this phenomenon, see Richard Steele's *The Theatre* #3 (Saturday 9 January 1720) in *Richard Steele's* The Theatre, 9–14, esp. 12–13; Hill, *The Actor*, 255–56; and Goldsmith, *Remarks on our Theatres* 2 (13 October 1759), 1: 389–91.

55. Garrick, *An Essay on Acting*, 5.

56. For this notion of "stamping" in relation to the actor, see Hill, *The Art of Acting*.

57. Worthen, 72.

58. Worthen, 72. In her discussion of Garrick's definition, Shearer West emphasizes the same point: "The detail with which critics and biographers discussed an actor's facial expression, gesture and by-play has rarely been equalled since, and this particular obsession with the externals of dramatic action related directly to the last vestiges of Cartesian theory, which saw the movements of the soul as expressing themselves through the actions of the body. But it was the actions themselves, rather than their fundamental source, that Garrick himself stressed when he defined the art of acting." See West, *The Image of the Actor*, 3.

59. This incident occurs in Fielding's *Tom Jones*, Book 16, Chapter 5.

60. This condition is difficult for us even to apprehend, for, as Alan T. McKenzie has pointed out in "The Countenance You Show Me," we have lost the ability to read this code for the passions.

61. See, among others, Lloyd's *The Actor* and Churchill's *The Rosciad*. This view was, of course, firmly put to rest by Denis Diderot in his groundbreaking essay *Le Paradoxe sur le comédien*, or *The Paradox of the Actor* (1773). Diderot's revolutionary argument in this fascinating and complex essay was that the strongest actors must not and do not feel the emotion they express in the course of a performance. For an extended discussion of Diderot's *Paradoxe* and its implications, see Roach, *The Player's Passion*, chapter 4.

62. For two more striking instances of such critique, see [Samuel Foote's] complaint in *A Treatise on the Passions*, against Garrick's King Lear as built on the trick of premeditated displays of effeminate tears (18–24), and [Thaddeus Fitzpatrick's] compilation of letters from *The Craftsman* and the *Gray's Inn Journal*, in *An Enquiry into the Real Merit of a Certain Popular Performer*, in which Garrick is attacked for the "Clap-Cues" (35) embedded in his style of speech (see especially the Dedicatory Address, vi–vii). In each case, Garrick's acting technique is described as a potpourri of stage tricks and claptraps, providing evidence of the extent to which Garrick's characterizations were viewed as artificial, rather than natural, even in his own time.

63. Many of Garrick's most famous "points" were captured in theatrical portraits and conversation pieces that he commissioned and that were widely sold in the form of

popular prints. The evidence suggests not only that these prints shaped expectations of Garrick's performances but that his live performances were measured against these static prints. As Shearer West points out in her study of theatrical portraiture, "The function of the theatrical portrait in the theatre-conscious society of the 18th century was not to preserve accurately an actor's performance but to *suggest* such a performance for largely commercial reasons" (27).

64. See Woods, 12 and Lynch, "Overloaded Portraits," 137.

65. For this view of Garrick, see Wilson and Roach, *The Player's Passion*, as well as the latter's article "Theatre History and the Ideology of the Aesthetic."

66. Wilson, 383.

67. Cibber, *An Apology*, 82.

68. According to *A Biographical Dictionary*, 68–71, the actress to whom Cibber refers here is Jane Rogers. Purposefully conflating actress with role to undo her own pretensions, Cibber mockingly writes: "I have known an Actress carry this Theatrical Prudery to such a height, that she was, very near, keeping herself chaste by it: Her Fondness for Virtue on the Stage, she began to think, might perswade the World, that it had made an Impression on her private Life; and the Appearances of it actually went so far, that, in an Epilogue to an obscure Play, the Profits of which were given to her, and wherein she acted a Part of impregnable Chastity, she bespoke the Favour of the Ladies, by a Protestation, that in Honour of their Goodness and Virtue, she would dedicate her unblemish'd Life to their Example. . . . But alas! how weak are the strongest Works of Art, when Nature besieges it! for though this good Creature so far held out her Distaste to Mankind, that they could never reduce her to marry any one of 'em; yet we must own she grew, like *Caesar*, greater by her Fall! Her first heroick Motive, to a Surrender, was to save the Life of a Lover, who, in his Despair, had vow'd to destroy himself, with which Act of Mercy (in a jealous Dispute once, in my hearing) she was provok'd to reproach him in these very Words; *Villain! did not I save your Life?* The Generous Lover, in return to that first tender Obligation, gave Life to her First-born, and that pious Offspring has, since, rais'd to her Memory, several innocent Grand-children" (81–82).

69. See Straub, *Sexual Suspects*.

70. This biting incident occurred during a performance of *Venice Preserved* in which Rogers was cast as Belvidera to Wilks's Jaffeir. Straub's source here is the anonymous *Memoirs of the Life of Robert Wilks* (1732). See note 68 above for Colley Cibber's account of the offspring of this affair.

71. Hill, *The Actor*, 120.

72. For an extended history and discussion of the first actresses, see Elizabeth Howe, *The First English Actresses*. For extended discussions of the intertextual resonances generated through the bodies of women on stage, see Maus, "'Playhouse Flesh and Blood'"; Rosenthal, "'Counterfeit Scrubbado'"; and Payne, "Reified Object or Emergent Professional?"

73. Chetwood, *A General History of the Stage*, 28. These actresses were identified as Bracegirdle and Barry by Elizabeth Howe, through whose work, cited above, I first became aware of this anecdote. Chetwood cites this example to support his arguments that "Per-

formers of both Sexes, ought to imitate those virtuous Characters they represent upon the Stage. . . . Moral Virtue, and a decent Behaviour, will gain Esteem from People of every Rank, will add Weight to the Characters they represent, and even may atone for want of Excellency" (25–28).

74. Highfill et al., *Biographical Dictionary* notes that Clive was famous for her "militant chastity," 3: 345. For discussions of Bellamy and Charke see Straub, chapters 6 and 7.

75. For an extensive discussion of William Hogarth's series of paintings of *The Beggar's Opera*, see Paulson, *Hogarth: His Life, Art, and Times*, 1: 180–91.

76. This detail was first brought to my attention during a seminar lead by Peter Wagner at Northwestern University (2 April 1996) in which he discussed details of his study, *Reading Iconotexts*. For contemporary allusions to this phenomenon, see Churchill's, *The Rosciad*: "As passion, humour, int'rest, party sways. / Things of no moment, colour of the hair, / Shape of a leg, complexion, brown or fair; / A dress well chosen, or a patch misplac'd, / Conciliate favour, or create distaste" (2–3); and Steele's *The Lying Lover*, in which Penelope, played incidentally by Jane Rogers, affirms: "if it be true, as the Poet finely sings, That all the Passions in the Features are. We may shew, or hide 'em, as we know how to affix these pretty artificial Moles—" (III.i).

77. Gay, *The What D'Ye Call It?*, opening scene, p. 4. All subsequent references to this text will be cited parenthetically by act, scene, and page number.

78. *A Complete Key to the last New Farce The What D'Ye Call It. To which is prefix'd a Hypercritical Preface on the Nature of Burlesque and the Poets Design.* The authors of this tract have been identified as Benjamin Griffin and Lewis Theobald. It is not insignificant that they objected to the casting of the usually comic actor, Penkethman, in a heroic role as purposeful and as in violation of generic decorum. This charge provides further evidence for my earlier arguments about the overidentification of actors with the lines of business and about the extent to which audience expectations could be confounded by the "character" of the actor.

79. For Pope's letter to Congreve describing contemporary reactions to *The What D'Ye Call It?* and for Gay's and Pope's letter to Congreve on the publication of the "Key," see Documents 128 and 129 in Congreve, *William Congreve: Letters and Documents*.

80. See Hammond, "Politics and Cultural Politics" and Lewis, "Gay's Burlesque Method in *The What D'Ye Call It?*"

81. See Derrida, "The Law of Genre," 65.

82. Derrida, 65.

83. See Jauss's influential essay, "Literary History as a Challenge to Literary Theory."

84. See Jauss, Theses 3 and 4 (25–32).

85. Todorov, *Genres in Discourse*, 19. In his introduction to a special issue of *Genre* 15 (1982), Stephen Greenblatt has argued similarly that "These collective social constructions on the one hand define the range of aesthetic possibilities within a given representational mode and, on the other, link that mode to the complex network of institutions, practices, and beliefs that constitute the culture as a whole. In this light, the study of genre is an exploration of the poetics of culture" (6).

1. My text is taken from Richard Brinsley Sheridan, *The Critic*, I.i., pp. 134, 135. All subsequent references to this text will be cited parenthetically by act, scene, and page number.

2. Thesis 4 of Jauss's "Literary History as a Challenge" provides a theoretical justification for this method of historicization. Jauss posits, "The reconstruction of the horizon of expectations, in the face of which a work was created and received in the past, enables one . . . to pose questions that the text gave an answer to, and thereby to discover how the contemporary reader could have viewed and understood the work" (28).

3. Agnew, *Worlds Apart*, 154. See Sennett, *The Fall of Public Man*.

4. Here Agnew (112) borrows a phrase from Jonas Barish's *The Anti-Theatrical Prejudice*.

5. As discussed in the last chapter, John Gay's *The What D'Ye Call It?* provides one instance of the former practice, while examples of the latter include Colley Cibber "mimicking" himself in Miller's *The Coffee-House* (1737/1738), and Kitty Clive impersonating herself in her afterpiece *The Rehearsal; or, Bays in Petticoats* (1749/1750).

6. *Stage Mutineers, or, A Play-House to be Lett* (1733), 3.

7. Ross, "Authority and Authenticity," 236–37.

8. As might be evident from this brief outline, the plays I have selected for extended readings are not always those that were either most preeminent in their time or even prominent in subsequent dramatic criticism. Yet they all illustrate crucial aspects of the concerns I have delineated above and contribute to our understanding of the cultural work of plays about plays. By extending the scope of this study to plays beyond the canonical few, I hope, as I indicated already in my introduction, to provide a more illustrative, though not necessarily exhaustive, portrait of the dynamic and varied conditions of eighteenth-century theatrical production. It is also worth reiterating here that this is *not* a chapter on farce. Plays about plays specifically take as their subject stage practices and dramatic representation. Thus, while farces, such as Samuel Foote's *The Englishman in Paris* (1753) and *The Englishman Return'd from Paris* (1756), often touch on many of the same themes as plays about plays, they are not included in this discussion because their focus is not on the stage.

9. Van Lannep et al., *The London Stage 1660–1800* (3:2:661–62) records two performances of *The Madhouse*, by Richard Baker, at Lincoln's-Inn-Fields on April 22 and 25, 1737. In *Some Account of the English Stage*, Genest records *The Madhouse* as a "musical trifle . . . acted 2 or 3 times . . . printed without the names of the performers" (3: 514). An octavo edition of the play was printed in London in 1737, and it is from that print that I take my citations. All subsequent references to this playtext will be cited parenthetically by act and scene number.

10. See "Competence" and "Competent" in the *Oxford English Dictionary*, 2nd ed.

11. See "Competence" as above.

12. Donaldson, *The World Upside-Down: Comedy from Jonson to Fielding*, 7.

13. Habermas, *The Structural Transformation of the Public Sphere*, 54, 56.

14. See respectively Hassall, "Fielding's Puppet Image," 75; Hume, *Henry Fielding and the London Theatre, 1728–1737*, 62; and Rudolph, "People and Puppets," 38.

15. Ahern, "The Sense of Nonsense in Fielding's *The Author's Farce*," 53.

16. For instance, Valerie Rudolph opens her essay by taking offense at an earlier critic's characterization of the end of Fielding dramatic career as "providential": "Disastrous would be a more accurate epithet in terms of theatre history" (31). Robert Hume similarly laments the "incalculable" damage to English theater as a result of the Licensing Act and takes issue with those critics who consider Fielding's theatrical career a mere prelude to his real business as novelist. He concludes his study of Fielding: "in 1737 the arc of his theatrical career was upward, and by all indications a distinguished career in the theater lay ahead of him" (260). Rudolph and Hume are, of course, writing against those who insist on rationalizing the end of Fielding's career in the theater by speculating as to whether Fielding could even have developed further as a dramatist at all. See, for example, Hunter, *Occasional Form: Henry Fielding and the Chains of Circumstance*, where he concludes that Fielding's "plays pleased many, but they did not please long, and it is just as well that he came upon vehicles more amenable to his own temperamental possibilities" (74).

17. In making this argument, I am indebted to J. Paul Hunter, who has argued that Fielding was not merely interested in asserting mastery over a given text or group of characters. Rather, like the Augustans he admired so much, Fielding also sought actively to create a position of authority in which he would be perceived, and could operate as, a larger cultural force. As Hunter so eloquently explains: "Intrigued by the inherent ambiguities of action—how the same action might mean different things when performed by different people in different contexts—Fielding was primarily concerned with the question of knowing how to construe accurately" (69).

18. Smith, *Plays About the Theatre in England from* The Rehearsal *in 1671 to the Licensing Act in 1737*, 208. In conjunction with M. L. Lawhon, Farnsworth published the second volume on this subject, titled *Plays About the Theatre in England, 1737–1800 or, The Self-Conscious Stage from Foote to Sheridan*. The complete title of the play referred to by Smith is *Pasquin: A Dramatic Satire on the Times*.

19. It was a great success at first; *The London Stage* (3:1) records over fifty performances within a year of its premiere. However, interest in the work apparently waned, and there were fewer than ten performances of the new version during the 1733/1734 season.

20. In this reading of *The Author's Farce*, I take the more recent line of argument that Fielding did not practice a consistent ideological politics so much as he promoted a cultural and aesthetic politics that bolstered his own career in the theater. For this view, see especially, Hammond, "Politics and Cultural Politics" and Thomson, "Fielding, Walpole, George II and the Liberty of the Theatre." In the reading below, I will allude only briefly to the specific political and literary referents of Fielding's satire. For more extensive, act-by-act close readings, see especially, Rivero, *The Plays of Henry Fielding* as well as Lewis, *Fielding's Burlesque Drama*.

21. Fielding, *The Author's Farce*, Prologue, 21–34. I generally cite the original (1730) version of this play, but where appropriate, I will cite revised passages from the 1734

edition as they are provided in the appendix to this volume. All subsequent references to this text will be cited parenthetically by act, scene, and line number.

22. For a discussion of how Fielding extended his attack to include Theophilus Cibber in the 1734 revision, see Lewis, 89–93.

23. For a discussion of the intense relationship sustained between the theatrical world and politics in the early eighteenth century and of Fielding's particular role in this conflict, see Loftis, *The Politics of Drama in Augustan England*.

24. Thomson, 47.

25. For an insightful discussion that reads this attack on cultural corruption as a critique of an emergent capitalist ideology, see Canfield, "The Critique of Capitalism and the Retreat into Art in Gay's *Beggar's Opera* and Fielding's *Author's Farce*."

26. For a discussion of the relationship between Pope's *Dunciad* and Fielding's *The Author's Farce* see Sellery, "Language and Moral Intelligence in the Enlightenment."

27. For a complete catalogue of the persons represented, see Appendix B of the Woods edition.

28. For a similar argument, see Rivero, 34.

29. This scene is widely regarded as a satire of the recognition scene in Richard Steele's *The Conscious Lovers*.

30. Recall, for instance, the case of Addison's *Spectator*, about which Jean-Christophe Agnew points out, "anonymity . . . was the mask behind which his candid observations of the fashions and foibles of life could continue undetected; it was the voucher for their authenticity and the vehicle of their power" (172).

31. See Canfield's warning against "uncritical complacency" (332).

32. Campbell, " 'When Men Women Turn,' " 63.

33. In *Pasquin*, for instance, Fielding deepens his portrait of the female Goddess of Nonsense in the figure of the Queen of Ignorance. For a discussion of the volatile and negative resonances of these kinds of female figures in eighteenth-century discourse, see Ingrassia, *Authorship, Commerce, and Gender in Early Eighteenth-Century England*, 24–26, 48–49. Ingrassia's study explores the ways that an anxious concern for masculine authority in the eighteenth century found expression in a correspondent hostility toward female involvement in the literary marketplace.

34. Campbell, 64.

35. Jerrold and Jerrold, *Five Queer Women*.

36. The writers discussed are Aphra Behn, "The Incomparable Astrea"; Mary de la Riviere Manley, "Delia"; Susanna Centlivre, "The Cook's Wife of Buckingham Court"; Eliza Haywood, "Ouida"; and Letitia Pilkington, "Swift's Insolent Slut."

37. Clive's *The Rehearsal: Or, Bays in Petticoats* was first performed as an afterpiece during the 1749/1750 season at Drury Lane; it was last performed during the 1761/1762 season. I have found no record of its publication until 1753, when it was printed for Dodsley in London. While I do not discuss this play in depth, I do want to note a number of significant aspects of its performance. First, Clive's satire of female authorship is doubly ironic here as, in effect, it would constitute a satire of herself. Second, the layers of "character" explode in this play as Clive played her protagonist Mrs. Hazard, who in

turn is made to play "Kitty Clive" in her rehearsal when "Clive" fails to show up for her role.

38. Shevelow, *Women and Print Culture*, 1.

39. Jones, ed., *Women in the Eighteenth Century*, 140. See also Donkin, *Getting into the Act*, who writes about the more particular case of female playwrights: "Playwriting, as a profession, violated all the rules of conduct. It conferred on women a public voice. It gave them some control over how women were represented on stage. It required that they mingle freely with people of both sexes in a place of work that was not home. It made ambition a prerequisite, and, perhaps more importantly, it offered the possibility of acquiring capital" (18).

40. See Castle, *Masquerade and Civilization*.

41. Nancy Cotton invokes this phrase in her *Women Playwrights in England c. 1363–1750*.

42. These plays were *The Lost Lover; Or, The Jealous Husband* and *The Royal Mischief* by Manley; *Agnes de Castro* by Trotter; and *Ibrahim* and *The Spanish Wives* by Pix.

43. *The London Stage* (1: 467) briefly discusses the issue of when *The Female Wits* was actually performed and finally resolves that the first six-day run must have come during the early autumn, probably September, of the 1696/1697 season. The text was not printed, however, until 1704. All subsequent citations of this play are taken from a copy of the 1704 edition. This edition was reprinted in 1967 in the Augustan Reprint Series, edited by Lucyle Hook. With the preface, prologue and epilogue omitted, the play has also been reprinted, along with a number of other plays by women playwrights of the same period, in Morgan, *The Female Wits*.

44. *The Spectator* condemned women playwrights on this very basis when it commented, "It is remarkable, that the writers of least Learning are best skill'd in the luscious Way. The Poetesses of the Age have done Wonders in this kind; and we are obliged to the Lady [Mary Pix] who writ *Ibrahim*" whose "Bawdry, refined upon an Author [Aphra Behn] of the same Sex"; *Spectator* No. 51, Addison and Steele, 1: 215–20, 218.

45. This analogy worked both ways, however, as Catherine Gallagher has powerfully demonstrated in her article, "Who Was That Masked Woman?" Women playwrights often manipulated this commonplace figure to their own commercial advantage.

46. See Cotton, cited above, as well as Clark, *Three Augustan Women Playwrights*; and Hook, Introduction to *The Female Wits*.

47. Smith, *Plays About the Theatre*, 72.

48. This text and that which follows are both taken from Fidelis Morgan's anthology, *The Female Wits*, 390.

49. Ibid.

50. The *Oxford English Dictionary* supplies many meanings for the term "Engross," including "To write in large letters; and to gain or to keep exclusive possession of; to concentrate (property, trade, privileges, functions) in one's own possession (often with the notion of unfairness or injury to others."

51. See Chapter 2: "The Grotesque Body and the Smithfield Muse: Authorship in the Eighteenth Century," of Stallybrass and White, *The Politics and Poetic of Transgression*.

52. *A Comparison Between the Two Stages* (1702), 26. Some scholars have attributed this work to Charles Gildon. I was first made aware of this passage by Lucyle Hook in her introduction to *The Female Wits*.

53. All references to this text will be cited parenthetically by act and line number as they appear in John Gay, Alexander Pope, and John Arbuthnot, *Three Hours After Marriage*.

54. According to Edward Parker's *A Complete Key to the New Farce Call'd* Three Hours After Marriage, Phoebe Clinket is, "a very silly Imitation of *Bays* in the *Rehearsal*, but is design'd to Ridicule the Countess of W—n—ea [Winchelsea], who, *Pope* says, is so much given to writing of Verses, that she keeps a Standish in every Room of her House, that she may immediately clap down her Thoughts, whether upon *Pindaric, Heroic, Pastoral, or Dramatical* Subjects" (5).

55. A "fool's cap" is defined in the *American Heritage Dictionary* as a gaily decorated cap . . . formerly worn by court jesters and clowns," while a "foolscap" is defined as a sheet of writing paper. Thus the authors here play on the variety of significations and punning potentialities of the term. For the idea of running the gauntlet, see Porter, *English Society in the Eighteenth Century*, 22.

56. Elizabeth Montagu as quoted in Porter, 23.

57. All the following citations of Prologues to Centlivre's plays are taken as printed in *The Works of the Celebrated Mrs. Centlivre*.

58. See the preface to the above cited edition for this and all subsequent references to the anonymous address "To the World."

59. See Colley, *Britons*, particularly Chapter 1.

60. The author of this introduction offers a similar argument in comparison to the Catholic Spaniards as well as the Islamic followers of Mahomet, writing in the case of Spain, "When I reflect on the French, I cannot forbear mentioning, with Anger, the *Spaniards*, who, since the Time their Kingdom was over-run by the Moors, have immured and shut up their Wives as it were, in Prisons. Is not this a barbarous Practice? Can the Nation be called civilized, that confines as wild Beasts that Part of the Creation, always acknowledged to be the most mild and gentle . . . ?"

61. Paula R. Backscheider might refer to this use of convention as finding a way to make their "chains speak." See her essay, "Women Writers and the Chains of Identification," in which she includes a lengthy discussion of the status of women playwrights.

62. Smith, *Plays About the Theatre in England*, 189.

63. *The English Stage Italianiz'd*. All subsequent references to this text are taken from this edition and where appropriate will be cited parenthetically by act and scene number.

64. For a discussion of this specious attribution, see Nicoll, *Early Eighteenth Century Drama*, 257. For an enumeration of the characteristics of dramatic satire, see Kern, *Dramatic Satire in the Age of Walpole, 1720–1750*, 10, 15.

65. Nicoll notes that "Prices were raised for pantomimes, and the actors sometimes succeeded in gaining double the amount for a show of this sort than they did from an ordinary comedy or tragedy" (2: 251–52).

66. See, for example, the farcical works of Samuel Foote, particularly *The Englishman in Paris* (1753) and *The Englishman Return'd from Paris* (1756), as well as his two-act satire

Taste (1752). For one account of how anti-French myth was joined to anti-aristocratic sentiment to produce a discourse of English nationalism during this later period, see Newman, *The Rise of English Nationalism*.

67. Smith, *Plays About the Theatre in England*, 135.

68. Smith, 241.

69. Hill, *A Snake in the Grass*.

70. Sheridan, *The Discovery*, Prologue.

71. George Colman the Younger, *The Female Dramatist*. All subsequent references to this text will be cited parenthetically by act, scene, and page number.

72. Turner, *The Anthropology of Performance*, 21–22.

Chapter Three

1. See, for example, Mrs. Hoper's *Queen Tragedy Restor'd*, in which the malaise of the nation is emblematized by the sickly lethargy of "Queen Tragedy."

2. Hnatko, "The Failure of Eighteenth-Century Tragedy," 468.

3. Nicoll, *History of English Drama*, 2: 63.

4. In his essay, "Anxiety, Political Rhetoric, and Historical Drama Under Walpole," Alexander Pettit has argued similarly that tragedy "is often the study of sympathetic ideologies (or sound moral virtues) rendered useless by the inability of the community or its representatives to live up to them" (112).

5. Philips, *The Briton*. Portraying the Saxon King Vandoc's armed rebellion against the Roman Empire, Philips's play can be read as a fascinating allegory of the Protestant Succession in which the liberty of the nation becomes the crucial stake in an armed struggle against tyrannical Popish and French forces.

6. My citation of Dennis's preface to *Iphigenia* (1699/1700) is taken from the facsimile reprint of the 1700 London edition of the play in *The Plays of John Dennis*, ed. Johnson. I discuss the significance of representations of male friendship in eighteenth-century tragedies in later portions of this chapter.

7. Steele, *The Guardian* No. 43, 30 April 1713. Stephens, 174.

8. This text is taken from *The Fatal Extravagance* as found in *The Dramatic Works of Aaron Hill, Esq.*

9. Dennis, *Iphigenia*. I have reversed the italics in transcribing this portion of the text.

10. Guthrie, *An Essay Upon English Tragedy with Remarks upon the Abbé de Blanc's Observations on the English Stage*, emphasis added.

11. Anderson, *Imagined Communities*, 11.

12. In a more general sense, Joseph R. Roach has argued similarly, "One of the goals of bourgeois aesthetics is to make the historically produced seem natural, universal, timeless. . . . [A] principal instrument for the aestheticization of daily social life, for the micropolitical inculcation of the ideology of the aesthetic in the eighteenth century, was the theatre," "Theatre History and the Ideology of the Aesthetic."

13. Johnson, *The Formation of English Neo-Classical Thought*, 172.

14. See Addison, *Spectator* No. 39, 14 April 1711, Addison and Steele, 1: 163.

15. Aristotle's *Poetics* was often cited in the seventeenth century as the authoritative source for this contention. It is important to note, however, that Aristotle actually put the least emphasis on "character": "Dramatic action, therefore, is not with a view to the representation of character: character comes in as subsidiary to the actions. . . . Again, without action there cannot be a tragedy; there may be without character," Section VI. For a detailed account of tragedy and tragic theory in the seventeenth century, see Hume, *The Development of English Drama in the Late Seventeenth Century*; for the same with respect to the eighteenth century, see Green, *The Neo-Classical Theory of Tragedy in England During the Eighteenth Century*.

16. Rothstein, *Restoration Tragedy*, 21.

17. As early as May 26, 1710 Richard Steele writes in *Tatler* No. 172, "I was thinking it would be of great Use, (if any Body could hit it) to lay before the World such Adventures as befall Persons not exalted above the common Level. This, methought, would better prevail upon the ordinary Race of Men, who are so prepossessed with outward Appearances, that they mistake Fortune for Nature, and believe nothing can relate to them that does not happen to such as live and look like themselves." *The Tatler*, 2: 445.

18. For a survey of the impact of emerging bourgeois ideology on the conventions of serious drama in this period, see Canfield, "Shifting Tropes of Ideology in English Serious Drama, Late Stuart to Early Georgian."

19. See Samuel Johnson, *Rambler* No. 156, 14 September 1751, commonly referred to as "'Rules' of Writing," in which he states, "As the design of tragedy is to instruct by moving the passions, it must always have a hero, a personage apparently and incontestably superior to the rest." *The Rambler*, 5: 65–70.

20. Perhaps the most famous and cutting example of this critique of the modern hero occurs in Fielding's *The Tragedy of Tragedies; or The Life and Death of Tom Thumb the Great*, in which the great hero of the tragedy, Tom Thumb, is literally reduced to a height no higher "than a span" (see Fielding's preface to this tragedy about tragedies under his pseudonym H. Scriblerus Secundus). In *Occasional Form*, J. Paul Hunter astutely summarizes Fielding's satiric intent: "Fielding's theatrical visualization of the size-as-value metaphor thus operates in a cultural context prepared to disvalue itself before a grander vision of the past. . . . Watching the story of Tom Thumb meant at least temporary acceptance of the view that modern heroism was diminutive indeed and any age that could praise such heroes had a severe problem with its values" (39).

21. An excellent example of this pattern can be found in Mrs. Hoper's *Queen Tragedy Restor'd*, which concludes abruptly when Shakespeare rises exhorting, "Desist ye learned Sons of Physick: / This is our Province, *Tragedy* diseas'd, / Requires the *Nostrums* of *Shakespearian* Scenes."

22. Pocock, "Modes of Political and Historical Time in Early Eighteenth-Eentury England," 98.

23. See Habermas, "Excursus," 12–14. For a more empirical account of the status of the middle class during the late seventeenth and early eighteenth centuries, see Earle, *The Making of the English Middle Class*.

24. I am not arguing, however, for either a one-to-one correspondence or a simply mimetic relationship between events in the social realm and their representation within an aesthetic form. Rather, I am suggesting a dialectical relation between tragedy as an aesthetic form and the particular content that demands accommodation by that form. Michael McKeon offers an overview and an argument for the use of such a methodology in eighteenth-century studies in his essay, "Cultural Crisis and Dialectical Method: Destabilizing Augustan Literature."

25. Alexander Pope to John Caryll, 30 April 1713, *The Correspondence of Alexander Pope*, 1: 75. In light of the discussion in the previous section of this chapter, it is worth noting that Addison was said to have been motivated by love of liberty and country in producing *Cato* for the boards. Samuel Johnson records this motive in his "Life of Addison": "The time, however, was now come when those who affected to think liberty in danger affected likewise to think that a stageplay might preserve it; and Addison was importuned, in the name of the tutelary deities of Britain, to shew his courage and his zeal by finishing his design." Johnson, *Lives of the English Poets*, 2: 99.

26. Loftis, *The Politics of Drama in Augustan England*, 57.

27. Addison's *Cato* premiered at Drury Lane on 14 April 1713 and was an astounding success, with more than twenty performances before the end of that first season. The play was revived in the following season. As Lincoln Faller has reported, there were 234 performances of *Cato* from 1713 to 1751, though only 17 thereafter to 1776. See Faller, *The Popularity of Addison's* Cato *and Lillo's* The London Merchant, *1770–1776*, 12.

28. See, for example, Armistead, "Drama of Renewal"; Morton, "'Roman Drops from British Eyes'"; and Faller.

29. Johnson, *Neo-Classical Thought*, 95–96, 105. For a more recent account of the ambivalences associated with the propensity for Roman analogs in the eighteenth century, see Ayres, *Classical Culture and the Idea of Rome in Eighteenth-Century England*.

30. See Armistead, "Drama of Renewal."

31. See especially [George] Sewell, *A Vindication of the English Stage, Exemplified in The Cato of Mr. Addison* and *Observations Upon Cato* as well as [John Oldmixon], *An Essay on Criticism; As it Regards Design, Thought, and Expression*.

32. See, for instance, Lady Mary Wortley Montagu's commentary, "Marcus being the son of Cato is no Excuse for our hearing so much of his Affairs; the Loves of his sons are improperly represented in the play. . . ." reprinted in "[Critique of *Cato*]," 64.

33. I have taken the prologue from the first edition of Joseph Addison's *Cato* as reprinted in modernized form in *The Beggar's Opera and Other Eighteenth-Century Plays*. All subsequent citations from *Cato* will appear parenthetically by act, scene, and page number as given in this text. It is worth noting here that Pope's allusion to "dying laws" in the prologue calls our attention proleptically to the need to reconsider both the specific circumstances of Addison's eponymous hero and the nagging tensions that trouble the tragedy more generally with respect to its classical precedents.

34. Significantly, Pope asserted that the love scenes were inserted only for the sake of popular taste. See Spence, *Anecdotes*, 46. Samuel Johnson concurred with others that "the greatest weakness of the play is in the scenes of love," but, wisely I think, he undermined

Pope's claim that they had only been added-on after the fact when he opined, "Such an authority is hard to reject, yet the love is so intimately mingled with the whole action that it cannot be easily thought extrinsick and adventitious; for if it were taken away what would be left?" ("Life of Addison," 103).

35. For one study of this phenomenon, see Cohen, *Fashioning Masculinity*.

36. In an article that focuses on race and sentiment in *Cato*, Julie Ellison has made a similar argument, writing that the popularity of the tragedy "depended . . . on overlooking the relationship between republican motifs and the racial and sexual content dramatized through other characters." See "Cato's Tears," 575.

37. [Francis Gentleman], *The Dramatic Censor; or, Critical Companion*, 1: 453–54.

38. Dennis, *Remarks Upon Cato, A Tragedy* (London, 1713).

39. [Joseph Reeve], *Cato. A Tragedy. By Mr. Addison. Without the Love Scenes*. Even the publication format and prefatory apparatus of *Cato Without the Love Scenes* announce the exclusion of women from the very activity of reading neo-classical tragedy. Printed in 1764, the edition features corresponding Latin translations on the left-hand page facing the right-hand English text (see Figure 6a–c). This tactic deliberately situates the text outside a woman's reading range, and it was compounded by the author's invocation of Voltaire's harsh commentary on the love scenes in *Cato* as a means to authorize this revised edition of the tragedy. Voltaire's words are given in French and translated into English on the opposite page. He characterized the love scenes as the "insipid intrigue" that "murders the whole piece" and blamed Addison for "submit[ting] his austere genius to the manners of the age," that is, to the appetite of women for amorous spectacles: "Les femmes qui parent les spectacles, comme ici, ne veulent plus souffrir qu'on leur parle d'autre chose que d'amour." From this configuration of materials, the reader is to understand that the text to follow will present tragedy as it should be—exclusively by, for, and about men. The Latin translation and alteration of the text has been attributed to one Joseph Reeve in Allardyce Nicoll's hand-list of plays in *A History of English Drama 1660–1900*, 3: 301. The British Library Catalogue attributes the 1764 edition, from which I am reading, to Reeve, though he is not so-named in the text (see full citation below); the title page of the 1764 edition still authorizes Joseph Addison. However, a volume by Reeve titled *Miscellaneous Poetry in English and Latin*, Second Edition, was published in London in 1794 and included the second edition of *Cato. A Tragedy. By Mr. Addison. Done into Latin Verse Without the Love Scenes*.

40. The author of this edition explains these alterations by submitting:

The Love Scenes being entirely out, it has been necessary here and there to make some *small* change in the original expression, and sometimes to borrow verses from different Scenes, to make the transition and connection of the parts *natural*.

The chief changes are marked in the margin, and the places where the verses are to be found, which in this Version are read in other Scenes, if any desire to be satisfied about a *trifle* of this nature.

[Reeve], *Cato. A Tragedy*, viii, emphasis added. I have emphasized the terms "small," "natural," and "trifle" to illustrate the extent to which the author of this revision regarded the female characters as irrelevant, or "small," with respect to the larger idea he conceived for this tragedy. All subsequent citations from *Cato Without the Love Scenes* will be from this text and, where appropriate, will be cited parenthetically by act, scene, and page number.

41. I am referring here, of course, to the complex system of social exchange described and analyzed most prominently by Rubin, "The Traffic in Women"; Sedgwick, *Between Men*; Luce Irigaray, *This Sex Which Is Not One*.

42. See, for example, Faller, 55–56, as well as Kelsall, "The Meaning of Addison's *Cato*." Ian Donaldson offers a slightly more complicated view of this episode that takes into account some of the ambivalence associated with the figure of Cato in the eighteenth century, but he ultimately concludes that Cato's cold response to his son's death marks him as a "man who is at once preternaturally stoical about his private sufferings, and preternaturally sensitive to the sufferings of his country." See Donaldson's "Cato in Tears," 390. In the eighteenth century, the appropriateness of this particular utterance had been the subject of considerable debate and more than once functioned as the crux for either condemning or defending Addison's tragedy. In her ["Critique of *Cato*"], Lady Mary Wortley Montagu was of the opinion that "The distresse of Cato, and the greatnesse of Mind which he shews at the veiw [sic] of his dead son moves us more than any Griefe he could expresse on that occassion and we are more sensible of his Smothered Sorrow than we could be of any Expressions of it" (67). While her position was later supported by *The Dramatic Censor*, John Dennis found the expression outrageous and unnatural and argued, "Is not this a downright Rebellion against Reason, against Nature, against Providence? Is not this bringing an artificial Character upon the Stage, instead of a natural one? And is an artificial Character proper for Tragedy, which is an imitation of Nature, and whose chief Excellence consists in describing a natural sorrow?" (*Remarks Upon Cato*, 40).

43. *The Dramatic Censor* minces no words in reporting of this scene in *Cato*: "This resolution alarms the impatient feelings of Portius, who charges the fair one with coldness, and exclaims in terms frantically inconsistent with the idea we have hitherto formed of his character. The lady's fainting is a most laughable circumstance, and the whole scene, which ends as it began, is such a laboured, unfinished aim at unessential passion, that we heartily wish it annihilated" (1: 446).

44. That "brotherhood" is one of the crucial stakes in this tragedy can be seen in Portius's asides, first in I.i: "Thou seest not that thy brother is thy rival; / But I must hide it, for I know thy temper," and then in III.i: What should I do? If I disclose my passion, / Our friendship's at an end: if I conceal it, / The world will call me false to a friend and brother" (*Cato*, pp. 8, 31). Of the first incident, *The Dramatic Censor* offers, "Portius disgraces his dignity by mean dissimulation . . . it sinks under the denomination of plausible artifice; thus the elder brother becomes less an object of estimation in this scene than the younger" (1: 439). In Gentleman's view, Portius bears the more egregious fault of the two brothers, for his is not merely the defect of loving a woman, but rather the unforgivable offense of allowing that woman to cause not just a rift, but a *concealed* rift, between himself and his brother. We will see this figure emerge as central once again in our discussion below of Lillo's *The London Merchant*.

45. In and of itself this revision is significant, for it makes possible the omission of a

number of indecorous and lusty statements in which Sempronius, incited by Syphax, fashions himself a Pluto to Marcia's Proserpine. It also renders obsolete Syphax's taunts that Sempronius has become "soft" and "unmanly" due to his love for a "worthless woman."

46. This last substitution constitutes a direct borrowing from the original (III.i), where it served Lucia's melodramatic imagination as a vision of what Marcus would look like after committing suicide over her.

47. This consistent effort to assimilate Juba into Cato's familial circle comes poignantly into focus with the reassignment of Marcia's soliloquized prayer for Cato's soul to Juba.

48. I would be remiss if I did not note that the text's drive to produce such a bond between Juba and Portius, with Cato as the father figure for both, ultimately results in a singular slip that undermines the ideological program supported by the exclusion of women. As if unsure whether Juba's figurative baptism into Cato's familial circle accomplishes its end by matching Portius "tear for tear," *Cato Without the Love Scenes* completes and secures this process by including, almost without revision, Cato's final speech in which he sanctions marriages between Juba and Marcia and Lucia and Portius. That is, despite the argument that both motivates and justifies the publication of *Cato Without the Love Scenes*, that the tragic ideal can be better achieved if women are excluded from the discourse, the text inevitably falls back upon that conventional patterning of relations between men in which women serve as the tokens of symbolic exchange. The effect of this incursion is all the more astounding in that Cato's last speech is not edited to eliminate his direct address to Marcia. Instead, and despite the fact that the revision neither lists Marcia in the *dramatis personae* nor offers a stage direction indicating her entry onto the scene, we find Cato gasping, " . . . Marcia, my daughter . . . Juba loves thee, Marcia" (V.vii, p. 165). It remains unclear why this portion of text was not altered, as were many others, to read, for instance, "Juba . . . Marcia loves thee, Juba . . ." followed by an offer of his daughter's hand in marriage to the young Numidian. Instead, Cato addresses an absent figure whose very invocation usurps the solemn periods on Cato's life, punctuating this final scene instead with a great and paradoxical question mark.

49. Lillo, Dedication for *The London Merchant; or, the History of George Barnwell*, 3. All subsequent references to *The London Merchant* will be taken from this text of the 1731 edition and will be cited parenthetically by act, scene, and line number.

50. In its first performances, *The London Merchant* was titled *The Merchant; or, The True History of George Barnwell*. See Van Lennep et al., *The London Stage 1660–1800*, 3:1:147.

51. Whether the account analyzes the text as a struggle of Christian mercantilism against Hobbesian opportunism, duty against desire, sentimental emotionalism against neo-classical stoicism, antifeminist against feminist discourse, or simply good against evil, the primary structure driving most readings of *The London Merchant* has remained binary. Notable contributions to the criticism of *The London Merchant* include Rodman, "Sentimentalism in Lillo's *The London Merchant*"; Havens, "The Sentimentalism of *The London Merchant*"; Trainor, "Tears Abounding" and "Context for a Biography of George Lillo"; Borkat, "The Evil of Goodness"; Trudy Drucker, "Lillo's Liberated Women"; DeRitter, "The Cult of Dependence"; Fein, "George Lillo's *The London Merchant* and Feminist Debates";

Mack, "Such Wounds as Hell Can Equal. Discussions of the tragedy are also included in Bernbaum's *The Drama of Sensibility* and Laura Brown's *English Dramatic Form, 1660–1760*. Even those who take a more complicated and less agonistic approach to the text tend in their conclusions to assimilate any contradictions within the play to an account of irreducible opposites arranged in hierarchical formation. See, for instance, Flores, "Mastering the Self" and Richard Brown, "Rival Socio-Economic Theories in Two Plays by George Lillo." Two notable exceptions to this general pattern in criticism can be found in Hammer, "Economy and Extravagance" and Canfield, "Shifting Tropes of Ideology in English Serious Drama, Later Stuart to Early Georgian." I cite both later in this section.

52. Millwood's defiance, her refusal to repent, and the text's need to contain and impose moral meaning on that refusal come into even sharper focus in the gallows scene that Lillo had originally planned as the play's final scene. Despite the fact that Millwood goes defiantly to her death in this scene, refusing to repent, Barnwell insists that the lesson to be learned by others is that if they should find themselves "o'ertaken" by vice at some future point they must:

Lament their guilt and by repentance rise,
Th'impenitent alone die unforgiven;
To sin's like man, and to forgive like Heaven.

For a history of this scene and a discussion of its later inclusion in the fifth edition, see McBurney's Introduction to *The London Merchant*. The lines above were taken from Appendix B, lines 71–73, of McBurney's edition. For a recent article speculating about why the scene was omitted from the first performances and editions, see Burke, "*The London Merchant* and Eighteenth-Century British Law."

53. In an otherwise fascinating and thorough article that traces the reception history of *The London Merchant* in relation to the discourse on apprenticeship in the eighteenth century and beyond, Lucinda Cole writes, for instance, "by the time her part in the murder of Barnwell's uncle is uncovered, Millwood has ceased to function as a 'woman' at all." See "*The London Merchant* and the Institution of Apprenticeship." One reason that could account for the different conclusions reached in Cole's and my essays is that where she takes Millwood to be a foil for Barnwell, I read Millwood against the London Merchant, Thorowgood. Some of the most interesting and compelling readings of *The London Merchant* derive from approaches based in economic discourse. Yet even the best of these neglect to interrogate the gendered terms that structure the economic discourse of this dramatic narrative. Among these critics, Peter Szondi and David Wallace do consider Millwood, but they both do so in a reductive fashion that incorporates a variety of stereotypical notions about "woman" that were particular to representation in eighteenth-century culture and that have come under considerable scrutiny in recent years. Hence, while their analyses of *The London Merchant* are both insightful and valuable with respect to the socioeconomic currents that shape the tragedy in its time, they can offer little insight into the role gender plays in the tragedy's attempt to establish a class ideology as a national

ideology. See Szondi, *Die Theorie des bürgerlichen Trauerspiels im 18. Jahrhundert*, esp. 62–83; and Wallace, "Bourgeois Tragedy or Sentimental Melodrama?"

54. McKendrick, "Commercialization and the Economy," 16.

55. For some of the most recent contributions to scholarship with respect to these issues, see Bermingham and Brewer, *The Consumption of Culture, 1600–1800*, and Brewer and Porter, *Consumption and the World of Goods*.

56. For a discussion of the operation of a gray world/green world motif in romantic comedy see Northrop Frye's *Anatomy of Criticism*.

57. Colley, 60.

58. As Colley reports, historical records indicate that "95 per cent of the *increase* in Britain's commodity exports that occurred in the six decades after the Act of Union was sold to captive and colonial markets outside Europe," and "re-exports of colonial goods made up almost 40 per cent of total British exports" (69).

59. Canfield has pointed out the manner in which Millwood is constructed as the "antithesis" to "bourgeois ideology" (215). This argument, I believe, can only take us so far, for, as I will demonstrate below, the problem for Thorowgood and for bourgeois ideology more generally, is not that Millwood represents an agonistic opposite, but rather that her mode of operations and her motivations are frighteningly similar to those that move mercantilism and capitalism.

60. The 1713 Treaty of Utrecht created *el pacto del asiento de negros*, in which the English acquired the contract to supply slaves to Spanish America as well as to the subjects of Great Britain for thirty years; the *Asiento* had been reaffirmed as recently as the 1729 Treaty of Seville.

61. I am indebted to Jonathan Dollimore's work on sexual difference and sexuality for the articulation of this idea. See *Sexual Dissidence*, where he theorizes what he terms the mechanics of the perverse dynamic and transgressive reinscriptions: "The displacements which constitute certain repressive discrimination are partly enabled via a proximity which, though disavowed, remains to enable a perverse return, an undoing, a transformation . . . I call this transgressive reinscription" (33). I am not interested here in undoing the "perverse dynamic" so much as in unraveling a case in which it operates to constitute a binary.

62. In her linguistic approach to the text, Stephanie Hammer echoes this view, concluding, "*The London Merchant* imagines the demise of the very institution which it ostensibly seeks to glorify and protect; politically, morally, and biologically, the countinghouse seems to have no future. Thus the model bourgeois tragedy actually undermines the very bourgeois values which it appears to affirm" (93).

63. In an interesting, though I think ultimately too speculative, article, Lee Morrissey explores not just the homosocial, but also the homosexual resonance of this scene and others in *The London Merchant*. See Morrissey, "Sexuality and Consumer Culture in Eighteenth Century England."

64. Wilson, "The Good, the Bad, and the Impotent," 247.

65. In his Introduction to *The London Merchant*, McBurney anticipates this argument,

writing, "The double title, in fact, clearly indicates the ideal and the disastrous deviation from this ideal" (xvi).

66. This split accounts, I believe, for some of the difficulties that critics have had in interpreting she-tragedies. Canfield took an important first step toward addressing this split and acknowledging the ideological content of Restoration and eighteenth-century drama in "The Ideology of Restoration Tragicomedy."

67. For concurring opinions, see Hume, *Development*, 220 and Howe, *The First English Actresses*, chapter 5.

68. As far as anyone has been able to discover, the first use of the term "she-tragedy" occurred in Rowe's epilogue to *Jane Shore*.

69. Between 1688 and 1706, Elizabeth Barry and Anne Bracegirdle were cast as rivals in at least thirty new tragedies. This statistic can be found in Howe, *The First English Actresses*, 159, which contains extensive discussions of the careers of Elizabeth Barry and Anne Bracegirdle as well as an appendix of the major actresses and their roles in new plays. I have taken other information for this discussion from Highfill et al., *A Biographical Dictionary of Actors, Actresses, ...*

70. See Chapter 1, note 72 for Howe, Maus, Rosenthal, and Payne.

71. The standard source for this circumstance is a letter from George Berkeley to Sir John Percival, where he states: "Mr. Addison's play has taken wonderfully, they have acted it now almost a month, and would I believe act it a month longer were it not that Mrs Oldfield cannot hold out any longer, having had for several nights past, as I am informed, a midwife behind the scenes, which is surely very unbecoming the character of Cato's daughter." Berkeley's understatement is remarkable, as is that of twentieth-century biographer Joanne Lafler when she observes, "For some of the sterner moralists, it must have seemed a blatant reminder of the difference between herself and the character she was playing," especially in light of the fact that the unmarried Oldfield was pregnant with the child of her recently deceased lover Arthur Maynwaring, with whom she already had one illegitimate child. I have cited this anecdote as it appears in Lafler, *The Celebrated Mrs. Oldfield*, 110.

72. See Matlack, " 'Spectatress of the Mischief Which She Made' "; Laura Brown, "The Defenseless Woman and the Development of English Tragedy"; and Marsden, "Rape, Voyeurism, and the Restoration Stage."

73. Whether critics read this transition as sudden or as gradual, almost all agree that she-tragedy ought to be positioned in this way. For accounts of she-tragedy that take the notion of transition as the focus of their argument, see, for instance, Nicoll, *A History of English Drama, 1660–1900*, 2: 97–101; Schwartz, "An Example of Eighteenth-Century Pathetic Tragedy"; Laura Brown, *English Dramatic Form* and "The Defenseless Woman"; and Canfield, "Shifting Tropes of Ideology." One significant departure from the recent tendency to focus primarily on female character and identity formation can be found in Tumir, "She-Tragedy and Its Men."

74. It is worth noting here that *The Fair Penitent* and *The Tragedy of Jane Shore* were two of the most performed tragedies of the eighteenth, century with 261 and 279 performances respectively between 1702 and 1776. Along with Addison's *Cato* (226 perfor-

mances) and Lillo's *The London Merchant* (179 performances), they account for four of the ten most performed non-Shakespearean tragedies of the period. The standard source for these figures is Avery, "The Popularity of *The Mourning Bride* in the London Theatres in the Eighteenth Century," 115–16.

75. Rowe, *The Fair Penitent*, Prologue, 15–20. All subsequent references to this text will be cited parenthetically by act, scene, and line number.

76. For a sustained study of these issues and their impact on dramatic representation in the Restoration period, see Staves, *Players' Scepters*.

77. The critical tradition of determining Calista's level of repentance is a long one and has dominated interpretation of the tragedy and its themes. In the eighteenth century, Samuel Johnson found that Calista exhibited "more rage than shame" and, along with Richard Cumberland, Francis Gentleman, and Elizabeth Inchbald, found that Calista was not repentant. See Johnson, "Life of Rowe" in *The Lives of the English Poets*, 2: 68; Cumberland, *The Observer*, nos. 77–79; Gentleman, *The Dramatic Censor*, 1: 256–77; Inchbald, "Remarks" on *The Fair Penitent*, in *Remarks for the British Theatre*. The tide seems to have shifted somewhat in the twentieth century, for where Annibel Jenkins follows the eighteenth-century line and finds Calista unrepentant, Canfield and Laura Brown have each argued that Calista is repentant and submits to a dominant system of values, Christian or moral respectively. See Jenkins, *Nicholas Rowe*; Canfield, *Nicholas Rowe and Christian Tragedy* and "Female Rebels and Patriarchal Paradigms in Some Neoclassical Works"; and Laura Brown, "The Defenseless Woman." A third way out of this bind has been to argue that Calista is penitent, but that rather than submit to the moral values of her father, she transcends all orthodox systems of judgment and realizes her guilt in her own way. For two such views, see Kearful, "The Nature of Tragedy in Rowe's *The Fair Penitent*"; and Armistead, "Calista and the 'Equal Empire' of Her 'Sacred Sex.'"

78. Cumberland, 2: 955.

79. As a number of critics have noted, it appears to be no accident that this opening scene occurs in a "garden belonging to Sciolto's palace." For readings that trace this theme more extensively, see both Armistead and Canfield, *Nicholas Rowe and Christian Tragedy*.

80. Indeed, when Sciolto comes upon the scene of Altamont and Calista with Lothario's body, his first charge and concern is against Altamont for disclaiming his friendship with Horatio (IV.142–45).

81. Indeed, the case is so strong that Cumberland found it a troubling inconsistency in Horatio's character that "that image would have interceded no less powerfully for [Altamont] when, penetrated with remorse, he intercedes for pity and forgiveness and even faints at [Horatio's] feet with agony at his unrelenting obduracy" (II:966). Once again, though he quibbles over minor inconsistencies, Cumberland picks-up on Rowe's commitment to solidifying an ideology of patriarchal succession in the son.

82. See the first two lines of Alexander Pope's "Epistle to a Lady" (1735).

83. For two accounts of the ways the tale of Jane Shore had been represented in both popular and official forms prior to Rowe's play, see Rowan, "Shore's Wife" and, more recently, Helgerson, "Weeping for Jane Shore," 451–76. For a view of how Rowe reflects directly on the political situation in England and the ambivalence felt toward a female

monarch, see DeRitter, "'Wonder not, princely Gloster, at the notice of this paper brings you.'"

84. This phrase is taken from Act IV, scene i, p. 91 of Rowe, *The Tragedy of Jane Shore*. All subsequent references to this text will be taken from this edition and will be cited parenthetically by act, scene, and page number.

85. In this moral tale, virtue once lost or compromised can never be wholly recovered. Yet, it can, as Rowe's representation makes clear, be reconstituted in part. One of Rowe's contemporaries explains the logic of such a transformation as follows: "if the Behaviour be then mild, humble, submissive, penitent, with a due Sense of the Guilt, and a suitable Compunction of Sorrow for it, then not only Nature, but Morality stand forth and plead in behalf of the Sufferer. The guilty Person seems then to have paid the Price of his Crimes, and is no longer an Object of Justice, but Mercy, that is Compassion." In the case of Rowe's Jane Shore, moreover, the effect is so powerful and "so pleasing, as to force us to a Condolance of her Misery, almost as if her Character were free from Faults, and entirely Virtuous." Thus we condemn the sin and compassionate the sinner in this moral tale. See *A Review of the Tragedy of* Jane Shore *Consisting of Observations on the Characters, Manners, Stile, and Sentiments*, 6, 8. A notable exception to this general tendency to pass over Jane Shore's patriotism can be found in Jenkins, *Nicholas Rowe*, 106–7.

86. *A Review of the Tragedy*, 9.

87. That Rowe was merely following the historical record in his representation of the tragic causes of Hastings's downfall would only have strengthened the force of this sentiment for an eighteenth-century audience. Apparently, after Edward IV's death, Hastings had taken Jane Shore as his own mistress. In order to bolster and justify his summary execution of Hastings on charges of treachery, Gloucester had issued a proclamation in which he took advantage of Hastings's known libidinous proclivities and accused him of crimes including pandering, debauchery, adultery, and witchcraft in association with Jane Shore. This official proclamation concluded, "Lord Hastings had lived in continual incontinentcy . . . with SHORE'S WIFE and lay nightly with her and particularly the very night before his death, so that it was no marvel if his ungracious life brought him to so unhappy a death." For this account, I have relied on documentation found in Rowan's "Shore's Wife," 454. As Rowan demonstrates, other "official" representations, including *The Mirror for Magistrates*, also pointed to Hastings's relationship with Jane Shore as the cause of his downfall.

88. In *The Ends of Empire* Laura Brown has argued similarly that, "In this sense, a major historical event, the execution of Hastings and eventual execution of the royal children, seems shaped and directed by female passion" (83). Brown refers here both to the passion of Jane Shore and that of Alicia, whose treacherous actions in planting a letter of accusation against Jane Shore and Hastings contribute directly to the demise of both. Some have argued that Alicia is a foil for Jane Shore, that her treachery, uncontrollable jealousy, and madness are meant to highlight, by contrast, Jane's loyalty and penitence. I would argue, as I believe Brown would, that Alicia acts less as a foil for Jane Shore than as a device of extension through which to project some of the more virulent consequences of "female

passion." In short, Rowe articulates through Alicia how female passion once unleashed is a, "merciless, wild, unforgiving fiend / ... / ... a monster loose among mankind" that gives rise to "famine, war, or spotted pestilence / Baneful as death, and horrible as hell" (IV.i, p.91). By this method, Rowe can maintain Jane's sympathetic status, even as, through images of Alicia, he implicitly generates a causal link between Jane's transgressions and the tragedy we witness.

89. What can be gleaned from the records is that Matthew Shore was a goldsmith, sometimes referred to as William Shore, that he married Jane Shore when she was very young, and that, most likely, he fled England when Jane become Edward IV's mistress in 1476. For this information, see Rowan, "Shore's Wife."

90. Rowan, 451.

91. Janet E. Aikins has argued similarly, "By using Jane's husband in disguise as Dumont and as an observer of the action, Rowe offers us a figure whose point of view we may partially share. ... By functioning as perceiver, Dumont is the creator of the significance of the action for the audience." "To Know Jane Shore, 'think on all time backward,'" 272.

92. For a different but complementary view on the generic implications of this bourgeois couple, see Helgerson.

93. It is not insignificant, moreover, that in this scene of revelation and reconciliation the actor who played Shore in the first performances of the tragedy was made to wear a rich suit of silk and velvet, symbolizing the character's success as a goldsmith and thus the upright prosperity of the middling classes. For details related to this costume decision and others, see Milhous, "The First Production of Rowe's *Jane Shore*," 315.

94. Hnatko, 464–65.

Chapter Four

1. Collier, *A Short View of the Immorality and Profaneness of the English Stage*, 5, 2.

2. See the final chapter of Robert Hume's *The Development of English Drama in the Late Seventeenth Century*.

3. In *Genre and Generic Change in English Comedy, 1660–1710*, Brian Corman has echoed this view, arguing that the eighteenth century witnessed a modulation in the attitude taken toward humours characters from one that was punitive to one that verged on the sympathetic. For an earlier study of this transformation in the tone of comedy in the eighteenth century, see Tave, *The Amiable Humorist*.

4. For this history and its fallacies, see Robert Hume, "Goldsmith and Sheridan and the Supposed Revolution in 'Laughing' Against 'Sentimental' Comedy."

5. See Goldsmith, "An Essay on the Theatre; or, A Comparison Between Laughing and Sentimental Comedy."

6. Collier, 2.

7. See Kenny, "Humane Comedy."

8. Hume, *Development*, 474

9. Bull, *Vanbrugh and Farquhar*, 106. See also McVeagh, "George Farquhar and Commercial England." For a discussion of Farquhar's *The Twin Rivals* as a response to Collier's attacks, see Rothstein, "Farquhar's *Twin Rivals* and the Reform of Comedy."

10. For an account of the ideological preoccupations of the Restoration comic stage, see Canfield, *Tricksters and Estates*. See also Laura Brown, *English Dramatic Form, 1660–1770*, who notes a "general rejection of aristocratic judgments" in what she terms the "transitional comedy" of the late seventeenth and early eighteenth centuries (102). A number of critics have attributed the shift in the concerns of comedy to the change in the audience demographic. See, for instance, Loftis, *Comedy and Society from Congreve to Fielding*, 9.

11. Hume, *Development*, 474.

12. See Habermas, *The Structural Transformation of the Public Sphere*. One of Habermas's main insights has been that the formal articulation of separate public and private spheres in the eighteenth century actually obscured how deeply the one was implicated in and indebted to the other. He writes, "the bourgeois public sphere may be conceived above all as the sphere of private people come together as a public" (27).

13. See Collier, 5, for the charge that the stage had made "Lewdness a Diversion."

14. Cooke, *The Elements of Dramatic Criticism*, 133.

15. Dennis, "A Defence of Sir Fopling Flutter," 2: 245.

16. Zeitlin, "Travesties of Gender and Genre in Aristophanes' *Thesmophoriazousae*," 139.

17. Milhous and Hume, "*The Beaux' Stratagem*," 95. Significantly, though they allow for the possibilities of such irony, ultimately they argue that the "romp" takes precedent over the play's more serious implications. In the discussion and readings below, I argue, on the contrary, that, whether directly or indirectly, these ironies invariably disrupt the "straight" ending and the "straight" reading.

18. For a suggestive demonstration of the efficacy of the dialectical methodology I am advocating for the analysis of eighteenth-century comedies, see McKeon, "Marxist Criticism and *Marriage à la Mode*." This method has been employed more recently by James Thompson in, "'Sure I Have Seen That Face Before.'" Like myself, Thompson argues that comedy carries out a process of valuation; yet he concludes that a stable value can be located in these comedies in the internal worth of the female heroines. Thompson reaches this conclusion, I believe, because he reads the comedies "straight," in this case as texts, rather than as performances. Drawing on the model of character I presented in Chapter 1, I will argue, on the other hand, that these plays do not dramatize the fixing of internal value so much as they dramatize the surfaces that compete for primacy in the process of valuation.

19. In a certain sense, my selections of texts for reading are as arbitrary as they are deliberate. There are dozens of other playtexts that I might have chosen instead which would have illustrated just as vividly the representative patterns that I have observed in eighteenth-century comedies. Relatively, then, my choices are arbitrary. Yet they are deliberate, and, I hope, effective in the sense that I have paired them literally on the basis of their titles as a means to emblematize and exemplify the importance of doubling, mimicry and parody in eighteenth-century comedic representations. It might be said that I have

"twinned" the plays; yet they are neither identically nor fraternally related. Rather, to the extent that eighteenth-century playwrights did in fact play upon, borrow from, adapt, and imitate one another's productions, the relationship I am trying to capture is one of contiguity rather than continuity, contingency rather than dependency, refraction rather than reflection. The abiding arbitrariness of these pairings reveals itself in the fact that at one point prior to its performance Oliver Goldsmith's *She Stoops to Conquer* had been alternatively titled *The Belle's Stratagem*, a title taken nine years later by Hannah Cowley for the play I have paired for discussion with George Farquhar's *The Beaux' Stratagem*.

20. I have simply consulted the *American Heritage Dictionary of the English Language*, 3rd ed.

21. For a discussion of contemporary eighteenth-century references, see Thalia Stathas's Introduction to Susanna Centlivre's *A Bold Stroke for a Wife*. All references to Centlivre's play will be cited parenthetically from this edition by act, scene and line number.

22. On the unity of plot, see Stathas, xxiii. On the fairy-tale qualities of the play, see Hull, "*A Bold Stroke for a Wife*" as well as Nancy Copeland's Introduction, 20–21.

23. For similar observations, see Stathas, xxiii; Frushell, "Marriage and Marrying in Susanna Centlivre's Plays," 18; and Bowyer, *The Celebrated Mrs. Centlivre*, 212.

24. See Eve Sedgwick's ground-breaking work *Between Men*. For conceptually allied theories contributing to the idea of a homosocial economy, see also Rubin, "The Traffic in Women" and Irigaray, *This Sex Which Is Not One*.

25. For a similar comment on the "male-centeredness" of the play, see Copeland, 20–21. This aspect of the play became all the more obvious in subsequent adaptations of the comedy which nearly eliminated Ann Lovely's part altogether. For a description of these adaptations, see Copeland, 30.

26. Laura J. Rosenthal anticipates this reading when she writes of Centlivre in *Playwrights and Plagiarists in Early Modern England*, "Her drama tends to insist upon certain freedoms for women, but at the same time reveals, under the guise of romantic love, little more than a rejection of a paternal form of patriarchy in favor of a fraternal version of the same" (206).

27. Rosenthal, 225.

28. Here Ann Lovely's behavior follows a pattern theorized by Karen Newman in "Directing Traffic." In a critique of Sedgwick, Rubin, and Irigaray, Newman argues for a model of reading that can account for women in representation not merely as objects of desire, but also as subjects in desire. For a similar critique that has more direct bearing on Restoration and eighteenth-century drama, see Burke, "Wycherley's 'Tendentious Joke.'"

29. See Cumberland, "Critique on the *Bold Stroke for a Wife*," 151.

30. Gagen, "Hannah Cowley (1743–1809)," 104.

31. Headnotes to *A Bold Stroke for a Husband* in *The Works of Mrs. Cowley*. The editor indicates that this is particularly the case when the third, but minor, marriage plot involving Olivia's father Caesar and Marcella, a neighbor's daughter, was cut in the performance text, as was often the case.

32. For this discussion of the prologue, I refer to the text of prologue in the 1783 edition of the play as found in the Brown University Women Writers Project. It is not

insignificant that some of the most critical lines in this prologue were revised in subsequent editions of the play in such a way as to ameliorate this threatening attitude. All subsequent references will be to this text and will be cited parenthetically by act and scene number.

33. Nussbaum, *The Autobiographical Subject*, xxi. I ought to note here that it is not entirely clear whether Cowley wrote this prologue or whether, as given in the third edition, it was written by "two gentlemen."

34. Castle, "The Culture of Travesty," 157.

35. For recent studies of Charlotte Charke and the implications of her transvestism, see Baruth, *Introducing Charlotte Charke*.

36. Straub, "The Guilty Pleasures of Female Theatrical Cross-Dressing and the Autobiography of Charlotte Charke," 150. Beth H. Friedman-Romell has extended discussions of the cross-dressed part in her article, "Breaking the Code."

37. Castle, 169. The overwhelming anxiety that the cross-dressed actress provoked is evidenced in Hill's *The Actor* where he moves swiftly to preclude any subversive possibilities by asking and then insisting: "Why is it that a tender love-scene, tho' ever so well apply'd on both sides, is yet perfectly cold and insipid to us, when the person who represents the lover, is a woman in the habit of the other sex? Is it not evidently from the persuasion we are under, that the tenderness that character expresses, is all affected and forced, from the natural impossibility of one woman's feeling for another all that passion which she is to represent to us in the scene?" (123).

38. That Cowley may have been aware of the potentially subversive interpretation that could be attached to this passage can be seen in the fact that she revised these lines significantly in subsequent editions. In the third edition, printed in 1784, for instance, the same lines read: "To rival him was not my first motive. The Portugueze robbed me of his heart; I concluded she had fascinations which nature had denied to me; it was impossible to visit her as a woman; I, therefore, assumed the Cavalier to study her, that I might, if possible, be to my Carlos, all he found in her." See *A Bold Stroke for a Husband*.

39. I have substituted the term "female" for "feminine" so as to avoid the conflation of sexual with gender terminology.

40. Inchbald, "Remarks" on *A Bold Stroke for a Husband*, in *Remarks for the British Theatre (1806–1809)*.

41. Inchbald's gesture is repeated in the 1813 edition of *The Works of Mrs. Cowley*, where the editor introduces the play by noting, "The Author had hitherto confined herself within the range of English manners; but now, for Variety, she takes her flight to other realms, and customs differing from our own . . . the Scene laid in Spain, where to the romantic mind readily gives credit."

42. See Butler, *Gender Trouble*.

43. Farquhar, *The Beaux' Stratagem*, V.iv.279–80. All subsequent references to this text will be taken from this edition and will be cited parenthetically by act, scene, and line number.

44. As a number of critics have already pointed out, an actual divorce was out of the question in this period. Though it is often viewed as a divorce or as tantamount to divorce,

the dissolution of the Sullens' marriage consists only in a formal separation. For an informative discussion of representations of marriage and divorce on the stage in this period, see Backscheider, "'Endless Aversion Rooted in the Soul.'" For a discussion of the divorce as a critical crux, see Milhous and Hume, "*The Beaux' Stratagem.*" For discussions of the influence of Milton's divorce tracts on *The Beaux' Stratagem*, see Rothstein, *George Farquhar*, 142–59 as well as Larson, "The Influence of Milton's Divorce Tracts on Farquhar's *Beaux' Stratagem*," 174–78.

45. For more on Farquhar's response to the changing economic situation in England, see McVeagh, "George Farquhar and Commercial England."

46. Cordner, Introduction to *The Beaux' Stratagem*, xviii.

47. Donaldson, *The World Upside-Down*, 7.

48. Donaldson, 8.

49. See Derrida, "The Law of Genre."

50. In this dedicatory letter, Cowley announces that her purpose in this comedy was "to draw a FEMALE CHARACTER, which with the most lively Sensibility, fine Understanding, and elegant Accomplishments, should unite that beautiful Reserve and Delicacy which, whilst they veil those charms, render them still more interesting." Hannah Cowley, "To THE QUEEN," *The Belle's Stratagem* (1782). All subsequent references to *The Belle's Stratagem* will be from this text and will be cited parenthetically by act and scene number.

51. See Pollak, *The Poetics of Sexual Myth.*

52. Spacks, "Female Changelessness; Or, What Do Women Want?" 281.

53. *The Rivals* actually failed at its first performance and was withdrawn after its second night, revised, and restaged at the end of the month, whereupon it became a success with an additional thirteen performances in its initial season (Van Lennep et al., *The London Stage*, 4: 1862–65). For a complete account of this performance history and of the revisions Sheridan made to the play, see *The Rivals, A Comedy, Edited from the Larpent MS.* This edition of the play provides the texts from the Larpent MS and the first printed edition of 1775 in juxtaposed columns. The most significant revisions involved tempering the characters of Sir Lucius O'Trigger and Sir Anthony Absolute.

54. See Auburn, *Sheridan's Comedies*, and Loftis, *Sheridan and the Drama of Georgian England.*

55. Auburn, 36. The tradition of reading the play in this manner could be said to have begun with Sheridan's first biographer, Thomas Moore, who wrote in *Memoirs of the Life of the Right Honourable Richard Brinsley Sheridan* (1825): "The characters of *The Rivals . . .* are *not* such as occur very commonly in the world; and, instead of producing striking effects with natural and obvious materials, which is the great art and difficulty of a painter of human life, he has here overcharged most of his persons with whims and absurdities, for which the circumstances they are engaged in afford but a very disproportionate vent" (cited in Auburn, 36).

56. The use of the term "pleasure" in this context comes from Auburn, 36–37. See also his article on the performance history of *The Rivals*, "The Pleasures of Sheridan's *The Rivals.*"

57. Hogan, "Plot, Character, and Comic Language in Sheridan," 277.

58. Sheridan, *The Rivals*, I.i.25–26, 35–37. All subsequent references to this play will be taken from this text and will be cited parenthetically by act, scene, and line number.

59. Not insignificantly, of course, the problem of the romance heroine's fantastic self-absorption had already been amply thematized and explored by Charlotte Lennox in her 1752 novel *The Female Quixote*.

60. Anne Parker makes a similar argument in "'Absolute Sense' in Sheridan's *The Rivals*": "In *The Rivals*, the serious scene 'imitates' the comic one, and Sheridan thereby undermines Julia's sentiments" (16).

61. Malek, "Julia as Comic Character in *The Rivals*," 12. In an insightful article that explores Sheridan's experimentation with comic language, Christine S. Wiesenthal provides additional support for this argument when she points out that, "A substantial measure of the 'divisive effect' of language which critics have noted in *The Rivals*, then, may be seen to arise from the ironic undertow created by a comic language so exuberant that it drags upon the rhetoric of sublimity, interfering with the readers wholly sympathetic response to Julia and Faulkland." See Wiesenthal, "Representation and Experimentation in the Major Comedies of Richard Brinsley Sheridan," 315.

62. Kaul, *The Action of English Comedy*, 147–48.

63. The view of Jack Absolute as the epitome of common sense in the comedy is one that has dominated critical interpretations. See, for example, Parker and Auburn. One significant factor that could be weighed against these arguments is that Henry Woodward, the actor who originated the role of Jack Absolute, was sixty-five years old at the first performance of *The Rivals*. That the plot involving Absolute failed to appear commonsensical to some who witnessed Woodward in the role is evidenced by the following remarks in the *Morning Chronicle*: "Mr. Woodward is certainly a very confined actor, and altho' he acquitted himself with ease in Absolute, he neither looked the young, gay, handsome Officer, likely to captivate a romantic girl, nor could assume that enthusiasm in his flights of conversation with her absolutely necessary to deceive her." By "One of the Pit," in the *Morning Chronicle*, 27 January 1775, as reprinted in *The Dramatic Works of Richard Brinsley Sheridan*, 47.

64. Vanbrugh and Cibber, *The Provoked Husband*, V.iv.218–22. That I cite lines here from *The Provoked Husband* is not altogether insignificant, as Cibber's revision and completion of Vanbrugh's unfinished play amply illustrates the turn, described in the beginning of this chapter, away from the harsh, biting cynicism of a Restoration sensibility and toward the good-natured moral didacticism that shaped the eighteenth-century comic perspective.

Chapter Five

1. The phrase in quotation marks is taken from Collier, *A Short View of the Immorality and Profaneness of the English Stage*, 2.

2. This is, of course, because eleven years later John Dennis took this essay as his point

of departure in his attack on the exemplary hero of sentimental comedy in his "Defence of Sir Fopling Flutter."

3. The offending line came from the first edition of the play; it appears that, in keeping with his own critique, Steele revised the line in subsequent editions to eliminate the image.

4. Steele, *Spectator* No. 51, Saturday, April 28, 1711, Addison and Steele, 1: 215–16.

5. Here Steele seems to echo Collier's *A Short View*, for in his enumeration of the abuses of the stage Collier cited "Their Smuttiness of Expression . . . Their making their top Characters Libertines, and giving them Success in their Debauchery" (2).

6. In an essay that I will discuss in much greater detail below, Henry Fielding echoed this view, writing that double-entendres and obscene jests are "commonly the last Resource of impotent Wit, the weak Strainings of the lowest, silliest, and dullest Fellows in the World." See Fielding, "An Essay on Conversation," 148.

7. Steele deploys this phrase in his preface to *The Conscious Lovers* (1722), a preface that is as much about defending his idea of comedy as it is an introduction to the matter of the play. See full citation below in my discussion of the play.

8. Walpole, "Thoughts on Comedy," 2: 317.

9. For more detailed discussions of the distinguishing characteristics of sentimental comedy see Bernbaum, *The Drama of Sensibility*; Sherbo, *English Sentimental Drama*; and, more recently, Ellis, *Sentimental Comedy*.

10. John Sheriff makes this point as well in *The Good-Natured Man*, 67.

11. *Spectator* No. 10, Monday, March 12, 1711, Addison and Steele, 1: 44.

12. Fielding, "An Essay on Conversation," 152 (emphasis mine).

13. Fielding, 119. Here, Fielding echoes Shaftesbury's contentions about the "social love and common affection which is natural to mankind" in Section II of "Sensus Communis" in Anthony, Earl of Shaftesbury, *Characteristics of Men, Manners, Opinions, Times, etc.*, 1: 77.

14. See Pocock, *Virtue, Commerce, and History*, esp. chapter 2: "Virtue, Rights, and Manners," 37–50; Barker-Benfield, *The Culture of Sensibility*; Langford, *A Polite and Commercial People*; Klein, "Property and Politeness in the Early Eighteenth-Century Whig moralists"; and Klein, "Liberty, Manners, and Politeness in Early Eighteenth-Century England."

15. Langford echoes this idea, writing, "In theory politeness comprehended, even began with, morals, but in practice it was as much a question of material acquisitions and urbane manners. It both permitted and controlled a relatively open competition for power, influence, jobs, wives, and markets" (4–5).

16. Miller's play was among the first to be licensed and produced following the Stage Licensing Act of 1737. The play barely received one performance, at Drury Lane on 16 February 1738, and the evidence suggests that it was shouted off the stage as much because Miller's earlier play *The Coffee-House* (1737/1738) had given offense to a group of Templars, who were then determined to ruin his next effort, as because audiences were resolved to express their opposition to censorship by damning the first licensed plays. For

a discussion of the reaction to *Art and Nature* as well as to the first few licensed plays, see Conolly, *The Censorship of English Drama, 1737–1824*, 165. For other details of *Art and Nature*, see Nicoll, *Early Eighteenth Century Drama*, vol. 2 of *A History of English Drama 1660–1900*, 13, 146, 181–82, 203 and Van Lennep et al., *The London Stage*, 3:2.703.

17. In the prologue Miller acknowledges borrowings from the French stage. Nicoll (146, 203) has identified these sources as Rousseau's *Le Flatteur*, Delisle's *Arlequin Sauvage*, and Chollet's *L'Art et la Nature*.

18. Miller, *Art and Nature*, I.2. All subsequent references to this play will be cited parenthetically by act and scene number as indicated in the 1738 text.

19. For just one example where Shaftesbury expresses views similar in tone, see "Miscellany III" of "Miscellaneous Reflections" in vol. 2 of *Characteristics of Men, Manners, Opinions, Times, etc.* As Klein has pointed out in *Shaftesbury and the Culture of Politeness*, the "proximity of ethics and aesthetics" was a "characteristic Shaftesburian theme" (35).

20. See Fielding, "Essay on Conversation," 128–31.

21. Walpole made this analogy explicit when he wrote in his "Thoughts on Comedy" that "good-breeding, which seems the current coin of humanity, is no more than bank bills real treasure: but it increases the national fund of politeness, and is taken as current money; though the acceptor knows it is no more addressed to him than the bill to the first person to whom it was made payable; but he can pay it away, and knows it will always be accepted" (2: 318).

22. For one concise formulation of the "premises of political economy," see Karl Marx's essay "Estranged Labour": "We presupposed private property, the separation of labour, capital and land, and of wages, profit of capital and rent of land—likewise division of labour, competition, the concept of exchange value, etc. On the basis of political economy itself, in its own words, we have shown that the worker sinks to the level of a commodity and becomes indeed the most wretched of commodities; that the wretchedness of the worker is in inverse proportion to the power and magnitude of his production . . . that the whole of society must fall apart into the two classes—the property-*owners* and the property-less *workers*" (70).

23. Pocock, "The Mobility of Property and the Rise of Eighteenth-Century Sociology," 108–9.

24. For two views on the emergence of the middling classes, see Earle, *The Making of The English Middle Class* and Rogers, "Money, Land, and Lineage."

25. See Klein, "Property and Politeness." For other approaches taken to the intersection of aristocratic or land-based ideologies with the commercial project, see Lieberman, "Property, Commerce, and the Common Law" and Raven, "Defending Conduct and Property."

26. Klein, "Property and Politeness," 229.

27. See Langford: "Politeness conveyed upper-class gentility, enlightenment, and sociability to a much wider élite whose only qualification was money, but who were glad to spend it on acquiring the status of gentleman" (4).

28. Markley, "Sentimentality as Performance," 217.

29. See Brewer and Porter, Introduction to *Consumption and the World of Goods*, 5. For a

series of accounts of the growth of consumerism in the eighteenth century, see McKendrick, Brewer, and Plumb, *The Birth of a Consumer Society*.

30. See Staves, "Pope's Refinement," 146. Staves doesn't provide a definition for these terms, but I take it to indicate a hybrid class of persons that was neither strictly bourgeois nor exclusively aristocratic, but rather, as discussed above, one that adapted traditionally aristocratic forms of social behavior and expression to suit a commercial or middling class agenda.

31. Plumb, "The Commercialization of Leisure in Eighteenth-Century England," 269. See also,Langford, 464.

32. For a discussion of sentiment and sensibility which has influenced this argument, see Barker-Benfield, *The Culture of Sensibility*.

33. This phrase is taken from Steele's *The Conscious Lovers*, I.ii.16. In what follows, I discuss the outrage directed toward Steele's pretensions.

34. Dennis, "Remarks on a Play, Call'd, *The Conscious Lovers*, a Comedy," 2: 253.

35. It is important to note here, as I did in Chapter 4, that this perception was a false one and may have been propounded either for rhetorical purposes or out of economic interest. For a pivotal demonstration of this case, see Robert Hume, "Goldsmith and Sheridan and the Supposed Revolution of 'Laughing' Against 'Sentimental' Comedy."

36. Goldsmith, "An Essay on the Theatre; or, a Comparison between Laughing and Sentimental Comedy," 3: 209.

37. Cooke, *The Elements of Dramatic Criticism*, 141.

38. Dennis, "Sir Fopling Flutter," 1: 249.

39. This view of comedy receives extensive treatment in Dennis's, "A Large Account of the Taste in Poetry, and the Causes of the Degeneracy of It," 2: 282, as well as at mid-century in Foote's *The Roman and English Comedy Consider'd and Compar'd*, 11–12.

40. See Hobbes's account "On Laughter" in chapter 9 of his long essay *On Human Nature*.

41. Goldsmith, *The Good Natur'd Man*, Preface, v.

42. This point has been documented extensively already by Stuart Tave in *The Amiable Humorist*: esp. chapter 5: "True Humor and English Liberty." The following argument has been influenced by Tave's reading of the connections between humour and liberty, but we diverge on a critical point. Where Tave argues that humour was transformed in the period, I argue instead that what occurred was a solidification of the distinction between humour and good-humour.

43. Congreve to Dennis (July 10, 1695), *William Congreve: Letters and Documents*, 185.

44. For a decisive study of this phenomenon, see Colley, *Britons*.

45. Davies, *A Genuine Narrative of the Life and Theatrical Transactions of Mr. John Henderson* (1777), as cited in Tave, 96.

46. In this context we can begin to make sense of some of the more unusual allusions that appear both in the defences of humour and comedy and in the attacks on sentimental comedy. These include the barb Dennis throws at Steele, maligning his credentials as an Englishman by reminding the reader that Steele was of Irish birth; Cooke's fascinating analogy in which he likens the rise of sentimental comedy to the irrational, fraudulent,

and tyrannical enthusiasms that made Cromwell's reign possible; as well as countless direct and oblique references to the incursions of French influence on English comedy. Each of these allusions makes it clear that English liberty was at stake in the representation of humour in comedy; all threats to humour constituted threats to liberty and prosperity. See, Dennis, "Defence of Sir Fopling Flutter," 2: 245, and Cooke, 149.

47. Shaftesbury's ethos was encapsulated in his singular pronouncement in "Sensus Communis" that "All politeness is owing to liberty." Anthony, Earl of Shaftesbury, "Sensus Communis; An Essay on the Freedom of Wit and Humour," *Characteristics of Men, Manners, Opinions, Times, etc.*, 1: 46. For a subtle account of the complexity with which Shaftesbury incorporated a discourse of liberty into his works, see Klein, "Liberty, Manners, and Politeness."

48. Klein, "Liberty, Manners and Politeness," 603, 588.

49. All references to Steele's *The Conscious Lovers* (1722) will be taken from Shirley Strum Kenny's edition, as cited above, and will be indicated parenthetically by act, scene, and line number.

50. Indeed, as John Loftis suggests, *The Conscious Lovers* might best be viewed as a culminating achievement in Steele's efforts to reform the stage, "providing as it does a pattern of comedy—exemplary comedy—in which the action and characters are designed as models for and incentives to virtuous behavior." Loftis, *Steele at Drury Lane*.

51. Steele, *Tatler* No. 8, 26 April to 28 April 1709, *The Tatler*, 1.

52. Inchbald, "Remarks" on *The Conscious Lovers*, *Remarks for the British Theatre*.

53. Kenny, Introduction to *The Conscious Lovers*, xxiii.

54. For a brief reading that follows a similar line of thought with respect to Cimberton, see Canfield, "Shifting Tropes of Ideology in English Serious Drama, Late Stuart to Early Georgian," esp. 220–22.

55. For a discussion of Steele's extended preparations for *The Conscious Lovers*, see Loftis, *Steele at Drury Lane*, 183–93.

56. For Colley Cibber's brief allusion to this event see his *An Apology for the Life of Mr. Colley Cibber*, 314.

57. See Loftis, 184–89 and Steele, *The Theatre*, Nos. 1–3, 19, 28, *Richard Steele's The Theatre 1720*. While the play would undergo at least two title changes in the next two years and Sir John Edgar would become Sir John Bevil, the main characters featured in *The Conscious Lovers* appear to be substantially the same as those described in these essays.

58. Steele, *The Theatre* No. 3, 12.

59. I am quoting here from British Library, Additional MS. 5145 C, fol. 198 as provided in *Steele's The Theatre*, 126–27.

60. In his attack on *The Conscious Lovers*, Dennis singles Bevil, Jr.'s obedience out as most improbable; he argues not only that Bevil, Jr.'s restraint was unrealistic, but that once children come to "full Use of their Reason, they are only bound to obey them in what is reasonable." Not insignificantly, and as might be anticipated from earlier portions of this chapter, Dennis transforms this issue into a question of liberty, charging, "what Obligations can be binding enough to make a Man of great Estate part with Liberty, with the very

Liberty of his Choice, in the most important Action of his Life, upon which the Happiness of all the rest depends?" ("Remarks on . . . *The Conscious Lovers*," 2: 263–65).

61. For Isabella's suspicions, see, II.ii.1–125. Again, it is not insignificant that Isabella's expectations appear to be shaped by the conventions of Restoration plots and by her own experience as a maiden in that period. That her expectations are not fulfilled only strengthens the case that this play deliberately marks its turn away from the Restoration comedy of breeding in which all men are "hypocrite[s]" to a sentimental comedy of good breeding in which a man loves with "sincerity and honor" (II.ii.55, 24–25).

62. Indiana's comments associate the popular taste for opera with a mindless desire for sensation and speak to the kind of rational tastes Steele meant to appeal to in developing sentimental comedy: "in the main, all the pleasure the best opera gives us is but mere sensation. Methinks it's pity the mind can't have a little more share in the entertainment (II.ii.199–201).

63. The second iteration occurs at V.iii.224–28.

64. Joseph Wood Krutch has put this view perhaps even more cynically, writing: "Nothing is more characteristic of sentimental comedy than this sudden discovery that a disinterested sacrifice made nobly turns out to be no sacrifice at all. . . . Hence the undeniable namby-pambyness of sentimental comedy. The moral always seems to be that nobleness pays, that the best way to look out for yourself is to appear unselfish, and that the plum will always drop into your mouth if you appear not to desire it" in *Comedy and Conscience After the Restoration*, 213. See also Susan Staves, who observes of these unrealistic sentimental endings, "no economic scarcity ever mars the happy resolution" in "Resentment or Resignation?" 212.

65. Moore, *The Foundling*, II.i. All subsequent references to *The Foundling* will be taken from this text and will be cited parenthetically by act and scene number.

66. See Chapter 1, where I discuss Thompson's discussion of coinage and value in relation to the concept of character at greater length.

67. James Thompson, " 'Sure I Have Seen That Face Before,' " 285, 281.

68. Nicoll, 2: 206, Bernbaum, 179.

69. Colman, *The English Merchant*, I.i.

70. For discussion of the West Indian as fictional type in representation, see Sypher, "The West-Indian as a 'Character' in the Eighteenth Century." For a more recent critical discussion of the discursive significance of the "torrid zones" in relation to questions about identity and nation, see the introductory chapter of Nussbaum, esp. 7–14.

71. Cumberland, *Memoirs of Richard Cumberland, Written by Himself*, 142.

72. David Hume, "Of National Characters," 1: 250.

73. See Hume on the "circumstances . . . which render a peculiar set of manners habitual to us" (1: 244). Hume's dissatisfaction with this explanation and his reversion to a racialized biological determinism came to be expressed in a note which he added to later editions of this essay: "I am apt to suspect the negroes, and in general all the other species of men . . . to be naturally inferior to whites. There never was a civilized nation of any other complexion than white, nor even any individual eminent either in action or speculation.

. . . Such a uniform and constant difference could not happen, in so many countries and ages, if nature had not made an original distinction betwixt these breeds of men" (1: 252).

74. All references to this text are taken from Cumberland's *The West Indian* as found in *British Dramatists from Dryden to Sheridan*, and will be cited parenthetically by act, scene, and line number.

75. See Donohue's reading of *The West Indian*, in *Dramatic Character in the English Romantic Age*, 108–10.

76. Donohue, 109–10.

77. See Parnell, "The Sentimental Mask," 285–97.

78. Steele, *The Tender Husband*, I.i.

Epilogue

1. Turner, *From Ritual to Theatre*, 13.

Bibliography

Plays Cited

Addison, Joseph. *Cato*. London, 1713. *The Beggar's Opera and Other Eighteenth-Century Plays*. Sel. John Hampden, intro. David W. Lindsay. 1928. London: Dent-Everyman's Library, 1988.

Baker, Robert. *Rehearsal of a New Ballad-Opera burlesqu'd, called The Mad-House*. London, 1737.

Centlivre, Susanna. *The Beau's Duel*. *The Works of the Celebrated Mrs. Centlivre*. 3 vols. London, 1760/61.

——. *A Bold Stroke for a Wife*. 1718. Ed. and intro. Thalia Stathas. Lincoln: University of Nebraska Press, 1968.

——. *A Bold Stroke for a Wife*. Ed. and intro. Nancy Copeland. London, Ont.: Broadview Press, 1995.

——. *The Cruel Gift*. *The Works of the Celebrated Mrs. Centlivre*. 3 vols. London, 1760/61.

Clive, Katherine. *The Rehearsal; or, Bays in Petticoats*. London, 1753.

Colman, George the Elder. *The English Merchant*. London, 1767.

——. *New Brooms (1776) and The Manager in Distress (1780)*. Intro. J. Terry Frazier. Delmar, N.Y.: Scholars' Facsimiles and Reprints, 1980.

Colman, George the Younger. *The Female Dramatist*. 1782. *The Plays of George Colman, the Younger*. Ed. and intro. Peter A. Tasch. 2 vols. New York: Garland, 1981. Vol. 1.

Cowley, Hannah. *The Belle's Stratagem*. 1782. *The Plays of Hannah Cowley*. Ed. Frederick M. Link. 2 vols. New York: Garland, 1979. Vol. 1.

——. *A Bold Stroke for a Husband*. 1783. *The Works of Mrs. Cowley*. London, 1813. Providence, R.I.: Brown University Women Writers Project, 1990.

Cumberland, Richard. *The West Indian*. 1771. *British Dramatists from Dryden to Sheridan*, ed. George H. Nettleton and Arthur Case, rev. George Winchester Stone, Jr. Carbondale: Southern Illinois University Press, 1969.

Dennis, John. *Iphigenia*. 1700. *The Plays of John Dennis*. Ed. and intro. J. W. Johnson. New York: Garland, 1980.

The English Stage Italianiz'd. London, 1727.

Farquhar, George. *The Beaux' Stratagem*. 1707. Ed. and Intro. Michael Cordner. London: Ernest Benn Limited-Mermaid Editions, 1976.

——. *The Twin Rivals*. London, 1703.

The Female Wits; or The Triumvirate of Poets at Rehearsal. 1704. Ed. Lucyle Hook. Augustan Reprint Society Series 124. Los Angeles: William Andrews Clark Library, 1967.

Fielding, Henry. *The Author's Farce*. 1730/1734. Ed. Charles B. Woods. Lincoln: University of Nebraska Press, 1966.

——. *Pasquin: A Dramatic Satire on the Times: Being the Rehearsal of Two Plays, Viz. A Comedy Called The Election; and a Tragedy, Called the Life and Death of Common-Sense*.

1736. *The Complete Works of Henry Fielding, Esq.* Drury Lane Edition. New York: Croscup Sterling, 1902.

——. *The Tragedy of Tragedies; or, The Life and Death of Tom Thumb the Great.* 1731. *The Beggar's Opera and Other Eighteenth-Century Plays.* Intro. David W. Lindsay. London: Dent-Everyman's Library, 1974.

Foote, Samuel. *The Englishman in Paris.* 1753. *The Plays of Samuel Foote.* Ed. Paula R. Backscheider and Douglas Howard. New York: Garland, 1983.

——. *The Englishman Return'd from Paris.* 1756. *The Plays of Samuel Foote.* Ed. Paula R. Backscheider and Douglas Howard. New York: Garland, 1983.

——. *Taste.* 1752. *The Plays of Samuel Foote.* Ed. Paula R. Backscheider and Douglas Howard. New York: Garland, 1983.

Gay, John. *The Beggar's Opera.* 1728. Ed. Bryan Loughrey and T. O. Treadwell. London: Penguin Books, 1986.

——. *The What D'Ye Call It? A Tragi-Comi-Pastoral Farce.* London, 1715.

Gay, John, Alexander Pope, and John Arbuthnot. *Three Hours After Marriage.* 1717. *Burlesque Plays of the Eighteenth Century*, ed. and intro. Simon Trussler. Oxford: Oxford University Press, 1969.

Goldsmith, Oliver. *The Good Natur'd Man.* London, 1768.

——. *She Stoops to Conquer.* 1773. Ed. Tom Davis. 1979. London: A & C Black, 1986.

Hill, Aaron. *The Fatal Extravagance. The Dramatic Works of Aaron Hill, Esq.* London, 1760. Facsimile reproduction in *The Plays of Aaron Hill.* Ed. and intro. Calhoun Winton. New York: Garland, 1981.

——. *A Snake in the Grass.* London, 1760.

Hoper, Mrs. *Queen Tragedy Restor'd.* London, 1749.

Lillo, George. *The London Merchant; or, The History of George Barnwell.* London, 1731. Ed. and intro. William H. McBurney. Lincoln: University of Nebraska Press, 1965.

Lynch, Francis. *The Independent Patriot; or, Musical Folly.* London, 1737.

Miller, James. *Art and Nature.* London, 1738.

——. *The Coffee-House.* London, 1737.

Moore, Edward. *The Foundling.* London, 1748.

Odingsells, Gabriel. *Bay's Opera.* London, 1730.

Philips, Ambrose. *The Briton.* London, 1722.

——. *The Distrest Mother.* London, 1712.

Reeve, Joseph. *Cato. A Tragedy. By Mr. Addison. Done into Latin Verse Without the Love Scenes.* London, 1764.

Rowe, Nicholas. *The Fair Penitent.* 1703. Ed. Malcolm Goldstein. Lincoln: University of Nebraska Press, 1969.

——. *The Tragedy of Jane Shore.* 1714. *The Beggar's Opera and Other Eighteenth-Century Plays.* Intro. David W. Lindsay. London: Dent-Everyman's Library, 1988.

Sheridan, Frances. *The Discovery.* London, 1763.

Sheridan, Richard Brinsley. *The Critic.* 1781. *The School for Scandal and Other Plays.* Ed. and intro. Eric Rump. London: Penguin, 1988.

——. *The Rivals.* 1775. Ed. Elizabeth Duthie. 1979. New York: W.W. Norton, 1994.

Stage Mutineers, or, A Play-House to be Lett. London, 1733.

Steele, Richard. *The Conscious Lovers.* 1722/1723. Ed. and intro. Shirley Strum Kenny. Lincoln: University of Nebraska Press, 1968.

——. *The Funeral*. London, 1702.

——. *The Lying Lover*. London, 1704.

——. *The Tender Husband*. London, 1705.

Vanbrugh, John and Colley Cibber. *The Provoked Husband*. 1728. Ed. and intro. Peter Dixon. Lincoln: University of Nebraska Press, 1973.

Villiers, George, Duke of Buckingham. *The Rehearsal*. 1671. *British Dramatists from Dryden to Sheridan*, ed. George H. Nettleton and Arthur E. Case, rev. George Winchester Stone, Jr. Carbondale: Southern Illinois University Press, 1969.

Wycherley, William. *The Country Wife*. 1675. Ed. and intro. Marvin T. Herrick. Woodbury, N.Y.: Barron's Educational Series, 1970.

Other Primary Materials

Addison, Joseph and Richard Steele. *The Spectator*. Ed. Donald F. Bond. 5 vols. Oxford: Clarendon Press, 1965.

Boyer, Abel. *The English Theophrastus: or, the Manners of the Age*. London, 1702.

Centlivre, Susanna. *The Works of the Celebrated Mrs. Centlivre*. 3 vols. London, 1760/1761.

Chetwood, William. *A General History of the Stage*. Dublin, 1749.

Churchill, Charles. *The Rosciad*. London, 1761.

Cibber, Colley. *An Apology for the Life of Mr. Colley Cibber*. London, 1740.

Collier, Jeremy. *A Short View of the Immorality and Profaneness of the English Stage*. 1698. New York: AMS Press, 1974.

A Comparison Between the Two Stages. London, 1702.

Congreve, William. *William Congreve: Letters and Documents*. Ed. John C. Hodges. London: Macmillan, 1964.

Cooke, William. *The Elements of Dramatic Criticism*. London, 1775.

Cumberland, Richard. *Memoirs of Richard Cumberland, Written by Himself*. 1807. Philadelphia: Parry and McMillan, 1856.

——. *The Observer*. Nos. 77–79. *Eighteenth-Century Critical Essays*. Ed. Scott Elledge. 2 vols. Ithaca, N.Y.: Cornell University Press, 1961. 2: 948–70.

Dennis, John. "A Defence of Sir Fopling Flutter." 1722. *The Critical Works of John Dennis*. Ed. Edward Niles Hooker. 2 vols. Baltimore: Johns Hopkins University Press, 1943. 2: 241–50.

——. "A Large Account of the Taste in Poetry, and the Causes of the Degeneracy in It." 1702. *The Critical Works of John Dennis*. Ed. Edward Niles Hooker. 2 vols. Baltimore: Johns Hopkins University Press, 1943. Vol. 2.

——. "Remarks on a Play, Call'd, *The Conscious Lovers*, a Comedy." *The Critical Works of John Dennis*. Ed. Edward Niles Hooker. 2 vols. Baltimore: Johns Hopkins University Press, 1943. Vol. 2.

——. *Remarks Upon Cato, A Tragedy*. London, 1713.

Diderot, Denis. *The Paradox of the Actor*. 1773. *Selected Writings on Art and Literature*. Trans. and intro. Geoffrey Bremner. London, Penguin, 1994.

Earle, John. *Microcosmography*. London, 1733.

Fielding, Henry. "An Essay on Conversation." *Miscellanies of Henry Fielding*. Ed. Henry

Knight Miller. Wesleyan Edition of the Works of Henry Fielding. Oxford: Clarendon Press, 1972. 1: 119–52.

——. "An Essay on the Knowledge of the Characters of Men." Vol. 14 of *The Complete Works of Henry Fielding, Esq.* New York: Croscup Sterling, 1902. 279–305.

——. *The Historical Register for the Year 1736.* 1737. Ed. William W. Appleton. Lincoln: University of Nebraska Press, 1967.

——. *Tom Jones.* 1749. Ed. Sheridan Baker. New York: W. W. Norton, 1973.

Fielding, Sarah. *Remarks on Clarissa, Addressed to the Author.* 1749. New York: Garland, 1970.

[Fitzpatrick, Thaddeus]. *An Enquiry into the Real Merit of a Certain Popular Performer.* London, 1760.

Foote, Samuel. *The Roman and English Comedy Consider'd and Compar'd.* London, 1747.

——. *A Treatise on the Passions.* London, n.d.

Garrick, David. *An Essay on Acting in which will be considered the Mimical Behavior of a certain Fashionable Faulty Actor.* London, 1744.

Genest, John. *Some Account of the English Stage.* 10 vols. Bath, 1832.

Gentleman, Francis. *The Dramatic Censor; or Critical Companion.* 2 vols. London, 1770.

Goldsmith, Oliver. "An Enquiry into the Present State of Polite Learning in Europe." *Collected Works of Oliver Goldsmith.* Ed. Arthur Friedman. 5 vols. Oxford: Clarendon Press, 1966. 1: 243–341.

——. "An Essay on the Theatre; or, a Comparison between Laughing and Sentimental Comedy." 1733. *Collected Works of Oliver Goldsmith.* Ed. Arthur Friedman. 5 vols. Oxford: Clarendon Press, 1966. 3: 209–13.

——. *Remarks on Our Theatres. Collected Works of Oliver Goldsmith.* Ed. Arthur Friedman. 5 vols. Oxford: Clarendon Press, 1966. Vol. 1.

[Griffin, Benjamin and Lewis Theobald]. *A Complete Key to the Last New Farce The What D'Ye Call It. To which is prefix'd a Hypercritical Preface on the Nature of Burlesque and the Poet's Design.* London, 1715.

Guthrie, William. *An Essay Upon English Tragedy with Remarks upon the Abbé de Blanc's Observations on the English Stage.* London, 1757.

Hall, Joseph. *Characters of Virtues and Vices.* London, 1608.

Hill, Aaron. *The Art of Acting.* London, 1746.

Hill, John. *The Actor: A Treatise on the Art of Playing.* London, 1750.

Hobbes, Thomas. *On Human Nature.* 1650. *Restoration and Eighteenth-Century Comedy,* ed. Scott McMillin. 2nd ed. New York: W.W. Norton, 1997. 457–58.

Hume, David. "Of National Characters." 1742. Vol. 1 of *Essays Moral, Political and Literary.* Ed. T. H. Green and T. H. Grose. 2 vols. London: Longman, Green, 1875. 244–58.

Inchbald, Elizabeth. *Remarks for the British Theatre (1806–1809).* Intro. Cecilia Macheski. Delmar, N.Y.: Scholars' Facsimiles and Reprints, 1990.

Johnson, Samuel. *Lives of the English Poets.* Ed. George Birkbeck Hill. 3 vols. Oxford: Clarendon Press, 1905.

——. *The Rambler.* Vols. 3–5, *Yale Edition of the Works of Samuel Johnson.* Ed. W. J. Bate and Albrecht Strauss. New Haven, Conn.: Yale University Press, 1969.

Lennox, Charlotte. *The Female Quixote.* 1752. Ed. Margaret Dalziel, intro. Margaret Anne Doody. Oxford: Oxford University Press, 1989.

Lichtenberg, Georg Christoph. *Lichtenberg's Visits to England as described in His Letters and*

Diaries. Trans. and annotated Margaret L. Mare and W. H. Quarrell. Oxford: Clarendon Press, 1938.

Lloyd, Robert. *The Actor*. London, 1760.

Montagu, Lady Mary Wortley. "[Critique of *Cato*]." *Lady Mary Wortley Montagu: Essays and Poems and* Simplicity, *a Comedy*. Ed. Robert Halsband and Isobel Grundy. Oxford: Clarendon Press, 1993. 62–68.

Moore, Thomas. *Memoirs of the Life of the Right Honourable Richard Brinsley Sheridan*. London, 1825.

[Oldmixon, John]. *An Essay on Criticism; As it Regards Design, Thought, and Expression*. London, 1728.

Overbury, Sir Thomas. *Miscellaneous Works*. Ed. E. F. Rimbault. London, 1890.

Parker, Edward. *A Complete Key to the New Farce Call'd* Three Hours After Marriage. London, 1717.

Pope, Alexander. *The Correspondence of Alexander Pope*. Ed. George Sherburn. 5 vols. Oxford: Clarendon Press, 1956.

——. *The Poems of Alexander Pope*. Ed. John Butt. 1963. London: Routledge, 1992.

A Review of the Tragedy of Jane Shore *Consisting of Observations on the Characters, Manners, Stile, and Sentiments*. London, 1714.

Sewell, [George]. *Observations Upon Cato*. London, 1713.

——. *A Vindication of the English Stage, Exemplified in* The Cato *of Mr. Addison*. London, 1716.

Shaftesbury, Anthony, Earl of. *Characteristics of Men, Manners, Opinions, Times, etc.* Ed. and intro. John M. Robertson. 2 vols. 1900. Gloucester, Mass.: Peter Smith, 1963.

Sheridan, Richard Brinsley. *The Dramatic Works of Richard Brinsley Sheridan*. Ed. Cecil Price. 2 vols. Oxford: Clarendon Press, 1973.

——. *The Rivals, A Comedy Edited from the Larpent MS*. Ed. Richard Little Purdy. Oxford: Clarendon Press, 1935.

Spence, Joseph. *Anecdotes*. Ed. Samuel Weller Singer. London, 1820.

Steele, Richard. *The Guardian*. Ed. and intro. John Calhoun Stephens. Lexington: University Press of Kentucky, 1982.

——. *The Tatler*. Ed. Donald F. Bond. 3 vols. Oxford: Clarendon Press, 1987.

——. *Richard Steele's* The Theatre. Ed. John Loftis. Oxford: Clarendon Press, 1962.

Walpole, Horace. "Thoughts on Comedy." 1775/76. *The Works of Horatio Walpole, Earl of Orford*. 5 vols. London, 1798. 2: 315–22.

Secondary Sources

Agnew, Jean-Christophe. *Worlds Apart: The Market and the Theatre in Anglo-American Thought, 1550–1750*. Cambridge: Cambridge University Press, 1986.

Ahern, Susan K. "The Sense of Nonsense in Fielding's *The Author's Farce*." *Theatre Survey* 23, 1 (May 1982): 45–54.

Aikins, Janet. "To Know Jane Shore, 'think on all time backward.'" *Papers in Language and Literature* 18, 3 (Summer 1982): 258–77.

Anderson, Benedict. *Imagined Communities: Reflections on the Origin and Spread of Nationalism*. Rev. ed. London: Verso, 1990.

Aristotle. *Poetics*. Trans. S. H. Butcher; intro. Francis Fergusson. New York: Hill and Wang, 1985.

Armistead, J. M. "Calista and the 'Equal Empire' of Her 'Sacred Sex.'" *Studies in Eighteenth-Century Culture* 15 (1986): 173–85.

——. "Drama of Renewal: *Cato* and Moral Empiricism." *Papers on Language and Literature* 17 (1981): 271–83.

Armstrong, Nancy. *Desire and Domestic Fiction*. Oxford: Oxford University Press, 1987.

Auburn, Mark S. "The Pleasures of Sheridan's *The Rivals*: A Critical Study in the Light of Stage History." *Modern Philology* 72 (1975): 256–71.

——. *Sheridan's Comedies: Their Contexts and Achievements*. Lincoln: University of Nebraska Press, 1977.

Avery, Emmett L. "The Popularity of *The Mourning Bride* in the London Theatres in the Eighteenth Century." *Research Studies of the State College of Washington* 9 (1941): 115–16.

Ayres, Philip. *Classical Culture and the Idea of Rome in Eighteenth-Century England*. Cambridge: Cambridge University Press, 1997.

Backscheider, Paula R. "'Endless Aversion Rooted in the Soul': Divorce in the 1690–1730 Theater." *Eighteenth Century: Theory and Interpretation* 37 (1996): 99–135.

——. *Spectacular Politics: Theatrical Power and Mass Culture in Early Modern England*. Baltimore: Johns Hopkins University Press, 1993.

——. "Women Writers and the Chains of Identification." *Studies in the Novel* 19 (1987): 245–62.

Barish, Jonas. *The Anti-Theatrical Prejudice*. Berkeley: University of California Press, 1981.

Barker-Benfield, G. J. *The Culture of Sensibility*. Chicago: University of Chicago Press, 1996

Barrett, Dene. *The Art of Gesture: The Practices and Principles of 18th-Century Acting*. Heidelberg: Carl Winter, 1987.

Baruth, Philip E., ed. *Introducing Charlotte Charke: Actress, Author, Enigma*. Afterword by Felicity Nussbaum. Urbana: University of Illinois Press, 1998.

Bate, Jonathan. *Shakespearean Constitutions: Politics, Theatre, Criticism 1730–1830*. Oxford: Clarendon Press, 1989.

Bender, John. *Imagining the Penitentiary*. Chicago: University of Chicago Press, 1987.

Bermingham, Ann and John Brewer, eds. *The Consumption of Culture, 1600–1800: Image, Object, Text*. London: Routledge, 1995.

Bernbaum, Ernest. *The Drama of Sensibility*. Gloucester, Mass.: Peter Smith, 1958.

Borkat, Roberta F. S. "The Evil of Goodness: Sentimental Morality in *The London Merchant*." *Studies in Philology* 76 (1979): 288–312.

Bowyer, John Wilson. *The Celebrated Mrs. Centlivre*. Durham, N.C.: Duke University Press, 1952.

Boyce, Benjamin. *The Theophrastan Character in England to 1642*. Cambridge, Mass.: Harvard University Press, 1947.

Braudy, Leo. "Penetration and Impenetrability in *Clarissa*." *Modern Essays on Eighteenth-Century Literature*, ed. Leopold Damrosch, Jr. New York: Oxford University Press, 1988. 261–81.

Brewer, John. "Commercialization and Politics." *The Birth of a Consumer Society: The Commercialization of Eighteenth-Century England*, ed. Neil McKendrick, John Brewer, and J. H. Plumb. Bloomington: Indiana University Press, 1982. 197–262.

Brewer, John and Roy Porter, eds. *Consumption and the World of Goods*. London: Routledge, 1993.

Brewer, John and Susan Staves, eds. *Early Modern Conceptions of Property*. London and New York: Routledge, 1996.

Brown, Laura. "The Defenseless Woman and the Development of English Tragedy." *SEL* 22 (1982): 429–43.

———. *The Ends of Empire: Women and Ideology in Early Eighteenth-Century English Literature*. Ithaca, N.Y.: Cornell University Press, 1993.

———. *English Dramatic Form, 1660–1760*. New Haven, Conn.: Yale University Press, 1981.

Brown, Richard E. "Rival Socioeconomic Theories in Two Plays by George Lillo." *Tennessee Studies in Literature* 24 (1979): 94–110.

Bull, John. *Vanbrugh and Farquhar*. New York: St. Martin's Press, 1998.

Burke, Helen. "*The London Merchant* and Eighteenth-Century British Law." *Philological Quarterly* 73 (1994): 347–66.

———. "Wycherley's 'Tendentious Joke': The Discourse of Alterity in *The Country Wife*." *Eighteenth Century: Theory and Interpretation* 29 (1988): 227–41.

Butler, Judith. *Gender Trouble: Feminism and the Subversion of Identity*. New York: Routledge, 1990.

Campbell, Jill. "'When Men Women Turn': Gender Reversals in Fielding's Plays." *The New Eighteenth Century*, ed. Felicity Nussbaum and Laura Brown. New York: Methuen, 1987. 62–83.

Canfield, J. Douglas. "The Critique of Capitalism and the Retreat into Art in Gay's *Beggar's Opera* and Fielding's *Author's Farce*." *Cutting Edges: Postmodern Critical Essays on Eighteenth-Century Satire*, ed. James E. Gill. Tennessee Studies in Literature 37. Knoxville: University of Tennessee Press, 1995. 320–334.

———. "Female Rebels and Patriarchal Paradigms in Some Neoclassical Works." *SECC* 18 (1988): 153–66.

———. "The Ideology of Restoration Tragicomedy." *ELH* 51 (1984): 447–64.

———. *Nicholas Rowe and Christian Tragedy*. Gainesville: University Presses of Florida, 1977.

———. "Shifting Tropes of Ideology in English Serious Drama, Late Stuart to Early Georgian." *Cultural Readings of Restoration and Eighteenth-Century English Theater*, ed. J. Douglas Canfield and Deborah Payne. Athens: University of Georgia Press, 1995. 195–227.

———. *Tricksters and Estates: On the Ideology of Restoration Comedy*. Lexington: University of Kentucky Press, 1997.

Canfield, J. Douglas and Deborah C. Payne, eds. *Cultural Readings of Restoration and Eighteenth-Century Drama*. Athens: University of Georgia Press, 1995.

Carlson, Marvin. *Places of Performance: The Semiotics of Theatre Architecture*. Ithaca, N.Y.: Cornell University Press, 1989.

Castle, Terry. "The Culture of Travesty: Sexuality and Masquerade in Eighteenth-Century England." *Sexual Underworlds of the Enlightenment*, ed. G. S. Rousseau and Roy Porter. Chapel Hill: University of North Carolina Press, 1988. 156–80.

———. *Masquerade and Civilization: The Carnivalesque in Eighteenth-Century English Culture and Fiction*. Stanford, Calif.: Stanford University Press, 1986.

Clark, Constance. *Three Augustan Women Playwrights*. New York: Peter Lang, 1986.

Cloud, Random (Randall McLeod). "'The very names of the Persons': Editing and the

Invention of Dramatick Character." *Staging the Renaissance*, ed. David Scott Kastan and Peter Stallybrass. New York: Routledge, 1991. 88–96.

Cohen, Michele. *Fashioning Masculinity: National Identity and Language in the Eighteenth Century*. London: Routledge, 1996.

Cole, Lucinda. "*The London Merchant* and the Institution of Apprenticeship." *Criticism* 37 (1995): 57–84.

Coleman, Patrick. "Character in an Eighteenth-Century Context." *Eighteenth Century: Theory and Interpretation* 24 (1983): 51–63.

——. "The Idea of Character in the *Encyclopédie*." *Eighteenth-Century Studies* 13 (1979): 21–47.

Colley, Linda. *Britons: Forging the Nation 1707–1837*. New Haven, Conn.: Yale University Press, 1992.

Conolly, L. W. *The Censorship of English Drama, 1737–1824*. San Marino, Calif.: Huntington Library, 1976.

Corman, Brian. *Genre and Generic Change in English Comedy, 1660–1710*. Toronto: University of Toronto Press, 1993.

Cotton, Nancy. *Women Playwrights in England c. 1363–1750*. Lewisburg, Pa.: Bucknell University Press, 1980.

Craik, T. W. and Clifford Leech, gen. eds. *The Revels History of Drama in English*. Vols. 5–6. London: Methuen, 1975–76.

DeRitter, Jones. "The Cult of Dependence: The Social Context of *The London Merchant*." *Comparative Drama* 21, 4 (Winter 1987–88): 374–86.

——. "'Wonder not, princely Gloster, at the notice this paper brings you': Women, Writing, and Politics in Rowe's *Jane Shore*." *Comparative Drama* 31 (1997): 86–104.

Derrida, Jacques. "The Law of Genre." Trans. Avital Ronell. *Critical Inquiry* 7 (1980): 55–81.

Dobson, Michael. *The Making of the National Poet: Shakespeare, Adaptation, and Authorship, 1660–1769*. Oxford: Clarendon Press, 1992.

Dollimore, Jonathan. *Sexual Dissidence*. Oxford: Clarendon Press, 1991.

Donaldson, Ian. "Cato in Tears: Stoical Guises of the Man of Feeling." *Studies in the Eighteenth Century II*, ed. R. F. Brissenden. Canberra: Australian National University Press, 1973. 377–95.

——. *The World Upside-Down: Comedy from Jonson to Fielding*. Oxford: Clarendon Press, 1970.

Donkin, Ellen. *Getting into the Act: Women Playwrights in London, 1776–1829*. London: Routledge, 1995.

Donohue, Joseph. *Dramatic Character in the English Romantic Age*. Princeton, N.J.: Princeton University Press, 1970.

Downer, Alan S. "Nature to Advantage Dressed: Eighteenth-Century Acting." *PMLA* 58 (1943): 1002–37.

Drucker, Trudy. "Lillo's Liberated Women." *Restoration and Eighteenth-Century Theatre Research* 1, 2 (Winter 1986): 42–43.

Earle, Peter. *The Making of the English Middle Class: Business, Society and Family Life in London 1660–1730*. London: Methuen, 1989.

Elam, Keir. *The Semiotics of Theatre and Drama*. 1980. London: Routledge, 1988.

Ellis, Frank H. *Sentimental Comedy*. Cambridge: Cambridge University Press, 1991.

Ellison, Julie. "Cato's Tears." *ELH* 63 (1996): 571–601.

Faller, Lincoln. *The Popularity of Addison's* Cato *and Lillo's* The London Merchant. New York: Garland, 1988.

Fein, Mara H. "George Lillo's *The London Merchant* and Feminist Debates." *Restoration and Eighteenth-Century Theatre Research* 6, 2 (Winter 1991): 17–25.

Flores, Stephan. "Mastering the Self: The Ideological Incorporation of Desire in Lillo's *The London Merchant*." *Essays in Theatre* 5, 2 (May 1987): 91–102.

Fried, Michael. *Absorption and Theatricality: Painting and the Beholder in the Age of Diderot*. Chicago: University of Chicago Press, 1980.

Friedman-Romell, Beth H. "Breaking the Code: Toward a Reception Theory of Theatrical Cross-Dressing in Eighteenth-Century London." *Theatre Journal* 47 (1995): 459–79.

Frushell, Richard C. "Marriage and Marrying in Susanna Centlivre's Plays." *Papers on Language and Literature* 22 (1986): 16–38.

Frye, Northrop. *Anatomy of Criticism*. Princeton, N.J.: Princeton University Press, 1957.

Gagen, Jean. "Hannah Cowley (1743–1809)." *Restoration and Eighteenth-Century Dramatists*, ed. Paula R. Backscheider. Vol. 89 of *The Dictionary of Literary Biography*. 3rd. ser. Detroit: Gale Research, 1989.

Gallagher, Catherine. *Nobody's Story: The Vanishing Acts of Women in the Marketplace, 1670–1820*. Berkeley: University of California Press, 1994.

——. "Who Was That Masked Woman? The Prostitute and the Playwright in the Comedies of Aphra Behn." *Women's Studies* 15 (1988): 23–42.

Gelley, Alexander. "Character and Person: On the Presentation of Self in Some Eighteenth-Century Novels." *Eighteenth Century: Theory and Interpretation* 21 (1980): 109–27.

Gill, Pat. *Interpreting Ladies: Women, Wit, and Morality in the Restoration Comedy of Manners*. Athens: University of Georgia Press, 1994.

Green, Clarence C. *The Neo-Classical Theory of Tragedy in England during the Eighteenth Century*. Cambridge, Mass.: Harvard University Press, 1934.

Greenblatt, Stephen. "The Forms of Power and the Power of Forms in the Renaissance." *Genre* 15 (1982): 3–6.

Habermas, Jürgen. *The Structural Transformation of the Public Sphere*. Trans. Thomas Burger with Frederick Lawrence. Cambridge, Mass.: MIT Press, 1989.

Hammer, Stephanie Barbe. "Economy and Extravagance: Criminal Origin and the War of Words in *The London Merchant*." *Essays in the Theatre* 8, 2 (May 1990): 81–94.

Hammond, Brean. "Politics and Cultural Politics: The Case of Henry Fielding." *Eighteenth-Century Life* 16 (1992): 76–93.

Hassall, Anthony J. "Fielding's Puppet Image." *Philological Quarterly* 53 (1974): 71–83.

Havens, Raymond D. "The Sentimentalism of *The London Merchant*." *ELH* 12 (1945): 183–87.

Helgerson, Richard. "Weeping for Jane Shore." *SAQ* 98 (1999): 451–76.

Highfill, Philip H., Kalmin A. Burnim, and Edward A. Langhans. *A Biographical Dictionary of Actors, Actresses, Musicians, Dancers, Managers and Other Stage Personnel in London, 1660–1800*. 16 vols. Carbondale: Southern Illinois University Press, 1973–93.

Hnatko, Eugene. "The Failure of Eighteenth-Century Tragedy." *SEL* 11 (1971): 459–68.

Hogan, Robert. "Plot, Character, and Comic Language in Sheridan." *Comedy from Shakespeare to Sheridan*, ed. A. R. Braunmuller and J. C. Bulman. Newark: University of Delaware Press, 1986. 274–85.

Holland, Peter. *The Ornament of Action: Text and Performance in Restoration Comedy*. Cambridge: Cambridge University Press, 1979.

Howe, Elizabeth. *The First English Actresses: Women and Drama 1660–1700*. Cambridge: Cambridge University Press, 1992.

Hull, William. "*A Bold Stroke for a Wife*: Centlivre's Satiric Fairy Tale." *Restoration and Eighteenth-Century Theatre Research* 6 (1991): 41–49.

Hume, Robert D. *The Development of English Drama in the Late Seventeenth Century*. 1976. Oxford: Clarendon Press, 1990.

———. "Goldsmith and Sheridan and the Supposed Revolution of 'Laughing' Against 'Sentimental' Comedy." *Studies in Change and Revolution: Aspects of English Intellectual History, 1640–1800*, ed. Paul J. Korshin. Menston: Scolar Press, 1972. 237–76.

———. *Henry Fielding and the London Theatre, 1728–1737*. Oxford: Clarendon Press, 1988.

———. "The Multifarious Forms of Eighteenth-Century Comedy." *The Stage and the Page: London's 'Whole Show' in the Eighteenth-Century Theatre*, ed. George Winchester Stone, Jr. Berkeley: University of California Press, 1981. 3–32.

Hunter, J. Paul. *Occasional Form: Henry Fielding and the Chains of Circumstance*. Baltimore: Johns Hopkins University Press, 1975.

Ingrassia, Catherine. *Authorship, Commerce, and Gender in Early Eighteenth-Century England: A Culture of Paper Credit*. Cambridge: Cambridge University Press, 1998.

Irigaray, Luce. *This Sex Which Is Not One*. Trans. Catherine Porter. Ithaca, N.Y.: Cornell University Press, 1985.

Jameson, Fredric. *The Political Unconscious: Narrative as a Socially Symbolic Act*. Ithaca, N.Y.: Cornell University Press, 1981.

Jauss, Hans Robert. "Literary History as a Challenge to Literary Theory." 1970. *Toward an Aesthetic of Reception*. Trans. Timothy Bahti, intro. Paul de Man. Theory and History of Literature 2. Minneapolis: University of Minnesota Press, 1982. 3–45.

———. *Toward an Aesthetic of Reception*. Trans. Timothy Bahti, intro. Paul de Man. Theory and History of Literature 2. Minneapolis: University of Minnesota Press, 1982.

Jenkins, Annibel. *Nicholas Rowe*. Boston: G.K. Hall, 1977.

Jerrold, Clare and Walter Jerrold. *Five Queer Women*. London: Brentano's, 1929.

Johnson, James William. *The Formation of English Neo-Classical Thought*. Princeton, N.J.: Princeton University Press, 1967.

Jones, Vivien, ed. *Women in the Eighteenth Century: Constructions of Femininity*. London: Routledge, 1990.

Kaul, A. N. *The Action of English Comedy*. New Haven, Conn.: Yale University Press, 1970.

Kearful, Frank J. "The Nature of Tragedy in Rowe's *The Fair Penitent*." *Papers in Language and Literature* 2, 4 (Fall 1966): 351–60.

Kelsall, M. M. "The Meaning of Addison's *Cato*." *Review of English Studies* n.s. 17 (May 1966): 149–62.

Kenny, Shirley Strum. "Humane Comedy." *Modern Philology* 75 (1977): 29–43.

Kern, Jean. *Dramatic Satire in the Age of Walpole, 1720–1750*. Ames: Iowa State University Press, 1976.

Klein, Lawrence E. "Liberty, Manners, and Politeness in Early Eighteenth-Century England." *Historical Journal* 32 (1989): 583–605.

———. "Property and Politeness in the Early Eighteenth-Century Whig Moralists: The Case of the *Spectator*." *Early Modern Conceptions of Property*, ed. John Brewer and Susan Staves. London: Routledge, 1996. 221–33.

———. *Shaftesbury and the Culture of Politeness*. Cambridge: Cambridge University Press, 1994.

Krutch, Joseph Wood. *Comedy and Conscience After the Restoration*. New York: Columbia University Press, 1924.

Lafler, Joanne. *The Celebrated Mrs. Oldfield: The Life and Art of an Augustan Actress*. Carbondale: Southern Illinois University Press, 1989.

Langford, Paul. *A Polite and Commercial People: England, 1727–1783*. Oxford: Clarendon Press, 1989.

Larson, Martin A. "The Influence of Milton's Divorce Tracts on Farquhar's *Beaux' Stratagem*." *PMLA* 39 (1924): 174–78.

Lewis, Peter. *Fielding's Burlesque Drama: Its Place in the Tradition*. Edinburgh: Edinburgh University Press, 1987.

———. "Gay's Burlesque Method in *The What D'Ye Call It*." *Durham University Journal* n.s. 29 (1967–68): 13–25.

Loftis, John. *Comedy and Society from Congreve to Fielding*. 1959. New York: AMS Press, 1979.

———. *The Politics of Drama in Augustan England*. Oxford: Clarendon Press, 1963.

———. *Sheridan and the Drama of Georgian England*. Cambridge, Mass.: Harvard University Press, 1977.

———. *Steele at Drury Lane*. Berkeley: University of California Press, 1952.

Lynch, Deidre Shauna. *The Economy of Character: Novels, Market Culture, and the Business of Inner Meaning*. Chicago: University of Chicago Press, 1998.

———. "Overloaded Portraits: The Excesses of Character and Countenance." *Body and Text in the Eighteenth Century*, ed. Veronica Kelley and Dorothea E. Von Mücke. Stanford, Calif.: Stanford University Press, 1994. 112–143.

Mack, Robert L. "Such Wounds as Hell can Equal: Tragic Guilt in the Drama of George Lillo." *Restoration and Eighteenth-Century Theatre Research* 7,1 (Summer 1992): 35–53.

Malek, James S. "Julia as Comic Character in *The Rivals*." *Studies in the Humanities* 7.1 (December 1978): 10–13.

Markley, Robert. "Sentimentality as Performance: Shaftesbury, Sterne, and the Theatrics of Virtue." *The New Eighteenth Century*, ed. Felicity Nussbaum and Laura Brown. New York: Methuen, 1987. 210–230.

———. *Two-edg'd Weapons: Style and Ideology in the Comedies of Etherege, Wycherley, and Congreve*. Oxford: Clarendon Press, 1988.

Marsden, Jean. "Rape, Voyeurism, and the Restoration Stage." *Broken Boundaries: Women and Feminism in Restoration Drama*, ed. Katherine M. Quinsey. Lexington: University of Kentucky Press, 1996. 185–200.

———. *The Re-Imagined Text: Shakespeare, Adaptation, and Eighteenth-Century Literary Theory*. Lexington: University of Kentucky Press, 1995.

Marshall, David. *The Figure of Theater: Shaftesbury, Defoe, Adam Smith, and George Eliot*. New York: Columbia University Press, 1986.

Marx, Karl. "Estranged Labour." *The Marx-Engels Reader*. Ed. Robert C. Tucker. 2nd ed. New York: W.W. Norton, 1978. 70–81.

Matlack, Cynthia. "'Spectatress of the Mischief Which She Made': Tragic Women Perceived and Perceiver." *Studies in Eighteenth-Century Culture* 6 (1977): 317–30.

Maus, Katherine Eisaman. "'Playhouse Flesh and Blood': Sexual Ideology and the Restoration Actress." *ELH* 46 (1979): 595–617.

McKendrick, Neil, John Brewer, and J. H. Plumb, eds. *The Birth of a Consumer Society: The Commercialization of Eighteenth-Century England.* Bloomington: Indiana University Press, 1982.

McKenzie, Alan T. "The Countenance You Show Me: Reading the Passions in the Eighteenth Century." *Georgia Review* 32 (1978): 758–73.

McKeon, Michael. "Cultural Crisis and Dialectical Method: Destabilizing Augustan Literature." *The Profession of Eighteenth-Century Literature*, ed. Leo Damrosch. Madison: University of Wisconsin Press, 1992. 42–61.

——. "Generic Transformation and Social Change: Rethinking the Rise of the Novel." 1985. Reprint in *Modern Essays in Eighteenth Century Literature*, ed. Leopold Damrosch, Jr. New York Oxford University Press, 1988. 159–80.

——. "Marxist Criticism and *Marriage à la Mode*." *Eighteenth Century: Theory and Interpretation* 24 (1983): 141–62.

——. *The Origins of the English Novel 1600–1740.* Baltimore: Johns Hopkins University Press, 1987.

McVeagh, John. "George Farquhar and Commercial England." *Studies in Voltaire and the Eighteenth Century* 217 (1983): 65–81.

Milhous, Judith. "The First Production of Rowe's *Jane Shore*." *Theatre Journal* 38 (1986): 309–21.

Milhous, Judith and Robert D. Hume. "*The Beaux' Stratagem*: A Production Analysis." *Theatre Journal* 34 (1982): 77–95.

Morgan, Fidelis. *The Female Wits: Women Playwrights of the Restoration.* London: Virago Press, 1981.

Morrissey, Lee. "Sexuality and Consumer Culture in Eighteenth Century England: 'Mutual Love from Pole to Pole' in *The London Merchant*." *Restoration and Eighteenth-Century Theatre Research* 13, 1 (Summer 1998): 25–40.

Morton, Richard. "'*Roman* drops from *British* Eyes': Latin History on the Restoration Stage." *The Stage in the Eighteenth Century*, ed. J. D. Browning. New York: Garland, 1981. 108–32.

Newman, Gerald. *The Rise of English Nationalism: A Cultural History 1740–1830.* New York: St. Martin's Press, 1987.

Newman, Karen. "Directing Traffic: Subjects, Objects, and the Politics of Exchange." *differences* 2 (1990): 41–54.

Nicoll, Allardyce. *A History of English Drama 1660–1900.* 3rd ed. 5 vols. Cambridge: Cambridge University Press, 1952.

Novak, Maximillian E. "Sincerity, Delusion, and Character in the Fiction of Defoe and the 'Sincerity Crisis' of His Time." *Augustan Studies: Essays in Honor of Irvin Ehrenpreis*, ed. Douglas Lane Patey and Timothy Keegan. Newark: University of Delaware Press, 1985. 109–26.

Nussbaum, Felicity. *The Autobiographical Subject.* Baltimore: Johns Hopkins University Press, 1989.

———. "Heteroclites: The Gender of Character in the Scandalous Memoirs." *The New Eighteenth Century*, ed. Felicity Nussbaum and Laura Brown. London: Methuen, 1987. 144–67.

———. *Torrid Zones: Maternity, Sexuality, and Empire in Eighteenth-Century English Narratives*. Baltimore: Johns Hopkins University Press, 1995.

Nussbaum, Felicity and Laura Brown, eds. *The New Eighteenth Century*. New York: Methuen, 1987.

Oakleaf, David. "Marks, Stamps, and Representations: Character in Eighteenth-Century Fiction." *Studies in the Novel* 23 (1991): 295–311.

Parker, Anne. "'Absolute Sense' in Sheridan's *The Rivals*." *Ball State University Forum* 27, 3 (Summer 1986): 10–19.

Parnell, Paul E. "The Sentimental Mask." *Restoration Drama: Modern Essays in Criticism*, ed. John Loftis. London: Oxford University Press, 1966. 285–97.

Paulson, Ronald. *Hogarth: His Life, Art, and Times*. 2 vols. New Haven, Conn.: Yale University Press, 1971.

———. *Popular and Polite Art in the Age of Hogarth and Fielding*. Notre Dame, Ind.: University of Notre Dame Press, 1979.

Payne, Deborah. "Reified Object or Emergent Professional? Retheorizing the Restoration Actress." *Cultural Readings of Restoration and Eighteenth-Century English Theater*, ed. J. Douglas Canfield and Deborah Payne. Athens: University of Georgia Press, 1995. 13–38.

Pedicord, Harry William. *The Theatrical Public in the Time of Garrick*. New York: King's Crown Press, 1954.

Peters, Julie Stone. *Congreve, the Drama, and the Printed Word*. Stanford, Calif.: Stanford University Press, 1990.

Pettit, Alexander. "Anxiety, Political Rhetoric, and Historical Drama Under Walpole." *1650–1850: Ideas, Aesthetics, and Inquiries in the Early Modern Era* 1 (1993): 109–36.

Plumb J. H. "The Commercialization of Leisure in Eighteenth-Century England." *Birth of a Consumer Society: The Commercialization of Eighteenth-Century England*, ed. Neil McKendrick, John Brewer, and Plumb. Bloomington: Indiana University Press, 1982.

Pocock, J. G. A. *Virtue, Commerce, and History*. Cambridge: Cambridge University Press, 1985.

Pollak, Ellen. *The Poetics of Sexual Myth*. Chicago: University of Chicago Press, 1985.

———. "Pope and Sexual Difference: Woman as Part and Counterpart in the 'Epistle to a Lady.'" *SEL* 24 (1984): 461–81.

Porter, Roy. *English Society in the Eighteenth Century*. Rev. ed. London: Penguin, 1990.

Raven, James. "Defending Conduct and Property. The London Press and the Luxury Debate." *Early Modern Conceptions of Property*, ed. John Brewer and Susan Staves. London: Routledge, 1996. 301–19.

Rivero, Albert J. *The Plays of Henry Fielding: A Critical Study of His Dramatic Career*. Charlottesville: University of Virginia Press, 1989.

Roach, Joseph R. *The Player's Passion: Studies in the Science of Acting*. 1985. Reprint Ann Arbor: University of Michigan Press, 1993.

———. "Theatre History and the Ideology of the Aesthetic." *Theatre Journal* 41 (1989): 155–68.

Rodman, George Bush. "Sentimentalism in Lillo's *The London Merchant*." *ELH* 12 (1945): 45–61.

Rogers, Nicholas. "Money, Land and Lineage: The Big Bourgeoisie of Hanoverian London." *Social History* 4 (1979): 437–54.

Rosenthal, Laura J. "'Counterfeit Scrubbado': Women Actors in the Restoration." *Eighteenth Century: Theory and Interpretation* 34 (1993): 3–22.

——. *Playwright and Plagiarists in Early Modern England*. Ithaca, N.Y.: Cornell University Press, 1996.

Ross, Marlon B. "Authority and Authenticity: Scribbling Authors and the Genius of Print in Eighteenth-Century England." *The Construction of Authorship: Textual Appropriations in Law and Literature*, ed. Martha Woodmansee and Peter Jaszi. Durham, N.C.: Duke University Press, 1994. 231–57.

Rothstein, Eric. "Farquhar's *Twin Rivals* and the Reform of Comedy." *PMLA* 79 (1964): 33–41.

——. *George Farquhar*. New York: Twayne, 1967.

——. *Restoration Tragedy: Form and the Progress of Change*. Madison: University of Wisconsin Press, 1967.

Rowan, D. F. "Shore's Wife." *SEL* 6 (1966): 447–64.

Rubin, Gayle. "The Traffic in Women: Notes on the 'Political Economy' of Sex." *Toward an Anthropology of Women*, ed. Rayna R. Reiter. New York: Monthly Review Press, 1975. 157–210.

Rudolph, Valerie C. "People and Puppets: Fielding's Burlesque of the 'Recognition Scene' in *The Author's Face*." *Papers on Language and Literature* 11 (1975): 31–38.

Schwartz, Alfred. "An Example of Eighteenth-Century Pathetic Tragedy: Rowe's *Jane Shore*." *MLQ* 22 (1961): 236–47.

Sedgwick, Eve Kosofsky. *Between Men: English Literature and Male Homosocial Desire*. New York: Columbia University Press, 1985.

Sellery, J'nan. "Language and Moral Intelligence in the Enlightenment: Fielding's Plays and Pope's *Dunciad*." *Enlightenment Essays* 1, 2 (1970): 17–26, 108–19.

Sennett, Richard. *The Fall of Public Man*. 1974. New York: W.W. Norton, 1992.

Sherbo, Arthur. *English Sentimental Drama*. East Lansing: Michigan State University Press, 1957.

Sheriff, John. *The Good-Natured Man: The Evolution of a Moral Ideal, 1660–1800*. University: University of Alabama Press, 1982.

Shevelow, Kathryn. *Women and Print Culture*. London: Routledge, 1989.

Silverman, Kaja. *The Subject of Semiotics*. New York: Oxford University Press, 1983.

Smeed, J. W. *The Theophrastan 'Character': The History of a Literary Genre*. Oxford: Clarendon Press, 1985.

Smith, Dane Farnsworth. *Plays About the Theatre in England from* The Rehearsal *in 1671 to the Licensing Act in 1737 or, The Self-Conscious Stage and Its Burlesque and Satirical Reflections in the Age of Criticism*. London: Oxford University Press, 1936.

Smith, Dane Farnsworth and M. L. Lawhon. *Plays About the Theatre in England, 1737–1800 or, The Self-Conscious Stage from Foote to Sheridan*. Lewisburg, Pa.: Bucknell University Press, 1979.

Spacks, Patricia Meyer. "Female Changelessness; Or, What Do Women Want?" *Studies in the Novel* 19 (1987): 273–83.

Stallybrass, Peter and Allon White. *The Politics and Poetics of Transgression*. Ithaca, N.Y.: Cornell University Press, 1986.

Staves, Susan. *Players' Scepters: Fictions of Authority in the Restoration*. Lincoln: University of Nebraska Press, 1979.

———. "Pope's Refinement." *The Eighteenth Century: Theory and Interpretation* 29 (1988): 145–63.

———. "Resentment or Resignation? Dividing the Spoils Among Daughters and Younger Sons." *Early Modern Conceptions of Property*, ed. John Brewer and Susan Staves. London: Routledge, 1996. 194–218.

Stone, George Winchester, Jr. and George M. Kahrl. *David Garrick, A Critical Biography*. Carbondale: Southern Illinois University Press, 1979.

Straub, Kristina. "The Guilty Pleasures of Female Theatrical Cross-Dressing and the Autobiography of Charlotte Charke." *Body Guards: The Politics of Gender Ambiguity*, ed. Julia Epstein and Kristina Straub. New York: Routledge, 1991. 142–66.

———. *Sexual Suspects: Eighteenth-Century Players and Sexual Ideology*. Princeton, N.J.: Princeton University Press, 1992.

Styan, J. L. *The English Stage: A History of Drama and Performance*. Cambridge: Cambridge University Press, 1996.

Sypher, Wylie. "The West-Indian as a 'Character' in the Eighteenth Century." *Studies in Philology* 36 (1939): 503–20.

Szondi, Peter. *Die Theorie des bürgerlichen Trauerspiels im 18. Jahrhundert*. Ed. Gert Mattenklott. Frankfurt am Main: Suhrkamp, 1977.

Tave, Stuart. *The Amiable Humorist: A Study in the Comic Theory and Criticism of the Eighteenth and Nineteenth Centuries*. Chicago: University of Chicago Press, 1960.

Taylor, George. "'The Just Delineation of the Passions': Theories of Acting in the Age of Garrick." *The Eighteenth-Century English Stage*, ed. Kenneth Richards and Peter Thomson. London: Methuen, 1972. 51–72.

Thompson, James. *Models of Value: Eighteenth-Century Political Economy and the Novel*. Durham, N.C.: Duke University Press, 1996.

———. "'Sure I Have Seen That Face Before': Representation and Value in Eighteenth-Century Drama." *Cultural Readings of Restoration and Eighteenth-Century Drama*, ed. J. Douglas Canfield and Deborah C. Payne. Athens: University of Georgia Press, 1995. 281–308.

Thomson, Peter. "Fielding, Walpole, George II and the Liberty of the Theatre." *Literature and History* 3rd ser. 2 (1993): 42–67.

Todorov, Tzvetan. *Genres in Discourse*. Trans. Catherine Porter. Cambridge: Cambridge University Press, 1990.

Trainor, Stephen L. "Context for a Biography of George Lillo." *Philological Quarterly* 64 (1985): 51–67.

———. "Tears Abounding: *The London Merchant* as Puritan Tragedy." *SEL* 18 (1978): 509–21.

Tumir, Vaska. "She-tragedy and Its Men: Conflict and Form in *The Orphan* and *The Fair Penitent*." *SEL* 30 (1990): 411–29.

Turner, Victor. *The Anthropology of Performance*. New York: PAJ Publications, 1987.

———. *From Ritual to Theatre: The Human Seriousness of Play*. New York: PAJ Publications, 1982.

Van Lannep, William, Emmett L. Avery, Arthur H. Scouten, George Winchester Stone, Jr., and Charles Beecher Hogan, eds. *The London Stage 1660–1800: A Calendar of Plays, Entertainments and Afterpieces*. 5 parts in 11 vols. Carbondale: Southern Illinois University Press, 1960–68.

Wagner, Peter. *Reading Iconotexts: From Swift to the French Revolution*. London: Reaktion Books, 1995.

Wallace, David. "Bourgeois Tragedy or Sentimental Melodrama? The Significance of George Lillo's *The London Merchant*." *Eighteenth-Century Studies* 25 (1991–92): 123–43.

Warner, William. *Licensing Entertainment: The Elevation of Novel Reading in Britain, 1684–1750*. Berkeley: University of California Press, 1998.

Watt, Ian. *The Rise of the Novel*. Berkeley: University of California Press, 1957.

Weinsheimer, Joel. "Theory of Character: *Emma*." *Poetics Today* 1 (1979): 185–211.

West, Shearer. *The Image of the Actor: Verbal and Visual Representation in the Age of Garrick and Kemble*. London: Pinter, 1991.

Wiesenthal, Christine S. "Representation and Experimentation in the Major Comedies of Richard Brinsley Sheridan." *Eighteenth-Century Studies* 25 (1992): 309–30.

Wilson, Kathleen. "The good, the bad, and the impotent: Imperialism and the politics of identity in Georgian England." *The Consumption of Culture 1600–1800: Image, Object, Text*, ed. Ann Bermingham and John Brewer. London: Routledge, 1995. 237–262.

Wilson, Michael S. "Garrick, Iconic Acting, and the Ideologies of Theatrical Performance." *Word and Image* 6 (1990): 368–94.

Woods, Leigh. *Garrick Claims the Stage: Acting as Social Emblem in Eighteenth-Century England*. Westport, Conn.: Greenwood Press, 1984.

Worthen, William B. *The Idea of the Actor: Drama and the Ethics of Performance*. Princeton, N.J.: Princeton University Press, 1984.

Zeitlin, Froma. "Travesties of Gender and Genre in Aristophanes' *Thesmophoriazousae*." *Writing and Sexual Difference*, ed. Elizabeth Abel. Chicago: University of Chicago Press, 1982. 131–57.

Index

character (*continued*)
22–24, 26–27, 39–40, 223, 230; and property relations, 16, 18–19, 237; and represen-
tation, 23–24, 27, 39–41, 50, 56, 64, 93,
147–48, 150, 164, 169, 170, 171–72, 179,
182, 183, 190–91, 221, 237
character sketches, 22–23
Charke, Charlotte, 39, 162
Charlotte, Queen (of England), 179
Chetwood, William, 38, 245–46 n. 73
Churchill, Charles, *The Rosciad*, 246 n. 76
Cibber, Colley, 216; *Apology*, 32, 37–38, 61,
242 n. 43, 245 n. 68; *The Provoked Husband*,
192
Cibber, Theophilus, 51
Clark, Constance, 70, 71
Clive, Catherine, 39; *The Rehearsal: Or, Bays in
Petticoats*, 67, 71, 73, 249–50 n. 37
Cole, Lucinda, 258 n. 53
Coleman, Patrick, 241 n. 32
Colley, Linda, *Britons*, 74, 75, 78, 117, 259 n.
58
Collier, Jeremy, 145, 146, 269 n. 5
Colman, George the Elder: *The English Merchant*, 227; *New Brooms*, 83
Colman, George the Younger, *The Female Dramatist*, 84–85
colonialism, 93, 118, 122, 228, 229, 232, 233
comedies of manners, humours, and intrigue.
See comedy
comedy, 9–10, 17, 42–43, 145–92 passim,
193, 194, 204; and class, 170–73, 176–79,
180, 192; constitutional parodies of identity
in, 9, 150, 170, 173, 179, 182–83, 192; conventions of, 55–56, 140–96 passim, 208–
11; cultural work of, 145, 147, 150–51, 152,
153, 156, 172, 177, 178, 190, 192; and gender, 154–60 passim, 160–70 passim, 179–
83 passim, 192; national identity in, 159–60,
169–70, 180, 182, 183, 208–11; and notions of heroism, 153, 184–85, 190; and patriarchal ideology, 154–62 passim, 167, 168,
170, 179, 181, 195–96; and valuation of
character, 9, 146, 147, 149, 150, 152, 159,
171–72, 176, 183
commercial culture, 5, 21, 49, 52–53, 56, 57,
61, 62, 95–96, 115–22 passim, 146, 155–
57, 172, 173, 192, 197, 199, 203, 204–5,
214, 236
Comparison Between the Two Stages, A, 71, 76–
78
Congreve, William, 43, 209
Conscious Lovers, The (Steele), 10, 18, 206, 207,
211, 212–19, 220, 221, 227

Cooke, William, *Elements of Dramatic Criticism*,
207–8
Corman, Brian, 263 n. 3
Cotton, Nancy, 68
Cowley, Hannah, 9; *The Belle's Stratagem*, 151,
170–71, 179–83; *A Bold Stroke for a Husband*, 151–52, 160–70, 179
Critic, The (Sheridan), 47
cross-dressing, 67, 68, 160, 162–63, 164, 165,
167–69, 233
cuckoldry, 155–57, 159, 163, 164
Cumberland, Richard, 127, 159, 261 n. 81; *The
West Indian*, 228–33

daughters, 54, 130, 132–34, 154, 219–21,
222, 225–28, 234
Davies, Thomas, 210
Dennis, John, 147–48, 207–9; "A Defence of
Sir Fopling Flutter," 206; *Iphigenia*, 89–91;
Remarks Upon Cato, 101–2, 256 n. 42; "Re-
marks on . . . The Conscious Lovers," 206,
272–73 n. 60
Derrida, Jacques, 44
Descartes, René, 14
Desire and Domestic Fiction (Armstrong), 15
Diderot, Denis, 13, 258 n. 61
Discovery, The (Frances Sheridan), 84
divorce, 171
Dollimore, Jonathan, 259 n. 61
domestic drama. *See* bourgeois drama
Donaldson, Ian, 56, 256 n. 42
Donkin, Ellen, 250 n. 39
Donohue, Joseph, 231, 232
Downer, Alan, S., 37
D'Urfey, Thomas, 80

economic theory, 20–21, 24, 48–49, 57, 95,
116, 199, 202, 203
eighteenth-century drama: absence of realism
in, 17; absence of subjectivity in, 7, 8, 11, 17,
19, 34, 35, 43, 45, 48, 150, 237; authority in,
49–53; cultural work of, 5, 8, 48–49, 235;
and genre, 44–46; and market culture, 61,
62; study of, 1–2, 5–6, 7, 85. *See also* comedy; plays about plays; sentimental comedy;
tragedy
Elam, Keir, 240–41 n. 21
Elements of Dramatic Criticism (Cooke), 207–
8
Ellison, Julie, 255 n. 36
English Merchant, The (Colman the Elder), 227
English Stage Italianiz'd, The, 53, 79–82
"Essay on Conversation" (Fielding), 197–99,
201

realism, 13, 14, 63–65, 240 n. 17; and the novel, 14–15; reconfiguration of, 14

Reeve, Joseph, 255 n. 39, 255–56 n. 40

rehearsal play, 41, 42, 50, 54, 59, 85

Rehearsal, The: Or, Bays in Petticoats (Clive), 67, 71

Remarks on Clarissa, 18

Restoration drama, 5, 94, 100, 123, 125–26, 145, 146, 194, 196, 213, 215, 216, 217–18

Review of the Tragedy of Jane Shore, A, 262 n. 85

Rich, Christopher, 78

Rise of the Novel, The (Watt), 6, 14, 15, 240 n. 17

Rivals, The (Sheridan), 151, 183–92

Roach, Joseph, 252 n. 12; *The Player's Passion*, 32, 34–36, 243 n. 53

Rochester, earl of, 123

Rogers, Jane, 38

romance narrative, 185, 186–88, 189, 192

Rosenthal, Laura J., 265 n. 62

Ross, Marlon, 52

Rothstein, Eric, 94

Rowe, Nicholas, 9, 144; *The Fair Penitent*, 96, 125–34, 139, 143; *The Tragedy of Jane Shore*, 96, 125, 134–43, 144

Rudolph, Valerie, 248 n. 16

"Salic Law of Wit," 68, 74

satire, 76, 80, 81

Sedgwick, Eve, 153, 154, 155, 159, 163

Sennett, Richard, 48

sentimental comedy, 10, 17, 145, 184, 185, 193–234, 235; attack on, 206–11; and class, 212–14, 216–17; conventions of, 194–96, 200, 203, 219, 220–21, 227, 233–34; cultural work of, 193, 196–97, 200, 203–6, 210, 211, 219–21, 227–29, 232–34, 236; emergence of, 204–17, 235–36; and good breeding, 194, 196, 199, 203–6, 211–20 passim, 227, 233–34; national identity in, 205, 211, 228–29, 231–34; notions of heroism in, 194, 200, 215, 218, 229; and patriarchal ideology, 10, 195–96, 219–21, 224–34 passim; and property relations, 200, 201, 203, 213–14, 219–34 passim; and valuation of character, 10, 195, 197, 220–27 passim, 230, 233, 234

sentimental love plot, 185, 188–89, 191

sentimental theory, 197–98

Sewell, George, 73

Shaftesbury, third earl of, 197, 198, 201, 211, 269 n. 13, 272 n. 47

Shakespeare, William, 6, 95; *Richard II*, 137

she-tragedy, 123–43

Sheridan, Frances, *The Discovery*, 84

Sheridan, Richard Brinsley, 9; *The Critic*, 47; *The Rivals*, 151, 183–92

Shevelow, Kathryn, 67

Short View of the Immorality . . . of the English Stage, A (Collier), 145, 146

Siddons, Sarah, 39

Smeed, J. W., 242 n. 33

Smith, Adam, 13, 198, 200; *Theory of Moral Sentiments*, 198–99

Smith, Dane Farnsworth, 59, 62, 69, 76, 82

Southerne, Thomas, 123

Spacks, Patricia, 181

Spectator, 11, 37, 193–94, 196–97, 200, 204, 206, 236

spectatorship, 13, 41, 85, 181–83, 236–37

Stage Licensing Act, 4, 49, 50, 58, 83

Stage Mutineers, 51

Stallybrass, Peter, 70, 75, 82

Staves, Susan, 204, 273 n. 64

Steele, Richard, 11, 19, 26, 37, 90–91, 193–98, 212–13, 216, 241 n. 23, 253 n. 17; *The Conscious Lovers*, 10, 18, 206, 207, 211, 212–20, 221, 227; *The Funeral*, 193; *The Lying Lover*, 246 n. 76

Stone, George Winchester, Jr., 33–34

Straub, Kristina, 38, 41, 162

Szondi, Peter, 258–59 n. 53

taste, 76, 81, 82, 100, 180, 182, 200, 204–18 passim

Tatler, 212–13

Tave, Stuart, 210

Taylor, George, 34

Theatre (Steele), 216

theatricality: in eighteenth-century life, 11, 12–13, 14, 16, 17, 19, 21, 24, 40, 45, 48–50, 57, 61–62, 65, 85, 183, 235, 236; and the modern subject, 13–16, 17; in the novel, 12–13

Theophrastus, 22

Thompson, James, 20–21, 220, 224

Thomson, Peter, 61

"Thoughts on Comedy" (Walpole), 195, 210–11

Three Hours After Marriage (Gay, Pope Arbuthnot), 53, 71–72

Todorov, Tzvetan, 44

tragedy, 9, 17, 87–144, 146, 148, 149, 209; cultural work of, 87–97, 99, 101, 113, 122, 123, 134–135, 140, 143–45; and gender, 91, 92, 96, 97, 102–16 passim, 119–20, 121–23, 125–44 passim; national identity in, 9, 87, 89–101, 112–14, 117, 118, 122, 123,

tragedy (*continued*)
125, 134–38, 141, 143, 144; and notions of heroism, 87, 89, 90, 94–100, 102, 111, 112, 114, 122, 125, 143, 144; and patriarchal ideology, 126–34
Trotter, Catherine, 68, 69, 70
Tumir, Vaska, 128
Turner, Victor, 5, 85, 235

Vanbrugh, John, *The Provoked Husband*, 192
Villiers, George, second duke of Buckingham, *The Rehearsal*, 50, 67
Voltaire, 255 n. 39

Wallace, David 258–59 n. 53
Walpole, Horace, "Thoughts on Comedy," 195, 210–11, 212, 270 n. 21
Walpole, Robert, 50, 51, 61
Warner, William B., 6

Watt, Ian, 6, 14, 15, 240 n. 17
Welsted, Leonard, 212
West Indian, The (Cumberland), 228–33
West, Shearer, 244 n. 58, 244–45 n. 63
What D'Ye Call It?, The (Gay), 7, 12, 41–44, 49, 59, 62, 149
White, Allon, 70, 75, 82
whiteness, 228, 273–74 n. 73
Wiesenthal, Christine S., 268 n. 61
Wilks, Robert, 32, 38
Wilson, Kathleen, 122
Wilson, Michael, 243 n. 51
Woods, Charles, 63, 66
Worlds Apart (Agnew), 12, 13, 24, 48–49, 241 n. 29, 249 n. 30
Worthen, William B., 4, 31

Zeitlin, Froma, 149, 174

Acknowledgments

This book has been a long time in the making, and the debts I have incurred over the years have been many. For support while this project was in its earliest stages, I am grateful to the Woodrow Wilson Foundation for a Mellon Fellowship in the Humanities as well as to the Penn-in-London fellowship program. As a faculty member at the University of Illinois at Chicago, I have received grants from the Campus Research Board and, even more fortuitously, a year's fellowship support from the Institute for the Humanities. A four-month fellowship at the Huntington Library was critical to moving this project forward; these were surely some of the most pleasurable months spent in study. For the assistance of the staff at that collection as well as at the British Library, the Newberry Library, the Yale University Libraries, the Harvard Theatre Collection, and the Theatre Museum in Covent Garden, I am forever grateful.

Many people have either read my work or provided me with invaluable advice about the project. First amongst this group is the Folger Group, a scholarly collective devoted to women's writing and feminist concerns that I was fortunate enough to participate in and learn from when my ideas for this book were just forming. At the University of Pennsylvania, I benefited from the care and vision of Phyllis Rackin and Stuart Curran. Together they taught me how to be a scholar, a teacher, and a thinker. For reading my work and offering both useful comments and encouragement at various stages along the way, I extend my thanks to Toni Bowers, Judith Kegan Gardiner, Jean Howard, Susan Lanser, Deidre Lynch, Jean Marsden, John Richetti, Joseph Roach, Mary Beth Rose, and Laura Rosenthal. I am especially grateful to Kristina Straub, one of the readers for the University of Pennsylvania Press, who was able to capture the importance of this work better than I ever could. Also at the press, I want to thank my anonymous second reader as well as my editor Jerry Singerman for seeing this project through in such a timely fashion.

For their remarkable kindness and generosity, I thank my friends, old and new, academic and nonacademic: Lisa Blansett, Sara Beasley, Jennifer Brody, Jill Campbell, Naomi Diamant, Jody Greene, Sharon Holland, Nicole King, Debbie Nelson, and Alok Yadav. For the fact that this book got finished at all, I must thank Anne Cubilié, Jamie Owen Daniel, Andrea Henderson, Rene Lederman, and Jon Rosner. Their friendship, their faith, and their love has meant the world to me; they have given me courage and kept me strong. There are some debts that can hardly be put into words; Blakey Vermeule thus remains in a category of her own.

Finally, I want to thank my family for their love and support at all times and in all things: Laurie, Yoji, Evan, and Ken Shimizu; Jodie, Howard, Emma, Ben, and Sam Adler; Robert Freeman; and Philippa Smith. This book is dedicated to my parents, Jack and Ellen Freeman, whose love has ever been unconditional and sees me through each and every day.

Earlier forms of portions of Chapter 3 appeared as "What's Love Got to Do with Addison's *Cato*?" *SEL: Studies in English Literature, 1500–1900* 39 (1999): 463–82; and "Tragic Flaws: Genre and Ideology in Lillo's *The London Merchant*," *SAQ: South Atlantic Quarterly* 98 (1999): 539–61.